Processes in Language Acquisition and Disorders

Processes in Language Acquisition and Disorders

Robin S. Chapman, Ph.D.
Professor
Department of Communicative Disorders
University of Wisconsin
Madison, Wisconsin

Mosby Year Book

St. Louis Baltimore Boston Chicago London Philadelphia Sydney Toronto

Mosby Year Book

Dedicated to Publishing Excellence

Sponsoring Editor: David K. Marshall
Assistant Editor: Julie Tryboski
Associate Managing Editor, Manuscript Services: Deborah Thorp
Production Supervisor: Carol A. Reynolds
Proofroom Manager: Barbara Kelly

Mosby-Year Book, Inc.
11830 Westline Industrial Drive
St. Louis, MO 63146

1 2 3 4 5 6 7 8 9 0 CL PP 96 95 94 93 92

Library of Congress Cataloging-in-Publication Data

Processes in language acquisition and disorders /
[edited by] Robin S. Chapman.
p. cm.
Includes bibliographical references and index.
ISBN 0-8151-1617-9
1. Language acquisition. 2. Language disorders in children.
3. Children—Language. I. Chapman, Robin S.
[DNLM: 1. Language Development. 2. Language Disorders. WS 105.5.C8 P963]
RJ496.L35P76 1992 92-12743
618.92'855—dc20 CIP
DNLM/DLC
for Library of Congress

To John and Josh

CONTRIBUTORS

Leonard Abbeduto, Ph.D.
Associate Professor
Department of Educational Psychology
Waisman Center on Mental Retardation and Human Development
University of Wisconsin at Madison
Madison, Wisconsin

Glenis Benson, M.Phil.
Doctoral Student
Educational Psychology
University of Wisconsin
Madison, Wisconsin

Robin S. Chapman, Ph.D.
Professor
Department of Communicative Disorders
University of Wisconsin
Madison, Wisconsin

Elizabeth R. Crais, Ph.D.
Assistant Professor
Division of Speech and Hearing Sciences
University of North Carolina
Chapel Hill, North Carolina

Christine A. Dollaghan, Ph.D.
Assistant Professor
Department of Communication
University of Pittsburgh
Pittsburgh, Pennsylvania

Alan G. Kamhi, Ph.D.
Associate Professor
Audiology and Speech Pathology
Memphis State University
Memphis, Tennessee

Raymond D. Kent, Ph.D.
Professor, Communicative Disorders
University of Wisconsin at Madison
Madison, Wisconsin

Laurence B. Leonard, Ph.D.
Professor, Audiology and Speech Sciences
Purdue University
West Lafayette, Indiana

Jon F. Miller, Ph.D.
Professor, Communicative Disorders
University of Wisconsin at Madison
Madison, Wisconsin

Linda M. Milosky, Ph.D.
Assistant Professor
Communication Sciences and Disorders
Syracuse University
Syracuse, New York

Nanette A. Negri, Ph.D.
Educational and Behavioral Consultant
Integrated Student Services
Madison Metropolitan School District
Madison, Wisconsin

Rhea Paul, Ph.D.
Associate Professor
Director, Portland Speech and Hearing Sciences Program
Language Development Project
Portland State University
Portland, Oregon

Diane Salmon, Ph.D.
Assistant Professor
Educational Psychology
National-Louis University
Evanston, Illinois

Richard G. Schwartz, Ph.D.
Professor, Doctoral Program in Speech and Hearing Sciences
City University of New York
New York, New York

Edythe A. Strand, Ph.D.
Assistant Professor
Speech and Hearing Sciences
University of Washington
Seattle, Washington

Nancy W. Streim, Ph.D.
Graduate School of Education
University of Pennsylvania
Philadelphia, Pennsylvania

Susan Ellis Weismer, Ph.D.
Assistant Professor
Department of Communicative Disorders
Waisman Center on Mental Retardation and Human Development
University of Wisconsin at Madison
Madison, Wisconsin

PREFACE

This is a book that focuses on *process* in child language: how children understand and use language. Initial chapters take up modeling of the processes of listening and talking, and the question of whether these processes are best thought of as holistic, modular, or interactive. In subsequent sections, organized around the specific linguistic domains of phonology, semantics, syntax, and pragmatics, chapters consider acquisition and the ways in which the knowledge structures of one domain may interact with other linguistic and nonlinguistic domains in children's communication. Evidence from both language development and language disorders is considered.

Process approaches to adult language use have long been the norm. Child language research, in contrast, has traditionally focused on modeling the child's linguistic competence, rather than use. The chapters here illustrate newer approaches to studying children's language acquisition. Not all these investigators adopt the same interactive model of process, but they share an approach that focuses on accounting for performance.

In addition, these investigators emphasize the nonlinguistic factors that influence what children understand and say: the interactive roles of world knowledge, situational context, communicative goals, personal knowledge, affect, topic, conversational history, and the biological constraints on the form that talk takes.

These are topics on which our knowledge is rapidly evolving, as new research paradigms, connectionist modeling of acquisition and disorders, and brain imaging are brought to bear on the questions raised here. This book offers students in the communication and cognitive sciences an opportunity to join researchers in posing and thinking through questions that a process approach to child language acquisition raises.

The context of discussion encouraged is wide-ranging. In these chapters, students will encounter investigators working to broaden their own understanding of the ways in which acquisition within one traditional linguistic domain interact with acquisition and processing in other domains, and with the child's developing world knowledge. Fundamental questions are raised about the models by which we choose to represent children's linguistic skills and language disorders—those creative fictions of the scientist that dictate the subsequently interesting lines of research.

This book is an invitation to the student to join that process of exploration and clarification. We hope for our readers to continue the collaboration out of which this book arose, for its roots lie in the seminar tradition: the coming together of scholars to share their curiosity, their questions, and their diverse knowledge in discussion and debate. The informal seminar in which the Child Talk model had its origins continued over three semesters, drawing on a widening community of scholars. As this book took shape and additional contributions were invited, the discussion of issues took place in writing and revision.

I am grateful to all who participated in this extended examination of our beliefs about children's language learning and to those who made this discussion possible. To my teachers in Swarthmore College's honors programs thirty years ago, who gave me a love for the interactive process of learning that a seminar constitutes, I offer my thanks: Hans Wallach, Solomon Asch, Henry Gleitman, Richard Solomon, and Irvin Rock among them. To Dan Slobin and Susan Ervin-Tripp at Berkeley, who took their seminar students with them into the creation of the new discipline of developmental psycholinguistics: my admiration and gratitude.

To the students whose continued curiosity and enthusiasm led the Child Talk seminar to new questions, my coauthors of Chapter 1, Betsy Crais, Nan Negri, Diane Salmon, Edie Strand, Nancy Streim: my great appreciation for the opportunity of shared learning. To the colleagues named at the end of Chapter 1 who patiently commented, expostulated, and critiqued our thinking: our thanks.

To the colleagues who joined us in the chapters of this book, for your shared willingness to think about process models and implications for clinical practice, for your efforts to be clear and your willingness to participate: my gratitude.

To the National Institutes of Health (Grant R01 HD 23353), the Waisman Center of Mental Retardation and Human Development, and the Department of Communicative Disorders, who have supported my work in children's language development and disorders over the period of this book's preparation: my thanks.

To Kevin Kline, David Marshall, Julie Tryboski, and the anonymous reviewers of Mosby-Year Book, Inc. who have made publication possible and the text shapely: my appreciation.

To the reader beginning this book: welcome.

Robin S. Chapman, Ph.D.

CONTENTS

SECTION III: INTERACTIVE PROCESSES IN LEXICAL ACQUISITION *139*

SECTION IV: INTERACTIVE PROCESSES IN SYNTACTIC DEVELOPMENT *217*

SECTION V: INTERACTIVE PROCESSES IN PRAGMATIC DEVELOPMENT *255*

SECTION I

Modeling Children's Language Performance

1 Child Talk: Assumptions of a Developmental Process Model for Early Language Learning

Robin S. Chapman, Ph.D.

Nancy W. Streim, Ph.D.

Elizabeth R. Crais, Ph.D.

Diane Salmon, Ph.D.

Edythe A. Strand, Ph.D.

Nanette A. Negri, Ph.D.

Child Talk, as a label, is a sort of promissory note, the name given to an evolving process model of children's language production collectively created in seminar discussions. When we first started this task, our rationale was simple: We wanted to integrate the work on adult language process models of production with the work on children's language that had focused on structural accounts. We wanted to create a developmental process model of language production that accounted for everyday conversation in all its diversity. And we wanted to do so in a radical way, questioning closely the assumptions taken for granted in each field, to see, for example, what happened if we threw out linguistic constructs such as syntax, or phonemes, or the semantic dictionary.

This chapter is by way of a progress report, or travel diary, of that journey, wherein we sketch briefly some of the issues we encountered, our struggles with them, and the assumptions we chose to discard or retain. Our quest was for that elusive promised land in which we might be able to answer the questions: (1) What is the nature of the child's knowledge of language? (2) How is it organized? (3) Why does it change? by examining the question (4) How is knowledge actually used in children's talking?

Many adult models set more limited goals than our own of accounting for discourse aspects of language production. Speech production models, for example, typically ignore problems associated with message selection and utterance formulation by setting, as their goal, accounting for behavior only in repetitive tasks or only in errors of speech production. Models of language production frequently turn out to be sentence-level models that ignored discourse context, situational context, and speaker intent or that assumed that the processes of utterance planning and speaking did not interact. Nor did these models typically comment on the relationship between the processes of production and language comprehension. We believed that such simplifications did violence to what we already knew about adult and child talk. Our first problem became that of constructing plausible assumptions for a model that could be applied more broadly to young children.

We wanted to ask: What is the process by which a child decides to talk, finds something to say, a way to say it, and with more or less success, says it? What are the developmental changes in this process, and why do they occur? What individual differences arise?

CLASSICAL STRUCTURAL MODELS OF CHILD TALK

Classical accounts of children's spoken acquisition have made the following claims: (1) children's language formulation is creative, (2) the units of production are linguistic in nature, (3) what the child learns are rules for combining these units, and (4) the process of acquisition is one of generating and applying hypotheses about rules.

The classical account is consistent with the general shape of sentence production models much like those advanced for adults by Garrett (1982) in which words are retrieved and assembled into sentence frames that are phonologically realized. Bock (1982, 1987) has argued against the modularity of separate linguistic domains implied in this view. In the modular Garrett account, semantic representations are retrieved without relation to phonologic representations. Sentence frame selection does not influence lexical selection. Bock (1982) has cited a number of adult studies that lead to the conclusion that such processing must be, at least, interactive. Are there also reasons to reject linguistic modularity as it arises in the classical view of children's language acquisition? And if other assumptions are warranted, what are their consequence for a process model? We make arguments for and against the classical view briefly, taking one aspect at a time.

Creativity

The conclusion that children created language was consistent with the emphasis at the time on the generativity of linguistic knowledge: the ideal speaker-listener's ability to produce an infinite number of well-formed sentences, some of infinite length, had he but world enough and time. Several lines of evidence converge on the conclusion that children are active creators of their language. Errors of overgeneralization—*two mouses, I goed, who deaded my cat?*—that reflect novel constructions by the child have been taken as paradigm examples of the language production process. Errors of underextension, for example, settling on a narrower category for accusative case when the language the child hears does not require such a constraint, as in Gvozdev's report of children learning Russian (Slobin, 1986a), were also taken as support for the view of the child actively discovering his or her language system. Reports of spontaneous creation of signing systems by deaf children not exposed to sign language (Goldin-Meadow and Feldman, 1977) were added.

So what's wrong with this view? Only the fact that it oversimplifies the picture of children's language learning, taking the exceptional instance as the paradigm case. Ervin-Tripp (1977) has argued persuasively from videotapes of family dinner hours that far more language use is formulaic than one might expect, viewing instances of play with novel toys. Nelson (1986), Peters (1984), Bruner (1978), and Snow (1977) have called attention to the routine expressions in early child language and their original sources in the predictable interaction sequences of parent-child play: scripts or scaffolds afforded by object exchanges, peekaboo games, and reading the same book over and over. In these instances, over time we see the child come to produce first his or her part of the dialogue and later the parent's part. Thus, children do not always create utterances from scratch; frequently they say what they have said before in the situation or what someone else has said. Creativity, then, becomes a more rarely encountered phenomenon—one required when past experience as a listener and talker does not provide the words or sentence frame necessary to the current communicative task. Ervin-Tripp (1977) describes such instances and calls them "bursts of syntax" that arise occasionally in the child's interacting day. Children, then, are both reproducers and creators of their utterances rather than either one or the other.

A standard objection to such proposals in the past has been to point out how rapidly the child learns language—far too rapidly to benefit from limited, possibly ill-formed, input. When we had reached this point in our thinking, we became curious about just how much talk a child heard and produced in 1 day: Just what is the size of the experiential data bases? There are some data available for the number of words spoken in a typical 12-hour waking day by 2-year-olds (Wagner, 1985); they range from 10,000 to 20,000/day. If input is estimated conservatively at twice that (mothers typically take two speaking turns to the child's one and contribute two morphemes more than the child in each utterance on average), a typical listening day might include 20,000 to 40,000 words. Translating these figures to the 1,000 days of the brief language learning period that the classical account recognizes, we are talking about children who have spoken, by age 4 years, 10 to 20 million words and who have listened to potentially 20 to 40 million words in context—hardly instantaneous acquisition. This is a healthy data base, particularly given the demonstration that word meanings and use can be acquired in one to a few novel presentations (Carey, 1978; Dollaghan, 1985; Streim and Chapman, 1986). Thus, it does not seem so implausible to invoke history of previous experience with talking and listening in a situation as a source for the words and structures available in that situation.

This conclusion has important consequences for a model of the formulation process: it should permit the production of both kinds of utterances, the one created on the spot and the one heard or said before. It seems that the child needs access to the conversational history of an interaction sequence as a basis for constructing current talk and that history is a record both of what has been comprehended before and what has been produced before.

Linguistic Units

The assumption that children learn units corresponding to linguistic levels of analysis has had strong support from two observations about language development. The first was that children learn to talk one word at a time, that is, they began with single words stripped of inflection. Second was the demonstration that grammatical complexity and early stages of language learning were well predicted by measures of mean utterance length based on morphemes.

So what is wrong with the assumption that children are learning morphemes? Again, the problem is one of oversimplification, because the children also learn phrases as unanalyzed wholes, as, indeed, we treat phrases like *night-night, allgone, alldone, thankyou,* and *wanna.* They can also produce prosodic contours with syllables empty of morphemic content, as in Allison's use of *wida,* reported by Bloom (1973), or undifferentiated, unstressed syllables inserted at points where grammatical morphemes will come later. As Peters (1984) has elegantly analyzed this problem in her book on the units of language acquisition, the central problem is the assumption that the unit of production is fixed at some one linguistic level of analysis. In fact, she argues, the same utterance, morphemically transcribed, may be produced with different degrees of unitization of sound, syllable, morpheme, word, or phrase.

We need to turn to the methodologies of speech acoustic analysis for the evidence that might allow us to decide what planning units underlie a production of *Wannago?*, *Wantago?*, or *Whatchadoing?*, for example. It is likely that the frequency with which the phrase is encountered in input, or produced, unaltered, is going to be an important determinant of larger size units, but the same utterance, orthographically speaking, could be produced on the basis of entirely different planning units by the same speaker at different times. For on-line segmentation decisions that critically affect attribution of productive syntactic patterns and the complexity measures of multiword speech, our current methods of word utterance determination are inadequate.

This issue is a particularly important one in modeling individual differences in sentence formulation by children whose approach to language acquisition is gestalt or formulaic, some 10% of normal children who have been studied, a large proportion of second-language learners, and, in extreme form, the immediate and delayed echolalia of autism. It increases in importance in thinking about adult utterance formulation. Surely the stuff out of which we construct our sentences is sometimes larger than morphemic units—idioms, often used expressions, whole clauses, or texts. It is made more complicated by the recognition that preference for gestalt vs. analytic approach is not simply a property of the language learner but a reflection of the characteristics of language input. One of Peters' students studied a trilingual child learning Finnish from a typical mother-child interaction, Japanese from a father given to repeating activities and formulaic language, and English from a teenage babysitter who fell somewhere in between, in the repetitiousness of interaction. The child learned Finnish in the analytic, one word at a time mode; Japanese in a gestalt, formulaic style; and English in between. The conclusion, then, is that units of language production (viewed linguistically) may vary from syllables to sentences as long as they correspond to meaning in some global fashion.

This conclusion requires a model of language production to either enter longer phrases and constructions in the lexicon, so that they may be encountered as giant "words," or to include phonological assemblies larger than the word. Either way, it becomes a problem to predict when the smaller and when the larger units will be chosen.

Rule-Governed Combinations of Units

The assumption that children learn rules for utterance formulation has been retained through many successive revisions of the nature of the rules themselves: from early, pivot grammars through combinations based on syntactic categories, case grammar categories like agent and object of action, to semantically, lexically, and pragmatically constrained categories. However, these accounts have introduced rules less and less motivated by linguistic categories.

Ervin-Tripp (1977) describes a child, for example, who says *I do it* only to announce her achievements and *you do it* only to request action, reflecting the specificity with which form and communicative intent can be linked. Schieffelin (1979) children, learn Kaluli, an ergative language in which the agents of highly transitive, dynamic events (actions on objects like chopping, hitting, tearing as opposed to sleeping or reading) are marked. These children never overextend the ergative marker to agents of the less dynamic events, meaning that their category for sentence initial position is not subject, not nominative case, not even agent of action, but something more restricted, which Slobin (1986b) suggests is not a linguistic category at all but a property of a dynamic transitive event structure that they are trying to put into words. It is the person's role in the event rather than the word's role in the sentence that is the basis for the ergative marker's inclusion. By this view, then, the child's early rules for including and ordering words and morphemes apply to the roles of the referents in events as they conceive them. The ordering frame is not derived from linguistic universals but from conceptual universals, the way in which young children see commonalities in the events around them: the child's event knowledge (Nelson, 1986). Ervin-Tripp's (1977) example highlights the fact that the child's own participation in the event, his or her role and communicative goals, may further contribute to the "rule" by which sentences are constructed.

Thus, representation of goals and events become important inputs to the production model for a child; without them, the production rule cannot be characterized at all.

Having satisfied ourselves that the rules the child uses must be constrained in terms other than linguistic ones, we go on to the problem that variability in utterance production within children is not predicted by rule-based accounts. To return to the examples of creative overextensions of plurals and past tense, the original data that Cazden (1968) reviewed contained such instances, but they were infrequent, constituting maybe 5% of the examples. At the same stage that children were overextending such forms, they were failing to do so, doing so correctly, or doing so in multiple fashion, such as the child who said *break, breaked,* and *broke.* The rules of the classical account were created to account for interesting departures from adult language but not for the simultaneous occurrence of a variety of forms or for frequency characteristics in general.

Klima and Bellugi's (1966) account of question development is such an example, where a stage in which children use but do not invert an auxiliary element is proposed: *Why he can't do that?* rather than *Why can't he do that?*. As Tyack and Ingram (1977) have shown, such productions are vanishingly rare in transcripts, and most of Bellugi's examples can be accounted for by the method of eliciting the sample (E: *Ask me why he can't do that?* C: *Why he can't do that?*). But there are, rarely, for some children, unprompted instances. They are exceptions rather than the rule when frequency is taken into account.

Illustrated here is a problem with the methodology by which the rule-governed account was constructed. At the time, the enterprise was that of describing competence or what could be produced rather than what was usually produced. Rule-based accounts were constructed to generate the range of combinations attested but not to reflect the very different frequencies of those combinations. This characteristic, however, makes such rule-based accounts potentially flawed when used to predict performance. Such problems can be resolved in a process model by limiting the scope of the rules more narrowly (if linguistic bases can be found) and allowing the forms to compete or by adopting connectionist approaches that give the appearance of rule-based behavior, together with exceptions and prototypical effects.

The Nature of the Acquisition Process

The least-studied and most troublesome aspects of the classical account are its claim that rules are acquired through the process of hypothesis generation and testing. This metaphorical invocation of scientific inquiry has certain limitations; the conscious construction of a hypothesis and deliberate testing of it—formal operational thinking in Piaget's sense—is clearly not what is meant. But if not, what could be meant?

A problem with the hypothesis-generating account is the claim that children must choose and discard hypotheses without the benefit of negative feedback. This view of the child's learning predicament came from the early search by Brown and Hanlon (1970) for parent utterances explicitly rejecting or correcting a child's attempt at language, in the way parents occasionally protested, for example, *ain't*. These instances were few and confined to corrections of truth value *(That's not a spoon, it's a fork.)* rather than syntactic or phonological well formedness in the Brown corpus. In older children, of course, socially appropriate uses are frequently corrected *(We don't say that word in front of Grandma.)* But the Brown and Hanlon view of negative feedback was quite narrow. It excluded repetitions or requests for confirmation or clarification that offered the corrected version. Demetras et al. (1986) have shown that such utterances frequently attend a child's incorrect form. Bowerman (1987) and Hirsch-Pasek et al. (1984) expand the scope of what might be considered negative feedback by pointing out that late errors can arise after "failure-driven" mastery and that failure to encounter such forms in other speakers might over time serve a disconfirming function.

Even if the existence of negative feedback is granted, however, it is not clear that it serves the function of leading a child to revise his hypotheses. An example of this comes from Chapman's notes on her younger son's pronoun use. For several months he talked about *my shoes, your shoes,* but *were canoe* (the boat we all owned; our canoe). This form came, I hypothesized, from an incorrect but reasonable analysis of the English pronoun system as inflected for possession: if *you* goes to *your,* surely *we* goes to *were;* just as, more commonly, other children may decide that if *it* becomes *its shoe,* surely *she* becomes *she's shoe.* But did Josh make such a hypothesis, as opposed to simply an analogous production? If so, he clearly was not testing it; over the months, clearly, patiently, the mother would say, "Oh, you mean *our canoe?*" *"Yes,"* he would beam, *"were canoe."* Similarly, her older son, as he tackled the auxiliary system, heard the neighborhood baby-sitter say a few times *ain't,* a form happily usable with any personal pronoun—*I ain't; you ain't, he, she, it ain't; we ain't; they ain't*—a much more consistent marking of a notion than, for example, *I'm not; you aren't; he, she, it, isn't; we aren't; they aren't.* A few examples of consistent marking of the notion he wanted to express were enough to prompt him to adopt the word despite his mother's more persistent and directive feedback *(no, no, say isn't).* Slobin (1978) cites many examples in his notes of his child's development of incorrect uses that persisted despite adult feedback of the correct form. Analogy or overextension can be invoked to explain the forms the children adopt, but these uses, unlike hypotheses, do not appear to be provisional and are not abandoned on correction. (Variation, of course, exists. Sometimes they are produced correctly, as noted previously. Even this is not sufficient to lead to the abandonment of the misanalyzed version.)

The innate solution of the controversy is to argue that, therefore, the hypotheses generated by the child must be innately constrained to a likely-to-be correct subset of hypotheses, embodied, for example, in parameter-setting theories of universal grammar (Hyams, 1986). This solution has certain appeal to those studying languages but relatively less for those studying children's communication. Rather, what seems to be wrong with both versions—those in which feedback exists or in which it does not—is the belief that the child's rules are generated as hypotheses for test. An alternative is to view the child's "rules" as being far narrower than these accounts or not rules at all in the sense of separate sets of syntactic instructions for well-formed sentence construction.

WHAT IS LEFT OUT OF THE CLASSICAL ACCOUNT

The way in which young children's syntactic rules appear restricted by particular words, particular semantic categories (often idiosyncratic ones), and particular communicative goals has already been pointed out. So too have the variations with which a given form, such as regular past tense, is produced or overextended. There are many other interesting aspects of developmental change in child performance that are simply ignored in the classical account. Included in this left-out category is the amount of talk—how many communicative attempts the child typically makes in a ½ hour of free play, for example, or in a day's observation, or how many utterances or total words he produces in conversation with an examiner. This neglected variable is one that shows the most striking change in the second year of life, when children triple the number of communicative vocalizations recorded in play between 10 and 21 months (Chapman et al., 1981). Miller's (1986) reference data base records on 3- to 13-year-olds demonstrate an increase in amount of talk per unit time throughout the preschool and early school-age period. Because the number of different words increase per unit time at the same rate as total words, type/token ratios typically conceal the great developmental change in the size of vocabulary that can be recruited for talk. Separated, the measures of different words and total words reveal the increasing number of different things a child can think of to say and his or her increasing willingness to contribute to the conversation during the language learning period. These are important changes in language use that a developmental process model should capture. It is as though we are seeing an increase not just in what is learned but in access to what has been learned, both about the world and about words.

A second aspect of children's language development neglected in classical accounts is the situational specificity of talk: the early appearance of language in routine contexts of bye-bye and peekaboo and allgone games, the learning of names in the book-reading routine, indeed, the toddler's sheer joy of producing a known name for the person, pet, or object that comes into view. Later, as Ninio and Bruner (1978), Nelson and Gruendel (1979), and Snow and Goldfield (1983) have shown, children produce language during a particular event or on a topic that they have heard earlier, such as taking over the questioning in the book-reading game *(What's that?),* usurping the adult comments at lunchtime, or giving back to the adult historical information about the dinosaur. Not only is the language used often specific to a given topic or situation, but it is often just the language that has been previously encountered with respect to that topic or in that situation. Every parent who reads to children during that stage in which the same book must be read again, night after night, is familiar with the ferocious tenacity of the young child's memory for verbatim talk, cued by context; it is not possible, even if one is fatigued, to skip sentences, shorten the dialogue, omit words, without protest and, often, provision.

These observations and studies suggest that conversational histories are stored with the objects and events that are their focus and that those histories are evoked when the objects and events are encountered again. Those histories, the findings make clear, contain words and sentences. What if this is the typical way in which access to words is obtained by children? And there is much reason to argue that this is so, particularly for younger children. Then the problem of access to words in sentence formulation is very different from searching for a meaning through a dictionary; instead, meaning and word are to be found in the encyclopedia entry the child is currently consulting.

Speaker specificity of talk is also characteristic of young children's expectations for the language that they hear. Even at age 3 months, the infant expects expressive, "baby-talk" voice quality to go with the mother's face. Children's later solutions to dialect differences among speakers can arise only if speaker characteristics are part of the record. So too must later records be kept of what has been said already—the conference goer keeping straight whom he or she has already told this joke to, the 4-year-old exclaiming in disgust, *You already told me that!*

Indeed, it is only by keeping event-based conversational histories that the humor of the following account can be appreciated. This is a story Annie Dilliard (1987) tells of her parents in her memoirs entitled *An American Childhood:*

> There was another very complicated joke, also in a select category, which required a long weekend with tolerant friends.
>
> You had to tell a joke that was not funny. It was a long, pointless story about a construction job that ended with someone's throwing away a brick. There was nothing funny about it at all, and when your friends did not laugh, you had to pretend you'd muffed it. (Your husband in the crowd could shill for you: "Tain't funny, Pam. You told it all wrong.")
>
> A few days later, if you could contrive another occasion for joke telling, and if your friends still permitted you to speak, you set forth on another joke, this one an old nineteenth-century chestnut about angry passengers on a train. The lady plucks the lighted, smelly cigar from the man's mouth and flings it from the moving train's window. The man seizes the little black poodle from her lap and hurls the poor dog from the same window. When the last passengers draw unspeaking into the station, what do they see coming down the platform but the black poodle, and guess what it has in its mouth? "The cigar," say your friends, bored sick and vowing never to spend another weekend with you. "No," you say triumphant, "the brick." This was Mother's kind of joke. Its very riskiness excited her. It wasn't funny, but it was interesting to set up, and it elicited from her friends a grudging admiration.*

The point of this example, of course, is that comprehension, like production, takes place in the context of a framing event, and that speaker, communicative goal (and its outcome), and referents all can serve to pull up or activate a prior history of talk. At another level, we offer this example as a metaphor for what words, like bricks, might do—haul into the middle of one discussion the history associated with their prior use in another, not the whole history but the specific, useful encyclopedic entry that fits the current context.

At this point in our thinking we had very serious cause to challenge the assumptions of classical theory about the existence and organization of the lexicon, or mental dictionary, on the basis of per-

*From Dilliard A: *An American Childhood.* New York, Harper & Row, Publishers, 1987, pp 53–54. Used by permission.

formance data. The claim of domain-specific linguistic modularity seemed wrong. Whatever the organization of the dictionary, we reasoned, it should facilitate or retard lexical search; what sort of organization could account for access, say, to 125 words/minute? Could such rates of access be shown for semantically related words likely to be stored together in such a mental dictionary? Readers should pause here and test this conclusion for themselves by taking out a paper and pencil and writing down as many animal names as they can think of in the next 60 seconds. Ready? Now.

So what happened? Did you find ready access to 100 animal names? 60? More like 20? Did you get stuck in the process? How did you get unstuck? How did you find more entries? If your performance was like our own, you realized your animals were organized by some larger topic, usually place encountered: house pets, farm animals, zoo animals, or possibly extensive dinosaur lists for those still reading to preschoolers. Do you conclude that you were searching a dictionary or an event-based encyclopedia?

Discrepancies between what the child can say and what he or she will say have been observed, even in situations (e.g., the production of modal verbs [Maratsos and Kuczaj, 1978]) where the child is cooperative and saying something. He or she just does not produce in one setting the modal verb that has been elicited in another. Such cases, apparently not accounted for by motivational factors, are a problem for the classical account that believes all words come from the modular lexical core and that any observed occurrence means the word is in there or available. The Child Talk prediction is that such differences in accessibility can be accounted for by the history of comprehended experience in that situation previously on that topic.

As a final entry in the list of phenomena ignored by classical structural accounts of child language, there are differences between children's comprehension and production of words, and word order, which have been a continuing puzzle for a classical account in which syntactic competence is a single domain-specific model. Overextension of words in production is usually not accompanied by a similar overextension of meaning in comprehension. Failure to attend to word order in comprehension but not in production is a replicable phenomenon for certain verbs. There are a number of ways to attempt to explain these observations, but we take them as symptomatic of a deeper, underlying problem with the classical account: it is the processes of talking and listening that appear modular in the sense of information encapsulation and continuity of prediction through time (Bates et al., 1988) rather than the domains of syntax and semantics. Similarly, processes in reading comprehension may differ significantly from listening comprehension. Jakimik and Glenberg (1990) found evidence for differential, and more difficult, processing of temporal anaphors (e.g., the former; the latter) in reading than listening.

CHILD TALK'S CLAIMS ABOUT MODULARITY

To summarize the foregoing discussion, modular models of linguistic knowledge (e.g., Fodor, 1983) typically contain abstract core semantic, syntactic, and phonological features associated with words (themselves organized as a dictionary or lexicon), together with representations of grammatically acceptable structures into which entries can be inserted. Syntactic categories and relationships divorced from meaning typically form the content of sentence structure representation. These models are modular in the sense of domain specificity.

The modular accounts are compact, economical representations of linguistic knowledge and, as such, offer useful intellectual tools to anyone dealing with language. Their adoption as accounts of user knowledge, however, creates major problems for a developmental process model of production.

There are a number of things that modularity might mean in a model. Bates et al. (1988) offer a good discussion, and in Chapter 3 Kamhi discusses his own views. Importantly, we believe that the different tests for modularity reveal different answers. Our own tests for modularity have included domain specificity and informational encapsulation. A third test might be the evidence for selective deficits in language disorders as a function of brain structure or function differences. Both adult speech production models and the classical child account have adopted domain specificity and informational encapsulation as characteristics of the linguistic system. Bock (1982, 1987) has challenged the second assumption but not the first. She has shown that interactive effects not predicted for encapsulated systems occur. Linguistic modules of lexicon and sentence frames remain in Bock's model, but now they interact.

Child Talk has interpreted similar data among children in an opposite way, given the strong evidence of context-specific language use. We see it as evidence against the modularity of language in the sense of domain specificity and are prepared to set aside notions of a lexicon impervious to detailed world knowledge and syntax unconnected to situation, speaker roles, or goals. But, in a sense, we have retained modularity: the modularity conferred by event representation in memory, which act as encapsulated systems representing words and sentence frames embedded in them in memory. What classical accounts left out of the language module—intentions, emotions, personal history of the self and other, and world knowledge generally—become the very stuff of which linguistic knowledge is made, as one brick, perhaps, in the complex constructions by which we make sense of our lives. The performance analysis forces another kind of modular claim, one antithetical to the search for linguistic competence: this is the recognition that the processes of comprehension and production are dissociable in both development and disorder and must be modeled separately, as well as together.

ASSUMPTIONS OF CHILD TALK

Child Talk is a model that assumes that early language learning is part of learning about the social and physical world: the world of people, the world of people, objects, events that involve them, the sounds and gestures that characteristically accompany them, and the vocal and gestural means by which one can bring about desired results. Early language learning is contextualized, that is, it is nonmodular with respect to knowledge domain. Early linguistic knowledge is part of the representation of the world's speakers, actions, events, situations, feelings, and goals. It is specific, episodic knowledge of what other people do in situations and the procedural knowledge of how to do things oneself in a situation. Let us to pursue the metaphor of knowledge organization: there is no dictionary or grammar book originally in which one can look up words, their pronunciation, their meaning, or allowable ways of combining them. There is only an encyclopedia of topics, those in which we are biologically endowed to take an interest (friendly people and animals, frightening people and animals, food, drink, objects to act on, certain sounds and facial expressions) and those in which culture and experience dictate an interest (familiar, moderately novel, or entirely new people, places, objects, and events of our 1-, 2-, or

3-year-old lives); goals we entertain; and ways we, and others, achieve them. The metaphor is even then not very good, because an encyclopedia implies a particular system of indexing or entry—topics and names, say—for access to its information rapidly; otherwise, one hunts through indexes, cross-references, and the alphabet to find some scrap of information. In contrast, the young child's access to past experience is multiply cued: by reinstantiation of setting, person, state and affect, goal, activity, topic, and prior talk in ways that pull up interaction histories, expectations of what will happen next, what could be done next (including talk) as means to an end.

What is modular, from Child Talk's view, are the child's knowledge schemas. This is the notion of modularity that meets the tests of encapsulation of information and, possibly, mandatory application of knowledge rather than the test of specificity of knowledge domain. Schemas, as they develop, can be instantiated by partial cues. Activated, they suggest the "local" meanings and interpretation in comprehension and the usual means for reaching a goal in production; current action and outcomes confirm or disconfirm these expectations and update the schema. To the extent that listening is an activity different from talking, the two processes are dissociable from one another, a kind of process modularity that Bates et al. (1988), among others, have argued for. But in the Child Talk view, it is their contextualized occurrence in a particular event that is modular; when the event expands to include expectations of dialogue sequence, expectations for listening and talking in that situation may become tied, and even switched, as the child takes on the other's role.

The fundamental assumption of the Child Talk model, then, is that linguistic knowledge is developed in the context of and embedded in world knowledge and is acquired like any other developing knowledge of how to plan and carry out goal-directed action.

We believe that knowledge of how to talk is:

1. Process based (understanding or production)
2. Embedded in world knowledge
3. Multiply entered in memory, including the context of understanding or production
4. Automatized by use
5. Generalized by lexical scripts
6. Generalized as utterance frames, given experiences that are based on the individual's knowledge of functional, pragmatic, discourse, and semantic relations or conceptual categories

We believe that the process of utterance formulation:

1. Is goal directed
2. Results in communicative action
3. Assembles units drawn from talk representation available in working memory
4. Contains the portion of the knowledge network activated in a spreading fashion by speaker goals, speaker affect, addressee identity, topic, setting, and the communicative events that the speaker believes to be taking place

It is attractive to think that a connectionist account of language acquisition might ultimately be possible, incorporating these assumptions. In our view, success would likely depend on including world knowledge in the connectionist net, as well as restricting early experience of the world and talk to that typically encountered by the child. Recent work in connectionist modeling (e.g., Elman, 1989; McClelland, 1991) has been promising.

Connectionist accounts can be viewed

as summations of experience reflecting the inherent structure in it but not separable from it and hence not disconfirmable in single instances in the way a rule might be. This is the attractive promise of connectionist accounts, in which the output of some module reflects the weights its connections have acquired through experience and the current input, leading to output behaviors that appear rule governed but are not, summations that, depending on the input, can also yield exceptions, mistakes, and variations.

If connectionist accounts make tangible the possibility of conceiving of knowledge representations that yield rulelike or prototype behaviors without being themselves rules or prototypes, they have their current limitations as well. As Bever has pointed out in recent colloquia, they fail, in current forms, to specify what the input structures are or what the output should be. These are left to the creativity and choice of the model maker, and they require many learning trials with perfect feedback in their current form to acquire the proper weighting. These are not the characteristics of the language learning child, who may need only one trial with no feedback to acquire some comprehension of and memory for a word. The child, however, has more than 1 year of experience of people, objects and events, babbling, and voices; these, if supplied, might create a rather different set of starting weights. And there are kinds of knowledge—phonological, morphological, and syntactic—that appear to require just such extended experience.

IMPLICATIONS FOR PROCESS MODELS

Interaction

The Child Talk model shares with other interactive models the claim that differing linguistic domains will appear to interact in the formulation of talk and in its comprehension. In Chapter 2, Milosky elaborates the evidence for an interaction of linguistic domains and world knowledge in comprehension. In Chapter 3, Kamhi offers a critical reconsideration of interactionism, modularity, and holism. Subsequent chapters in this book are organized around evidence for each traditional linguistic domain that interactions with other linguistic domains take place. Not all other authors in this book share the massively interactive view that Child Talk proposes, in which the schema building of early contextualized knowledge contributes to the appearance of interacting domains. For many theorists, interaction arises in the trade-offs when limited resources are stretched; this too is a kind of interaction that arises in the Child Talk model as lexical and utterance frame schemas begin to emerge from experience. Almost all, however, find persuasive evidence of interaction among linguistic domains in the child's process of talking and listening.

The interactions between phonologic and lexical development, in particular, are explored from a variety of perspectives in this volume: Kent (see Chapter 4) considers the biologic origins of speech, Strand (see Chapter 5) reviews adult models of speech motor control in relation to language, and Schwartz (see Chapter 6) considers the theoretical frameworks of nonlinear phonology and connectionism.

Lexical interactions are further explored in this book in Dollaghan's chapter on adult-based models of the lexicon and in Crais's review of fast mapping (the early phase of word learning). Streim (see Chapter 12) and Paul (see Chapter 13) consider the interactions that arise between syntax and other domains in children's talk. Streim also reviews evidence in support of Child Talk's predictions that more abstract syntactic categories are not available to younger children.

Further predictions that the Child Talk model might make await experimental investigation. For example, the model would claim that fast mapping of words in separate event contexts would make word recognition (with context supplied) easier in early acquisition stages than fast mapping of the same words in the same event context (hence, requiring more auditory experience to build auditory representations complete enough to distinguish the words from one another).

Language Disorders

A consequence of the Child Talk assumptions about language production is the prediction for early development that delays in cognitive and social development and limitations of linguistic cognitive and social experience will be associated with later language delay. Because early language representations are embedded in the child's developing representations of people, objects, events, settings, and associated affect and goals, delays in the construction of these representations will limit the comprehension, acquisition, and use of associated language. In addition, these limitations in later language acquisition are more likely to be revealed in measures of language production used for young children that are reflecting frequency and variety of talk across topics, speakers, or communication goals. By this argument, prelinguistic delays in development should be related to later linguistic delay for causal reasons, and early language development should reveal the continuous influence of earlier learning and experience in a variety of domains.

Miller (see Chapter 11) and Abbeduto and Benson (see Chapter 14) review some of the evidence for this relationship and further evidence for specific language impairment among children with mental retardation. Negri (see Chapter 15) discusses the cognitive, social, and emotional development of children with autism and their language use, including the surprisingly different view of their skills that is arising from the use of reading and writing with facilitated communication.

With its emphasis on process, the Child Talk model is consistent with the view that specific language impairments can have their origins in process-based sources that affect multiple language domains. Leonard (see Chapter 10) examines competing linguistic and process-based accounts for language impairment cross-linguistically. Weismer (see Chapter 7) considers the role that prosodic variables, including stress and rate, may play in the acquisition of language-impaired children.

IMPLICATIONS FOR CLINICAL PRACTICE

Assessment

The Child Talk model, with its emphasis on performance learning rather than competence, carries implications for assessment. Importantly, it implies that both spoken comprehension and spontaneous talk, as well as reading and writing, should be assessed. Further, it directs attention to aspects of these performances not normally assessed in our standardized tests of language, though contextual, naturalistic approaches such as Lund and Duchan's (1988) make some of these same recommendations. How much does the child talk? How rapidly? These developmentally changing indices may reflect the degree of automatization of talk.

Other assessment questions that Child Talk would lead one to include are: How diverse a vocabulary does the child bring to bear on a topic? How frequently do types and tokens of words and sentence structures occur across contexts? When a new word is first acquired, how is it generalized across addresses, affect, communicative goal, topic, event, object, action, utterance, and discourse context? Systematic data on frequency of use across linguistic (and nonlinguistic) contexts will allow a much more sensitive quantification of the connectivity of linguistic knowledge.

With respect to comprehension, the Child Talk model's focus on process raises the question of how rapidly the child comprehends and what sort of support for short-term memory is necessary. Further, comprehension is viewed as a constructive process requiring the child to infer plausible contexts, as Milosky (see Chapter 2) points out. Thus, it is important to assess inferential and pragmatic aspects of comprehension, including inferences about the speaker's beliefs and communicative goals. (In Chapter 14, Abbeduto and Benson review the latter research literature.)

Intervention

The Child Talk model is consistent with much that is already recommended in clinical practice. It would reemphasize the developmental maxims that children first acquire new functions for old forms and first use new forms for old functions. These might be translated into the clinical advice to work on only one new aspect at a time. If, for example, new vocabulary is to be modeled, it should correspond to familiar concepts and uses. If new communicative goals are the target of intervention, familiar words and sentence structure should be used. Basically one is working to modify existing schemas through incremental change; for this reason, a developmental sequencing of intervention goals is strongly advised (with, of course, the modifications appropriate to clients' communicative tasks).

A second implication of the Child Talk model for intervention is the claim that *practice* is an important component of treatment—practice in the sense of increased opportunity for talk. Practice of newly acquired words and structures in old contexts should increase the automaticity of talk, permitting additional increases in the complexity of the talk. Practice of old words and structures in new contexts should increase the generalizability of these.

A third implication is that language should be modeled in naturalistic communicative contexts, on topics of relevance, and that the size, or chunkiness, of this context should conform to the increasing variety and complexity of discourse goals the child is able to pursue. Thus, one should work at the level of discourse rather than sentence planning: the retelling or invention, with variation, of simple stories; the inclusion of increasingly elaborated talk in the children's sociodramatic play; repeated opportunities to offer instruction at increasingly complex tasks; and models of persuasive language use.

A fourth implication of the Child Talk model, and one for which there is the least current evidence, is that indirect work to increase the connectedness and elaboration of world knowledge should increase access to the diverse vocabulary and records of talk connected with each. Of course, the opportunity to hear talk in these new contexts should increase its subsequent availability even further, as would the opportunity to produce talk in these new contexts.

SUMMARY

Four assumptions of a classical, competence-based account of children's linguistic knowledge were examined and rejected in favor of a process-based set of assumptions for children's language production. The major claim made by the Child Talk model is that knowledge structures subserving talk are not separate from but linked to the developing network of world knowledge and that the organization of this network determines access to the talk formulated or produced. Implications for language disorders and clinical practice were discussed.

Acknowledgment

The preparation of this chapter was supported by NIH grant R01 HD23353-01 to R. S. Chapman and by Core Support grant no. 5P30HD03352 to the Waisman Center on Mental Retardation and Human Development. Earlier versions have been presented to the University of Wisconsin's Psychology Department brown bag lunch series, the American Speech-Language-Hearing Association's Annual Convention in its 1986 research issue seminar, and the Robert Wood Johnson conference on predicting language/communication ability, June 1987. This was an invited address to the Wisconsin Child Language Disorder Symposium, Madison, Wisconsin, June 3, 1988. We thank our colleagues Dee Vetter, Mick McNeil, Gary Weismer, Jon Miller, Rich Lehrer, Helen Goodluck, Jola Jakimik, Art Glenberg, Gregg Oden, Chi-Pang Chiang, Linda Milosky, Marilyn Shatz, and Michael Lewis for patient commentary on our ideas as they evolved.

REFERENCES

Bates E, Bretherton I, and Snyder L: *From First Words to Grammar: Individual Differences and Dissociable Mechanisms.* New York, Cambridge University Press, 1988.

Bloom L: *One Word at a Time.* The Hague, Mouton, 1973.

Bock JK: Toward a cognitive psychology of syntax. *Psychol Rev* 1982; 89:1–47.

Bock JK: Co-ordinating words and syntax in speech plans, in Ellis AW (ed): *Progress in the Psychology of Language.* Hillsdale, NJ, Lawrence Erlbaum Associates, vol 3, 1987, pp 337–390.

Bowerman M: Commentary, in MacWhinney B (ed): *Mechanisms of Language Acquisition.* Hillsdale, NJ, Lawrence Erlbaum Associates, 1987, pp 443–446.

Brown R, Hanlon C: Derivational complexity and order of acquisition in child speech, in Hayes J (ed): *Cognition and the Development of Language.* New York, John Wiley & Sons, 1970.

Bruner J: On prelinguistic prerequisites of speech, in Campbell RN, Smith PT (eds): *Recent Advances in the Psychology of Language.* New York: Plenum Press, vol 4a, 1978, pp 199–214.

Carey S: The child as word learner, in Halle M, Bresnan J, Miller G (eds): *Linguistic Theory and Psychological Reality.* Cambridge, Mass, MIT Press, 1978, pp 264–293.

Cazden C: The acquisition of noun and verb inflections. *Child Dev* 1968; 39:433–448.

Chapman RS, Miller JF, MacKenzie H, et al: The development of discourse skills in the second year of life. Paper presented at the Second International Congress for the Study of Child Language, Vancouver, Canada, August 1981.

Demtras MJ, Post KN, Snow CE: Feedback to first language learners: The role of repetitions and clarification questions. *J Child Lang* 1986; 13:275–292.

Dilliard A: *An American Childhood* New York, Harper & Row, Publishers, 1987, pp 53–54.

Dollaghan C: Child meets word: "Fast-mapping" in preschool children. *J Speech Hear Res* 1985; 28:449–454.

Elman JL: Representation and structure in connectionist models. Technical Rep no 8903, San Diego, Center for Research in Language, University of California, 1989.

Ervin-Tripp S: From conversation to syntax. *Pap Rep Child Lang Dev* 1977; 13:K1–K21.

Fodor J: *The Modularity of Mind.* Cambridge, Mass, MIT Press, 1983.

Garrett M: A perspective on research in language production, in Mehler J, Walker E, Garrett M (eds): *Perspectives on Mental Retardation.* Hillsdale, NJ, Lawrence Erlbaum Associates, 1982, pp 185–199.

Goldin-Meadow S, Feldman H: The development of language-like communication without a language model. *Science* 1977; 197:401–403.

Hirsch-Pasek K, Trieman R, Schneiderman M: Brown and Hanlon revisited: Mother's sensitivity to ungrammatical forms. *J Child Lang* 1984; 11:81–88.

Hyams N: *Language Acquisition and the Theory of Parameters.* Dordrecht, D Reidel, 1986.

Jakimik J, Glenberg A: Verbal learning meets psycholinguistics: Modality effects in the comprehension of anaphora. *J Memory Lang* 1990; 29:582–590.

Klima E, Bellugi U: Syntactic regularities in the speech of children, in Lyons J, Wales RJ (eds): *Psycholinguistic Papers.* Edinburgh, Edinburgh University Press, 1966.

Lund N, Duchan J: *Assessing Children's Language in Naturalistic Contexts,* ed 2. Englewood Cliffs, NJ, Prentice-Hall, 1988.

Maratsos M, Kuczaj S: Against the transformationalist account: A simpler analysis of auxiliary overmarkings. *J Child Lang* 1978; 5:337–346.

McClelland JL: Connectionist models of developmental change. Paper presented at the 1991 Biennial Meeting of the Society for Research in Child Development, Seattle, April 1991.

Miller JF: Reference data base for SALT. Language Analysis Laboratory, Waisman Center on Mental Retardation and Human Development, Madison, Wis, 1986.

Nelson K: *Event Knowledge.* New York, Academic Press, 1986.

Nelson K, Gruendel J: At morning it's lunchtime: A scriptal view of children's dialogues. *Discourse Processes* 1979; 2:73–94.

Ninio A, Bruner J: The achievement and antecedents of labeling. *J Child Language* 1978; 5:1–16.

Peters AM: *The Units of Language Acquisition.* New York, Cambridge University Press, 1984.

Schieffelin B: Getting it together: An ethnographic approach to the study of the development of communicative competence, in Ochs E, Schieffelin B (eds): *Developmental Pragmatics.* New York, Academic Press, 1979, pp 73–108.

Slobin DI: A case study of early language awareness, in Sinclair A, Jarvella RJ, Levelt WJM (eds): *The Child's Conception of Language.* New York, Springer-Verlag New York, 1978.

Slobin DI: Why study acquisition crosslinguistically? in Slobin DI (ed): *The Cross-Linguistic Study of Language Acquisition: The Data.* Hillsdale, NJ, Lawrence Erlbaum Associates, 1986a.

Slobin DI: Cross-linguistic evidence for the language-making capacity, in Slobin DI (ed): *The Cross-Linguistic Study of Language Acquisition: Theoretical Issues.* Hillsdale, NJ, Lawrence Erlbaum Associates, 1986b.

Snow C: The development of conversation between mothers and babies. *J Child Lang* 1977; 4:1–22.

Snow CE, Goldfield BA: Turn the page please: Situation-specific language acquisition. *J Child Lang* 1983; 10:551–570.

Streim N, Chapman RS: A case study of acquisition of novel action verbs: The roles of event and discourse context. Boston University Conference on Language Development, Boston, Oct, 1986.

Tyack D, Ingram D: Children's production and comprehension of questions. *J Child Lang* 1977; 4:221–224.

Wagner K: How much do children say in a day? *J Child Lang* 1985; 12:475–487.

2 Children Listening: The Role of World Knowledge in Language Comprehension

Linda M. Milosky, Ph.D.

Using information from context is critical to the process of understanding language. The physical surroundings, social relationships, the nature of events, and the prior utterances of discourse all comprise context; an individual's past and present knowledge about those aspects of context is the world knowledge that is used in interpreting a given utterance. For a listener to successfully understand an utterance, world knowledge relevant to the context must be activated and used. The Child Talk model has described how such world knowledge is necessary in explaining children's talk. The model also would predict that world knowledge is consistently required for comprehension of language.

One might choose to characterize the child's development as a listener as a process of "decontextualization," of increasing independence from situational context in discerning meaning (Owens, 1990). For example, children more than 18 months of age can comprehend the names of familiar objects not only when those objects are directly in front of them but also when they are in another room. The child also becomes able to identify previously unfamiliar exemplars of a word such as "ball." Later the child is able to understand and act out sentences about improbable and unexpected events (e.g. "The boy bites the dog.") (Tager-Flusberg, 1989). School language has been referred to as decontextualized language (Wallach and Miller, 1988). Thus, the child is seen as being freed up from reliance on context to ascertain meaning. However, I will argue in this chapter that by its very nature, language cannot be decontextualized; it must occur in a context. Because of the inherent vagueness or indeterminacy of language, context is critical for accurate comprehension of a speaker's intent. Although in one sense the child's recognition of the meaning of the word "ball" no longer depends on the presence of that object or the presence of certain specific related cues (Huttenlocher and Smiley, 1987), and the school-aged child does deal with language that is expository (Wallach and Miller, 1988), the task of the maturing child is not to simply decode messages and assign referents correctly but to interpret messages. To do so, the increasingly sophisticated communicator needs to identify and use the *relevant* aspects of context to accurately interpret a speaker's or writer's message. He or she also must become increasingly sensitive to context to discern the goals of a speaker or of a prose passage.

WHAT IS CONTEXT?

Context is comprised not only of the physical context (the room, the objects present) but also the social context (the people and the listener's history with those people), the event context, the affective context (the listener's emotional state and goals), and the prior linguistic context. For example, if an adult asks the child, "Can you show me the ball?," the child activates knowledge relevant to the context to interpret the request. The child uses his knowledge of adult speakers to judge that this utterance is likely to be a request for action rather than information.

Context, then, is evidenced in the present situation, but it activates the listener's history that accompanies the words and the aspects of the situation. When we speak of a word or a situation as having a history, we are speaking of prior experiences, which create world knowledge. It is critical to consider how inextricably comprehension is woven together with world knowledge and how selective aspects of world knowledge are activated in a given situation.

I will argue in this chapter that it is necessary to reconceptualize the developmental process. It is necessary to abandon the notion of decontextualization of language and instead to consider the developmental process as one of increasingly sophisticated uses of context. Development will be characterized in terms of increasing fluidity or lack of rigidity in using context and by changes in the amount and kinds of knowledge children acquire and use for dealing with the basic indeterminacy of language. I will begin by elaborating on what is meant by the basic indeterminacy of language and then will discuss the role of context in utterance processing and interpretation, with examples of adult language processing models. Next, context will be considered in the broad sense of the term, with the various elements of context being illustrated. I will then discuss the nature of the developmental process in terms of how use of context changes with experience. Finally, I will consider the implications of this view for process models and for clinical practice.

THE INDETERMINACY OF LANGUAGE

Language is indeterminate, or open to many different interpretations, and the human language processing mechanism, if it is to be successful, must deal with that basic indeterminacy. The frequency with which potential ambiguity occurs is truly startling when one begins to consider utterances carefully. Table 2–1 illustrates the many potential sources of ambiguity. A typical communicator might be tempted to say that most words have one or perhaps two meanings, with three meanings considered very rare. Indeed, because ambiguous words have been a frequent focus of study in the language processing literature, one may consider them as a small, or at least distinct, subset of words. In fact, when viewed in isolation rather than in the context of a specific interaction, most words can be seen to take on many potential meanings or senses. For example, Table 2–2 illustrates the many potential senses of the words "bugs" and "approaches." Some researchers (e.g., Hogaboam and Perfetti, 1975; Simpson, 1981) have advocated that ambiguous words have a context-independent dominant meaning. Crain and Steedman (1985) have argued, however, that when individuals are forced to determine a

TABLE 2–1.
Sources of Ambiguity or Indeterminacy in Language

Source	Example
Phonologic	
Segmentation	What flower likes to be kissed? *Tulips* (two lips).
Individual lexical items	
Ambiguous words	She was looking for *bugs.*
Novel uses of words	She did a *Reagan* on the budget.
Phrasal	
Idioms	Stacy *spilled the beans.*
Metaphors	She was a summer's day.
Sentential syntax	
Surface structure ambiguity	She approached the man (looking for bugs). vs. She approached (the man looking for bugs.)
Deep structure ambiguity	Visiting relatives can be boring.
Pragmatic/contextual	
Indirect requests	Can you tell me the time?
Irony	You wrecked my car? *Thanks a lot.*
Determining relevance	The answer to "Where's New York?" varies depending on where it is asked.
Indeterminate reference	"The procedure is actually quite simple. First you arrange things into different groups. Of course, one pile may be sufficient depending on how much there is to do. If you have to go somewhere else due to lack of facilities that is the next step, otherwise you are pretty well set" (a passage about laundry from Bransford & Johnson, 1972).

meaning in the absence of context (or rather, within the context of a psychological experiment), they create a context.

Figurative language, or instances of language in which the literal meaning of words is different from the intended meaning, provides another source of potential ambiguity. Pollio et al. (1990, p. 143) demonstrate that instances of figurative speech such as metaphors, irony, idioms, and hyperbole are pervasive in oral and written communication, citing data from written text that suggest that "the average third grader will have to deal with one figure of speech every two pages. The average 11th grader will have to deal with approximately 5 per page." Milosky and Hardy (1990) reported 55 uses of figurative language in 5 minutes of dialogue in a prime-time family television show. Pollio et al. (1990) argue that figurative language is not a special case of language input but that it needs to be viewed as part of the ongoing creative process in communicative interaction.

In a similar vein, in a specific discourse context, words may be used in syntactically novel ways, but their meanings will be clear. Clark (1983, pp. 303–304) demonstrates the common use of so-called contextual expressions in everyday communication; his examples include indirect nouns ("One water, please," "Last night they played a Beethoven."), nouns, verbs, and adjectives derived from concrete nouns ("saxophonist," "to graphite the locks," "impish,"), and verbs and adjectives derived from names of people or places ("The photographer asked me to do a Napoleon for the camera," "She is very San Francisco."). A favorite of mine occurred recently when an acquaintance, in talking about the slow pace of renovations on his house, said, "I'm being a bit

TABLE 2–2.
Possible Meanings of Ambiguous Words

Bugs	
	Vermin
	Insects
	Electronic surveillance devices
	Bugs Bunny
	Bugs Malone (gangster)
	Annoying (e.g., "He really bugs me.")
	Computer glitches
	Hobgoblin (dialectical or literary)
	Defects or difficulty (e.g., "I still need to work the bugs out.")
	Volkswagen cars
Approach	
	To come near or nearer to (e.g., "He approached the city.")
	To come near to in quality, character, time or condition (e.g., "He approaches Shakespeare as a poet.")
	To begin work on; set about (e.g., "to approach a problem")
	To bring near to something
	To make advances or a proposal to
	To come nearer, or draw near (e.g., "The storm approaches.")
	To approximate (e.g., "a fair approach to accuracy")
	To prepare to ask about

Eeyore about the work on the house lately." Clark (1983) persuasively makes the case that such expressions are routine and not rare anomalies in linguistic communication.

These examples reflect the potential difficulties arising from only lexical ambiguity. Syntactic or structural ambiguity also is rife ("The elephant is ready to lift," "They talked about the problem with the mechanic."), with context and intonation or punctuation providing the necessary cues for interpretation.

Pragmatic ambiguity occurs, for example, when a listener does not know whether to consider a question (e.g., "Is your mother home?") as a request for action or information. Similarly, when a speaker makes an ironic remark, the listener may not know whether to consider the remark as sincere or sarcastic. Even an apparently straightforward question—"Where is New York?," for example—requires the listener to use context to understand what kind of answer the speaker wants: "the next turnpike exit," "on the East coast," "in the United States" (Shannon, 1983).

Despite the fact that language is filled with all kinds of ambiguities—phonologic, semantic, syntactic, and pragmatic—and despite the fact that language may not fully specify referents, listeners usually do not notice these ambiguities and rarely have trouble negotiating shared meaning.

HOW IS MEANING UNIQUELY DETERMINED?

Autonomist Models

Researchers in language comprehension are divided in their views about how listeners use different sources of information to determine meaning (Table 2–3). One possibility is that listeners first perform a separate linguistic analysis of a message and then compare the outcome of that analysis with the context. That is, listeners first decode by assigning meaning to each of the words in an utterance.

TABLE 2–3.
Types of Processing Models: Some Examples

Autonomist	
Serial autonomist	Preferred meaning for each word in a sentence is accessed and single preferred parse generated based on parsing heuristics, independent of context; then compared with context for consistency of meaning. If mismatch, then sentence is reparsed or alternate word meaning retrieved (e.g., Cairns, 1983; Ford et al., 1982; Holmes, 1984; Rayner et al., 1983).
Parallel autonomist	All possible word senses and all possible parses are generated independent of context, and then context is consulted to choose correct parse. Contextually independent "dominant" meaning may be chosen faster than others (e.g., Tanenhaus et al., 1985).
Interactive	Continual interaction among lexical and syntactic selection processes and context. Only contextually relevant senses of words and parses of sentences are generated (e.g., Chapman et al., 1981 see Chapter 1; Crain and Steedman, 1985; Marslen-Wilson and Tyler, 1980).
Compromise	Lexical and syntactic processors construct all possible interpretations for first sentence constituent. Contextual knowledge then inhibits exhaustive analyses and multiple interpretations from being generated for each subsequent constituent (e.g., Sperber and Wilson, 1986).
	Activation of many potential senses of words but also posits a role for context in the resolution of the list of possible senses *before* the actual lexical item is accessed. Lexical selection is the result of two independent (autonomous) processes—featural or sensory analysis and contextually based semantic analysis (e.g., Rueckl and Oden, 1986).

By using the sentence syntax (and perhaps the sentence semantics), they figure out how those meanings go together and then check the meaning to see if it makes sense in context. This so-called autonomous model implies a modularity of processing.

Serial autonomist models (Cairns, 1983; Ford et al., 1982; Holmes, 1984; Rayner et al., 1983) propose that the preferred meaning for each word in a sentence is accessed first and the preferred syntactic representation or parse is generated. Then the resulting representation is compared with context to determine if meaning is appropriate. For example, for the sentence "Jane approached the man looking for bugs," the autonomous subcomponents would determine that the preferred meaning for "bugs" would be "insects," the preferred meaning for "approached" would be "came close to," and the preferred parse might be "Jane approached the man (looking for bugs)," with Jane as the one looking for the insects. Then that interpretation would be checked with the context, and if there had been discussion of electronic surveillance devices, and if the man had been sweeping the room for them, the original arrived-at meaning would be rejected and the sentence would be sent back for reprocessing.

Parallel autonomist models (Tanenhaus et al., 1985) propose that several possible representations are generated. For example, when listeners hear the sentence "Jane approached the man looking for bugs," parallel autonomist models propose that a lexical module generates all the possible interpretations of each word (see Table 2–2), and simultaneously a syntactic module sends forth all possible syntactic parses of the sentence (Table 2–4), resulting in numerous possible representations of the meaning of that sentence (Table 2–5). Then the listener must choose among all the resulting interpretations in light of the situation. Clearly, autonomous models

TABLE 2–4.
Possible Parses of an Ambiguous Sentence

Jane approached (the man looking for bugs.)
Jane approached the man (looking for bugs).

must assume a finite and relatively small number of meanings for each word. However, as illustrated in Tables 2–2, 2–4, and 2–5, this assumption is questionable. Indeed, because of the ubiquity of ambiguity, some autonomist claims have been modified, with models suggesting that the dominant or most frequent meanings of words are generated first and subordinate meanings accessed later. Thus, although parallel parsing and sense selection would be occurring, the dominant meaning would be arrived at most quickly. However, none of these models addresses the problem that Clark (1983) raised for the language processor—the relatively common case of *nonce sense,* or novel uses of words to convey meanings (e.g., "He's Watergating it," to describe someone

TABLE 2–5.
A Subset of Possible Meaning Representations for Sample Sentence

Jane came close to the man who was looking for insects.
Jane came close to the man who was looking for electronic surveillance devices.
Jane came close to the man who was looking for computer glitches.
Jane came close to the man who was looking for defects.
Jane came close to the man who was looking for annoying people.
Jane came close to the man who was looking for Bugs Bunny.
Jane came close to the man who was looking for Bugs Malone.
Jane came close to the man who was looking for Volkswagens.
Jane was looking for insects and came close to the man.
Jane was looking for electronic surveillance devices and came close to the man.
Jane was looking for computer glitches and came close to the man.
Jane was looking for computer glitches and came close to the man.
Jane was looking for defects and came close to the man.
Jane was looking for annoying people and came close to the man.
Jane was looking for Bugs Bunny and came close to the man.
Jane was looking for Bugs Malone and came close to the man.
Jane was looking for Volkswagens and came close to the man.
Jane prepared to ask about the man who was looking for insects.
Jane prepared to ask about the man who was looking for electronic surveillance devices.
Jane prepared to ask about the man who was looking for computer glitches.
Jane prepared to ask about the man who was looking for annoying people.
Jane prepared to ask about the man who was looking for Bugs Bunny.
Jane prepared to ask about the man who was looking for defects.
Jane prepared to ask about the man who was looking for Bugs Malone.
Jane prepared to ask about the man who was looking for Volkswagens.
Jane made a proposal to the man who was looking for vermin.
Jane made a proposal to the man who was looking for insects.
Jane made a proposal to the man who was looking for Bugs Bunny.
Jane made a proposal to the man who was looking for annoying people.
Jane made a proposal to the man who was looking for computer glitches.
Jane made a proposal to the man who was looking for Hobgoblin.
Jane made a proposal to the man who was looking for defects.
Jane made a proposal to the man who was looking for Bugs Malone.
Jane made a proposal to the man who was looking for Volkswagens.
Jane resembles the man who was looking for insects.
Jane resembles the man who was looking for vermin.
Jane resembles the man who was looking for electronic surveillance devices.
Jane resembles the man who was looking for Bugs Bunny.

getting information in a nefarious manner.)

Interactionist Models

Another possible explanation of how we comprehend is that only certain relevant senses of the words and the syntax arise because the context has guided the retrieval of the meaning or has been used to predict meaning. The Child Talk model is one example. Consider the story beginning:

> Jane was a school nurse. She was concerned about an outbreak of lice among the teachers and children in the elementary school. Her next patient was the fourth grade teacher. Jane approached the man looking for bugs.

Will listeners immediately arrive at the correct interpretation of "bugs" because only the relevant sense of the word was activated? Will the sentence be automatically parsed because Jane was the person doing the looking and she was coming close to the man? Interactionist models say "yes."

Interactionist models (Chapman et al., see Chapter 1; Crain and Steedman, 1985; Marslen-Wilson and Tyler, 1980) propose that decisions about sentence syntax and word meanings interact with each other and with information from the context.

Data from lexical ambiguity studies have been used to support interactionist claims, as well as autonomist claims. The goal of lexical ambiguity studies is to determine whether all potential meanings of an ambiguous word are activated, with one then chosen, or if only the relevant sense of the word is activated and then accessed. The primary experimental paradigm used in these studies is the priming paradigm. As the name implies, the paradigm assumes that a word or sentence primes, or prepares, a listener for a second word that is related. Subjects might be presented briefly with an ambiguous word as a prime (e.g., "ring") and then are shown a word, called the target, that is related to one sense of the ambiguous word (e.g., "finger"). They may be asked to name the target word as rapidly as possible (naming task) or to say whether the target word is a real word or not (lexical decision task). The dependent measure of response time is compared across the different senses of the word. For example, using the prime word "ring," response time to the target word "finger" would be compared to the target word "phone." If only one sense of the word "ring" is accessed, one would expect a difference in response time between the two targets.

Studies supporting interactionist models (Schvaneveldt et al., 1976; Tabossi, 1988) show that in a biasing context (e.g., "For her engagement, the woman received a beautiful diamond ring."), not all meanings of a word are activated; only the relevant sense of the word is activated and therefore accessed. These data have been subject to much scrutiny, because autonomist proponents claim that two stages are involved in sense selection of ambiguous words. In the first stage, potential lexical items are activated or accessed within the autonomous lexical module, and in the second stage, a decision is made regarding the correct lexical item (postaccess decision). Autonomist proponents have claimed that lexical decision tasks reflect post–lexical access decisions, and if one is to refute an autonomist model, experimental paradigms must truly reflect the processing that occurs in the access phase. Naming tasks, in contrast, have been considered by some to be sensitive to the earlier access phase of processing. However, the validity of this distinction between tasks continues to be questioned (Foss, 1988).

Biasing context also has been shown to facilitate syntactic processing. In a series of studies, Crain and Steedman

(1985) reported on the kinds of semantic and pragmatic information they found the parser to use in making decisions about syntactically ambiguous sentences. Hoppe and Kess (1986) found interaction of context with parsing decisions in a dichotic listening task; Milosky (1986) found biasing context to facilitate story continuation, with ambiguous and unambiguous sentences being facilitated equally, and with preferred vs. nonpreferred interpretations equally facilitated. These findings are not consistent with an autonomous, heuristically driven parser.

Compromise Models

Sperber and Wilson (1986) suggest that a modular view of processing may be partially maintained by having lexical and syntactic processors that are capable of constructing all possible interpretations for constituents of an utterance. The first sentence constituent generates such an exhaustive activation. However, after presenting all possible interpretations to a more central unit that has access to contextual knowledge, this central unit feeds information back to the input modules and inhibits exhaustive analyses and multiple interpretations from being generated for each subsequent constituent. Instead, for the second and subsequent constituents, the sense consistent with the first constituent is being generated, with others being inhibited. Thus, the input module still does not have broad access to contextual information (is not driven by all the contextual information), but context could affect processing.

Another model, the fuzzy propositional model, recently suggested by Rueckl and Oden (1986) still allows for activation of many potential senses of words but also posits a role for context in the resolution of the list of possible senses before the actual lexical item is accessed. Rueckl and Oden (1986) posit that contextual information affects lexical selection but that lexical selection is the result of two independent (autonomous) processes—featural or sensory analysis and contextually based semantic analysis. The results of these two analyses are then integrated to lead to a lexical choice. This model is different from models that have claimed that resolution of meaning is accomplished in a post–lexical access decision phase. Instead, context operates during the access phase by restricting the features that possible upcoming word candidates (meanings) may have and by facilitating those words that meet these constraints. This model is different from a strict interactionist model in that it posits activation of all senses unless context does not allow so. Strong interactionist positions, on the other hand, propose an active searching of context to allow construction of meaning, with prediction of candidates (Crain and Steedman, 1985). The findings of Simpson et al. (1989) indicate that sentence context does facilitate the selection of a lexical candidate in an active way.

Comparing the Models

As one seeks to categorize or differentiate models of processing, it becomes clear that one major source of confusion is the kind of knowledge or information that is retrieved when a word is accessed from the lexicon (Gerrig, 1986). Some autonomous accounts have modified their claims about exhaustive access of potential meanings by arguing that although all meanings are available, the context-independent dominant meaning is available first. However, one must consider the nature of meaning frequency or dominance as a mediating variable. Meaning frequency results from experiences in specific contexts. Therefore, the dominance of a given meaning would depend on the context in which that meaning was experienced and in which it was elicited. The meaning that is dominant in the context of a psychological experiment in which words are presented in isolation may not be the meaning that is dominant in other contexts. Thus, it is necessary to consider that not only frequency is stored but also other aspects of experience that are intimately tied to frequency. Gernsbacher (1984) has demonstrated that word frequency, which has been studied extensively in word recognition studies, is confounded with experiential familiarity and that experiential familiarity of words, as rated by subjects, provides the most reliable effect on word recognition latencies. Thus, the inclusion of meaning frequency suggests a role for experience in lexical storage and retrieval. The nature of that experience is relevant for activation of meaning. Other words can prime meanings, but many other aspects of communicative experience also can prime certain meanings. This leads to a second consideration, namely, the nature of natural communicative context.

THE NATURE OF CONTEXT

Context as it has been operationalized in most psycholinguistic experiments is vastly different from the nature of context in real-life communication situations. Many studies have considered context to be the use of a single sentence in contrast with a no-context condition of an isolated word. For example, Swinney (1979) used the sentence "The man was surprised when he found several spiders, roaches, and other bugs in the corner of his room" to disambiguate "bugs." Other studies, particularly those examining syntactic ambiguity, have used short passages, like the one provided earlier for Jane and the bugs, to disambiguate sentences. However, these stimuli are very impoverished compared with everyday communication.

In most comprehension situations, listeners have a very rich context, not just the prior words in a single sentence or a few sentences. Listeners may use a speaker's prosody, gestures, facial expression, accent, body posture, and interpersonal distance to aid in determining meaning. Listeners use their knowledge of the situation, the event in which the talk is occurring, and the physical objects present. They often have knowledge of the speaker and of other listeners in the situation, and they may share considerable history with those individuals. In addition, an utterance may have been preceded by several other utterances on the same topic, and the current listeners, in their prior turns as speaker, may have just spoken the word or words, using a specific sense, which they are then hearing spoken by another.

Thus, communicative context provides an enormous amount of information compared with studies examining so-called contextual effects. According to autonomist models, even when listeners have all of this knowledge, they would still be generating every possible meaning for every occurrence of a word. Autonomist models also rely exclusively on the decoding of linguistic input to form a primary representation of the sentence. However, in everyday communication, the linguistic input may be distorted or disrupted or may be competing with noise. Interactionist models, in contrast, propose that the listener uses whatever knowledge sources are available or most salient to arrive at meaning.

Ultimately, as Clark (1983) has pointed out, any model of comprehension must deal successfully with the basic indeterminacy of language. Hence, models that propose activation of all likely candidates seem untenable, given the potentially infinite number of senses a word may convey. Many of the studies on which arguments about processing are being based do not use language of the sort that listeners typically process. Models of processing need to address such effects, given the nature of talk. A strong interactionist perspective allows maximal use of experience, activation of relevant features, and allows models to better approximate real-life communication, in which repetition is rife.

THE ROLE OF SALIENCE IN COMPREHENSION

As one considers how world knowledge is used in the comprehension process, it is clear that the entire history of each situational element or each word in an utterance is not activated in any one situation. Some aspects of the context are more *salient* than others, and some aspects of the context and of world knowledge are more *relevant* than others. Salience, or what is highlighted or noticed in the present situation, may in part be determined by elements of the utterance (e.g., emphatic stress), by aspects of the situation (e.g., unexpected occurrences, shocking colors), or by prior experience (e.g., the word "notes" having different salient meanings for a musician vs. a researcher). Listeners may use whatever information sources are available to them, because one source or another is often unavailable, incomplete, distorted, or noisy.

The notion of salience provides a means for determining meaning in a given situation. The basic, decontextualized indeterminacy of language is evident when we speak of "shades of meaning" that words can have. For example, as we become more sophisticated language users, it becomes clear that a word's synonyms often only approximate the meaning of that word. Implied within many models of language processing is the concept of word meaning as a unitary phenomenon, in which a referent or list of referents is retrieved on recognition of a word. However, such a model does not lend itself well to differentiating shades of meaning. An alternate way of modeling meaning is a featural approach, in which a meaning is not unitary but is instead composed of several features, some of which are more salient in a given comprehension situation. However, for a compositional approach to word meaning to be viable, the nature and source of what are defined as features must be expanded, consistent with Clark's (1983) observations.

The traditional features that have been proposed in semantic feature theory are based solely on a decontextualized semantic organization. In contrast, this model proposes that features are derived from the experience of hearing words in context; on any one occasion, that context may provide additional features for use of the word in that situation. The context also makes salient particular features. Thus, meaning is constructed from salient features present from previous experience, activated by use of words in utterances, plus salient features present in the ongoing experience. Clark's (1983) example of a passage by Erma Bombeck provides evidence of the need to be flexible in defining features. The passage begins:

> We thought we were onto a steam iron yesterday, but we were too late. Steam irons never have any trouble finding roommates. She could pick her own pad and not even have to share a bathroom. Stereos are a dime a dozen. Everyone's got their own system.

It quickly becomes clear to the reader that she must read the inanimate nouns as "persons possessing that inanimate noun."

The construction of meaning, rather than simple retrieval of a fixed stored image, is consistent with parallel distributed processing models of memory and forms the basis for Rosenfield's (1988, p. 127) arguments against modularity and computational approaches to processing: "Modularity, like the earlier doctrine of localization, implies that the ways in which we can understand the world—the possible categories of knowledge—are relatively fixed. And yet, as the historical record shows, we not only create new environments but our ways of understanding any given scene or event, at a particular time, are very different from person to person." Rosenfield (1988) goes on to argue that the computational approach does not allow explanation of all the possible ways we have of categorizing our perceptions and that it does not explain how experience affects perception.

The effect of salience in context is to determine which features of words or utterances are to be activated and which are to be inhibited, hence determining meaning. MacWhinney (1989) presents a cue competition model of language comprehension in which items from the lexicon are matched to input as a result of activation and summation of cues for a specific meaning. These cues may include syntactic expectations and the presence of associated words in the surrounding discourse, but in MacWhinney's (1989) account, they do not include physical objects present, knowledge of the speaker, or the nature of the event in which the talk is embedded. Given the broadly contextualized base of meaning being suggested here, what is the nature of the features used for determining meaning?

The nature of features has been the subject of much debate, and this chapter proposes to review only some of the possibilities. Sternberg (1987) has identified seven types of cues that context provides. These are exemplified in Table 2–6, and an eighth cue type has been added, event-based or associative cues, which are based on events or objects occurring together. Rueckle and Oden (1986) have considered basic orthographic information as featural cues. For an oral message, features might include basic acoustic information and prosodic elements (stress, intonation, and juncture). However, Sternberg's cues encompass only those features provided by prior text. The present model would also include features that reflected how those words might be used in social or interpersonal aspects of communicative experience. For example, a listener may become accustomed to hearing certain words said in a certain tone of voice, and that tone of voice may become very salient for those words. One case in point was Gilda Radner's production of the phrase "never mind" on the television show "Saturday Night Live." I have frequently observed that after someone says "Never mind," another speaker will mimic that phrase using Radner's prosody. Another example might be the use of the phrase "thanks a lot." This phrase is more likely to be taken ironically as opposed to sincerely based on its conventional usage (Ford and Milosky, 1991). Another example might be the child's recognition of

TABLE 2–6.

Cues for Learning Vocabulary From Linguistic Context*

1. Temporal cues: "in the morning"
2. Spatial cues: "in the kitchen"
3. Value cues: "It smelled wonderful."
4. Stative descriptive cues: "It was strong."
5. Functional descriptive cues: "She needed it to get going."
6. Class membership: "What a beverage!"
7. Equivalence cues: "The song about it is called 'Java Jive'."
8. Associative (event) cues: "You may drink it with cream or sugar in it."

*Adapted from Sternberg R: Most vocabulary is learned from context, in McKeown M, Curtis M (eds): *The Nature of Vocabulary Acquisition*. Hillsdale, NJ, Lawrence Erlbaum Associates, 1987.

"whydoncha" from an adult as a request for action rather than information. Thus, the definition of what comprises a feature is broader than in traditional accounts of lexical learning and development. Depending on an individual's experience, a feature may consist of typical speaker information (who is likely to say the words, what kind of attitude this speaker is likely to be expressing about the content, e.g., sincere vs. ironic), event information (under what circumstances the word is likely to be said), or goal information (for what purposes the words, the phrase, or the structure is likely to be used, e.g., hyperpolite forms.).

The strength of any one feature will depend on the individual's prior experiences and on the number and strength of situational cues activating that feature. Thus, context determines the salience of certain meanings or certain aspects of a situation.

RELEVANCE

In the previous account, a listener is surrounded by overwhelmingly large amounts of information that may bear on the interpretation of a remark. However, all salient information is not necessarily relevant to the comprehension task at hand. The listener uses only specific aspects of context by identifying and using only what is relevant to the immediate comprehension task. The relevance, or degree of importance, of various meanings of words, of prior experiences, and of various aspects of the current situation is determined by the speaker's intent and by the listener's goals, attention, and affective state. Comprehension is maximal when what is most salient is also most relevant. Hence, the listener's interpretation of any utterance is an interaction among the utterance, the salient (and hopefully relevant) aspects of the present context, and all the salient (and hopefully relevant) aspects of experience—experience with words, sentence frames, people, places, things, and events.

The central role of relevance in processing language is explicated by Sperber and Wilson (1986, p vii): "Human cognitive processes . . . are geared to achieving the greatest possible cognitive effect for the smallest possible processing effort. To achieve this the individual must focus his attention on what seems to him to be the most relevant information available." In Sperber and Wilson's (1986) terms, the comprehender creates context from what is relevant in the available information. The developmental question that arises, then, is how to capture what is relevant in the child's eyes, and how does a child come to recognize what information is relevant to achieving a particular goal? With specific reference to language, how does one consider the multiple sources of information and then determine their relevance for communicative meaning? Contextualized models of processing would suggest that knowledge gained from experience interacts with the individual's goals and the information available in the current context to determine what information is relevant (Rosenfield, 1988.)

Relevance, therefore, is determined by an individual's goals and by what is of interest to the individual. Rosenfield (1988, p. 121) states, "Information must be formed out of the stimuli in terms of individual needs and desires. Goals determine the kinds of information—in a very broad sense—that the brain is capable of deriving from environmental clues."

The importance of goal-based processing has been recognized in cognitive psychology. Numerous investigations of discourse processing have revealed the centrality of characters' goals in accounting for what listeners remember of a passage. Information that is relevant to achieving a character's goal is remembered better than information that is not directly linked to a central goal (Trabasso et al., 1984; Trabasso and Stein, 1981; Trabasso and Van Den Broek, 1985). Goals also would seem to play an important role in evaluations of message adequacy. When listeners are asked to judge messages and to state whether they are "good," they may well ask themselves, "Good enough for what?" For example, Milosky et al. (1986) examined children's judgments about four types of explanations offered in response to indirect requests for information about a math worksheet. The findings suggested that children's perceptions of the goal of the task (e.g., to get an answer to a math problem vs. to understand the mathematical reasoning for the problem solution) may have influenced how they rated the explanations that were offered.

Closely related to goals is a listener's level of involvement in a situation. As we speak about words having a history, it is only natural to ask how one's level of involvement affects memory for and comprehension of the words and the situation. Bower (1978) has found that when individuals read stories, the meaning that the reader obtains for a story depends on which character she identifies with. When a reader identifies with a character, she is more likely to remember the thoughts of the character, describe events from that character's point of view, and interpret that character's actions sympathetically. Also, the mood of the reader affects which character an individual identifies with. When subjects in Bower's study were induced into either happy or sad moods via posthypnotic suggestion, they chose the character with the mood similar to their own as the central focus of the story; that was the character they remembered the most about.

Degree of involvement also seems to determine listener's memory for conversations. Keenan et al. (1977) recorded a conversation among a group of academic psycholinguists and then selected utterances that were judged to be of high vs. low involvement (utterances in which the speaker made fun of some portion of his experiment vs. utterances that focused solely on the content). Individuals who had been listeners in the conversation were much better able to recall exact wording of high involvement interpersonal statements than low involvement expository statements. Thus, evidence suggests that emotional involvement affects comprehension and memory for exact wording.

The following anecdote provides an example of the effects of salience and relevance on comprehension. A student recently reported entering her 5-year-old son's room, her arms filled with sheets, and asking him, "Can you make your bed?" Without looking up from the cars with which he was intently playing, he said, "Yes," and continued making motor noises. She was surprised at his failure to read her indirect request correctly, but because she was engaged in a study of comprehension of nonliteral intent, she reported that she was sensitive to the fact that he failed to understand because his attention was heavily engaged by his play. She stated that ordinarily she might have considered his response as being purposely obtuse.

HOW DO CHILDREN DEAL WITH LINGUISTIC INDETERMINACY? AMBIGUITY RESOLUTION IN CHILDREN

Most models of language processing in children typically have not addressed how potential ambiguities are resolved by nonlinguistic information. In the early stages of language comprehension, we do see evidence of children's use of context to respond to language that is not necessarily ambiguous but is only partially understood. Children respond to requests by doing what they usually do in the situation or by putting objects where they usually belong (Chapman, 1988). They combine their single-word comprehension skills with what they know about the situation to respond to their communicative partners.

At the utterance level, children's comprehension of ambiguous utterances has been studied primarily in the context of referential communication, metaphorical language, and indirect requests. These all represent communicative occurrences in which either reference is not clear or more than one meaning can exist. Yet these studies have often employed metalinguistic tasks and have presented stimuli in highly decontextualized fashion.

On-line processing tasks have been used to investigate children's word recognition in isolation and in sentence context. These investigations (Schwantes, 1981; Simpson and Lorsbach, 1983; Stanovich et al., 1981) generally have found that as children get older and their word recognition skills improve, there is less difference between context and no-context conditions in word recognition studies. However, Simpson and Foster (1986) have proposed that there may be age-related changes in the kind of information that older children use or in the manner in which they use contextual information. Merrill et al. (1981) compared the features of words that good vs. poor readers encoded when the words appeared in sentences. They found that good readers encoded only features of words that were relevant to the sentence context, whereas poor readers encoded irrelevant, as well as relevant, features. Simpson and Foster (1986) sought to determine developmental trends in context use. Although older children may be relying on context less (equal facilitation with and without context), they also may be using context more efficiently. They propose that older children may use context to activate only the most directly relevant information about a word. Although Simpson and Foster (1986) do not discuss the trade-offs in processing between devoting resources to decoding vs. devoting resources to higher level processes, including use of context, it may be that their suggestion about efficiency amounts to just that. It may be that younger children are using context to aid in the decoding process, but older children (or better readers) do not need to use context for decoding and instead may use context at a higher level to restrict or focus on specific meaning. Certainly the findings of developmental reading research (cited later) support such a hypothesis.

Simpson and Foster (1986) investigated age-related changes in processing of lexical ambiguities using a priming paradigm and defined context as a prime related to the target word. They report findings consistent with access to all meanings, although the time course of activation was slower in younger children. They also found that older children then selected the dominant meaning and inhibited other meanings, with no evidence of that process occurring in younger children. Although Simpson and Foster (1986) followed the course of activation for only 750 ms, in a previous study, Simpson and Lorsbach (1983) found that younger children did not show inhibition for unrelated words even at 2,000 ms. In absence of context, older children use meaning frequently to focus on relevant aspects of word processing. Simpson and Foster (1986) acknowledge that all words, not just so-called ambiguous words, "take on at least slightly different meanings in different contexts." Yet they still propose that all meanings of all words are initially activated, but they do suggest that further exploration of the developmental effects of sentence context is needed. The considerations raised earlier about the nature of dominance or word frequency effects and about the nature of context also are relevant in interpreting their findings. Context in this study consisted of one word.

CONTEXT EFFECTS ON CHILDREN'S COMPREHENSION

Studies that have examined somewhat broader context effects in children's comprehension of various kinds of ambiguous language still have considerably restricted context. For example, Kahan and Richards (1986) report on the referential communication strategies of subjects aged 5 through 18 years "in a variety of communication contexts." These contexts consisted of manipulations of the type of distractor items in a forced-choice task and whether or not the distractor items were present when subjects had to describe the target stimulus. The subjects were told to provide a description that would allow a listener to choose the target item from among four similar items. They found that even 9- to 11-year-old children persisted in simply naming the target and did not provide any contrastive description when the target was presented without the context of the distractor items.

Anderson et al. (1978), Dreher (1985), and Martin-Rehrmann (1989) have examined children's ability to instantiate a specific exemplar (e.g., "Christmas tree") when a general term is given in the context of a sentence (e.g., "The tree was covered with lights and tinsel.") All of these studies have found an effect of sentential context on children's instantiation of a specific sense of a word.

In studies examining the effects of context on children's comprehension of figurative language (Ackerman, 1982; Nippold and Martin, 1989), the task usually consists of children listening to a series of very short narratives (often only two or three sentences long) in which the target figurative language has been embedded. Ackerman (1982) found that context was necessary for 6- and 8-year-old subjects to interpret idioms correctly, and Nippold and Martin (1989) found slight improvement in adolescents' performance when idioms were embedded in context. Hardy and Milosky (1991) provided two sentences of social background information in narratives containing ironic remarks and found that the likelihood of interpreting the remark ironically varied with the nature of the social relationship between the interactants in the story.

Another task that has been used to investigate context effects has provided the figurative language and asked children to select the appropriate context for such language. When Nippold et al. (1988) provided subjects with a proverb and then asked them to choose the appropriate context from among four one-sentence contexts, they found proverb comprehension at much younger ages (i.e., fourth grade) than had previously been reported in the literature.

NEED FOR NATURALISTIC CONTEXTS

Despite the relatively meager contexts employed in the previously cited studies and other psycholinguistic experiments, context consistently has been found to affect processing. The previous operational definitions of context are fairly typical of the comprehension literature and are in sharp contrast to the very naturalistic contexts examined in the language production literature. This difference is not surprising, given the difficulty of determining whether and how a child has comprehended an utterance, but it is troubling given the statements we are seeking to make about children's comprehension.

Within developmental psychology, investigators have begun to consider the need for embedding experimental studies of children's cognition in the settings in which the experimental tasks are likely to occur in real life. For example, Ceci and Bronfenbrenner (1985) examined children's development of prospective memory (their ability to remember to do something in the future, e.g., taking cupcakes out of the oven) both in a laboratory setting and in their homes. They also compared children's performance on sex-typed tasks (taking cupcakes out of the oven vs. charging a motorcycle battery). They found that when children are in a familiar context, they are able to employ more sophisticated cognitive strategies on a time-monitoring task. Significant interaction effects (among age, sex, task), when they occurred, occurred only in the laboratory setting. They conclude that "the laboratory, as an unfamiliar and thereby somewhat anxiety-arousing environment, is more likely to activate variation in research findings as a function of characteristics of both the person (e.g., age and sex) and the immediate situation (e.g., the nature of the task.)" (p. 158).

Ceci and Bronfenbrenner (1985) examined the broad physical context with reference to performance on a task basically unrelated to many aspects of that context (i.e., one can bake cupcakes anywhere as long as there is a working stove in that location). They demonstrate that aspects of context that are, in a strict sense, irrelevant to the task at hand still affect performance. As we continue to refine our language processing models, it becomes important to predict the specific aspects of context that will affect a listener's interpretation of an utterance but also to recognize that processing may be subject to such general effects as familiarity of surroundings.

CONTEXT AND EXPERTISE OR EXPERIENCE

Familiarity with events, specific objects or tasks, and individual speakers develops with experience with those entities. The role of experience in cognitive processing has been examined extensively in studies comparing performance of experts vs. novices on a variety of tasks. These studies have often been motivated by the debate regarding domain-specific vs. domain-general cognitive processing. At issue in this debate is whether knowledge (most often gained through experience) of an area, a skill, or a process affects the nature and efficiency of cognitive processing within that domain. These studies arose in response to the broad stage theories of Piaget and others, who proposed general modes of processing at different stages of development, regardless of the specific domain.

What is the evidence that more expert individuals process language differently from novices? One source of evidence that will be cited is drawn from the cognitive psychology literature that has examined many of the processes that are central to language comprehension, including inferencing, causal reasoning, classification, and constructive memory. Ceci and Bronfenbrenner (1985) and Chi and Ceci (1987) maintain that when children have considerable experience with a body of knowledge, they then can employ more efficient cognitive processing strategies. For example, Chi et al. (1989) explored the differences in knowledge structure of children who were experts on dinosaurs vs. those who were novices. They found that because experts had more hierarchically structured knowledge, they offered better causal explanations, they reasoned using information about categories, and their inferences about novel dinosaurs were based on domain-specific information. Although novices also engaged in causal reasoning and inferencing, they were more likely to use irrelevant features and general world knowledge, resulting in less accurate performance. Hence, the characteristics that were salient for novices tended to be less relevant to successful completion of the tasks at hand.

Chi and Ceci (1987) cite many examples from the work of cross-cultural cognitive psychologists and anthropologists demonstrating that the ability to reason and to classify is highly dependent on the nature of the materials. Scribner's (1977) work showed that nonliterate adults and children, who did not infer using abstract entities, did infer when they were asked to reason using personal experiences or real-world knowledge. Ceci and Liker (1986) found that a group of individuals of low, albeit normal, IQs (80s) engaged in very sophisticated reasoning similar to that required for using multiple regression when picking winners at a racetrack, a favorite pastime of theirs. These examples clearly cause us to question the nature of expertise, the criteria we may use to label someone as an expert, and the nature of the domain in which that person has expertise. Traditional accounts of language processing often have considered the areas of syntax, semantics, phonology, morphology, and pragmatics to be the domains for which we construct modules in a modular account. Bates et al. (1988) recently proposed that language might be modularized in terms of comprehension and production, given the developmental evidence for dissociations between comprehension and production. However, if one considers the nature of children's experiences, it is likely that more specific domains (or subdomains) exist, reflecting children's "expertise" with certain situations. The existence of such experientially based domains of language is the claim of the Child Talk model.

For the very young child, the domains are likely to be event-based experiences, with processing ease determined by the familiarity with the event and the nature and purposes of the talk accompanying that event. Huttenlocher and Smiley (1987) have taken such an approach in explaining early word meanings and the process by which children seem to overextend words in early talk. They argue that what seem to be overgeneral uses (e.g., saying "cookie" when one sees a pocketbook) may, in fact, be the child remembering a prior event (the pleasant surprise of having a cookie appear out of a pocketbook) and requesting the object in that event again. The child is not, however, creating a complexive meaning for the word "cookie" in which the word is taken to mean the cookie, the pocketbook, and all the objects and events associated with cookie. Nelson and Gruendel's (1986) scriptal model of children's knowledge representations also is based on the importance of recurring events. These kinds of domains are very content specific and thus would imply a major role for the importance of specific content in modeling processing. Yet such an approach has not typically been considered in our theorizing or our investigation of language. It is a goal of this book to argue that it should be.

Keil (1984), in discussing the likelihood of a child comprehending a metaphor, argues that the degree of elaboration of knowledge relevant to the metaphor is a key determinant of comprehension rather than the presence of a putative general metaphoric skill. Keil (1984, p. 90) states that "one cannot speak of learning mechanisms in isolation, independent of the content of the knowledge they operate on." Yet many models and predictions regarding children's processing performance do not acknowledge this consideration. For example, Simpson and Foster (1986) predict that "older children and adults would be more likely than younger children to use biasing sentence context to select more rapidly the contextually appropriate meaning of an ambiguous word." Their model assumes two stages in processing: a stage in which all meanings are accessed and then a stage in which context is used to select the appropriate meaning. They propose that younger children do not engage in the second stage, but they do not consider that the processing may be material specific, with perhaps younger children showing such contextual effects when the material is sufficiently familiar to them.

The effect of world knowledge on syntactic comprehension has been demonstrated repeatedly within the comprehension strategy literature (Chapman, 1988). Children use their knowledge of events in the real world to enact sentences in psycholinguistic studies. When findings are compared across studies, for example, of children's use of word order to interpret noun-verb-noun sequences, it seems that children's strategies vary depending on the stimulus materials and, in particular, the verbs used (Chapman, 1988; Roberts, 1983). Within the domain of academic performance, Siegler (1989) has demonstrated the value of using a multistrategy approach to account for children's arithmetic performance; the data are accounted for much better by a model that considers that the strategy used may depend on the particular math problem.

Children's figurative language understanding provides another example of how world knowledge and experience may affect language processing. Early studies of children's metaphorical understanding indicated that such understanding was not achieved until the late elementary school years. Studies have reported conflicting findings about young children's metaphoric abilities. Vosniadou (1987) argues that young children may take metaphoric statements literally not because they lack some metaphorical mode but because their experience is insufficient to allow them to distinguish between the possible and the impossible. She also points out that earlier studies often have confounded children's inability to understand metaphor with their lack of relevant background knowledge about entities used in the metaphors. Vosniadou et al. (1984) found that 4-year-old children could show evidence of metaphor comprehension when they were asked to demonstrate that comprehension by enacting metaphors with toys in a toy-world environment. They also found that metaphorical sentences conveying predictable story endings were much more easily understood than those conveying unpredictable story endings.

Another relevant issue for modeling language comprehension is to consider the trade-offs that may exist between expert and novice processing. Sternberg (1989) points out that experts may become "entrenched," that is, they may lose a valuable flexibility. Some evidence of such effects may be seen in tasks requiring processing of passages. Ross and Berg (1990) examined the nature of individual differences in event knowledge for two common events, a doctor's appointment and an airplane trip. They found that idiosyncrasies in event knowledge may interfere with recall of stories in which the event description is not similar to the individual's event knowledge. Ceci et al. (1981) assessed children's memory for familiar characters' (e.g., Bionic Woman) actions when those actions were consistent vs. inconsistent with their previous knowledge of the characters. When actions were inconsistent with the children's knowledge of the characters, they were remembered less well than when actions were consistent.

Anderson et al. (1977) tested the role of experience in interpreting passages by presenting two passages to students majoring in either physical education or music education. One passage could have been interpreted as being about either a prison break or a wrestling match, and the other could have been interpreted as being about either an evening of card playing or a rehearsal of a woodwind ensemble. After reading each passage, students were asked to recall it and then answer a series of multiple-choice comprehension questions about it. The effects of background on interpretation were striking. Physical education majors understood the first passage to be about wrestling, whereas other individuals generally understood it to be about a prison escape. Music education majors understood the second passage to be about a woodwind ensemble, whereas other understood it to be about card playing. Thus, as the various aspects of a situation and the incoming language activate those aspects of past experience that are relevant, that past experience in turn strongly shapes expectations of what is yet to come in an interaction.

Chi and Ceci (1987) argue that the influence of content knowledge on task performance has been considered negligible by many researchers. In addition, they maintain that researchers have often assumed that children possess adequate knowledge to perform a task but are lacking in some processing skill when they do not perform it. Rather, they propose that children who do not perform a task may not have the knowledge needed for that task. For example, memory recall studies often have claimed to assess children's knowledge of categories on a sorting task after administration of the experimental memory task and then have claimed that younger subjects do have categorical knowledge but did not use that knowledge on the memory task. However, Chi and Ceci (1987) maintain that these tasks may not adequately assess the nature of the child's representation or the organization of knowledge. They propose that a single such measure is not adequate and that a series of tasks is needed to thoroughly capture children's knowledge structures and to prevent faulty assumptions about their knowledge.

IMPLICATIONS FOR PROCESS MODELS OF CHILDREN'S COMPREHENSION

I have argued that the development of comprehension skill is not a process of increasing decontextualization but a process of gaining familiarity and experience with increasingly diverse contexts of language use; that context is inherently necessary to the disambiguation of language. From this point of view, the skilled adult comprehender's ability to understand a word or sentence that is isolated from surrounding context is as much a result of his or her ability to invent its context as it is a result of linguistic knowledge. I have suggested that only interactionist models can capture this flexibility of the skilled listener.

Further investigations are necessary to delineate how both normal and language disordered children use context and how they access their prior knowledge in the comprehension task. Certainly findings from the reading literature are suggestive. Stanovich (1980) proposed an interactive compensatory hypothesis of contextual effects in which poor readers are more likely to *rely* on context for word decoding, whereas good readers have automatic decoding skills and thus may be more *sensitive* to context. They therefore can use context in the service of higher level comprehension monitoring strategies while reading.

Comparisons of good vs. poor readers (Leu et al., 1986; Merrill et al., 1981) have found differences in the manner and degree to which context is used. Leu et al. (1986) presented good and poor readers with repetitive, predictable texts and found that both benefited from the predictability, although in different ways. Good readers had automatic word decoding skills that allowed them to pay attention to the meaning of the story from the very beginning. Initially, poor readers decoded slowly, using the repetitive nature of the sentences to facilitate word recognition. During the second part of the story, their reading speeds increased because of the repetitive nature of context, and thus resources ordinarily used for decoding were made available for comprehending story meaning. Goldsmith-Phillips (1989) found a similar pattern when investigating developmental trends among second, fourth, and sixth grade children. Thus, it is not that, overall, reading abilities become more "decontextualized" but that context is used to accomplish more cognitively sophisticated goals. Studies using oral language stimuli, which clearly differ in their decoding demands, have identified some of the comprehension strategies that children use. However, we do not yet have a cohesive picture of how children use contextual information and world knowledge to meet the simultaneous demands of linguistic processing, determining message meaning and relevance, and comprehension monitoring.

IMPLICATIONS FOR CLINICAL PRACTICE

Of what relevance is experience and world knowledge in explaining or remediating language disorders? Presumably language disordered children's experiences do not differ. They also, by definition, are considered normal cognitively. Traditionally we have considered the deficit to be a purely "linguistic" one. However, it may be that the nature and accessibility of knowledge representations may account for some of the language deficits exhibited by the children. Kail and Leonard (1986) concluded that the word-finding difficulties exhibited by language-impaired children were not caused by retrieval deficits per se. Instead, it seemed that their semantic representations were not very well elaborated and that this basic knowledge structure deficit accounted for their poor performance on naming tasks. Rosenfield (1988, p. 142), in discussing adult aphasics, argues that "it is the inability to establish contexts, not the loss of any memory images of words, that is the reason patients have difficulties naming things." This suggestion is consistent with views of aphasia that maintain that processing inefficiency rather than language loss is at the heart of the aphasic's difficulties (McNeil, 1982). Similarly, in discussing the performance deficits of learning disabled children, Rabinowitz and Chi (1987) argue that accessibility of knowledge is a key variable in accounting for strategic processing performance.

An interactionist view of language processing requires that we investigate not only purely linguistic sources of deficit but also the knowledge that underlies the linguistic organization and the processes by which that knowledge is accessed. I suggest that language disorders can arise not just from slowed acquisition of linguistic information but from limited elaboration of the associated contexts, thus reducing access to information. The previously cited findings from the reading literature indicate that individual differences in ability are associated with different uses of context in processing.

Intervention, therefore, should focus on defining context as part of the target, not simply as the incidental "activity" in which the targets are presented. Lund and Duchan (1988) have developed a model and methods of assessment based on this premise. Garner (1990) stresses the importance of setting or context in metacognitive and metalinguistic strategy instruction; such instruction is common in treatment of language–learning disabled children. Clinicians must carefully choose which aspects of context to make salient in association with the linguistic target or task, choosing those aspects that are likely to be maximally relevant to both the child and the language target to be learned. Constable (1986) provides excellent examples of contextually sensitive intervention using children's scriptal knowledge.

I was educated about the value of such an approach by a 14-year-old severely retarded client with whom I was working. Ron was a great basketball aficionado, who spoke telegraphically and often repeated slogans of the local teams. One day, while working on production of prepositions, we were cleaning up after having made fruit salad. In a playful manner, I wadded up my paper towels, held them close to the garbage bag, and then dunked them in the bag, saying in a sports announcer–like intonation, "in the bag." Ron was delighted with this and promptly and spontaneously repeated the phrase several times with other garbage items. One month later, while working in his classroom with another student, I observed him carrying his garbage to the wastebasket. He tossed it in and then turned to us and said, "in the basket." Generalization of the preposition to other linguistic contexts also was noted. Thus, using his relevant world knowledge and making salient the relevant aspects of the current context resulted in far more rapid learning and spontaneous use than I was accustomed to with him. To be maximally effective, intervention and research on intervention must consider the true nature of communicative input, as defined by Bransford and Nitsch (1978), that of situation plus linguistic input. In the Child Talk model, situation and linguistic input cannot be divorced.

REFERENCES

Ackerman B: Children's use of contextual expectations to detect and resolve comprehension failures. *J Exp Child Psychol* 1982; 33:63–73.

Anderson R, Reynolds R, Schallert D, et al: Frameworks for comprehending discourse. *Am Educ Res J* 1977; 14:367–381.

Anderson RC, Stevens KC, Shifrin Z, et al: Instantiation of word meanings in children. *J Reading Behav* 1978; 10:149–157.

Bates E, Bretherton I, Snyder L: *From First Words to Grammar: Individual Differences and Dissociable Mechanisms.* New York, Cambridge University Press, 1988.

Bower G: Experiments on story comprehension and recall. *Discourse Processes* 1978; 1:211–231.

Bransford JD, Johnson MK: Contextual prerequisites for understanding: Some investigations of comprehension and recall. *J Verbal Learn Verbal Behav* 1972; 11:717–726.

Bransford JD, Nitsch KE: Coming to understand things we could not previously understand, in Kavanaugh J, Strange W (eds): *Speech and Language in the Laboratory, School, and Clinic.* Cambridge, Mass, MIT Press, 1978.

Cairns H: Research in language comprehension, in Naremore R (ed): *Language Science.* San Diego, Calif, College Hill Press, 1983, pp 211–242.

Ceci SJ, Bronfenbrenner U: "Don't forget to take the cupcakes out of the oven": Prospective memory, strategic time-monitoring, and context. *Child Dev* 1985; 56:152–164.

Ceci SJ, Caves RD, Howe MJA: Children's long-term memory for information that is incongruous with their prior knowledge. *Br J Psychol* 1981; 72:443–450.

Ceci SJ, Liker J: A day at the races: The study of IQ, expertise, and cognitive complexity. *J Exp Psychol (Gen)* 1986; 115:255–266.

Chapman R: Language acquisition in the child, in Lass N, Northern J, Yoder D, et al (eds): *Handbook of Speech-Language Pathology and Audiology*. Philadelphia, BC Decker, 1988, pp 309–353.

Chi M, Ceci SJ: Content knowledge: Its role representation, and restructuring in memory development. *Adv Child Dev Behav* 1987; 20:91–142.

Chi M, Hutchinson J, Robin A: How inferences about novel domain-related concepts can be constrained by structured knowledge. *Merrill-Palmer Q* 1989; 35:27–62.

Clark H: Making sense of nonce sense, in Flores d'Arcais G, Jarvella R (eds): *The Process of Language Understanding*. New York, John Wiley and Sons, 1983, pp 297–332.

Constable C: The application of scripts in the organization of language intervention contexts, in Nelson K (ed): *Event knowledge: Structure and Function in Development*. Hillsdale, NJ: Lawrence Erlbaum Associates, 1986.

Crain S, Steedman M: On not being led up the garden path: The use of context by the psychological syntax processor, in Dowty D, Karttunen L, Zwicky A (eds): *Natural Language Parsing*. New York, Cambridge University Press, 1985, pp 320–358.

Dreher MJ: Spontaneous instantiation of general terms, in Singer H, Ruddell RB (eds): *Theoretical Models and Processes of Reading*, ed 3. Newark, International Reading Association, 1985, pp 426–433.

Ford J, Milosky L: Intonation and the development of irony comprehension. Presented at the American Speech-Language-Hearing Association, Atlanta, Nov, 1991.

Ford M, Bresnan J, Kaplan R: A competence based theory of syntactic closure, in *The Mental Representation of Grammatical Relations*. Cambridge, MIT Press, 1982, pp 727–796.

Foss D: Experimental psycholinguistics. *Am Rev Psychol* 1988; 39:301–348.

Garner R: When children and adults do not use learning strategies: Toward a theory of settings. *Rev Educ Res* 1990; 60:517–529.

Gernsbacher MA: Resolving 20 years of inconsistent interactions between lexical familiarity and orthography, concreteness, and polysemy. *J Exp Psychol (Gen)* 1984; 113:256–281.

Gerrig R: Process and products of lexical access. *Lang Cognitive Processes* 1986; 1:187–195.

Goldsmith-Phillips J: Word and context in reading development: A test of the interactive-compensatory hypothesis. *J Educ Psychol* 1989; 81:299–305.

Hardy D, Milosky L: Social background information and the development of irony. Presented at the American Speech-Language-Hearing Association convention, Atlanta, Nov, 1991.

Hogaboam T, Perfetti C: Lexical ambiguity and sentence comprehension. *J Verbal Learning Verbal Behav* 1975; 14:265–274.

Holmes V: Parsing strategies and discourse context. *J Psycholinguistic Res* 1984; 13:237–257.

Hoppe R, Kess J: Biasing thematic contexts for ambiguous sentences in a dichotic listening experiment. *J Psycholinguist Res* 1986; 15:225–241.

Huttenlocher J, Smiley P: Early word meanings: The case of object names. *Cognit Psychol* 1987; 19:63–87.

Kahan L, Richards D: The effects of context on referential communication strategies. *Child Dev* 1986; 57:1130–1141.

Kail R, Leonard L: Word finding abilities in language-impaired children. *Am Speech Lang Hear Assoc Monogr* 1986; 25.

Keenan J, MacWhinney B, Mayhew D: Pragmatics in memory: A study of natural conversation. *J Verbal Learn Verbal Behav* 1977; 16:549–560.

Keil F: Mechanisms in cognitive development and the stucture of knowledge, in Sternberg R (ed): *Mechanisms in Cognitive Development.* New York, WH Freeman, 1986, pp 81–100.

Leu Jr D, Simons H, DeGroff L: Predictable texts and interactive-compensatory hypotheses: Evaluating individual differences in reading ability, context use, and comprehension. *J Educ Psychol* 1986; 78:347–352.

Lund N, Duchan J: *Assessing Children's Language in Naturalistic Contexts.* Englewood Cliffs, NJ, Prentice-Hall, 1988.

MacWhinney B: Competition and teachability, in Rice M, Schiefelbusch R: *The Teachability of Language.* Baltimore, Brookes Publishing Co, 1989, pp 63–104.

Marslen-Wilson W, Tyler L: The temporal structure of spoken language understanding. *Cognition* 1980; 8:1–71.

Martin-Rehrmann J: The effects of context on the spontaneous instantiation of general terms by third, fifth, and seventh graders. Doctoral dissertation, Syracuse, NY, Syracuse University, 1989.

McNeil M: The nature of aphasia in adults, in Lass N, Northern J, Yoder D, et al (eds): *Speech, Language and Hearing.* Philadelphia, WB Saunders Co, 1982, pp 692–740.

Merrill E, Sperber R, McCauley C: Differences in semantic encoding as a function of reading comprehension skill. *Memory Cognit* 1981; 9:618–624.

Milosky L: The effect of context on resolution of syntactic ambiguity. Doctoral dissertation, Madison, University of Wisconsin, 1986.

Milosky L, Hardy D: A rose by any other name: Understanding nonliteral communication. Paper presented at the Annual Meeting of the American-Speech-Language-Hearing Association, Seattle, 1990.

Milosky L, Wilkinson L, Chiang C, et al: School-age children's understanding of explanation adequacy. *J Ed Psychol* 1986; 78:334–340.

Nelson K, Gruendel J: Children's scripts, in Nelson K (ed): *Event Knowledge: Structure and Function in Development.* Hillsdale, NJ, Lawrence Erlbaum Associates, 1986.

Nippold M, Martin S: Idiom interpretation in isolation versus context: A developmental study with adolescents. *J Speech Hear Res* 1989; 32:59–66.

Nippold M, Martin S, Erskine B: Proverb comprehension in context: A developmental study with children and adolescents. *J Speech Hear Res* 1988; 31:19–27.

Owens R: Development of communication, language and speech, in Shames G, Wiig E (eds): *Human Communication Disorders.* Columbus, Ohio, Charles E Merrill Publishing Co, 1990, pp 30–73.

Pollio H, Smith M, Pollio M: Figurative language and cognitive psychology. *Lang Cognit Processes* 1990; 5;141–167.

Rabinowitz M, Chi M: An interactive model of strategic processing, in Ceci S (ed): *Handbook of Cognitive, Social, and Neuropsychological Aspects of Learning Disabilities.* Hillsdale, NJ, Lawrence Erlbaum Associates, 1987, pp 83–102.

Rayner K, Carlson M, Frazier L: The interaction of syntax and semantics during sentence processing: Eye movements in the analysis of semantically biased sentences. *J Verbal Learning Verbal Behav* 1983; 22:358–374.

Roberts K: Comprehension and production of word order in stage I. *Child Dev* 1983; 54:443–449.

Rosenfield I: *The Invention of Memory*. New York, Basic Books, 1988.

Ross B, Berg C: Individual differences in script reports: Implications for language assessment. *Top Lang Dis* 1990; 10:30–44.

Rueckl J, Oden G: The integration of contextual and featural information during word identification. *J Memory Lang* 1986; 25:445–450.

Schvaneveldt R, Meyer D, Becker D: Lexical ambiguity, semantic context, and visual word recognition. *J Exp Psychol (Hum Percept)* 1976; 2:243–256.

Schwantes FM: Locus of the context effect in children's word recognition. *Child Dev* 1981; 52:895–903.

Scribner S: Modes of ways of thinking and ways of speaking: Culture and logic reconsidered, in Johnson-Laird PN, Wason PC (eds): *Thinking: Readings in Cognitive Science*. New York, Cambridge University Press, 1977, pp 483–500.

Shannon B: Answers to where questions. *Discourse Processes* 1983; 6:319–352.

Siegler R: How domain-general and domain-specific knowledge interact to produce strategy choices. *Merrill-Palmer* 1989; 35:1–25.

Simpson G: Meaning dominance and semantic context in the processing of lexical ambiguity. *J Verbal Learning Verbal Behav* 1981; 20:120–136.

Simpson G, Foster M: Lexical ambiguity and children's word recognition. *Dev Psychol* 1986; 22:147–154.

Simpson G, Lorbach T: The development of automatic and conscious components of contextual facilitation. *Child Dev* 1983; 54:760–772.

Simpson G, Peterson R, Casteel M, et al: Lexical and sentence context effects in word recognition. *J Exp Psychol (Learn Mem Cogn)* 1989; 15:88–97.

Sperber D, Wilson D: *Relevance: Communication and Cognition*. Cambridge, Mass, Harvard University Press, 1986.

Stanovich KE: Toward an interactive-compensatory model of individual differences in the development of reading fluency. *Reading Res Q* 1980; 16(1):32–71.

Stanovich KE, West RF, Feeman DJ: A longitudinal study of sentence context effects in second-grade children: Tests of an interactive-compensatory model. *J Exp Child Psychol* 1981; 32:185–199.

Sternberg R: Most vocabulary is learned from context, in McKeown M, Curtis M (eds): *The Nature of Vocabulary Acquisition*. Hillsdale, NJ, Lawrence Erlbaum Associates, 1987.

Sternberg R: Domain-generality versus domain-specificity: The life and impending death of a false dichotomy. *Merrill-Palmer Q* 1989; 35:115–130.

Swinney D: Lexical access during sentence comprehension: (Re)consideration of contextual effects. *J Verbal Learn Verbal Behav* 1979; 18:645–659.

Tabossi P: Effects of context on the immediate interpretation of unambiguous nouns. *J Exp Psychol* 1988; 14:153–162.

Tager-Flusberg H: Putting words together: Morphology and syntax in the preschool years, in Gleason J (ed): *The Development of Language*. Columbus, Ohio, Charles E Merrill Publishing Co, 1989.

Tanenhaus M, Carlson G, Seidenberg M: Do listeners compute linguistic representations? in Dowty D, Kartunnen L, Zwicky A, (eds): *Natural Language Parsing*. New York, Cambridge University Press, 1985.

Trabasso T, Secco T, Van Den Broek P: Causal cohesion and story coherence, in Mandl H, Stein N, Trabasso T (eds.): *Learning and Comprehension in Text*. Hillsdale, NJ, Lawrence Erlbaum Associates, 1984.

Trabasso T, Stein N: Children's knowledge of events: A causal analysis of story structure, in Bower G (ed): *The Psychology of Learning and Motivation*. New York, Academic Press, 1981.

Trabasso T, Van Den Broek P: Causal thinking and the representation of narrative events. *J Memory Lang* 1985; 24:612–630.

Vosniadou S: Children and metaphors. *Child Dev* 1987; 58:870–885.

Vosniadou S, Ortony A, Reynolds RE, et al: Sources of difficulty in children's comprehension of metaphorical language. *Child Dev* 1984; 55:1588–1606.

Wallach G, Miller L: *Language Intervention and Academic Success*. Boston, College-Hill Press, 1988.

3 Three Perspectives on Language Processing: Interactionism, Modularity, and Holism

Alan G. Kamhi, Ph.D.

For many linguists and psycholinguists, a dominant issue has been whether the language processing system is best characterized as a highly interactive one in which different sources of knowledge communicate freely or as a highly modular one composed of autonomous subsystems (Bates et al., 1988; Fodor, 1983; Frazier, 1987; Tanenhaus et al., 1987). Current theories vary along several dimensions. In terms of the architecture of the system, proposals range from highly modular and structured systems with accompanying subsystems to nonmodular, monolithic, fully interactive systems. Most models implicitly or explicitly assume that there are processing principles involving pragmatic and conceptual notions concerning the expression of communicative functions and the influence of world knowledge. In less modular systems, such principles govern virtually all aspects of language processing (Bates and MacWhinney, 1982; Chapman et al., see Chapter 1). In more modular systems, such principles are implicitly assumed but are thought to operate only in relatively late stages of language processing. Early stages of processing are governed by nonpragmatic principles, such as structure or frequency-based strategies.

In this chapter, I will begin with a brief review of interactionist perspectives, focusing on the research motivated by an interactionist, limited capacity process model. This will be followed by a summary of Fodor's views on modularity and a description of some models of intelligence (Gardner, 1983) and language learning (Bates et al., 1988; Chapman et al., see Chapter 1) that have incorporated modular notions. Holistic principles will be discussed next. The chapter will conclude with a discussion of the various perspectives on language processing and some implications these perspectives have for clinical practice.

INTERACTIONIST VIEWS

Interactionist views lie somewhere on a continuum between a strong nativist view at one end and a behaviorist view at the other. Interactionists acknowledge that many factors (e.g., social, cognitive, biological, linguistic) affect development and that these factors interact with and modify one another (Bohannon and Warren-Leubecker, 1989, p. 181). Thus, not only are these factors interactive, but the causal relationships among them are also reciprocal. Bohannon and Warren-Leubecker (1989) describe three basic interactive approaches: (1) Piaget's cognitive approach, (2) a social interactionist approach, and (3) an information processing approach. In the Piagetian view, a child constructs cognitive structures using the processes of accommodation and assimilation. Structures of language can be viewed as emergent solutions to the problem of mapping certain nonlinguistic cognitive meanings and social intentions onto linguistic forms (Bates and Snyder, 1987).

The Piagetian approach has fostered considerable research examining the relationship between cognitive and linguistic attainments, especially in very young children (Bates et al., 1979; Bates and Snyder, 1987; Gopnik and Meltzoff, 1986, 1987; Johnston, 1985; Kelly and Dale, 1989). This research has uncovered strong associations between certain cognitive and linguistic attainments. For example, Kelly and Dale (1989) found significant differences in play behaviors between children using no words and children using single words. The data tend to support the *correlational hypothesis,* which holds that there is no causal relationship between attainments in language and cognition. In other words, a particular cognitive skill that is temporally associated with a particular linguistic ability can emerge before, at the same time, or after the associated linguistic ability. Although the Piagetian approach has been useful in focusing attention on cognitive-linguistic interactions, the approach does not lead to specific predictions about interactions within and across different language domains (i.e., syntax, morphology, semantics, phonology, and pragmatics).

The social-interaction approach has alternatively been called a functionalist approach (Bates and MacWhinney, 1982). The basic claim is that the language structures are seen as a by-product of the social-communicative functions of language. These rules can develop from simple rote associations and imitations learned within the social context. The mother's role in providing the child with appropriate language experience is emphasized by the social-interaction approach. Much of the research on the characteristics of mothers' speech to young children has been motivated by the social-interaction approach. Bohannon and Warren-Leubecker (1989) provide an even-handed review of this literature. As with the Piagetian approach, the social-interaction perspective does not have much to say about language processes and relationships between these processes.

An information processing approach, with its obvious emphasis on processing, is not surprisingly the approach most conducive to conducting research about language processes. A limited-capacity information processing model, as initially proposed by LaBerge and Samuels (1974), has been accepted, either implicitly or explicitly, by most child language researchers who study language processes. The basic notion of the limited-capacity view, as stated by LaBerge and Samuels (1974, p. 293), is as follows:

> During the execution of a complex skill, it is necessary to coordinate many component processes within a very short period of time. If each component process requires attention, performance of the complex skill will be impossible because the capacity of attention will be exceeded. But if enough of the components and their coordinations can be processed automatically, then the loads on attention will be within tolerable limits and the skill can be successfully performed.

More recent information processing approaches emphasize parallel rather than serial processing. These parallel-distributed models involve a parallel series of "activation nodes," with each node connected to other nodes in a hierarchical network (McClelland and Rumelhart, 1986). The competition model proposed by Bates and MacWhinney (1987) is a specific adaptation of a parallel-distributed processing system. The basic notion of the competition model is that learning is dependent on the probability of form-function matches. More frequently used forms are learned over rarer forms. The major predictive construct in the model is cue validity, which is divided into two components: cue availability and cue reliability. The model predicts that available and reliable cues should be learned first. A comprehensive review of several cues (e.g., case marking and word order) across a number of different languages (English, French, Italian, Turkish, and Hungarian) have supported the prediction (Bates and MacWhinney, 1987; MacWhinney, 1987). However, as Bohannon and Warren-Luebecker (1989) note, because the competition model is relatively new, there is little other evidence in support of it and no evidence against it.

THE INTERACTIONIST, LIMITED PROCESSING CAPACITY APPROACH TO LANGUAGE DISORDERS

An interactionist approach and the limited-capacity model have been extremely popular for researchers and clinicians interested in disordered populations (Crystal, 1987; Masterson and Kamhi, 1989, in press; Panagos and Prelock, 1982; Schwartz, 1988, in press). Schwartz (in press, p. 2), for example, states that "in many cases, understanding the interactions of language components is critical to our understanding of disordered speech and, more practically, to assessment and intervention." The recognition that language is a highly interactive system has made clinicians more sensitive to the relationships that exist among the various language domains. However, the nature of the specific interactions can quickly become very complex as the number of levels increases and different types of interactions are considered. Crystal (1987) has pointed out that the number of levels (i.e., content domains) and how best to define these levels continues to be a controversial issue. Levels can include any number of language domains (e.g., syntax, semantics, phonology, and prosody), different units of language (e.g., sound, syllable, word, and phrase), and related cognitive, neurological, social levels. It should be apparent that the potential existence of many levels has serious consequences for anyone wishing to make sense of the notion of interaction. The more levels that are identified, the greater the number of possible interactions there will be between levels. As Crystal (1987) notes, a 3-level model allows for only 3 interactions, whereas a 6-level model allows for 15 interactions, and a 9-level model, 36 interactions.

To make the study of interactions a manageable endeavor, one must focus attention on selected interactions (e.g., syntax-phonology). The actual interactions examined can be motivated by interest (e.g., Schwartz looks at interactions most likely to be encountered in disordered populations) or by a theoretical perspective that focuses attention on particular interactions. For example, the Piagetian view focuses attention on the relationship between certain cognitive attainments and language, whereas the social-interaction perspective focuses attention on the relationship between environmental inputs and language. Another way that has been used to reduce the number of potential interactions is to organize levels hierarchically, the assumption being that higher levels influence or constrain lower levels. Hierarchical models are common in depicting processes involved in language comprehension (Clark and Clark, 1977) and production (Bock, 1982; Foss and Hakes, 1978). Syntactic, semantic, and conceptual processes are usually considered higher-order levels, whereas phonetic and phonological processes are usually referred to as lower-level processes.

Hierarchical models in which limited capacity resource allocation is assumed have been used to explain linguistic interactions and trade-offs that occur in children's speech. Early anecdotal reports (de Villiers and de Villiers, 1978; Waterson, 1978) provided examples of children's longer utterances containing more phonological errors than shorter utterances. These reports were followed by more systematic investigations of linguistic trade-offs by Panagos and Prelock (1982). In these early studies, children were asked to imitate a series of sentences that varied in syntactic (e.g., clause structure) and phonological complexity (e.g., number of syllables). The basic finding was that increases in syntactic and phonological complexity were associated with more syntactic errors (e.g., word omissions) and more misarticulations. These findings led Panagos and Prelock (1982, p. 176) to conclude that:

> During sentence production syntactic and phonological structures influence one another such that complexity added on either level disrupts performance on the other and cumulative complexity disrupts performance on both. The dominant outcome of complexity mismanagement is the simplification of sentence structures at all levels of hierarchical organization.

Panagos and Prelock's (1982) claim about complexity mismanagement had a certain appeal to it because it made intuitive sense and was consistent with the limited capacity processing model that was in its peak of popularity 10 to 15 years ago. There were a number of limitations, however, in the experimental procedures and stimuli used in the studies that raised questions about the results (Kamhi et al., 1984; Schwartz, in press). For example, Schwartz (in press) has noted that some of the sentences were quite complex and thus not representative of normal sentence production. There was also a likely confounder between word length and familiarity. Kamhi et al. (1984) suggested that the way in which a given child managed sentence production demands was influenced by several factors, including (1) the sensitivity of the measures used to detect the effect of processing demands; (2) the developmental level of the child's speech production skills, linguistic knowledge, and cognitive abilities; and (3) the extent to which the child tolerated variability in speech productions.

The sensitivity of the measures used has obvious importance. For example, imperceptible changes in phonological accuracy can be detected only through the use of sensitive instrumentation. Most studies, however, have been concerned with perceptible changes in phonological accuracy because the variability in phonological accuracy has been sufficient to be reflected in phonemic-level changes.

Developmental factors also have an obvious influence on how children manage processing demands. The limited resource theorist views development as the gradual automatization of processes or functions; automatization frees up processing resources, which can then be allocated to other functions. Using this framework, one can conceptualize the development of language as a gradual automatization of certain sentence formulation processes (e.g., planning, execution, and articulation). The extent to which a child has automatized these processes thus might influence how vulnerable these processes are to increases in higher-level processing demands. The findings reported on linguistic interactions in spontaneous speech (see later discussion) support these points.

Developing cognitive abilities should also influence children's management of processing demands. Schwartz and Folger (1977) found that stage VI sensorimotor children showed more consistency in the production of sounds and syllable structure than stage V children. They attributed this decrease in variability to an improvement in children's ability to create and maintain accurate phonological representations.

The extent to which a child tolerates variability also has direct bearing on how processing demands are managed. For example, Scollon's (1976) child appeared to accept more variability in his speech than Waterson's (1978) son, who seemed to "know" his processing limits and attempted not to exceed them. Ferguson (1979) has suggested that a child who shows a looser and more variable phonological system exhibits an unanalytic, risk-taking style of language acquisition. This style is contrasted by the child who takes a more cautious, analytic approach to language acquisition. Such a child would exhibit a more rigid, less variable phonological system. These style differences can be extended to other aspects of language and behavior (Weiss et al., 1983).

My colleagues and I (Kamhi et al., 1984; Masterson and Kamhi, 1991, in press; Nelson and Kamhi, 1984, 1985) addressed some of the factors that affect the kinds of linguistic interactions children exhibit and how they manage sentence production demands in a series of studies. In the first study (Kamhi et al., 1984), we examined the effect that increases in language complexity had on the accuracy and consistency of young children's target word productions using an elicited imitation task. An imitation task was used to see if we could replicate Panagos' findings with young normally developing children. We predicted that children with more advanced speech, language, and cognitive skills would be less influenced by variations in language complexity than children with less advanced skills in these areas. Seven children aged 22 to 34 months were followed for 4 months.

The sentence imitation task consisted of 144 sentences grouped in 18 stimulus conditions. Each stimulus condition consisted of a stimulus word that occurred in eight utterances, reflecting different levels of language complexity: single word, two-word (modifier + noun [N]), simple sentence (subject, verb, object [SVO]), SVO + subject modifier, SVO + negative contraction, yes/no question with *did,* and two passives. The eight sentence types were chosen to reflect forms that children were both currently producing and not producing. The stimulus words contained nine late-emerging word initial phonemes, such as /ʒ/, /ʤ/, /ʋ/; one half of the word was bisyllabic.

Phonetic accuracy and consistency of the words were scored for each stimulus condition. Five patterns were possible: (1) consistent word production, (2) inconsistent word production, (3) increase in phonological accuracy, (4) decrease in phonological accuracy, and (5) unscorable. There were few unscorable patterns. The basic finding was that the younger, less mature children were less consistent in their target word productions than the older, more advanced children. Less than half (43%) of the younger children's word productions stayed the same across changes in language complexity compared with 79% of the older children's word productions. For all children, the most frequent effect of increases in language complexity was no change in word productions. When increases in language complexity did have an effect, there were as many improvements in phonological accuracy as there were decreases in accuracy.

The findings supported our initial hypothesis that children with more advanced speech-language and cognitive abilities would be less influenced by variations in language complexity than children with less advanced linguistic and cognitive abilities. Within-stage differences between children were also found, however. For example, one of the younger children showed twice as much variability in her misarticulated words than the other two children at her language level. We suggested that this child showed a higher tolerance for variability in her system.

In a speculative discussion section (Kamhi et al., 1984, pp. 336–337), we raised the question of the interdependence and autonomy of the processes involved in sentence production. We began by noting that in a limited-capacity system, one has two choices: (1) operate within the limits of one's processing capabilities or (2) exceed the limits and suffer the consequences. Our data suggested that a child's speech-language and cognitive level defines the capacity limits of the system (i.e., sentence production), whereas the extent to which a child tolerates variability determines whether these limits are typically observed or exceeded. This claim predicts that a child's language and cognitive level and tolerance for variability determine how interdependent and autonomous sentence production processes will be.

In a subsequent study, Nelson and Kamhi (1984) examined the relationships among several syntactic, semantic, and phonological variables in imitated and spontaneous utterances of four 2-year-old normally developing children. Previous studies had not evaluated linguistic interactions in spontaneous speech. Subjects were seen eight times over 4 months. During each session, a spontaneous speech sample was obtained and a sentence imitation task administered. The sentence imitation task consisted of four nonsense words with low phonological complexity (e.g., "tam," "muke") and four words with high phonological complexity (e.g., "jaften," "fifalo"). The words were presented in four sentences of varying length and complexity.

On the sentence imitation task, all four subjects made more speech errors (as reflected by percent consonant correct [PCC] scores) as the syntactic complexity of the sentences increased. During the course of the study, children gradually became able to produce the phonologically simple words accurately in all of the sentences. The children still made errors producing the phonologically complex words at the end of the study. Data from the spontaneous speech samples indicated that trade-offs between sentence length and speech production accuracy occurred primarily during developmental transitions from one language stage to another. (Stages were assigned based on procedures described by Crystal et al., 1976.) Trade-offs were not as likely to occur during more stable periods of development.

Nelson and Kamhi (1985) reanalyzed the data to determine whether certain discourse factors effected children's production of complex sentences and speech sound accuracy. Utterances that shared the topic and/or syntactic structure, or both of the immediately preceding utterance were found to be syntactically more complex than utterances unrelated to the prior discourse topic. Information in the preceding utterance had no effect, however, on children's production of speech sounds. The findings from both of these reports clearly indicated that the pattern of linguistic interactions was quite different in spontaneous speech than it was in the sentence imitation task.

Having identified some of the factors

that influence linguistic interactions in young normally developing children, Masterson and Kamhi (1991, in press) examined the interrelationship among linguistic components and the influence of certain contextual variables in older children with language and learning disabilities. Subjects were ten children with spoken and written language impairments, language learning disabled (LLD), ten children with only written language impairments, reading disabled (RD), and ten normally developing children (ages 6–9 years old). Data came from three sources: (1) a sentence imitation task adapted from Panagos and Prelock (1982), (2) a story-telling task in which children told two picture stories to the experimenter and two to another child, and (3) an event description task in which children were asked first to describe and then to explain three physical demonstrations. In addition to the usual measures of syntactic and phonological complexity, measures of fluency were also included.

As in the Nelson and Kamhi (1984) study, there were fewer interactions, or trade-offs, in the spontaneous speech data than in the imitated data. Interestingly, for some linguistic levels, the interactions were in different directions. For example, morphophonemic accuracy decreased in complex clause structures in imitated utterances but increased in complex clause structures in spontaneous speech. Intelligibility, which was rarely sacrificed in spontaneous speech, was often poorer in imitated sentences. These findings are consistent with those just reported for younger normally developing children. It should be clear that imitating sentences that exceed processing capabilities cause interactions (or breakdowns) that are different from those that occur in spontaneous speech.

The patterns of linguistic interactions were similar across the three groups of children. As expected, the LLD children consistently made more errors than the RD and normally developing children. However, the relative number of breakdowns (e.g., misarticulations, morphophonemic errors, and disfluencies) was no higher in the LLD group than it was in the other two groups. These findings suggested that young school-aged LLD children were not more vulnerable to processing demands than nondisabled children, nor were their language systems more interdependent than those of nondisabled children.

Several interesting effects of context were also found (Masterson and Kamhi, 1991). For example, in the story-telling condition, children in all groups tended to use simpler structures when they were given appropriate props or referents to retell the story than when they were not given the props. Children in all groups tended to use simpler sentence structures when talking about old information than when talking about novel information. These findings extend those of Nelson and Kamhi by further specifying the influence of contextual factors on linguistic interactions. Sentence imitation tasks are obviously insensitive to contextual influences.

FINDINGS IN SEARCH OF AN EXPLANATION

The studies discussed in the previous section have led to a better understanding of the kinds of interactions that occur within and across language domains, as well as a better understanding of how biological, cognitive, and social factors affect language development. The inconsistencies across studies and the substantial differences that exist across subjects are troublesome, however. Schwartz (in press) is concerned that we have yet to establish the best approach to measuring linguistic interactions. I have three other concerns with research conducted within an interactionist, limited processing capacity perspective.

The first concern is with the adequacy of the limited-capacity models that are used to explain trade-off effects. Navon (1984) has raised some questions about the notion of resource dependence and competition. His basic argument is that the existence of a limited quantity of resources for processing is a theoretical claim that should be empirically tested. In the article, Navon (1984) considers alternative explanations for phenomena commonly attributed to resource limitations. For example, a deterioration in the performance of a task when the task is performed concurrently with another task is usually taken as evidence that both tasks draw from a common pool of resources. Navon (1984, p. 220) points out, however, that task interference may be caused by other factors, such as task outputs or side effects that inhibit the performance of the other task. He gives the example of how the pattern of activations driven by the processing of reading a word can inhibit the activation essential for a concurrent task of comprehending a verbally presented word. In light of his claims, there may be alternative explanations for the linguistic dependencies or trade-off effects that are now attributed to limited resources.

The second concern is that it is unclear how much we gain by continuing to study the nature of linguistic interactions. I do not agree with Crystal (1987), who argues that it is premature to assert priorities within the various language levels, because too many possible interactions have not yet been investigated. Crystal (1987, p. 20) goes on to say that "all that can be confidently asserted is that mutual influence between some levels exists, and that this factor should play a more dominant role in our search for a general explanation of language handicap." Although there is clearly a need for additional research that examines interactions between linguistic, cognitive, and biological variables, different theoretical frameworks are needed to focus the research and interpret the findings. There are some interactions that we know enough about, such as the importance of discourse context and conceptual factors on language productions. In contrast, there are some interactions that we know very little about, such as the influence of prosodic variables on segmental aspects of speech production. Importantly, the purpose of future studies should not be to reaffirm the highly interactive nature of language but to distinguish interactions that are highly individualistic or idiosyncratic from those that tend to be generalizable across children.

The third concern is that the interactionist approach can sometimes lead to fragmentation of language into small, uninteresting units that then get reified (i.e., their existence is assumed). Kent (1990), in a provocative paper on fragmentation in clinical service, expands on the problem of fragmentation and reification. He points out that interaction might need to be invoked because of our misconception of things. When two components are linked by double-headed arrows in flow or block diagrams, we need to ask if the two components should have been separated in the first place or even exist as independent entities. Interaction among things and processes reifies those things and processes. Kent (1990, p. 9) concludes his discussion of interaction by noting that:

> the postulation of rampant interactivity and interconnectedness may be more acceptable as a theoretical position if the emphasis is placed on the interactivity itself rather than on the objects related by interactivity.

In other words, we must be very careful in accepting the interactionist approach (i.e., interactivity) as a tenable theoretical position.

MODULARITY

An interest in modules provides a very different orientation to questions about the interactions and interrelationships among language, cognitive, biological, and social systems. When theorists acknowledge modularity of systems, they attempt to answer questions about the size and content of the modules and whether they are innate or acquired, vertical or horizontal, impenetrable or leaky. Although Fodor (1983) wrote the book on modularity, his is not the only view of modularity. Gardner (1983), for example, has based his theory of intelligence on modular notions. Modular notions have also been incorporated in recent interactionist views of language learning (Bates et al., 1988; Chapman et al., Chapter 1). These views will be discussed after a brief review of Fodor's view of modularity.

Fodor's Modularity

According to Fodor (1985, p. 3), "a module is *(inter alia)* an informationally encapsulated computational system—an inference-making mechanism whose access to background information is constrained by general features of cognitive architecture, hence relatively rigidly and relatively permanently constrained." In another passage, Fodor (1983, p. 37) writes: "Roughly, modular cognitive systems are domain specific, innately specified, hardwired, autonomous, and not assembled." He proposes nine criteria that define the extent to which a system is modular. These criteria include (1) domain specificity, (2) mandatory operation (e.g., you cannot hear speech as noise even if you would prefer to), (3) limited access to mental representations (i.e., relatively inaccessible to consciousness), (4) speed, (5) informational encapsulation (it is difficult to get information into the system), (6) shallow outputs, (7) neural architecture, (8) specific patterns of breakdown, and (9) characteristic pace and sequencing in ontogeny. As Bates et al. (1988, p. 24) note, the first six characteristics are typical of all overlearned skills, such as driving, tennis, and typing, whereas the last three characteristics are biological ones.

Because information encapsulation is the essence of a modular system, some further elaboration of this notion is necessary. An encapsulated system is one that does not allow most inputs to penetrate the system. This does not necessarily mean that all modular systems are impenetrable; rather, to the extent that input systems are informationally encapsulated, of all the information that might in principle bear on a problem solution, only a small and stereotyped portion is actually admitted for consideration (Fodor, 1983, p. 71). In this way, speed is achieved for input systems by permitting them to ignore lots of the facts. Fodor (1983) provides a clear example of how a perceptual system can be impervious to knowledge. He presents the scenario of a long-time friend who knows that under no conceivable circumstance would Fodor stick his finger in his eye. This belief is explicit and deeply felt. Yet if Fodor jabs his finger near enough to the friend's eyes and fast enough, he will blink. In this way, the blink reflex is mandatory and impervious to what is known about beliefs and expectations. Fodor does not deny the influence of world knowledge and other input sources; he simply does not find top-down effects interesting because they are not internal to the module.

Fodor's modules are "input systems." He (1983, p. 47) acknowledges, however, that if there are other psychological systems that fit the definition, then "of course, they are modular too." The modularity of output systems, such as speech production, is thus not an issue for him. He also makes no claims about the exact number of modules but suggests that candidates might include mechanisms for color perception, the analysis of shape, and the analysis of three-dimensional spatial relations. Candidates in audition might include computational systems that assign grammatical descriptions to token utterances or ones that detect the melodic or rhythmic structure of acoustic arrays.

A crucial aspect of Fodor's (1983) approach to modularity is the distinction he makes between modular and nonmodular processes. Whereas modular processes are autonomous, domain specific, very fast, and mandatory, nonmodular processes are slow, deep, global, largely under voluntary (executive) control, and unencapsulated. He makes some fairly outrageous claims about the nature of nonmodular central processes. Consider, for example, the generalization that he hopes will some day come to be known as Fodor's first law of the nonexistence of cognitive science (Fodor, 1983, p. 107): "The more global a cognitive process is, the less anybody understands it. *Very* global processes, like analogical reasoning, aren't understood at all." Fodor's argument here is that the closer one gets to higher, more intelligent, less reflexive, less routine exercises of cognition, the more these processes can draw from all previously established knowledge, truths, beliefs, or present whims. The highest cognitive processes are thus unbounded in the inputs from which they draw. In short, "Nature has contrived to have it both ways, to get the best out of fast dumb systems *and* slow contemplative ones, by simply refusing to choose between them" (Fodor, 1985, p. 4).

A modular approach to language processing would look something like Forster's (1979) model that consists of phonological, syntactic, and message-level processors. Each of these components operates independently with access only to its own information source and the output of the next lower processor. The output of each component is made available to a "general problem solver," which has access to real-world knowledge. Models such as these enjoy all sorts of explanatory advantages (Frazier, 1987). The limited task and information source of each component subsystem is consistent with modularity claims of fast, dumb, automatic processes, as well as claims suggesting independence in the use of theoretically distinct information types.

Gardner's Theory of Multiple Intelligences

Although Fodor (1984) is clearly one of the main proponents of modularity, many psychologists have embraced some of the basic notions inherent in Fodor's views. These notions are also inherent in the long tradition of faculty psychology tracing back to Gall (1758–1828) and more recently Thurstone (1938). Gardner's (1983) recent theory of multiple intelligences is an obvious offspring of faculty psychology. Gardner's intelligences include linguistic, logicomathematic, music, bodily kinesthetic, spatial, interpersonal, and intrapersonal. He proposes eight criteria for the identification of these separate intelligences that overlap somewhat with Fodor's criteria: (1) an identifiable core operation or set of operations, (2) susceptibility to encoding in a symbol system, (3) an evolutionary history and plausibility, (4) potential isolation by brain damage, (5) the existence of idiot savants, prodigies, and other exceptional individuals, (6) support from experimental psychological tasks, (7) a distinctive developmental history, along with a definable set of expert "end-state" performances, and (8) support from psychometric findings. Unlike Fodor, Gardner is interested in experimental and psychometric support for the existences of intelligence modules. However, it should be clear that some of Gardner's modules (e.g., personal intelligence) meet few of the eight criteria.

The Search of Bates et al. (1988) for Dissociable Mechanisms

In contrast to the vertical module biases of Fodor (1984) and other modern proponents of modularity, Bates et al. (1988) attempted to find horizontal modules that control individual differences in language. These horizontal modules are processes that language shares with other aspects of cognition. The specific goal of their research was "to identify associations and dissociations, synchronies and asynchronies, packages of abilities that 'hang together' over time" (Bates et al., 1988, p. 7). Toward this end, they examined individual differences in young children's language behaviors during the transition from first words to grammar.

Bates et al. (1988, p. 11) offer a looser, less constrained definition of a module than both Fodor (1984) and Gardner (1983). They characterize modules in terms of the processes and representations needed to operate in a specific content domain of particular importance for the organism. This definition has several implications for language processing and development. First, modules can develop and break down independently in children, even though they may interact with one another in real-time processing. Second, the nature of the modules is unspecified. In contrast to Fodor (1985) and other theorists who argue for highly specialized perceptual and linguistic modules, Bates et al. (1988) posit the existence of horizontal processing modules (i.e., processes that cut across the various subdomains of language). Third, this broader view of modularity allows for modules to be acquired and thus not have to be biologically specified. The notion of acquired modules has been advocated by several reading theorists (Seidenberg, 1989; Stanovich, in press). These theorists have suggested that the processes involved in word recognition reflect an acquired module.

The relationships Bates et al. (1988) find in their data lead them to conclude that children divide language in a way quite different from what researchers have previously thought. Traditionally language has been divided into separate domains such as phonology, lexical semantics, and grammar or, alternatively, phonology, semantics, syntax, morphology, and pragmatics. Bates et al. (1988), however, did not find support for the existence of vertical faculties in language; in particular, they found no evidence for a division between grammar and semantics. The data repeatedly showed that lexical development and grammar were closely linked within and across stages of development. The data did, however, suggest the existence of three partially dissociable language acquisition mechanisms (i.e., horizontal modules) that are emphasized to different degrees at different points in development. These were comprehension, rote production (i.e., routinized use of language), and analyzed production (i.e., lexical-conceptual sophistication of language). Because these mechanisms cut across the content domains of language, Bates et al. (1988) view them as horizontal, nonmodular processes rather than vertical ones.

Although Bates et al. (1988) found no evidence for vertical language modules in young children, they recognize that evidence for such modules exists in older children and adults (e.g., clear dissociations in language functions in aphasic adults). It follows that vertical modules are not born; they are made (Bates et al., 1988, p. 284):

> An independent and ultimately 'impenetrable' use of grammar is slowly constructed, piece by piece, practiced endlessly until it becomes as effortless and routine as any other fully acquired perceptual-motor skill.

Bates et al. (1988) conclude that the early stages of language acquisition are characterized primarily by dissociations among horizontal faculties, whereas later stages may be characterized by the development of vertical faculties that are learned rather than innate. These conclusions are consistent with the interactionist view that all aspects of language functioning can be accounted for by horizontal faculties that cut across different content domains. Bates et al. (1988) favor the interactionist view that emphasizes constructivist (Piagetian) principles.

Child Talk's Modularity

Child Talk is the name given to a process model of children's language production. Other chapters in this book will describe the model in greater detail. What is modular in Child Talk's view are children's knowledge schemas (Chapman et al., see Chapter 1). Modularity is conferred by event representations in memory that act as encapsulated systems representing words and sentence frames. Intentions, emotions, personal history of the self and other, and world knowledge in general, are part of the schema as module. According to Chapman et al. (see Chapter 1), this view of modularity meets the criteria of encapsulation and mandatory application of knowledge, but not specificity of knowledge domain. Their view of modularity is obviously quite different from the other views of modularity discussed.

The Good and the Bad About Modularity

The attractiveness of modular systems should be apparent. By being fast, dumb, and encapsulated, modular perceptual systems are protected from highly developed inferential systems. This allows the organism to stay tuned to the environment. As Tanenhaus et al. (1987, p. 85) put it: One does not want to fail to recognize a tiger when it appears unexpectedly. Linguists and psycholinguists who argue for autonomous linguistic systems are particularly attracted to modular systems because these systems can be distinguished from the more general-purpose cognitive system. These individuals do not favor highly interactive models because they blur the distinctions they find so interesting. The notion of highly encapsulated modular systems is also attractive to many psychologists because such systems reduce the number of potential interactions that need to be studied. Processing models that include modular systems thus tend to be more parsimonious than processing models without modular components.

Modular systems become less attractive when one begins to ask questions about the size and nature of modules, the extent to which modules leak (i.e., are not fully encapsulated), whether modules are innate or can be acquired, and so forth. Modular systems also become less attractive when one realizes, as Bates et al. (1988) point out, that there is no such thing as a totally nonmodular theory of mind because such a theory would imply that mind and brain are unbounded objects with no internal structure. An interactionist must accept, either implicitly or explicitly, the existence of general but nevertheless self-contained processes for perceiving, learning, and remembering. Even the most rabid interactionists (e.g., connectionists) must acknowledge the existence of "tiny modules, i.e., nodes or stored responses that can be connected to one another via some kind of associative process" (Bates et al., 1988, p. 12). The argument between proponents of modularity and interactionism thus must center instead on questions about the size and nature of the modules, their innateness, leakiness, and so forth.

The idea that modules can be acquired and are not necessarily innate is particularly appealing. Although the notion of acquired modules is inconsistent with Fodor's (1983) views on modularity, it seems a more elegant way (though not more testable) to portray highly automatized processes that operate within a particular content domain. As indicated in the previous section, word recognition and grammar seem to be excellent candidates for acquired modules (Bates et al., 1988; Seidenberg, 1989). Phonetic perception, on the other hand, is a good candidate for an innate module (Fodor, 1983).

The size of modules is a particularly important question. As Bates et al. (1988) have pointed out, all interactionists must acknowledge the existence of tiny modules. The smaller the module, however, the less controversial and less interesting it is. Not many people get worked up over whether or not tiny modules (e.g., connectionist nodes) actually exist. In contrast, rarely have claims about the existence of large modules gone unchallenged. This is because the existence of large modules have far-reaching consequences. Somewhere in between are claims about the modular status of entities such as schemas or other knowledge states. There is no disputing that language can be broken up into very small modules, such as words, phonemes, morphemes, or larger ones, such as schemas, scripts, or frames. It just seems that by attributing modular status to clusters of knowledge or specific linguistic units, the essence and with it the appeal of modularity are lost. The notion of modularity should not become a metaphor for coherent knowledge or representational units. Modular status should be reserved for innate and acquired systems that meet a large number of Fodor's modularity criteria. The task for child language investigators is to determine which language systems develop into modular systems. The notion of "developmental modularity" also needs to be incorporated into models of language performance.

HOLISM

In recent years, a growing number of theorists, researchers, and clinicians have become disenchanted with fragmentary, reductionist, mechanistic approaches to science, learning, and education (Heshusius, 1989; Kent, 1990, Norris and Damico, 1990; Poplin, 1988). The Newtonian, mechanistic view of the world breaks down complex behaviors into objective, measurable components and portrays development as as additive, sequential, and continuous. In reaction to the reductionist, mechanistic view, many people have embraced the principles embodied in holistic, humanist views of the world. A fundamental holistic assumption is that the properties of the parts can be understood only from the dynamics of the whole. The whole is different from and more than the sum of its parts (Heshusius, 1989, pp. 411–412). For many, the essence of holism, or wholeness, is a focus on the individual as a human organism rather than a machinelike mechanism. Wholeness is embodied in the word individual, which means "undivided" (Kent, 1990). A focus on the individual leads holists to emphasize the importance of self-regulatory, self-organizing, and self-evaluative behaviors.

The emergence of a holistic paradigm is often traced back to the discoveries about relativity and quantum physics that provided an alternative to the newtonian view of the world. As Kent (1990, p. 7) notes, Einstein's theory of relativity does not view the universe as a set of interacting constituent particles. The universe is more appropriately viewed as a universal field that has the essential quality of unbroken wholeness in flowing movement. The whole becomes the primary notion, whereas the parts are abstractions from the whole. Kent quotes Bohm (1985, p. 128), who makes the point that one cannot analyze the whole into distinct parts with preassigned interactions. Rather, "the whole organizes and even creates the parts."

The most prevalent application of holistic notions to language is found in the widely popular "whole language" approach to teaching reading in the early elementary school years (Goodman, 1986; Smith, 1982). Consistent with holistic principles, the whole language approach views language as an integrated system that is more than the sum of its component parts (Norris and Damico, 1990). Norris and Damico (1990, p. 213) describe several assumptions of the whole language approach:

1. Language is closely linked with other semiotic and cognitive abilities and is influenced by such things as motivation, experience, learning, and anxiety.
2. All of the components of language are always present and interacting in any instance of language use.
3. Language is not learned by first acquiring the smallest component parts but by exposing the child simultaneously to all language components in a meaningful context.
4. Language learning is viewed as an active constructive process.

Active constructive processing, a fundamental notion in Piaget's theory of cognitive development, is a theme that runs through all accounts of holistic accounts of learning. Heshusius (1989, p. 412) writes:

> Learning is understanding *relations* rather than pieces of knowledge. It is the personal/social/cultural construction of meaning by the child, based on who the child is and on what she or he knows. Learners always bring their own personal social, cultural, and political histories, purposes, and interpretations to the situation, whether we are aware of it or not. Learning occurs at various but equally valid levels, including kinesthetic, intuitive, and nondiscursive.

Kent (1990, p. 12) makes similar points about the practice of speech-language pathology:

> As practitioners we must respect and try to apprehend the values and beliefs of our clients. These values and beliefs are part of a life-story narrative and they are indivisible from a client's anatomy and physiology. . . . The results of a battery of tests (then) should be seen as disparate fragments of a person. The unity of personhood is beyond any approach to quantification.

Although it might appear that holism is most applicable to educational and clinical issues, holists also see important implications for research. Forms of inquiry that are consistent with holism include phenomenological research, qualitative and interpretative research, ethnography, naturalistic research, and case studies (Heshusius, 1989). According to Heshusius (1989, p. 413), the researcher who embraces holistic principles is not a measurer or controller of variables but a careful and aware listener, observer, and able narrator. Inquiry occurs in real-life settings and in relation to real-life events. Qualitative judgments and human rationality rather than quantification is seen as the best way to justify knowledge claims.

The Good and the Bad About Holism

There is an inherent appeal in holism. Being human, we are naturally attracted to assumptions and principles that emphasize humanism, unity, meaning, purpose, qualitative judgments, and so forth. Newtonian science with its emphasis on quantification and fragmentation has a tendency to proliferate experiments that isolate measurable variables. Many empirical studies appear to be narrowly focused, addressing questions far removed from real-life settings and events. Holistic assumptions are particularly attractive to educators and clinicians disenchanted with reductionist, fragmentary, programmatic approaches to teaching and learning. As indicated earlier, holistic assumptions provide the theoretical foundation for the whole language movement.

It seems difficult to find fault with holistic assumptions that emphasize wholeness rather than fragmentation, qualitative judgments rather than quantitative measurements, and so forth. Why would anyone want to be associated with mechanistic or reductionist assumptions (such nasty terms), when the alternative is holism and humanism (such nice terms). These terms, like whole language, seem to have been designed to be opponent proof. The problem is that the two views are not incompatible. Unfortunately, many holists, particularly advocates of whole language approaches, make it seem that empirical science and all non-holistic views (behaviorism, interactionism, nativism, etc.) are inconsistent with the assumptions that characterize holism.

Licht and Torgesen (1989), in their response to Heshusius' (1989) paper, show how quantitative empirical research can and does address many of the goals of holism. Licht and Torgesen (1989) argue that Heshusius (1989) confuses the broader natural science philosophy with the narrow philosophy of behaviorists who do not consider any variables that are not directly observable. There are large bodies of research in cognition, learning, and language that examine how values, feelings, and motives influence behavior. As an example, Licht and Torgesen (1989) cite the entire field of attribution theory, which is concerned with how personal interpretations of reality influence one's behavior. In another work, Licht and Kistener (1986) examined the impact of negative beliefs and motivational states on academic performance. Similarly, an interest in contextual effects is seen throughout the social sciences, as exemplified in the studies cited earlier that examined contextual influences on language productions (Masterson and Kamhi, 1991). Finally, the importance of in-depth interviews with clients or parents and detailed developmental histories or narratives, as Kent (1990) calls them, is indisputable in medicine and clinical fields such as speech-language pathology.

The essence of holism is its emphasis on the whole and the notion that the whole is more than the sum of its parts. Practically speaking, however, what does it mean to study the whole of language, treat language as a whole, or treat the whole child? How does one go about studying the whole without understanding its parts? What can we say about language without knowing about its components (syntax, semantics, etc.) and the factors (cognitive, social, biological, etc.) that influence these components? A holist might answer that one should focus on the purposes and functions of language, the culture and values of the individual, and the contexts of communication. To do so, however, one must have knowledge about which language forms are appropriate for which functions in which contexts.

Holists are correct when they say that knowledge of the parts does not lead to knowledge of the whole. What they fail to point out, however, is that knowledge of the whole is often not possible without knowledge of the parts. The holist rhetoric of meaning, purpose, and unity hides the inevitable reduction that must take place. Holists do not like small units, such as phonemes, syllables, words, and sentences or divisions between syntax, semantics, and phonology. They prefer larger, meaningful units of discourse contexts, concepts, and intentions. But these "larger" units are inevitably broken down by taxonomies that differentiate between various kinds of contexts, meanings, and intentions. Holistic rhetoric attempts to mask the reductionism that characterizes purportedly holistic research and teaching. But let us not be fooled: holistic assumptions notwithstanding, there is no such thing as a nonreductionist, nonfragmentary theory of language, just as there is no such thing as a nonmodular theory of mind. The controversy is thus not about whether one reduces something like language to specific components, but what the important components are and the extent to which these components are modular in nature. It is no coincidence that these are the same questions that many linguists and psycholinguists have been pondering.

IMPLICATIONS FOR PROCESS MODELS OF CHILDREN'S LANGUAGE

In this chapter, three perspectives about the language processing system and its complex interactions have been discussed. I began the chapter with a bias against the interactionist, limited-capacity perspective, because the research I have conducted using this perspective has given me first-hand experience with its limitations. This perspective has led to an increasing fragmentation of language and a proliferation of hierarchical, multilevel models with double-headed arrows that go every which way. In addition, limited resource notions are not without problems (Navon, 1984). Despite these shortcomings, the interactionist perspective has played an important role in focusing attention on the interactions and hierarchical (dependent) relationships that characterize language processing systems.

In contrast to an initial bias against the interactionist, limited-capacity perspective, I was attracted to the modular and holistic perspectives, despite their inherent incompatibility. The major appeal of modularity was the notion of highly encapsulated fast, dumb processing systems that are impervious to higher-level inferential systems, whereas the major appeal of holism was its emphasis on meaning, purpose, and human values rather than easily quantifiable and measurable units. As indicated earlier, it is difficult to find fault with holistic assumptions that stress wholeness over fragmentation and qualitative judgments over quantitative measurements.

The initial appeal of modularity and holism has been significantly tempered, however, by the realization that many modular and holistic notions are not easily validated. It is a lot easier to list a set of modularity criteria, as Fodor and Gardner have done, than to find actual systems that meet all or even most of the criteria. In the same vein, it is one thing to emphasize the wholeness and unity of a system such as language; it is another thing to study and make sense of the language system without knowing a lot about its parts. Some would argue that part of the appeal of modularity and holism is their resistance to empirical validation, a resistance that, of course, makes it very difficult to invalidate these views. Adherence to modular or holistic views in their idealized forms thus must be based, in large part, on faith (some would say blind faith).

My problem is that I lack the kind of fervor and commitment required to believe in modularity or holism. Unfortunately, without fervor it is easy to slip into tentacles of relativism, which holds that there are no right or wrong theories or explanations—that everything is relative. But everything is not relative; there is a difference between good explanations and bad ones. With complex issues, however, differentiating between good and not-so-good explanations is not so simple. Fortunately, a few people are trying to reconcile the disparate views. Bates and her colleagues, as discussed earlier, have shown how aspects of modularity can be incorporated into an interactionist perspective that emphasizes constructivist notions. Their position that certain language systems can become vertical modules is a compromise between the innate vertical modules proposed by Fodor and the absence of any vertical modules in interactionist models.

The principles embodied by connectionism and parallel processing systems also hold some promise for understanding the language processing system and its complex interactions. It is not coincidental that many of the earliest connectionists, such as Rumelhart (McClelland and Rumelhart, 1986), had strong early allegiances to interactive, limited capacity processing models. Rumelhart (1975) is still well known for his early work in schema theory and narrative structure. Rumelhart, like many other psychologists, however, realized the limitations of serial, top-down, bottom-up processing models for understanding the nature of highly interactive processing systems. Connectionist models, which are based on probabilistic activation levels, provide an empirical means to test specific predictions about linguistic interactions and perhaps some modularity claims as well. Unfortunately, connectionism is not user friendly. Although the basic principles of connectionism are not difficult to grasp, much of connectionist research involves computer simulations that require sophisticated mathematical and programming skills.

The Child Talk model developed by Chapman and her colleagues (see Chapter 1) represents another promising attempt to develop a unifying process model of child language. The Child Talk model includes principles and components from the interactionist, modular, and holistic perspectives. Child Talk takes as its starting point the strong evidence of context-specific language use. Intentions, emotions, actions, events, personal history of the self and other, and world knowledge are the building blocks of linguistic knowledge. As indicated earlier, what is modular in Child Talk are the child's knowledge schemas. The model is clearly an ambitious one. It is unclear, however, whether it is verifiable. Like Fodor's modularity and holism, the model appears to be somewhat resistant to empirical validation and, therefore, invalidation. For example, what kind of evidence would disprove the existence of modular knowledge schemas? What kind of decontextualized language knowledge (e.g., rules, principles, concepts) would it take to challenge the claims made by Child Talk? All language knowledge is obviously not context specific. The vitality and validity of the model will be determined by research that addresses these questions and tests the specific predictions Child Talk makes. Some of the other chapters in this book may, in fact, address some of these questions.

IMPLICATIONS FOR CLINICAL PRACTICE

One may ask, in conclusion, what all this talk of language processing and modular systems has to do with clinical practice. The answer is "a lot." The different processing views discussed in this chapter are each consistent with particular assessment and intervention practices. For example, belief in the existence of Fodor-like vertical language modules is consistent with assessment protocols that differentiate clearly among language content domains and intervention procedures that sequentially target specific content domains (e.g., first syntactic structures, then semantic relations, then pragmatic functions). In contrast, the various interactionist views would lead one to consider the interactions that occur within and between the various language domains. Assessment procedures would attempt to discover the particular relationships and trade-offs that exist among language components. Rather than sequentially targeting specific content domains in therapy, more than one domain of language would be targeted. For example, the use of various communicative functions might be the primary objective, and specific language forms would be learned to serve particular communicative functions (e.g., question forms would be taught to request information and clarification).

Adherence to holistic principles would lead one to evaluate more than just language abilities. There would be interest in learning about the whole child, the child's personal history, intentions, feelings, and so forth. Therapy objectives would probably incorporate many of the key elements of Child Talk, focusing on developing language to describe events, objects, situations, and feelings that are integral and meaningful aspects of the child's life.

As Johnston (1983) reminded us several years ago, all clinical practice operates within some theoretical perspective. We can pretend that clinical practice has no theoretical motivation, or we can examine the theoretical assumptions implicit in our clinical practice, evaluate them, and modify them when they do not work anymore. If an unexamined life is not worth living, unexamined clinical practice might not be worth practicing. The kind of commitment needed to link theory and practice is not an easy one, but it is well worth the effort.

REFERENCES

Bates E, Benigni L, Bretherton I, et al: *The Emergence of Symbols: Cognition and Communication in Infancy*. New York, Academic Press, 1979.

Bates E, Bretherton I, Snyder L: *From First Words to Grammar: Individual Differences and Dissociable Mechanisms*. New York, Cambridge University Press, 1988.

Bates E, MacWhinney B: Functionalist approaches to the acquisition of grammar, in Wanner E, Gleitman L (eds): *Language acquisition: The State of the Art*. New York, Cambridge University Press, 1982, pp 173–219.

Bates E, MacWhinney B: Competition, variation, and language learning, in MacWhinney B (ed): *Mechanisms of Language Learning*. Hillsdale, NJ, Lawrence Erlbaum Associates, 1987, pp 157–195.

Bates E, Snyder L: The cognitive hypothesis in language development, in Uzgiris I, Hunt J (eds): *Research With Scales of Psychological Development in Infancy*. Champaign, Ill, University of Illinois Press, 1987.

Bock K: Toward a cognitive psychology of syntax: Information processing contributions to sentence formulation. *Psychol Rev* 1982; 89:1–47.

Bohannon J, Warren-Leubecker A: Theoretical approaches to language acquisition, in Gleason J (ed): *The Development of Language*. Columbus, Ohio, Charles E Merrill Publishing Co, 1989, pp 327–359.

Bohm D: Hidden variables and the implicate order. *Zygon* 1985; 20:111–124.

Clark H, Clark E: *Psychology and Language*. New York, Harcourt, Brace, Jovanovich, 1977.

Crystal D: Towards a 'bucket' theory of language disability: Taking account of interaction between linguistic levels. *Clin Linguistics Phonetics* 1987; 1:7–22.

Crystal D, Fletcher P, Garman M: *The Grammatical Analysis of Language Disability*. New York, Elsevier North-Holland, 1976.

de Villiers J, De Villiers P: Simplifying phonological processes in the one- and two-word stage. Paper presented at the Boston University Conference on Child Language Development, Boston, October 1978.

Ferguson C: Phonology as an individual access system, in Fillmore C, Kempler D, Wang W (eds): *Individual Differences in Language Ability and Language Behavior*. New York, Academic Press, 1979.

Fodor J: *The Modularity of Mind: An Essay on Faculty Psychology*. New York, MIT Press, 1983.

Fodor J: Precis of the modularity of mind. *Behav Brain Sci* 1985; 8:1–42.

Forster K: Levels of processing and the structures of the language processor, in Cooper W, Walker E (eds): *Sentence Processing*. Hillsdale, NJ, Lawrence Erlbaum Associates, pp 27–85.

Foss D, Hakes D: *Psycholinguistics*. Englewood Cliffs, NJ, Prentice-Hall, 1978.

Frazier L: Theories of sentence processing, in Garfield J (ed): *Modularity in Knowledge Representation and Natural-Language Understanding*. Cambridge, Mass, MIT Press, 1987, pp 291–309.

Gardner H: *Frames of Mind*. New York, Basic Books, 1983.

Goodman K: *What's Whole in Whole Language?* Portsmouth, NH, Heinemann, 1986.

Gopnik A, Meltzoff A: Relations between semantic and cognitive development in the one-word stage: The specificity hypothesis. *Child Dev* 1986; 57:1040–1053.

Gopnik A, Meltzoff A: The development of categorization in the second year and its relation to other cognitive and linguistic developments. *J Verbal Lear Verbal Behav* 1987; 5:492–496.

Heshusius L: The newtonian mechanistic paradigm, special education and contours of alternatives: An overview. *J Learn Disabil* 1989; 22:403–415.

Johnston J: What is language intervention? The role of theory, in Miller J, Yuder D, Schiefelbusch (eds): *Contemporary Issues in Language Intervention*. ASHA Reports, 12. pp 52–57.

Johnston J: Cognitive prerequisites: The evidence from children learning English, in Slobin D (ed): *The Cross-Linguistic Study of Language Acquisition*. Hillsdale, NJ, Lawrence Erlbaum Associates, 1985, pp 961–1004.

Kamhi A, Catts H, Davis M: Management of sentence production demands. *J Speech Hear Res* 1984; 27:329–337.

Kelly C, Dale P: Cognitive skills associated with the onset of multiword utterances. *J Speech Hear Res* 1989; 32:645–656.

Kent R: The fragmentation of clinical service and clinical science in communicative disorders. *NSSLHA J* 1990; 17:4–16.

LaBerge D, Samuels S: Toward a theory of automatic information processing in reading. *Cognit Psychol* 1974; 6:293–323.

Licht M, Torgesen J: Natural science approaches to questions of subjectivity. *J Learn Dis* 1989; 22:418–419.

Masterson J, Kamhi A: Linguistic trade-offs in school-age children with and without language disorders. *J Speech Hear Res* (in press).

Masterson J, Kamhi A: The effects of elicitation condition on sentence production in normal and language-learning disabled children. *J Speech Hear Res* 1991; 34:549–559.

MacWhinney B: The competition model, in MacWhinney B (ed): *Mechanisms of Language Learning.* Hillsdale, NJ, Lawrence Erlbaum Associates, 1987, pp 249–303.

McClelland J, Rumelhart D: *Parallel Distributed Processing: Explorations in the Microstructure of Cognition.* Cambridge, Mass, MIT Press, 1986.

Navon D: Resources—a theoretical soup stone. *Psychol Rev* 1984; 91:216–234.

Nelson L, Kamhi A: Syntactic, semantic, and phonological trade-offs in preschool children's utterances. Paper presented at the Annual Convention of the American Speech-Language-Hearing Association, San Francisco, November 1984.

Nelson L, Kamhi A: Discourse information is a factor in preschool children's sentence production. Paper presented at the Biennial Meeting of the Society for Research in Child Development, Toronto, 1985.

Norris J, Damico J: Whole language in theory and practice: Implications for language intervention. *Lang Speech Hear Services Sch* 1990; 21:212–221.

Panagos J, Prelock P: Phonological constraints on the sentence productions of language-disordered children. *J Speech Hear Res* 1982; 25:171–177.

Poplin M: Holistic/constructivist principles of teaching/learning process: Implications for the field of learning disabilities. *J Learn Dis* 1988; 21:401–416.

Rumelhart D: Notes on schema for stories, in Brown D, Collins A (eds): *Representation and Understanding: Studies in Cognitive Science.* New York, Academic Press, 1975, pp 211–236.

Schwartz R: Phonological factors in early lexical acquisition, in Smith M, Locke J (eds): *The Emergent Lexicon: The Child's Development of a Linguistic Vocabulary.* New York, Academic Press, 1988, pp 185–224.

Schwartz R: Interactions among language components in phonological development and disorders, in Yavas M (ed): *Phonological Development and Phonological Disorders.* São Paulo, Brazil, Mereado Aberto (in press).

Schwartz R, Folger K: Sensorimotor development and descriptions of child phonology. *Pap Rep Child Lang Dev* 1977; 13:8–15.

Scollon R: *Conversations With a One-Year-Old.* Honolulu, University Press of Hawaii, 1976.

Seidenberg M: Visual word recognition and pronunciation: A computational model and its implications, in Marslen-Wilson W (ed): *Lexical Representation and Process.* Cambridge, Mass, MIT Press, 1989, pp 25–75.

Smith F: *Understanding Reading.* New York, Holt, Rhinehart, & Winston, 1982.

Stanovich K: Concepts in developmental theories of reading skills cognitive resources, automaticity, and modularity. *Dev Rev* (in press).

Tanenhaus M, Dell G, Carlson G: Context effects in lexical processing: A connectionist approach, in Garfield J (ed): *Modularity in Knowledge, Representation and Natural Language Understanding.* Cambridge, Mass, MIT Press, 1987, pp 83–111.

Thurstone L: Primary Mental Abilities. *Psychometric Monographs*, 1938.

Waterson N: Growth of complexity in phonological development, in Waterson N, Snow C, (eds): *The Development of Communication.* New York, John Wiley & Sons, 1978.

Weiss A, Leonard L, Rowan L, et al: Linguistic and nonlinguistic features of style in normal and language-impaired children. *J Speech Hear Disord* 1983; 48:154–164.

SECTION II

Interactive Processes in Phonological Development

4 Phonological Development as Biology and Behavior

Raymond D. Kent, Ph.D.

For the normally developing child, speech is the primary means by which language is learned and used. As a language modality, speech has two aspects: one perceptual and one productive. What the child learns about language comes largely through the perception of the sound patterns of the ambient or parent language. What the child learns in language expression is to produce satisfactory replicas of these sound patterns through appropriate regulation of the speech apparatus—the vocal tract and the phonatory-pulmonary system. The two aspects of perception and production are interwoven in phonological capability. In this chapter, their interrelationships will be discussed from a biological perspective. In other words, the perception and production of speech will be examined in terms of *ethology,* or the biological study of behavior. Hearing and producing speech sounds are biological processes that enable the acquisition of spoken language. In its general meaning, phonology is a term that denotes sound pattern, and this general meaning will be used in this chapter.

Although phonology can be isolated to some degree from other components of language or from the overall behavior of humans, phonology is best understood in relation to language in toto and in relation to human biology. Ohala (1990) has argued that phonology should not be regarded as an autonomous area of study but as one that is fully understandable only in relation to other areas, such as phonetics. The same can be said about phonological development. Phonological development in the child occurs in a larger developmental context, and it is with this context that this discussion begins.

Table 4–1 is a summary description of selected aspects of growth and maturation. The table has three parts, one pertaining to auditory perceptual development for speech, another to development of speech production, and a third to general development. The information in the table is drawn from a number of sources, the major ones being identified in the table legend. It is not possible to give detailed discussion in this chapter to the various entries in the table. Rather, major concepts will be reviewed as they relate to possible continuities, discontinuities, convergences, divergences, and interrelationships within and among the three table components. Reference will be made to this table throughout the chapter.

NEOTONY

The first general concept to be discussed is neotony, which literally means "holding onto youth." Human neotony is particularly evident in a comparison of the adult with the neonate. The neonate in many ways resembles the fetus as much as it resembles the adult. This is

TABLE 4–1.
Selected Accomplishments Within the First Year of Life in the Areas of Auditory Perception, Vocal or Speech Production, and General Development*

Age (mo)	Perception	Production	General Development
≤1	Categorical discrimination of some speech contrasts Discrimination of own mother's voice from other women's voices Discrimination of some foreign utterances from parent language	Phonation stage: crying, grunts, belches and other vegetative sounds	Possible imitation of facial gestures Eye movement and turning of head toward sound
1–4	Normalization for speaking rates and different talkers Detection of variations in intonational patterns Recognition of same syllable in different utterances Some switching of attentional focus for speech contrasts	Cooing stage: vowels, laughter, some velar sounds	Smiling Lifting of head in prone position at 1–3 mo Swiping arm movement in supine position Novelty preference for visual stimuli at 2–3 mo
4–6	Detection of prosodic markers for clausal units Preference for infant-directed over adult-directed speech Some matching of vocalizations with appropriate facial shapes	Expansion stage: increase in consonants, which often appear as a single articulation that accompanies a continuous or interrupted phonation Shift in proportion of utterances that contain glottal/phonatory modulation vs. proportion that contain supraglottal articulation	Righting of head when pulled to sitting position Sitting with some support Recognition of previously exposed visual stimuli Successful reaching and grasping Selective attending to form or color in visual displays

		Some conversational turn-taking behavior, e.g., matching of switching pauses	
6–8	Some use of prosodic features to distinguish foreign words from words in parent language	Multisyllable babble stage: rhythmic strings of alternating consonants and vowels (also called reduplicated babble or canonical babble) Phonetic characteristics of babble are influenced by infant's hearing status Both repetitive and variegated babble may be present	Sitting independently at 6–9 mo Crawling at 6–11 mo Adultlike reaching movements
8–10	Decline in ability to detect certain foreign contrasts Some ability to distinguish foreign from native words on the basis of phonetic cues	Babbling may take on sentencelike intonation Babbling takes on some phonetic characteristics of the native language	Changing from prone to sitting position
10–12	Possible reorganization of perceptual categories to match phonetic structure of parent language	Vocables, protowords, and phonetically consistent forms often evident First word appears at mean age 11 mo	Pulling of body to standing position Standing with support Independent walking at 10–14 mo

*Adapted from Jusczyk PW: Developing phonological categories from the speech signal, in Ferguson C, Menn L, Stoel-Gammon C (eds): *Child Phonological Development.* York Press (in press); Kent RD, Hodge M: The biogenesis of speech: continuity and process in early speech and language development, in Miller JF (ed): *Progress in Research on Child Language Disorders.* Austin, Tex, Pro-Ed, 1990; Oller DK: Metaphonology and infant vocalizations, in Lindblom B, Zetterstrom R (eds): *Early Precursors of Speech.* New York, Macmillan, 1986, pp 21–35; Werker JF, Pegg JE: Infant speech perception and phonological acquisition, in Ferguson C, Menn L, Stoel-Gammon C (eds): *Child Phonological Development.* Parkton, Md, York Press (in press).

not the case with many other species, in which the newborn is basically a miniature version of the adult. Neotony has several important implications for human development, some of which are as follows (reference to Table 4–1 may be helpful):

1. The brain grows as much after birth as it does during gestation, so that substantial changes occur in the brain while the child is experiencing life outside the womb. This circumstance allows for a strong experiential stamp on brain development.
2. The vocal tract is reshaped to a considerable degree during the first year of life and to a lesser degree as development continues. This means that the infant gradually takes on the adult-shaped vocal tract and, therefore, the adult potential for certain kinds of sound patterns.
3. The neonate and young infant can discriminate a broad range of phonetic contrasts used in the world's languages. The discrimination of some of these contrasts diminishes with maturity *(but can be relearned, often with some effort, at any time later in life).*

Neotony places certain limits on the infant's ability to acquire speech and language, but it also places certain limits on the methods used to study the development of speech and language behavior. For example, methods that draw heavily on characteristics of adult speech should be used cautiously. Many of the early studies of infant vocalizations used phonetic transcription, as though the infant sounds were like those of an adult natural language that was amenable to the methods of descriptive linguistics. The result was often confusing, with observers occasionally reaching quite contrary conclusions. One observer might conclude that infants can produce virtually any sound needed for a natural language; another might conclude that infants had a rather limited phonetic repertoire that was gradually augmented with age and experience. This is not to say that phonetic methods are inappropriate in themselves but only that they need to be used with care. Ultimately it is of great interest to record the phonetic quality of infant vocalizations to the adult ear.

CONTINUITY

Development is change, but change can be conceptualized in various ways, two of which have been central to discussions of vocal development in infants. First, change can be discontinuous, such that behaviors, processes, or structures at one point in development are substantially different from those at another point. Furthermore, the differences can appear abruptly, so that the developmental picture appears to be one of alternating periods of stability (plateau) and rapid change (steps). Stage descriptions of development generally assume, either explicity or implicitly, that this picture is correct. Stages are then identified, typically in relation to stabilized behaviors, that characterize the plateaus. Many (in fact, nearly all) depictions of vocal development have been formulated as stage models. Some examples are given in Table 4–2 for the development of vocalizations in the first year of life. These stage models are useful in conceptualizing patterns in the development of speech and language. In addition, they have potential clinical value in defining age-appropriate behaviors that can be reliably observed.

In contrast, change can be continuous, that is, behaviors, processes or structures at one point in development are closely related to those at another point. Much recent work has emphasized continuities in sound patterns over the period

TABLE 4–2.
Stages of Vocal Development in Infants

Stark (1979)	Oller (1978)	Elbers (1982)	Holmgren et al. (1986)	Kent (1990)
Reflexive crying, vegetative sounds (≤8 wk)	Phonation (≤4 wk)		Continuous phonation without articulation (≤ 4 wk)	Early phonation (≤4 wk)
Cooing and laughter (8–20 wk)	Gooing (4–12 wk)		Interrupted phonation without articulation (4–8 wk)	Late phonation (4–8 wk)
Vocal play (16–30 wk)	Expansion (12–24 wk)	Vocalizing	Continuous or interrupted phonation with one articulation (8–20 wk)	Articulation/phonation (8–24 wk)
Reduplicated babble (24–50 wk)	Canonical babble (24–40 wk)	Repetitive (28–38 wk)	Phonatory variants with or without articulation (20–26 wk)	Multisyllabic babble (≥24 wk)
Nonreduplicated babble and expressive jargon (40 wk)	Variegated babble (≥40 wk)	Concatenating (38–48 wk) Mixing (≥48 wk)	Continuous or interrupted phonation and reduplicated articulation (≥26 week)	Jargon (≥40 wk)

of infancy (Kent and Bauer, 1985; Kent and Hodge, 1990; Vihman et al., 1985, 1986). Arguments for continuity also have been made for other areas of development, including mental development (Bornstein and Sigman, 1986). Such continuities hold both theoretical and clinical interest. The theoretical interest lies in the understanding of the acquisition of spoken language, for which continuities are threads for exploration (Vihman et al., 1986). The clinical interest lies in the possibility that an infant's sound patterns at one age may be useful in predicting an eventual delay or disorder in spoken language acquisition. Frequently those who espouse a continuity view of development attempt to identify the underlying processes that connect developmental changes.

The discontinuity vs. continuity argument has been the subject of much debate, but this debate, like many others that are based on poorly defined criteria, has generated much heat but rather less light. In fact, the current literature on early vocal development is somewhat two-faced. Several recent investigations favor the hypothesis of developmental continuity at the same time that the majority of models of vocal development maintain the tradition of stages.

Perhaps one of the most significant questions one can ask about the development of spoken language is simply: At what point does language development begin? Locke (1983) proposed that language acquisition begins when a child's sound patterns are redirected from a biological path (presumably common to all infants) to one that is adjusted to the ambient language. In other words, evidence of language acquisition is at hand when the child's sound patterns move decisively in the direction of a particular language. If no language adjustment is made, the child would follow a biological path of least resistance, in which sounds are governed by biological factors such as ease of production. Locke (1983) suggested that this beginning of language typically occurs after the acquisition of 50 words or when the child is about 2 years of age. Implicit in Locke's remarks is the idea that vocalizations have a natural course, presumably determined by biological factors. The biological factors seem to predominate in early infancy until a time when the ambient language begins to mold the form and function of utterances.

Holding to Locke's (1983) criterion, de Boysson-Bardies et al. (1989) concluded from their acoustic data on vowels in infant babbling that language development begins by 10 months of life, much earlier than the age identified by Locke. Similar conclusions were drawn earlier on the basis of perceptual evaluations by de Boysson-Bardies et al. (1984). These results indicated that babbling is shaped by the ambient language in subtle but potentially important ways. We might say that infants' babbling is adjusted to the caregiver's language. Therefore, babbling is not solely the expression of the human genotype, although the genetic influence is certainly powerful, as indicated by the commonalities among babbling patterns in infants from very different languages and cultures (Locke, 1983). For example, infants from many different national origins tend to produce large numbers of labial sounds *([p b m])* in their babbling.

Piatelli-Palmarini (1989) suggested an even earlier onset of language, arguing that the capability for language is overdetermined, being substantially present in the human genome. According to this view, language is not really learned at all: "There is no *known* process, either in biology or in cognition, that literally amounts to learning in the 'traditional' sense, that is, to a transfer of structure *from* the environment *to* the organism" (Piatelli-Palmarini, 1989, p. 2; emphasis in the original). Piatelli-Palmarini (1989) argues, in fact, that there cannot be such a process. What there is instead is internal selection, which becomes a critical part of an innatist-selectivist theory. This theory holds that humans possess an innate capacity for language that is built around universal principles.

How can we reconcile these very different answers to the question "When does language begin?" The question is difficult to answer because language is not a sufficiently unitary behavior to permit identification of a determinate starting point. It may be more useful to consider the components of language behavior and to inquire into their relative developmental patterns. Perhaps language can be recognized as a necessary and sufficient combination or interaction of prerequisite functions, of behaviors that precede language and develop into it. Studdert-Kennedy (in press) takes a similar approach, proposing that language development should be studied as a kind of postnatal embryology of behavior.

This line of investigation has the added benefit of directing our attention to the various factors that might promote or impede the development of language. That is, the inquiry may very well bring into focus the various conditions that place an infant at risk for language delay or disorder. These factors include the following, with specific examples indicated in parentheses: sensory deficits (deafness), social deprivation (isolation during infancy), motoric incompetence (severe paralysis of the speech muscles), cognitive deficiency (mental retardation), structural deficit (cleft palate), and some factors probably yet to be identified.

PROCESSES IN EARLY SPEECH DEVELOPMENT

The components of language are not easily numbered or analyzed, but Table 4–3 shows seven processes, as well as some of their interactions and integrations, that significantly underlie the development of spoken language. Each line at the left of the table represents a component process. The processes are consolidated as spoken language. The intermediate entries at the center of the table indicate interactions of the component

TABLE 4–3.
Basic Processes, Their Interactions and Integrations, and Emergent Behaviors in the Development of Spoken Language*

Basic Processes	Interactions and Integrations	Emergent Behaviors
Speech system anatomy	Performance anatomy of speech system	
Speech system physiology	Perceptuomotor integration for speech	
Sensory processing	Neural regulation for speech	Speech production
Nervous system development	Neural functions for cognition	Speech perception
Cognitive functions	Social-cognitive events	Language development
Social interaction	Sociolinguistic experiences	
Language stimulation	Neural functions for language	

*Spoken language is rooted in the various functions and processes listed in the first two columns of the table.

processes at the left. Some of the interactions create *emergent* properties. An emergent property is a function that arises from preexisting properties but has capabilities not present in its predecessors. Emergent properties are potentially powerful explanations of complex behavior and usually are thought to result from a combination of earlier or more basic properties. As a simple example, consider imitation, as when an infant imitates a mother's sounds. For imitation to occur, the infant must listen to the mother's sound pattern and control his or her own vocal system. Therefore, sensory and motor processes are combined to result in an emergent behavior of imitation.

Language relies on both a production system and a perception system, each of which can be described in terms of anatomical and functional development. Therefore, inquiry into the origins of spoken language must consider how the capabilities for speech production and perception emerge from the biology of their respective systems.

Vocal Tract Anatomy and Physiology

As noted earlier and summarized in Table 4–1, the infant's vocal tract undergoes a remarkable transformation from a shape resembling that of a nonhuman primate to a shape more like that of an adult human. This transformation is illustrated in Figure 4–1. Much of this transformation is accomplished within the first 2 years of life, but important anatomical changes extend well beyond the period of infancy. One implication of this anatomical development is that the infant's early experiences with sound production are framed against a changing vocal tract anatomy, some features of which may contribute significantly to the acquisition of basic phonetic contrasts.

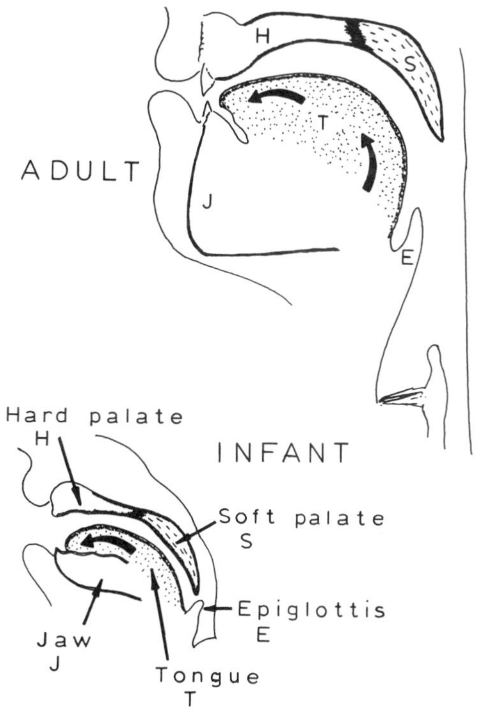

FIG 4–1.
Drawings of the infant and adult vocal tracts.

For example, the remodeling of the velopharynx may affect the infant's capability to make the nasal-nonnasal contrast, a contrast that is critical in its support of other phonetic contrasts, particularly for consonants. The changes in vocal tract anatomy are largely genetically determined, but Bosma (1975) asserts that the vocal tract also has a *performance anatomy,* that is, an anatomy shaped by its use, particularly by activities such as feeding, which generate rather large forces. Therefore, performance anatomy is represented in Table 4–3 as an interaction between the anatomy and physiology of the speech system.

Language Stimulation

Language stimulation refers to the infant's continuing experience with (usually) a particular language. The auditory signal is of paramount importance in the infant's growing familiarity with language. However, the infant's response to the auditory patterns of language is influenced by factors such as eye contact with adults who are speaking to the child (Bloom, 1974, 1975). By 18 to 20 weeks of age, infants relate the auditory and visual characteristics of speech sounds (Kuhl and Meltzoff, 1988). They appear to recognize that /*a*/ sounds are associated with a large mouth opening, /*i*/ sounds with a small mouth opening and retracted lips, and /*u*/ sounds with a small mouth opening and rounded lips. Furthermore, infants can apparently relate the sounds they hear to the articulatory movements that recreate the sound pattern, that is, they can imitate sounds made by adults. Kuhl and Meltzoff (1988) concluded that cross-modal perception (the infants' ability to link auditory and visual characteristics of speech sounds) and vocal imitation are related by a common representation of speech.

It is important to recognize that early exposures to spoken language commonly involve a combination of auditory, visual, and even tactile stimuli. Parent-child games often are carried out with concurrent speech, facial and manual gestures, and bodily contact. Multisensory cues are very likely the norm in a great deal of the language stimulation that infants receive from their parents. It can even be questioned if any one modality in isolation provides an effective learning situation. Massaro (1989, p. 753) addresses this issue as follows: "Experience with language must reduce ambiguity about both the utterance, the environment, and their pairing."

Sensory Processing

Sensory processing is a general term used here to represent sensory information related to speech and vocal function, including, but not limited to, auditory processing. However, space limitations permit only a narrow discussion on the auditory processing of speech patterns. Developmental changes in the perceptual system during infancy are somewhat unclear. On the one hand, some investigators, such as Kuhl (1988), have concluded that the human infant, even within the first few weeks or months of life, can make nearly all of the discriminations required for the phonetic contrasts of adult languages. This early proficiency is sometimes taken to be evidence of a "hard wiring" of the auditory system, as though the infant comes into the world with the requisite auditory discriminations to support language learning. In this view, the infant is ready to make some immediate decisions on the acoustic message of speech.

On the other hand, the infant's auditory performance apparently is not wired so hard as to be impervious to language exposure. Research by Werker and associates (reviewed by Werker, 1989, and Werker and Pegg, in press) indicates that an infant may "lose" some discriminations that are not supported by the ambient language. The discriminations are not irretrievably lost, because they may be recovered with appropriate training or exposure. Adults who learn a second language often will need to "hear" a phonetic contrast that is irrelevant to their first language.

Data on infant speech perception have been interpreted by Werker and Lalonde (1988) as indicative of an infant's ability to segment the acoustic signal of speech into discrete perceptual entities that are relevant to the task of language learning. Pisoni et al. (in press) take another view. They think it is unlikely that an infant segments the acoustic signal into small perceptual units for phonemic analysis, followed by analysis at the word level. Instead, they point to a developmental process of speech perception that proceeds from large undifferentiated units (e.g., words or prosodic structures) to smaller context-dependent units, such as the phonetic segment. Experimental results consistent with this idea have been reported by Liberman et al. (1974) and Walley et al. (1986). In the opinion of Pisoni et al. (in press), research on speech perception in infants has not gone much beyond revealing sensory capabilities. Studdert-Kennedy (in press) also has questioned the claim that infants are capable of an innate segmental analysis, arguing that studies of speech discrimination in infants have assessed psychoacoustic capacities relevant to speech processing but not segmental analysis itself. Similarly, Massaro (1989) questioned whether children perceive speech categorically (as some argue from the work of Eimas et al., 1971), arguing instead that young children's perception of speech is continuous.

In fact, these different points of view may lead in a common direction. They can be part of a conception of auditory speech processing that emphasizes an essential duality of unit and stream (Kent, 1991). This duality has an analogy in modern physics, which recognizes that light is both particle and wave. Light behaves as a particle in that it can be measured as quanta, or discrete pulses of energy. But light also demonstrates wave properties such as reflection and refraction. The two aspects of light are united in the modern theory of quantal electrodynamics. Basically this theory gives physicists their particle and their wave too. By recognizing one, the physicist does not have to sacrifice the other.

It seems unlikely that infants perceive the signal of speech as adults do, as a stream of segments linked to the phonological structure of the language. More likely, infants hear speech as a continuous stream of sounds carrying certain conspicuous spectral and temporal details that eventually are recognized as phonetic cues. This stream has a wavelike character in its precession of syllabic crests and margins that average about four per second. The intonation of speech also contributes to a wavelike aspect, in which local rises and falls of vocal pitch are integrated into a typically overall falling pattern (called pitch declination). The stream enables the infant to follow a speaker's voice, and it is the kinematic, prosodic, and paralinguistic features of this stream that "closely reflect the mother's communicative intentions and interpersonal affect" (Trevarthen and Marwick, 1986, p. 295).

The stream lends to the speech signal a very important property alluded to in Chapter 1—*predictive continuity*. The acoustic signal of speech coheres, or stays together, even if a detailed examination of its acoustic fabric reveals substantial differences among its constituent sounds, such as intervals of vowel resonance, noise for fricatives, brief silences for stops, and murmurs for nasal consonants. The signal tends to stay together in perception, and the power of this coherence is so strong that entire sounds can be replaced in a sentence without any recognition of this acoustic transplantation by listeners (Warren, 1976).

Adults, however, can recognize units in this stream. The units can be thought of as a condensate from the stream. Certain acoustic features are consolidated to be recognized as segments, even as accompanying acoustic features (like vocal pitch) maintain the continuity of the stream. For example, the stop consonant *t* in *toy* is a unit that consolidates several possible acoustic cues (brief silence, noise burst, aspiration, and formant transitions). Moreover, units of more than one kind can be recognized, depending on their familiarity and their expression in the acoustic signal. In particular, the infant might learn to recognize certain early phrases such as *night-night, allgone,* and *wanna* as units (see Chapter 1). Later, these phrases will be analyzed into smaller units. The stream of speech is not solely acoustic; it is also visual. From their earliest experiences with speech, infants typically have the opportunity to integrate the auditory and visual cues of speech. This integration is facilitated by the appearance of auditory and visual cues in co-occurring streams of information.

Attention to the spoken message is a helpful by-product of streaming. Attentional focus can be switched from one stream (mommy's talk) to another (daddy's talk) and can be placed on particular parts of an utterance (like the referent of a sentence). Figure 4–1 does not explicitly show attentional mechanisms, but they may be conceptualized as selectively operating across functions and processes. Jusczyk (1985, 1986) proposed that infants actively adjust the perceptual weights of acoustic features in accord with their language experience. Edelman (1989) also emphasizes the role of attention in sensory, motor, and conceptual activities. Edelman (1989, p. 200) notes that "a *single* sensory or perceptual channel is, in general, quite *unlikely* to be the pivot of attentional shift." Rather, he supposes that substantial parts of the nervous system and a flexible hierarchy of needs, values, and plans cooperate to shift attention. Attention is an important factor in reconciling an infant's sensory capability with the infant's responses to language stimuli. Words and prosodic structures probably have strong attentional significance, and they therefore influence an infant's behavior in connection with adult language behaviors. But segments are not irrelevant, as at least some segmental features of particular salience are needed for recognition of word shapes or prosodic shapes.

As shown in Table 4–1, the infant during the first year of life is capable of a variety of auditory discriminations pertinent to language development. A major challenge in accounting for the development of speech perception is to explain how infants possess such a remarkable discriminatory potential and how this potential is modified by language experience. The initial categories cannot be too rigid, or the child could not adapt to the phonetic patterns of a particular language. On the other hand, the categories must have a certain persistence, or they would be quickly dissipated by the richness of the auditory experience, which includes a universe of sound types and qualities, including noise. Carpenter and Grossberg (1987) discuss how interacting systems for attention and orientation can meet the requirements for a categorization that has the desired degrees of flexibility and stability. Briefly, the attentional subsystem recognizes familiar stimuli, thereby maintaining stable representations (categories) for them and allowing for expectations based on top-down processing. The orienting subsystem determines if a stimulus is unfamiliar (and possibly requiring a new category) or familiar (and adequately represented by the existing recognition code).

Because speech is an integrated perceptuomotor capability, perceptual processing is integrated with the production processes. The term in Table 4–3 labeled perceptuomotor integration reflects the perceptual and motor integration of speech. It appears that this integration begins at least by 6 months of postnatal life, so that the infant has begun to reconcile the auditory and motor aspects of vocal behavior at about the time that multisyllabic babbling appears. It seems reasonable that attention plays an important role in the integration of perceptual and motor events. This is an accomplishment with great potential and will be discussed from a neurological perspective in the following.

Nervous System

It is somewhat artificial to separate the nervous system from the other functions shown in Table 4–3, but this separation helps to make an extremely complicated process manageable for discussion. Therefore, neural maturation is identified as one component, although it is intimately related to the other components in the table. As the infant begins to experience life, vast changes are made in the nervous system. These changes must interact with the infant's sensory and motor experiences. The theory of neuronal group selection (Edelman, 1987, 1989) addresses the interactions in brain and behavior development. This theory proposes three mechanisms: *developmental selection, experiential selection,* and *reentrant mapping*. Each of these will be discussed in terms of its implications for the understanding of language development.

Developmental selection is a mechanism for the diversification of local neuronal connectivities or the patterns of synaptic connections among neurons. This mechanism involves the processes of cell division, cell death, cell migration, process extension, and elimination, which combine in their effects to yield a primary repertoire of large numbers of neuronal groups within a given brain region. These repertoires arise through genetic and epigenetic regulation.

In experiental selection, behavior causes a dynamic selection of neuronal groups, that is, populations of synapses are strengthened or weakened so that secondary repertoires are formed through a kind of differential amplification. Perceptual categorization develops as maps are generated in relation to receptor sheets. Receptor sheets are the neuronal populations related to a particular sensory system. For example, the auditory receptor sheet refers to the neurons of the auditory system. Maps are formed as representations on other neuronal populations. The interaction between maps and receptor sheets with one another is accomplished through a signal exchange called reentrant mapping. Reentrant mapping is a parallel signaling through ordered anatomical connections between separate maps. As signals pass across reentrantly connected maps, temporal correlations are formed among the neuronal selections within the maps. As applied to infant vocal experiences, this idea suggests that a parallel signaling develops among maps that relate to auditory, visual, and tactile sensations, all of which occur in a situational context defined by participants, interactions, and emotions. This is rich stuff for the beginning of language.

Edelman (1989, p. 179) wrote, "Speech rhythm, segmentation, categorization, and reentrant cycling may all have been closely linked in the evolution of the powerful speech specialization." The same factors would seem to have close linkage in the ontogeny of vocalization. For example, the early rhythmic sequences of babbling may be a vehicle for relating sensory and motor aspects of vocalization, as well as providing a training field for categorization and prosodic variations (Kent et al., 1991).

Figure 4–2 illustrates one way in which Edelman's theory of neuronal group selection might be applied to vocal development in the infant. The lowest level is that of the receptor sheet, which is constituted of neurons receiving input from the transducers (for present purposes, the eye, the ear, and an oral somatosensory collective). The receptor sheets are connected with maps, the next highest level of organization. The maps may be identified with particular sensory and motor functions. The local maps, in turn, are mutually connected within global maps. This illustration is one attempt to understand the *neural regulation of speech.* Note that the reentrant mapping could result in an experiential encyclopedia in which various sensory and motor responses are related to a given experience.

Cognition

Cognitive development, social interaction, and language stimulation are highly interactive. The study of cognitive development during infancy is a broad subject, but it suffices for present purposes to note that it may be entering a new theoretical period. Mandler (1990) wrote that the Piagetian school of thought that dominated cognitive theories for several years is being eclipsed by a different theory, one that emphasizes the capability of infants to *conceptualize the world.* The newer view is that at least by the age of 3 to 4 months, infants visually perceive objects as bounded, unitary, and distinct from the background. This perceptual capability is combined with perceptual analysis, or redescription, to form concepts (Mandler, 1988).

This thinking is consistent with the idea that a conceptual system is established before language is learned (Edel-

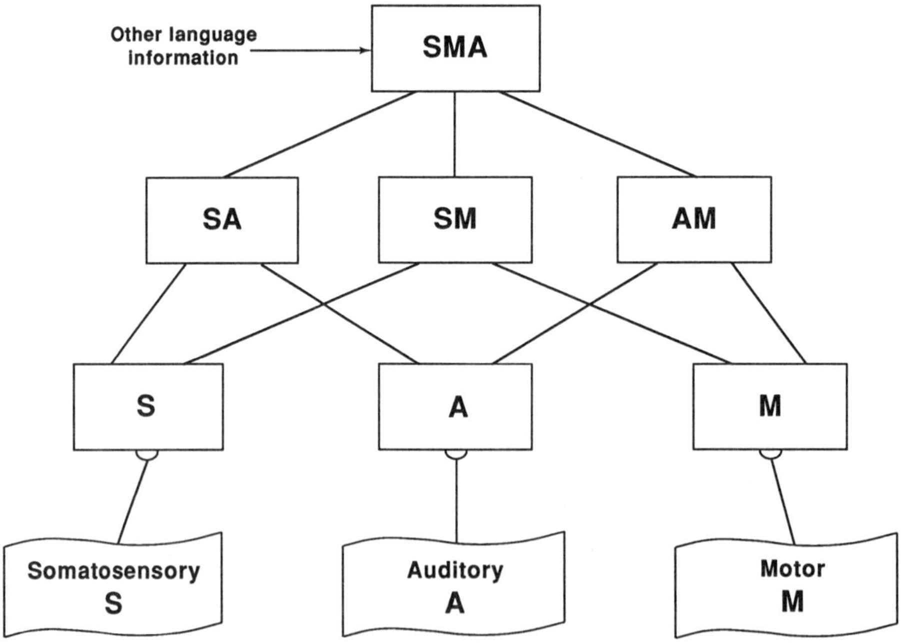

FIG 4–2.
A sketch showing how Edelman's theory of neuronal group selection might be applied to the neural processes underlying the development of language. See text for explanation.

man, 1989; Slobin, 1985). This becomes a key hypothesis in the study of the *neural functions for cognition.* However, the development of a conceptual system may be accompanied by certain changes in utterances that are commonly regarded as "prelinguistic." Blake and Fink (1987) concluded that babbling contained sound-meaning correspondences that were apparently invented by their infant subjects. That is, before "real" words are identified by caregivers, infants are at work producing sound patterns that relate to certain meanings. Recent evidence also suggests an early relationship between vocalization and significant experiences in infancy (Hilke, 1988). Infants vocalized more with concurrent significant changes in experience (external events were changing) than when no external cues for such changes were evident. Social interaction, particularly within the mother-infant dyad, is a rich source of experience.

Social Interaction

Exchanges between mother and infant are a milieu for language modeling, emotional attachment, and a variety of experiences that provide sensory and motor stimulation. Studies of interaction related to language development are reviewed by Chapman (1981) and Trevarthen and Marwick (1986). This topic is too large to be reviewed here, but some phenemena of immediate relevance can be mentioned. The mother and infant interaction frequently is characterized by rhythmic organization (including turn taking), prosodic exaggerations (one feature of "motherese," or the language behavior that mothers direct to their infants), mutual regard expressed through eye contact, vocalizations, and various body responses. The social context provided by the mother-infant interaction is a basis for a coordinated sensory-motor engagement, in which the mother and infant become attuned to one another. These and other experiences constitute the social-cognitive events in Table 4–3.

One possibility for a representation of language vis-à-vis experience comes from the theory of neuronal group selection (Edelman, 1987). A concept of special interest is that of a *global map* that coordinates local sensory and motor maps. Cross-modal perception would involve sensory maps for visual and auditory properties of speech. Imitation would involve additional maps for motor regulation of speech and the somatosensory representation of speech movements. The elaboration of these local and global maps with semantic and syntactic functions would then define the development of the *neural functions of language.* Turn-taking patterns of vocalization (Beebe et al., 1988) would assist infants to relate their own sound productions to those of adults. These patterns and a variety of other *sociolinguistic experiences* in which language accompanies or interprets social events are a critical part of the infant's early training for language.

Above all, Table 4–3 highlights areas that constitute a biological approach to the study of the development of spoken language. The next section addresses a field of study complementary to that considered so far. Much can be learned about the development of spoken language from a study of the atypical developmental process, as in the case of infants with sensory, motor, or cognitive disabilities.

CLINICAL PERSPECTIVE AND PROSPECTIVE

Vocalization is one of the earliest voluntary behaviors in infancy and has been used to assess an infant's state of health. The human behavior of vocalization is present throughout the life span, beginning with the birth cry, proceeding through language acquisition in the child, and continuing though adult language usage. The close association of vocalization with language makes vocalization a natural focus for investigations of child language development and the early identification of infants at risk for communication disorders. Clinical applications of measures of vocalization are expanding rapidly. Noninvasive studies of infant cry have been used to predict developmental outcome (Lester, 1987). A rather substantial normative data base on cry is available, and cry characteristics have been described for several clinical populations, including infants with asphyxia (Michelsson, 1971; Michelsson et al., 1977a), chromosomal abnormalities (Vuorenkoski et al., 1966), cleft palate (Michelsson et al., 1975), laryngitis (Raes et al., 1982), malnutrition (Lester, 1979), hypothyroidism (Michelsson and Sirvio, 1976), marijuana-using mothers (Lester and Dreher, 1989), meningitis (Michelsson et al., 1977b), prematurity or low birth weight (Lester, 1987), and sudden infant death syndrome (Colton and Steinschneider, 1980).

Cry may be studied throughout infancy, although many of the published studies pertain to cry in the first few days or weeks of life. Other vocalizations appear as infancy progresses, and these are of particular interest because they reflect the continuing interaction of the infants with their environment, particularly exposure to an ambient language and interaction with a caregiver. An infant's comfort-state utterances, such as solitary babbling or vocal exchanges with caregivers, may provide information on the infant's general state and the nature of the infant's interactions with the environment. A clinical interest lies in the possibility that an infant's sound patterns at one age may be predictive of delayed or abnormal spoken language acquisition (Camp et al., 1987; Jensen et al., 1988; Kent and Hodge, 1990; Menyuk et al., 1986; Murphy et al., 1983). Babbling and other prespeech vocalizations may not be language in the strictest sense of the word, but as discussed in relation to Table 4–3, they may prefigure components of language in important respects. This potential, paired with the demonstrated value of infant cry studies in distinguishing infants at risk for developmental disorder, lays the foundation for clinical studies of infant sound patterns.

To what extent are vocalizations such as babbling sensitive to conditions that place the infant at risk for developmental delay? It is now quite clear that severe hearing loss can affect the phonetic characteristics of babbling in the second half-year of life (Kent et al., 1986; Oller and Eilers, 1988; Oller et al., 1985; Stoel-Gammon and Otomo, 1986), contrary to earlier writings (Lenneberg et al., 1965; Mavilya, 1969). Craniofacial anomalies such as cleft palate also are associated with unusual sound patterns in babbling (Philips and Kent, 1984; Sancier, 1989). Another condition of special interest is tracheostomy, which is often used in circumstances requiring prolonged airway management. Infants with tracheostomies are aphonic and therefore have limited experience in supraglottal sound production, especially if the period of tracheostomy overlaps the period in which babbling normally occurs. The literature on the effects of tracheostomy on speech and language development is not completely consistent, but some reports indicate that this form of medical management may be associated with a deviant developmental pattern (Aradine, 1986; Fowler et al., 1985; Hill and Singer, 1990; Locke and Pearson, 1989; Ross, 1982). Surprisingly, especially in view of arguments that babbling reflects cognitive development (Elbers, 1982), the limited data available on babbling in infants with Down syndrome do not disclose marked differences from the babbling of more typically developing infants (Dodd, 1972; Oller and Seibert, 1988; Smith, 1984; Smith and Oller, 1981).

In summary, several investigations support the ideas that (1) vocalizations in the first year of life reflect processes in common with later spoken language development and that (2) babbling and other infant vocalizations may hold clinical significance in the identification of infants at risk for speech and language delay or disorder. The published data are limited, however, so much so as to place in question any immediate attempts to use detailed analyses of babbling as an index of speech readiness or as a clinical protocol to identify infants at risk for communication disorder. Much more data are needed on vocalizations in both normally developing infants and in infants with developmental disorders. In addition, and equally important, analysis procedures need to be standardized and tested for reliability.

Although more research needs to be done on phonological development in clinical populations, progress has been made. Mowrer (1980) wrote that "virtually nothing" was known about early phonological development in special populations, such as infants with hearing loss, autism, cerebral palsy, oral deformity, mental retardation, or emotional disturbance. The last decade has produced several reports pertaining to these populations, and the data confirm the fruitfulness of research in this direction.

SUMMARY

The study of language acquisition is in part the biological study of infant development or, even better, the ethological study of infant development. The biological study of behavior holds promise as a heuristic tool by which the components of language can be studied. This chapter has emphasized the study of infant vocalization as a joint product of a developing biology and an emerging behavioral system. The ideas are quite consistent with the process perspective discussed in Chapter 1. In particular, the analyses described in the present chapter suggest some ways in which the infant and young child might develop an experiential encyclopedia that is indexed to growing language capabilities. This approach can and should be applied to both the typically developing and the atypically developing infant. This dual focus can greatly stimulate progress in the understanding of the ontogeny of spoken language and may help to direct assessment and management for children with communicative disability.

REFERENCES

Aradine CR: Development of toddlers with long-term tracheostomies. Doctoral dissertation, Ann Arbor, University of Michigan, 1986.

Beebe B, Alson D, Jaffe J, et al: Vocal congruence in mother-infant play. *J Psycholingist Res* 1988; 17:245–259.

Blake J, Fink R: Sound-meaning correspondences in babbling. *J Child Lang* 1987; 14:229–253.

Bloom K: Eye contact as a setting event for infant learning. *J Exp Child Psychol* 1974; 17:250–263.

Bloom K: Social elicitation of infant vocal behavior. *J Exp Child Psychol* 1975; 20:51–58.

Bornstein MH, Sigman MD: Continuity in mental development from infancy. *Child Dev* 1986; 57:251–274.

Bosma JF: Anatomic and physiologic development of the speech apparatus, in Tower DB (ed): *The Nervous System.* vol 3: *Human Communication and Its Disorders.* New York, Raven Press, 1975.

Camp B, Burgess D, Morgan L, et al: A longitudinal study of infant vocalization in the first year. *J Pediatr Psychol* 1987; 12:321–331.

Carpenter GA, Grossberg S: Discovering order in chaos: Stable self-organization of neural recognition codes. *Ann NY Acad Sci* 1987; 504:33–50.

Chapman RS: Mother-child interaction in the second year of life: Its role in language development, in Schiefelbusch R, Bricker D (eds): *Early Language: Acquisition and Intervention.* Baltimore, University Park Press, 1981, pp 201–250.

Colton R, Steinschneider A: Acoustic relationships of infant cries to sudden infant death syndrome, in Murray T, Murray J (eds): *Infant Communication: Cry and Early Speech.* Houston, College-Hill Press, 1980.

De Boysson-Bardies B, Halle P, Durand C: A crosslinguistic investigation of vowel formants in babbling. *J Child Lang* 1989; 16:1–17.

De Boysson-Bardies B, Sagart L, Durand C: Discernible differences in the babbling of infants according to target language. *J Child Language* 1984; 11:1–15.

Dodd BJ: Comparison of babbling patterns in normal and Down-syndrome infants. *J Ment Defic Res* 1972; 16:35–40.

Edelman G: *Neural Darwinism: The Theory of Neuronal Group Selection.* New York, Basic Books, 1987.

Edelman G: *The Remembered Present: A Biological Theory of Consciousness.* New York, Basic Books, 1989.

Eimas PD, Siqueland ER, Jusczyk P, et al: Speech perception in infants. *Science* 1971; 171:303–306.

Elbers L: Operating principles in repetitive babbling: a cognitive continuity approach. *Cognition* 1982; 12:45–63.

Fowler S, Simon B, Handler S: Communication development in children, in Myers E, Stool S, Johnson J (eds): *Tracheostomy.* New York, Churchill Livingstone, 1985, pp 271–285.

Hilke DD: Infant vocalizations and changes in experience. *J Child Lang* 1988; 15:1–15.

Hill B, Singer L: Speech and language development after infant tracheostomy. *J Speech Hear Disord* 1990; 55:15–20.

Holmgren K, Lindblom B, Aurelius G, et al: On the phonetics of infant vocalization, in Lindblom B, Zetterstrom R (eds): *Precursors of Early Speech.* New York. Stockton Press, 1986, pp 51–63.

Jensen TS, Boggild-Andersen B, Schmidt J, et al: Perinatal risk factors and first-year vocalizations: Influence on preschool language and motor performance. *Dev Med Child Neurol* 1988; 30:153–161.

Jusczyk P: On characterizing the development of speech perception, in Mehler J, Fox R (eds): *Neonate Cognition: Beyond the Blooming Buzzing Confusion.* Hillsdale, NJ, Lawrence Erlbaum Associates, 1985, pp 199–229.

Jusczyk PW: Toward a model of the development of speech perception, in Perkell J, Klatt D (eds): *Invariance and Variability in Speech Processes.* Hillsdale, NJ, Lawrence Erlbaum Associates, 1986, pp 1–19.

Jusczyk PW: Developing phonological categories from the speech signal, Ferguson C, Menn L, Stoel-Gammon C (eds): *Child Phonological Development.* Parkton, MD York Press (in press).

Kent RD: The auditory processing of speech. Paper presented at Central Auditory Processing: A Transdisciplinary View, Buffalo, State University of New York, March 15–16, 1991.

Kent RD: The biology of phonological development, in Ferguson C, Menn L, Stoel-

Gammon C (eds): *Child Phonological Development.* Parkton, Md, York Press (in press).

Kent RD, Bauer HR: Vocalizations of one year olds. *J Child Lang* 1985; 12:491–526.

Kent RD, Hodge M: The biogenesis of speech: Continuity and process in early speech and language development, in Miller JF (ed): *Progress in Research on Child Language Disorders.* Austin, Tex, Pro-Ed, 1990.

Kent RD, Mitchell PR, Sancier M: Evidence and role of rhythmic organization in early vocal development in human infants, in Fagard J (ed): *The Organization of Temporal Patterns of Movements and Motor Development.* New York, Elsevier North-Holland, 1991, pp 135–149.

Kent RD, Osberger MJ, Netsell R, et al: Phonetic development in identical twins differing in auditory function. *J Speech Hear Disord* 1986; 52:64–75.

Kuhl PK: Auditory perception and the evolution of speech. *Human Evolution* 1988; 3:19–43.

Kuhl PK, Meltzoff AN: Speech as an intermodal object of perception, in Yonas A (ed): *Perceptual Development in Infancy.* vol 20: *The Minnesota Symposia on Child Psychology.* Hillsdale, NJ, Lawrence Erlbaum Associates, 1988.

Lenneberg EH, Rebelsky GF, Nichols IA: The vocalizations of infants born to deaf and hearing parents. *Hum Dev* 1965; 8:23–37.

Lester BM: Spectrum analysis of the cry sounds of well-nourished and malnourished infants. *Child Dev* 1979; 47:237.

Lester BM: Developmental outcome prediction from acoustic cry analysis in term and preterm infants. *Pediatrics* 1987; 80:529–534.

Lester BM, Dreher M: Effects of marijuana use during pregnancy on newborn cry. *Child Dev* 1989; 60:765–771.

Liberman IY, Shankweiler D, Fischer FW, et al: Explicit syllable and phoneme segmentation in the young child. *J Exp Child Psychol* 1974; 18:201–212.

Locke JL: *Phonological Acquisition and Change.* New York, Academic Press, 1983.

Locke JL, Pearson DM: Linguistic significance of babbling: Evidence from a tracheostomized infant. Boston, Neurolinguistics Laboratory, Massachusetts General Hospital, MGH Institute of Health Professions, 1989 (unpublished).

Mandler JM: How to build a baby: On the development of an accessible representational system. *Cognit Dev* 1988; 3:113–136.

Mandler JM: A new perspective on cognitive development in infancy. *Am Sci* 1990; 78:236–243.

Massaro DW: Multiple book review of *Speech Perception by Ear and Eye: A Paradigm for Psychological Inquiry. Behav Brain Sci* 1989; 12:741–794.

Mavilya M: (1969). Spontaneous vocalizations and babbling in hearing impaired infants. Doctoral dissertation, New York, Columbia University (University Microfilms no 70-12879).

Menyuk P, Liebergott J, Schultz M: Predicting phonological development, in Lindblom B, Zetterstrom R (eds): *Precursors of Early Speech.* New York, Stockton Press, 1986, pp 79–93.

Michelsson K: Cry analysis of symptomless low birth weight neonates and of asphyxiated newborn infants. *Acta Paediatr Scand* 1971; 216(suppl):1–45.

Michelsson K, Sirvio P: Cry analysis in congenital hypothyroidism. *Folia Phoniatr* 1976; 28:40–47.

Michelsson K, Sirvio P, Koivisto M, et al: Spectrographic analysis of pain cry in neonates with cleft palate. *Biol Neonate* 1975; 26:353–358.

Michelsson K, Sirvio P, Wasz-Hockert O: Sound spectrographic cry analysis of infants with bacterial meningitis. *Dev Med Child Neurol* 1977a; 19:309–315.

Michelsson K, Sirvio P, Wasz-Hockert O: Pain cry in full-term asphyxiated newborn infants correlated with later findings. *Acta Paediatr Scand* 1977b; 66:611–616.

Mowrer DE: Phonological development during the first year of life, in Lass NJ (ed): *Speech and Language: Advances in Basic Research and Practice.* New York, Academic Press, 1980, vol 4, pp 99–142.

Murphy R, Menyuk P, Liebergott J, et al: Predicting rate of lexical acquisition. Paper presented at the Biennial Meeting of the Society for Research in Child Development, Detroit, 1983.

Ohala J: There is no interface between phonology and phonetics: A personal view. *J Phonetics* 1990; 18:153–172.

Oller DK: Infant vocalizations and the development of speech. *Allied Health Behav Sci* 1978; 1:523–549.

Oller DK: Metaphonology and infant vocalizations, in Lindblom B, Zetterstrom R (eds): *Early Precursors of Speech.* New York, Macmillan, 1986, pp 21–35.

Oller DK, Eilers RE: The role of audition in infant babbling. *Child Dev* 1988; 59:441–449.

Oller DK, Eilers RE, Bull DH, et al: Prespeech vocalizations of a deaf infant: A comparison with normal metaphonological development. *J Speech Hear Res* 1985; 28:47–62.

Oller DK, Seibert JM: Babbling in prelinguistic mentally retarded children. *Am J Ment Retard* 1988; 92:369–375.

Philips BJ, Kent RD: Acoustic-phonetic descriptions of speech production in persons with cleft palate and other velophayrngeal disorders, in Lass NJ (ed): *Speech and Language: Advances in Basic Research and Practice.* New York, Academic Press, vol 10, 1984.

Piatelli-Palmarini M: Evolution, selection and cognition: From "learning" to parameter setting in biology and in the study of language. *Cognition* 1989; 31:1–44.

Pisoni DB, Logan JS, Lively SE: Perceptual learning of nonnative speech contrasts: Implications for theories of speech perception, in Nusbaum HC, Goodman G (eds): *Development of Speech Perception: The Transition From Recognizing Speech Sounds to Spoken Words.* Cambridge, Mass, MIT Press (in press).

Raes J, Michelsson K, Dehaer F, et al: Cry analysis in infants with infectious and congenital disorders of the larynx. *Int J Pediatr Otorhinolaryngol* 1982; 1:157–169.

Ross GS: Language functioning and speech development of six children receiving tracheotomy in infancy. *J Commun Disord* 1982; 15:95–111.

Sancier ML: A descriptive study of sound production in cleft palate infants: Patterns, productivity, and contrastivity. Master's thesis, Madison, University of Wisconsin, 1989.

Slobin DI: Crosslinguistic evidence for the language-making capacity, in Slobin DI (ed): *The Crosslinguistic Study of Language Acquisition.* Hillsdale, NJ, Lawrence Erlbaum Associates, 1985, vol 2, pp 1157–1256.

Smith BL: Implications of infant vocalizations for assessing phonological disorders, in Lass NJ (ed): *Speech and Language: Advances in Basic Research and Practice,* vol 2. Orlando, FL, Academic, 1984, pp 169–195.

Smith BL, Oller DK: A comparative study of premeaningful vocalizations produced by normally developing and Down's syndrome infants. *J Speech Hear Disord* 1981; 46:46–51.

Stark R: Prespeech segmental feature development, in Fletcher P, Garman M (eds): *Language Acquisition.* New York, Cambridge University Press, 1979, pp 15–32.

Stoel-Gammon C, Otomo K: Babbling development of hearing-impaired and normally hearing subjects. *J Speech Hear Disord* 1986; 51:33–41.

Studdert-Kennedy M: A note on linguistic nativism, in Hoffman R, Palermo D (eds): *Cognition and the Symbolic Processes.* Hillsdale, NJ, Lawrence Erlbaum Associates (in press).

Trevarthen C, Marwick H: Signs of motivation for speech in infants, and the nature of a mother's support for development of language, in Lindblom B, Zetterstrom R (eds): *Precursors of Early Speech.* New York, Stockton Press, 1986, pp 279–308.

Vihman MM, Ferguson CA, Elbert M: Phonological development from babbling to speech: Common tendencies and individual differences. *Applied Psycholinguist* 1986; 7:3–40.

Vihman MM, Macken MA, Miller R, et al: From babbling to speech: A reassessment of the continuity issue. *Language* 1985; 61:397–445.

Vuorenkoski V, Lind J, Partanen TS, et al: Spectrographic analysis of cries from children with maladie cu cri du chat. *Ann Paediatr Fenn* 1966; 12:174–180.

Walley AC, Smith LB, Jusczyk PW: The role of phonemes and syllables in the perceived similarity of speech sounds for children. *Memory Cognit* 1986; 14:220–229.

Warren RW: Auditory illusions and perceptual processes, in Lass NJ (ed): *Contemporary Issues in Experimental Phonetics.* New York, Academic Press, 1976.

Werker JF: Becoming a native listener. *Am Sci* 1989; 77:54–59.

Werker JF, Lalonde C: Cross-language speech perception: Initial capabilities and developmental change. *Dev Psychol* 1988; 75:1866–1878.

Werker JF, Pegg JE: Infant speech perception and phonological acquisition, in Ferguson C, Menn L, Stoel-Gammon C (eds): *Child Phonological Development.* Parkton, Md, York Press (in press).

5 The Integration of Speech Motor Control and Language Formulation in Process Models of Acquisition

Edythe A. Strand, Ph.D.

In introductory courses in linguistics, speech pathology, and psychology, speech and language are presented as very different entities, with speech being merely the output, or acoustic realization of a variety of complex language processes. The term "language" is used to represent the concept of arbitrary but conventional systems of symbols for communication. It implies cognitive and representational processes that result in a specific input to a motor control system. The term "speech" represents the spoken form of language, involving the processes of respiration, phonation, resonance, and articulation. It relates specifically to movement resulting in constriction of the air stream through the vocal tract to create an acoustic output. Although this dichotomous representation of language and speech is useful, it has been taken to the extreme in the representation of language and speech as separate, linearly occurring processes that are not necessarily related to each other as they occur. It is not surprising, then, that researchers who attempt to model how verbal language works have often separated the two as discrete processes. In fact, models of language formulation and models of speech production have developed relatively independently of one another. Elaboration and expansion in one area have had relatively little influence on refinement of the other.

This separation of language and speech has greatly influenced our thinking about how we produce verbal utterances. For example, language and speech have been studied as separate mental (language) and physical (speech) activity that occurs in a linear fashion. Mental processes, such as lexical selection and syntactic formulation, have been described as occurring first, resulting in some specific linguistic "input" to the motor control system. Speech motor control processes, then, have been described as converting linguistic input to acoustic output. This focus on seriality has led researchers to study language and speech separately. Little work has focused on examining the dynamic influences each may have on the other.

The major purposes of this chapter are to (1) propose a series of claims about early utterance production that posit that language formulation and speech motor control are interactive and parallel systems and (2) describe the implications of this interaction for developmental processes. The series of claims will be presented in the context of the Child Talk model. The claims reflect the position that there is no need to separate language and speech. In fact, these claims stress the importance of considering the *integration* of language processing and speech motor control when one is providing explanations of the acquisition of verbal utterance production. This is a shift away from many traditional explanations of early language, which have been focused on competence. That is, traditional explanations describe and predict particular semantic, syntactic, or phonological behaviors that may occur at a particular time. Such competence or stage models provide description of behaviors at different developmental stages but do not focus on modeling the interactive processes involved in early utterance production. This is especially true for the speech motor control processes that are operating during early language acquisition and work with language formulation processes to result in the acoustic output of verbal language. This lack of attention to the interactive influences of motor control and language formulation has limited our thinking about early speech performance at any one point in time during development. It has limited our understanding of how this important interaction influences development as it proceeds. Further, traditional approaches are less able to account for problems such as variability, regression, and progression in development and are less able to explain delay and deviance in the acquisition of early utterance production.

In this chapter, I will first review how *adult* models of language formulation and adult models of speech production vary in their attempts to account for specific aspects of spoken language. Then, evidence will be presented regarding the interactive influences of speech motor control and language formulation in early language acquisition. The third major section will present examples of specific claims that may be made for these interactive influences, using the Child Talk model. Finally, implications for clinical practice will be discussed.

The goal of this chapter is to suggest the nature of the interactive speech and language processes involved in early utterance production vs. specifying the form that interaction takes. Although at this point there is not a clear relationship between the seriation of abstract units (i.e., phonemes, syllables, words) and the observed sequencing of articulatory gestures resulting in acoustic output, suggestions will be made regarding how an integrative process model may come closer to explaining that relationship. The assumptions inherent in the Child Talk model regarding the interaction of speech motor control and language formulation are presented in the hope they will lead to the formation of experimental questions and further development of theories regarding the interaction of speech motor control and language formulation in early language acquisition.*

*The term modeling is used often throughout this chapter. The use of the word model in early language acquisition refers to a theoretical description of the mental, as well as physical, processes involved in the ideation, formulation, and execution of a verbal message. The term "utterance production" is used in lieu of either "language" or "speech" to reflect the integration of the two aspects of emerging talk, emphasizing that both language formulation and speech motor control should be reflected in approaches to modeling how early talk occurs.

ADULT MODELS OF LANGUAGE FORMULATION AND SPEECH PRODUCTION

The assumption evident from adult language formulation models and models of adult speech production is that there is a linguistic or representational component that serves as input to a motor process. One begins where the other ends. This implies a division between central and peripheral mechanisms. Central processes involve linguistic formulation, whereas peripheral processes involve activation of lower motor neurons, afferent feedback, and the movement resulting in the acoustic output. Inherent in this traditional view is a strictly serial system of processing, in which one stage must be completed before the next begins.

A brief review of some approaches to modeling language formulation and speech production illustrates this independence and shows how traditional approaches have failed to consider the integration of language and speech. Remember that most explanations of either language formulation or speech motor control focus on adult speech. To date, little attempt has been made to formulate acquisition models of early production of verbal utterances.

Models of Language Formulation

Models posited to explain language formulation in sentence production (Bock, 1982; Dell, 1985, 1986, 1988; Garrett, 1980; Stemberger, 1985) conceptualize basic elements important to formulation of an utterance, including intent, a knowledge network, processes of lexical selection, and syntactic processing. Most language formulation models also assume a phonological representation of lexical items, as well as a process of converting that phonological representation into phonetic segments. These segments are then converted to acoustic output. None of those models addresses how the transition is made, nor do they discuss how language formulation might influence that transition or the output itself.

Serial Models

In one approach to modeling sentence production, language formulation processes are described as sets of independent levels of processing. For example, Garrett (1975, 1980) describes two distinct processing levels, functional and positional, that he developed to account for the principal features of speech errors. At the functional level, the meanings of words (not their phonological form) are mapped from a conceptual representation to a linguistic representation. This involves the assembly of these semantic representations into syntactic structure by assigning them relational roles. At this level then, the phrasal membership and grammatical functions of words are determined. At the positional level, the serial order of words and some aspects of their form are determined. Included in this level are the insertion of the words into a grammatical frame and the retrieval of phonological representations from the lexicon. The grammatical, or planning, frame can be described as a pattern of function words and bound morphemes that create slots for content words. Consider the sentence "The boy is swinging the bat," as an example. The grammatical frame can be illustrated as The ____is ____ing the ____. Phonologically specified content words, then, are assigned to this grammatical frame, and results in the elaboration of the sentence's phonetic form.

Shattuck-Hufnagel (1979) proposes a similar model based on patterns in sublexical speech error data. In her model, serial ordering operates in a two-part representation of the planned utterance: the segments that make up the selected lexical items and the separate framework of sequentially ordered locations or slots with which the segments are to be associated. A serial ordering process operates to associate each segment with a slot in the structural framework over the length of some processing chunk of the utterance. Segmental interaction errors result from disruption in a system sensitive to structure rather than from misactivation of language elements at the wrong point in time. Both Garrett's (1975, 1980) and Shattuck-Hufnagel's (1979) models illustrate serial, autonomous levels of linguistic processing.

Interactive Serial Model

Other perspectives on language formulation, however, suggest less autonomous levels of language processing and take into account the cognitive and communicative factors influencing the processing of the intended utterance. Although many explanations of sentence production imply a hierarchical sequence of relatively independent processes, Bock (1982) presented evidence for the interaction of lexical and syntactical processing, including the influence of processing demands. In her model, she posits six major processes, which she terms "arenas," to be involved in sentence production: referential, semantic, phonological, phonetic, motor assembly, and syntactic (Fig 5–1).

A referential arena is responsible for coding nonlinguistic representational thought into a format that can be used by the linguistic system. That is, the ideational content of a message may be organized in some pattern before the translation to linguistic representation. Bock (1982) cites Chafe (1977), who posits processes of schematization and framing in this prelinguistic stage. Schemas organize nonlinguistic knowledge and memo-

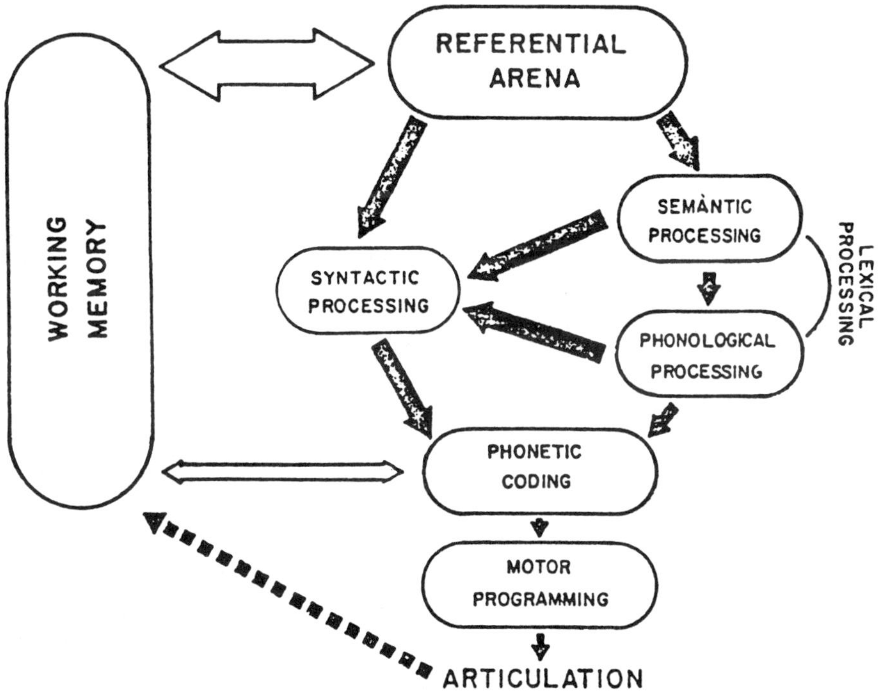

FIG 5–1.
Bock's model for the formulation of verbal utterances. Her figure illustrates interaction among levels of processing. Arrows pointing to working memory illustrate those levels requiring controlled processing. (From Bock JK: *Psychol Rev* 1982; 89:24. Used by permission.)

ries into "chunks" so that communicative goals and constraints are established. Framing involves the selection of participants and their roles (e.g., actor, action, object, location). Examples of additional information to be processed into linguistic representation at this referential stage include the speaker's intention (e.g., question, command, state), hierarchical relationships between related ideas, and verb tense.

The semantic arena is responsible for mapping those propositional relations formulated in the referential arena with lexical concepts. Selection of a particular word (lexical concept) is made based on the existence of related words in the speakers vocabulary. A phonological arena maps lexical concepts onto phonological representations. Bock (1982) notes that this is primarily an associative process and that phonological representation for novel derivations (e.g., plurals) is designated according to relational procedures that embody the morphological system of a given language.

The phonetic coding arena specifies phonetic representation that guides motor planning for speech production. In Bock's model, the motor program is constructed from the phonetic code in the motor assembly arena, which is responsible both for compiling and executing the motor program. Bock (1982) proposes two syntactic processing modes in adult language production. The first operates in parallel with the retrieval and assembly of semantic and phonological elements and is primarily an automatic function. A more controlled construction of syntactic plans also operates. Trade-offs between automatic and controlled syntactic processing are presented as an explanation for semantically similar but syntactically different sentences (e.g., active and passive sentences).

Important to Bock's model is the assumption that there is interaction among arenas. For example, she presents evidence that lexical accessibility influences syntactic structure. This is a move away from previous sentence production theories that posit serial, autonomous elements. Bock's model, in contrast, proposes an interactive system in which multiple levels of processing may affect syntax independently. Bock (1982) suggests that lexical processing has some influence over syntactic processing and that a valid theory of sentence formulation should describe interactions between representations and processing. Her approach suggests both top-down and bottom-up processes rather than the top-down hierarchies of autonomous serial models. This perspective also includes study of the influence of conceptual accessibility (Bock and Warren, 1985), activation processes (Bock, 1986), and lexical accessibility (Bock, 1987). Although speech motor control processes are not explicitly included in this description of interactive systems, Bock's approach motivates examination of how language formulation and speech motor control influence each other both in adult language models and in models of language development.

Connectionist Models

Another approach to modeling language production comes from theories of spreading activation (Dell, 1985; 1986, 1988; McClelland and Rumelhart, 1981; Stemberger, 1985, in press). Often termed connectionist models, this approach stresses the notion that processing activity results from the interactions occurring among large numbers of processing units. A basic feature of connectionist models of cognition is the notion of parallel distributed processing. This term refers to a large network of simultaneous and interactive processing elements or units (nodes) and their connections. This is in stark contrast to a system comprised of strictly serial steps. Processing results from the propagation of activity through the network. Each node maintains a state of activation based on activation it receives from other nodes and also transmits information to adjacent nodes through their connections.

Connectionist models have evolved from and are reminiscent of neuronal analogies. In the general model described by Smolensky (1988), for example, connections between nodes vary in strength and may be excitatory (carrying a positive weight) or inhibitory (carrying a negative weight). The activation level of a single node is a summation of the activation values of adjacent nodes multiplied by the strength of the respective connections. Thus, the weighted connections act to modify information within the processing system.

Although connectionist models vary in their specific characteristics, certain features are common to most. For example, activation values and weights are present in all connectionist models, although specific limitations on values allowed for node activation and connection weight vary from one application of connectionist modeling to another. One salient property of connectionist networks is that the activation value of a node reflects its past participation in processing and also information about its current processing environment. Proponents of connectionist modeling (McClelland, 1988; Smolensky, 1988) have argued that these properties facilitate modeling of cognitive processes in which different levels of processing are thought to interact (e.g., syntactic vs. phonological levels), as well as those in which learning is thought to play a critical role. In addition, it is believed that the features of connectionist modeling can greatly facilitate the modeling of linguistic performance (typically characterized by variability), as well as competence (typically characterized by rulelike consistency).

A brief description of one specific application of connectionist modeling may help readers better understand this approach for language production. Dell (1988) describes a model of phonological retrieval in spoken sentences. The network structure of the model is divided into a lexical network and a word-shape network. This distinction separates the phonological structure of a word into two components: (1) a sequence of slots that specifies the abstract shape of the word and (2) the number and kinds of syllables and phonemes. The lexical network, then, connects word nodes with their sounds.

Figure 5–2 illustrates a portion of Dell's (1988) model in which he describes the process by which a speaker retrieves the phonological composition of the phrase "deal back" before its production. (See Dell [1986] for a complex version of his model that includes additional levels of representation.) The figure illustrates some of the basic connectionist features described earlier in this section and some of the specific additional features used by one modeler.

In Dell's model, nodes in the lexical network are connected through bidirectional and excitatory connections with appropriate phonemes in the phonemic network and with appropriate word-shape headers in the word-shape network. This allows activation to spread in both a top-down and bottom-up fashion. Through this process of *spreading activation,* many words other than the correct ones become activated to some extent; however, only a single word is "selected" because it reaches a selection threshold first. Words that come later in the utterance being produced are "primed," that is, they receive some activation but not enough to trigger selection. The increasing levels of activation for words that are related (through their connections) to the actual word to be selected is the formal mechanism included in this model for explaining errors in performance. Sometimes words or phonemes that are highly activated but are not the target word are selected. To prevent ever-increasing lev-

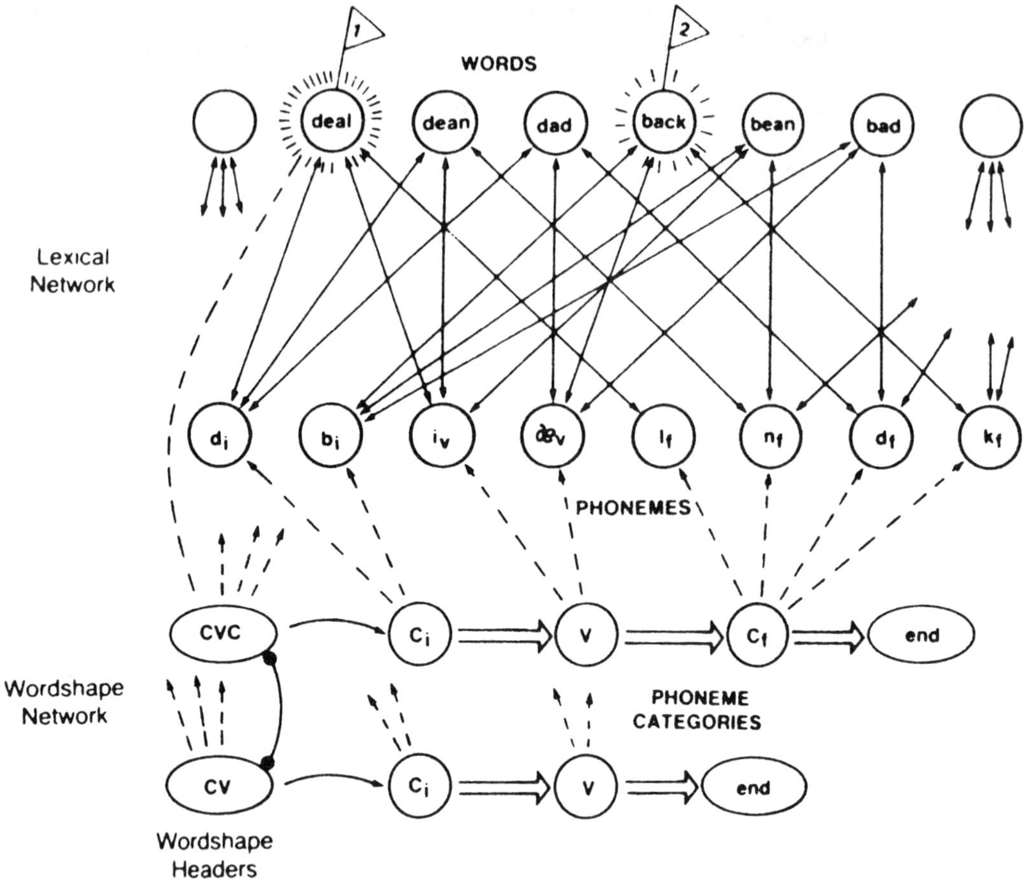

FIG 5–2.
Dell's model for phonological retrieval illustrating the lexical and word-shape networks in the model. This example shows the retrieval of the phonological composition of the phrase "deal back" before its production. (From Dell GS: *J Memory Lang* 1988; 27:128. Used by permission.)

els of activation for any node, two additional features have been included by Dell: *activation decay* and *postselection inhibition.* Activation decay affects activation levels so that a constant decrement in activation occurs for each node at a designated time interval. Postselection inhibition is related to activation decay but involves the active turning off of activation after selection. It is included to prevent repeated selection of a given node. Although this is only one example of a connectionist approach to modeling language processing, it illustrates a move toward emphasizing simultaneous and interactive processing in language formulation and production.

Table 5–1 summarizes the various approaches to modeling language formulation. These examples illustrate a variety of perspectives from which researchers describe the complex processes involved in talk. These perspectives range from strictly serial models, to those that add interaction among levels, to those that emphasize simultaneous interactive processing. However, none of these models explicitly considers the influence of speech motor control processing on language formulation. Also, to date, no ap-

TABLE 5–1.

Models of Language Formulation That Focus on the Activity Included in Formulating an Utterance.*

Serial models: Suggest independent levels of linguistic processing
- Garrett (1975, 1980)
- Shattuck-Hufnagel (1979)

Interactive Serial Model: Suggests interaction among serially organized levels of linguistic processing
- Bock (1982)

Connectionist models: Suggest that linguistic processing occurs as a result of a large network of simultaneous and interactive processing elements and their connections
- Stemberger (1985)
- Dell (1988)

*This includes intent, processes of lexical selection, and syntactic processing.

proach has attempted to describe development of language. That is, no approach

... hanges

rocess-

... spects

he se-

l pro-

motor

escrip-

n how

y, and

e air

t. The

guage

ted in

ler et

al., [illegible]; Kent and Minifie, 1977; MacNeilage, 1970; Nolan, 1982). All of these models assume an input from the language formulation systems, although they differ according to what they believe that linguistic input to be. Kent (1976) reports that the motor skills involved in speech are related to either temporal structure or the spatial structure of the utterance. He considers the two major problems in the motor control of speech production to be the seriation of elements and the articulatory representation of those elements. Seriation relates to the temporal aspects of speech motor control and involves the problems of patterning or sequencing of units. Seriation finds expression in the assembly of phonetic or syllable strings. Neuromuscular or articulatory representation involves the conversion of cortical control elements to specific vocal tract configurations at the peripheral level. Seriation, then, is related to the temporal structure, whereas neuromuscular representation is related to spatial structure. These two motor control issues must be addressed to model or describe the process of converting mental, linguistic representations to acoustic signals for communication.

Translation Models

Two major approaches have been offered in modeling speech production (Table 5–2). One perspective, often called *translation* models, has been most prevalent historically. Translation models assume a discrete and invariant input from the language formulation system and describe processes of conversion of that ab-

TABLE 5–2.

Models of Speech Production That Focus on How Movement of Specific Range, Velocity, and Direction Occurs to Constrict the Airstream for a Desired Acoustic Output

Translation models (MacNeilage, 1970)
- The model assumes a discrete invariant input from the language formulation system.
- It describes processes of conversion of that linguistic input to movement.

Action theory (Fowler et al., 1980)
- Linguistic units do not exist independent of the motor representation, so there is no conversion process.
- Groups of muscles perform as a unit to complete a specific task.

stract input to observable, measurable movements resulting in acoustic output. Concepts involved in this conversion include units of planning and production, motor programming; movement specification; the role of afferent, proprioceptive, and auditory feedback; and timing.

A number of models have been suggested that focus on one or more of these aspects of speech motor control (Kent and Minifie, 1977; MacNeilage, 1970; Sternberg et al., 1978). For example, MacNeilage (1970) offers a model of motor control for the serial ordering of speech. He posits a mechanism that is guided by invariant "targets." These targets control the generation of context-dependent movement patterns. In his view, a space coordinate system translates phonological information into spatial target specifications. The motor control system then generates movement command patterns so that the articulators reach specified targets in a required order. Finally, these command patterns are issued to the muscles. Important to this model is the role of open and closed loop control systems, both of which operate in speech motor control. Specifically, MacNeilage (1970) proposed that an open loop control system (in which commands are generated before execution and independent of the output) would operate by generating a "context-independent" command. Closed loop systems (in which information about the movement in the periphery is sent back to those systems generating the movement) continuously sample the current mechanical state of the articulatory system and adjust motor commands accordingly.

Action Theory

A second major contemporary approach to speech production is that of action theory (Fowler, 1980; Fowler et al., 1980; Kelso and Tuller, 1984; Kelso et al., 1986). In this approach, linguistic units are directly and invariantly represented in the speech output. They do not exist independent of the motor representation. The plan is not separate from the execution as it is in translation theory. That is, the "input" from the language formulation system is conceptualized as being the same as the motor output, thus involving no conversion process. Segments, which are both abstract and actual, are dynamic, qualitatively separate, and serially ordered. They are conceptualized as being four dimensional, with time being intrinsic to the segment itself. That is, movements are programmed without explicit specification of duration. The temporal regularities that result are caused by the biomechanical and physiological characteristics of the vocal tract and articulatory structures.

A concept central to action theory is that of *coordinative structures*. These may be described as groups of muscles that perform as a unit to complete a specific task. These groups are constrained to produce an activity of a certain type. Vowels and consonants are said to be differentiated in that they have separate systems of coordinative structures and that they are coproduced. That is, the system of coordinative structures for consonants is overlaid on the dynamic system for vowels.

Although these two perspectives on speech production are quite different in their explanations and predictions concerning "segments," movement specification, and control of movement, neither approach addresses interaction with verbal formulation processes or specifically relates their supporting data to language formulation models. Action theorists assume that there is no distinction between the plan and the utterance, but they still begin at roughly the same place as translation theorists—with a linguistic input that has already been formulated by a language formulation process. Although one view assumes a static, abstract, and discrete input (translation) and the other assumes a dynamic, context-free input (action), neither approach addresses how processes of language formulation may interact with their model of speech production. Further, as was illustrated for language formulation models, speech production models make no attempt to explain changes in the processes of speech motor control during the development of early talk.

THE INTERACTION OF SPEECH MOTOR CONTROL AND LANGUAGE FORMULATION IN DEVELOPMENT

The relationship between language development and motor development has been discussed primarily as co-occurring rather than interactive maturation. Molfese and Betz (1987) reviewed literature describing three separate views of language and motor development. One view suggests separate maturation and cerebral lateralization for language processes and motor process, and another describes language and motor development as processes that share overlapping hemisphere sites, allowing an index of hemisphere lateralization. They emphasize a third view, that language and motor development evolve synchronistically because of central nervous system maturation. Language development and motor development are ongoing processes; the co-occurrence of behaviors is best explained as a set of parallel developments in a developing organism.

Most evidence reviewed by Molfese and Betz (1987) compared language production with development of fine and gross motor skills in the limbs. Much data have been offered describing similarities in speech and limb systems with respect to timing patterns, responses to applied perturbations, and basic kinematic characteristics (see Ostry and Cooke, 1987, for review). Although these studies illustrate similarities in the control of movement in the two systems, they do not address how they may influence each other. Examination of how motor control develops in general and specifically how the development of speech motor control influences and is influenced by the development of language formulation is an important area for research.

Influence of Motor Control on Emerging Phonology and First Words

To incorporate the influence of speech motor control in a model for the development of early utterances, one must consider a variety of aspects of the developing motor system, including early musculoskeletal constraints, the maturation of neural control for speech production, and the development of skilled motor behavior. Although it is beyond the scope of this chapter to discuss these issues in detail, a review of some of the evidence for early influences of speech motor control on emerging phonological and lexical processing will illustrate the necessity for integrating the two processes in models of early talk.

Some evidence has been offered for the influence of speech motor control on emerging phonological and lexical production (Kent, 1984; MacNeilage et al., 1981; Smith, 1988; Studdert-Kennedy, 1986). The importance of this evidence has been pointed out by Smith (1988, p. 79), who argues against relying only on linguistic accounts of phonological and lexical development:

> A variety of factors influence the acquisition of sound production skills, and no individual one realistically accounts for all the observations that can be made concerning children's sound patterns associated with early lexical development. Unfortunately the importance of motor/physical factors often seems to be ignored

> because of the interest in finding higher order (i.e., linguistically, psychologically based) phonological rules or processes. As Ohala noted, however, by first looking for phonetically motivated explanations of sound patterns, it is possible to more realistically determine when higher level learning may be associated with early lexical productions.

The influence of early maturation of the central nervous system and biomechanical constraints of a rapidly changing vocal tract have been studied by a variety of investigators (see Kent, 1981, 1984, for reviews). Early talk evolves not only because of the development of cognitive and linguistic systems but also because of neuromotor and musculoskeletal changes. Phonetic development proceeds in course partly because of necessary changes in anatomy and neurophysiological changes (Kent, 1981, in press; Stark, 1986; Studdert-Kennedy, 1986).

Because neuroanatomical, neurophysiological, and musculoskeletal factors change extensively through the period of early language production, it is important to consider the effects that these physical factors have on production of early words. Sound production patterns of young infants are strongly affected by biological and physical characteristics of the vocal tract. Early sound production preferences may be explained by substantial changes in vocal tract anatomy during the first year of life (Kent, Chapter 4, 1984). For example, at first, sounds tend to be neutral vowel-like sounds because the larynx is set high in the vocal tract and the tongue fills most of the oral cavity. Back consonants occur quite frequently in early cooing and babbling but less frequently in late babbling and early words because of the initially high larynx position. Stark (1986) points out that this change in parameters of the vocal tract is accompanied by changes in neurophysiological development, which also may be explanatory of early discontinuities of vocal development. A model of early talk, then, should reflect changes in musculoskeletal anatomy, as well as the changes in central nervous system control from primarily reflexive to complex motor control strategies.

The influence of biomechanical and motor control constraints on emerging phonology has been examined by MacNeilage et al. (1981). They reviewed literature describing early sound production in the babbling of hearing infants and deaf infants in English-speaking and non-English-speaking environments and indicated that these early sound preferences are similar and therefore determined by production constraints. Kent (1984) reiterates this view by pointing out that acquisition of phonology interacts with the acquisition of motor control for speech and adds that development of the child's motor facility also depends in part on the need to utter sequences of sound contrast.

Speech production has been described as having two relatively independent stages (Kent, 1976): a *premotor stage,* during which selection and sequencing of speech segments occurs, and a *motoric stage,* which involves the control of movement for production of the segments. MacNeilage et al. (1981) investigated the extent to which the two-stage view could be extended to very early speech development. They reviewed evidence that a child may proceed gradually from a holistic stage of word production to a stage in which there is a separate premotor representation of individual sounds. They suggest early consonantal production preferences are the result of only motor constraints of the production system and not representation in a premotor stage.

The study of Leopold (1947) is often cited as an illustration that phonological production in early words may not be a pattern of gradual growth but one of growth and decay (Kent, 1984). In one example, Leopold's daughter produced her first word, "pretty," with accurate phonological production. About 1 year later, she omitted the /r/ and finally reduced precision of production to "biddy" in correspondence with the phonological production patterns she was using in other word production. This example is presented as evidence that the organization of phonetic production of early words is initially holistic in nature, where there is not separate representation of individual sounds (MacNeilage et al., 1981). The child proceeds from this holistic stage to one in which there is a premotor representation of individual sounds and sometimes deterioration of the output form. Other evidence for the word as the basic unit of contrast in early language production has been offered (Kent, 1984; Menn, 1983; Studdert-Kennedy, 1986).

Schwartz and Leonard (1981) have suggested that early lexical productions are those for which the child has both a *schema* and a motor *scheme*. The schema is a structural unit of perceptual or figurative knowledge. The motor scheme is the behavioral structure that permits the child to transfer and generalize actions to similar situations. A child develops a limited number of schemas representing a word. These schemas are subject to the child's perceptual limitations and input from the environment. These first schemas comprise the child's initial group of comprehended lexical items. Simultaneously the child constructs a limited number of motor schemes for vocalizations. These are initially independent of schemas. Eventually the child begins to coordinate these schemas and schemes. Early words will consist of those for which the child has both a schema and a coordinated scheme. Development proceeds by adding schemas and schemes and coordinating existing schemas and schemes.

Influence of Rhythmic Behavior

Early lexical development is also influenced by rhythmic behavior, which seems to be a precursor to voluntary motor control (Smith, 1988; Thelen, 1981). Lashley's (1951) concept of rhythmic action suggests that rhythm is the foundation for all perceptual-motor activities. Rhythmical stereotypies (rigid, programmed responses to a variety of eliciting contexts) have been viewed as transition behavior between uncoordinated activity and complex coordinated voluntary motor control (Thelen, 1981). Thelen (1981) points out that the large number of different rhythmical stereotypes and the nature of their development suggests that these movements track the emergence of functional synergisms in many muscle groups. Thus, the association of rhythmic movement with emerging voluntary control implies that this intrinsic patterning is more than a transient phenomenon. It is an essential coordination used in the later construction of skilled behavior.

Martin (1972) discusses rhythm as temporal patterning based on motor function. Temporal constraints operate in natural movement sequences, such as speech, some of which are based on biomechanical systems. Martin (1972, p. 488) states that "these constraints influence the segmental details of the acoustic signal, but they should be expected also to affect at least some aspects of the morphology and syntax of any language at the level of the syllable strings since they play a role in determining what can be naturally and easily spoken."

Rhythmic or cyclical patterns, then, are a natural basis for the organization of systems of movement and may contribute to the acquisition of skilled movement for speech production (Kent, 1984). Smith (1988) notes that the neural mechanism responsible for generating rhythmic motor behavior in infants may also be the basis for reduplicated babbling, which is observed in infant vocalization at about 6 to 7 months of age. This repetition of a basic syllable shape (e.g., *ba ba ba*) in premeaningful utterance production may gradually be associated with meaningful early words. Evidence that early word production is characterized by this pattern of syllable reduplication (Kent, 1984; Smith, 1988) suggests that processes important to the development of speech motor control are interactive with developing linguistic processes.

The management of rhythm and timing (temporal programs) and the management of neuromuscular commands (motor programs) have been central issues in attempts to describe the serial execution of movements for verbal utterance (MacNeilage, 1970; Shaffer, 1982). Martin (1972, p. 487) defined rhythm as "relative timing between adjacent and non adjacent elements in a behavior sequence." In his view, timing of speech is preset by central timing mechanisms. The temporal organization of an utterance is dominated by accented (stressed) elements that are planned before the other elements. Conception of accented syllables as the primary targets in the organization of articulatory programs leads to a prediction that decisions concerning function words (unaccented syllables) and content words (accented words) are ordered. Martin (1972) proposed that the actual rhythmic pattern for an utterance can be determined by rules that express the relation between the relative accent levels and the relative timing of the elements in a sequence. Although little empirical data exist to test models of rhythm or timing, research examining speech error data (Boomer and Laver, 1968; Fromkin, 1971) provides evidence for the importance of this type of approach and the probability of the dominance of stress or rhythmic programming.

The plan and execution of movements in a syllable structure are often described in terms of a motor program. This motor program may be characterized as central command patterns that generate specified patterns of movement. The concept of a motor program, although disputed and not easily tested, is often used to describe speech production. The process of motor programs is useful to conceptualize both in describing rhythm and temporal structure of utterances, as well as for describing the articulatory, spatial, and movement specifications during speech production.

The most extreme view of the motor program is that the central commands are generated completely without reliance on feedback. Other views conceptualize motor programming as involving both advance planning and continuous proprioceptive feedback that provides information about the current state of the vocal tract. Little data currently exist describing the nature of the motor program or how it is executed in speech production. This is primarily because of the lack of an accepted methodology for defining or measuring effects of impaired programming processes.

How does one incorporate temporal and motor planning into an acquisition model that makes specific claims regarding the interaction of language and motor control in development? The concept of *automaticity* is an important unifying factor. As the child proceeds through the early stages of language acquisition, he or she must initially use controlled processing requiring much attention and effort. Gradually the child develops increased automaticity in linguistic processing, in temporal and motor planning, and in motor skill for execution of movement. This leads to less demand on the limited capacity of the child, freeing up attentional mechanisms for continued development in linguistic and motor performance.

Integration of Processing Demands

Issues relating to processing capacity and the child's response to processing demands relate directly to the integration of speech motor control and language formulation in early acquisition of talk. During this period, the child is developing cognitive, semantic, phonological, and motor control processing simultaneously and interactively. The competing demand for allocation of attention or effort in each of these cognitive or linguistic systems necessarily taxes the child's limited capacity for processing.

Kahneman (1973) proposes a capacity theory to explain our limited ability to carry out multiple activities at the same time. In this theory, the total amount of attention that can be deployed at one time is limited. Kahneman (1973) offers a model of allocation of capacity to mental activity (Fig 5–3) describing the relationship of influence and control between components of a system. Not all activities require an input of attention (e.g., early stages of sensory analysis), and, therefore, processing or performance can be achieved automatically without conscious effort. Different mental activities impose different demands on the limited capacity of humans, yielding varying requirements for conscious processing. When the supply of attention does not meet the demands needed for such controlled processing, performance falters or fails entirely.

All skilled performance, including utterance production, involves both automatic and controlled processes. *Automatic processing* operates outside of conscious awareness. Schneider and Shiffrin (1977) note that during an automatic process, a sequence of nodes (processing units) becomes active in response to a

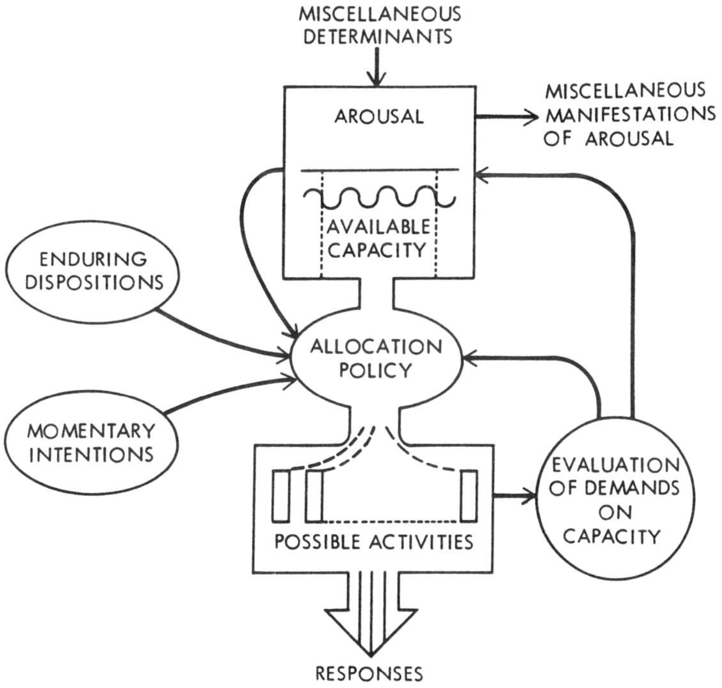

FIG 5–3.
Kahneman's model of the allocation of capacity to mental activity. (From Kahneman D: *Attention and Effort.* Englewood Cliffs, NJ, Prentice-Hall, 1973, p 10. Used by permission.)

particular input. The sequence is activated without requiring active control or attention by the person. Therefore, those cognitive and linguistic processes operating "automatically" demand no processing capacity and can be performed without control or attention by the speaker and without interference with other processes. *Controlled processing,* on the other hand, does require conscious attention. Schneider and Shiffrin (1977) define a controlled process as a temporary sequence of nodes activated under control of the person and through attention by the person. Although automatic processes require little or no processing capacity, controlled processes are capacity limited. These controlled operations require the use of short-term memory, and the nature of their limitation is in part caused by the capacity limitations of short-term store. Although controlled processing allows performance to occur in novel or less practiced situations, it is affected by additional tasks. Consider, for example, simple conversation at the supermarket checkout counter. While entering prices or bagging, the clerk may easily engage in fluent conversation. On beginning to count change, however, hesitations, revisions, and pauses in speech output occur. The increased need for controlled processing has taxed the limited-capacity system, reducing the quality of performance in utterance production.

Bock (1982) points out there is a growing awareness of the importance of processing automaticity in language production, especially with respect to developmental issues. She notes that automaticity and control may be viewed as defining the ends of a continuum. Early talk likely requires significant amounts of controlled processing. As the child develops, increased automaticity allows for more complex linguistic and motor processing.

Other researchers have also posited the importance of processing capacity in early utterance production (Campbell and Shriberg, 1982; Crystal, 1987; Hawkins, 1984; Levelt, 1989; Smith, 1988). Evidence has been provided for trade-offs in the quality of performance of language formulation and speech motor control processes during development of early talk. For example, Panagos et al. (1979) examined the extent to which sources of grammatical complexity at different levels of linguistic encoding separately and in combination influence articulatory performance. Their results indicated decreased performance in articulatory performance with increased grammatical complexity. Panagos et al. (1979, p. 846) concluded that this articulatory simplification "may be an outgrowth of information processing limitations." Evidence that phonological structure can influence the child's syntactic processing has also been offered (Panagos and Prelock, 1982). Their data indicate that "during sentence production, syntactic and phonological structures influence one another such that complexity added on either level disrupts performance on the other and cumulative complexity disrupts performance on both" (Panagos and Prelock, 1982, p. 176).

Kamhi et al. (1984) shed light on another aspect of limited capacity and its role in the development of utterance production. Their data showed that younger children were more influenced by changes in complexity than older children. Further, differences among children within the same language stage yielded support for the notion that the level of self-tolerance for articulatory variability influences the management of processing demands. Kamhi et al. (1984, p. 336) hypothesized that "the level of a child's speech, language and cognitive abilities defines the capacity limits of the sentence formulation process, whereas the extent to which the child tolerates variability in speech determines whether or not these limits are observed or exceeded." Kamhi's more recent reservations about limited-capacity models are described in Chapter 3.

Smith (1988) emphasizes the role of limited capacity in the development of skilled speech motor control. He notes that as automaticity of synergistic movement patterns develops, the number of movement parameters to be independently controlled is reduced. In early talk, when linguistic and motor processes operate without much automaticity, children rely more heavily on continuous sensory feedback information for error detection and correction. Smith (1988, p. 94) suggests that "if there is a maximum degree of linguistic processing that young children are capable of managing at any one time, which must be allocated among phonological, lexical, syntactic and other linguistic tasks, such feedback factors might affect any or all of those parameters. Some of the simplification that occurs in children's speech and language might, therefore, be the result of having to attend simultaneously to a number of linguistic processing tasks."

Crystal (1987) considers the role of limited capacity in children who are language delayed in his proposal of a "bucket theory" of language disability. He compares language processing capacity to a bucket containing a certain amount of linguistic (as well as cognitive, perceptual, and motor) information or processing demands. As the child develops, the amount in the bucket gets larger. In the case of the child exhibiting deviant language, he continues, there are a series of holes above a certain level in the bucket. As the processing demands rise, as would water in a bucket, and reaches the holes, any extra processing demands will cause some of the information or processing skill to "spill out." His theory makes no assumptions about hierarchy and considers all processing levels at once without predicting what process might suffer when limited capacity is exceeded. His account of language disability, then, puts great emphasis on the interaction of language and motor processes and how limited capacity affects the resulting performance in utterance production. This perspective not only calls for additional research in the *interaction* of levels of linguistic and motor processing but has important clinical implications as well.

IMPLICATIONS FOR PROCESS MODELS OF CHILDREN'S LANGUAGE

Speech and language development has traditionally been described in terms of stages. Kent (1984) suggests that a process model recognizing continuities in behavior may be preferable to a stage model based on discontinuities. This seems especially true given the rapid changes that occur in the variety of complex processes involved in early talk as maturation occurs. A process model focuses on the dynamic and interactive mental and physical activity that occurs during a particular behavior. A process model that takes into account the interactive influences of speech motor control and language formulation may go further in solving some of the problems of current utterance production models.

The literature reviewed in this chapter illustrates that increasing emphasis is being placed on the interaction of language and speech systems. The evidence that language development may be influenced by the movement system through which it is expressed leads to the assumption that the emergence of speech and language during early talk should not be modeled separately. Rather, emphasis should be placed on the development of a process model that incorporates the integration of speech motor control and language formulation. Further, that model should illustrate how such interaction is influenced by processing capacity and demands. Such a model may allow better understanding of why some children exhibit delays or deviancy in development and how clinicians may better approach remediation.

In the next section, a series of claims are made in the context of the Child Talk model. These claims regarding the interactive influence of motor control and language formulation are proposed as a framework from which to generate experimental questions and supporting data for continued refinement of a process model to explain early talk.

Assumptions of the Child Talk Model

The Child Talk model of children's language production is process-based and views talk as spontaneously initiated and goal directed. The major claim of the model is that linguistic knowledge is not modular or separated from world knowledge but embedded in it. This chapter has addressed issues regarding the acoustic realization of that linguistic knowledge. Although the processes of speech motor control are not the main focus of the Child Talk model, the interactive influences of language and speech necessitate the formulation of specific claims regarding the relationship of verbal formulation and its acoustic realization.

One of the great difficulties in the development of an acquisition model is accounting for changes in the nature of the relationship among interactive systems as the child proceeds through development. This is especially true of an acquisition model for utterance production, in which complex and rapid changes in cognition, perception, language, and motor skills are co-occurring. The claims of the Child Talk model regarding production of the child's early linguistic formulation are centered on the interactive influences of speech and language formulation, although it is recognized that cognitive, perceptual, and personality development are integrally involved in the processing of early talk.

The first claim is that the processes of verbal formulation do yield a "linguistic input" to the motor control system. Unlike translation models, this input is not an autonomous element in a serial input-output model. Rather, the processes of language formulation influence and are influenced by the processes of speech motor control. Further examination of the development of speech motor control, especially in relation to the changes in language that co-occur, will lead to the determination of the form of this early linguistic input. It is assumed, however, that this input quite probably varies, depending on stage of development, communicative goal, affect, and environmental influences.

In this model it is assumed that simultaneous, parallel and interactive neurophysiological and anatomical changes influence emerging phonology. At the same time, the development of rhythmical patterns of motor behavior strongly influence and are integral to the production of early meaningful utterances. The development of increased automaticity both in language formulation and speech motor control allow for continued interactive development of complex language and motor processes. That is, gradual increases in automatic processing facilitate growth in linguistic and speech motor control performance.

Important to the issue of development of increased automaticity in processing is the assumption that both temporal and motor programming develop interactively with language formulation. Models of speech production use the construct of "programs" (temporal, motor, or both) to explain how speech is planned and serially executed. Although refined methodology is needed to describe the nature and role of programming in speech production, the Child Talk model makes the claim that both temporal programs and motor programs operate to control utterance production. Further, it is assumed that temporal planning is the primary or dominant process in the motor control of the seriation of segments for production. These planning and control processes operate interactively and in parallel and are directly influenced by the linguistic processes also in progress during formulation and production.

Assumptions regarding temporal and motor programming lead to the claims regarding the notion of *hierarchy*. This term usually implies a sequence of stages or a series of levels in which adjacent members have a subordinate-superordinate relationship. For example, linguistic processes such as lexical and semantic or syntactic are often referred to as higher level cortical processes, whereas output, including speech motor control, is a later, peripheral, lower level process. In the Child Talk model, hierarchy is flexible and a product of the relative timing of different portions of an utterance's construction. This is the view of "hierarchy" suggested by Cromer (1978, p. 127): "The analysis of a complex behavior into its component parts in which the performance of some parts is postponed while performance in other parts takes priority." This is congruent with our argument for trade-offs in processing demands.

The simultaneous, parallel and interactive processes of verbal formulation and motor speech planning, then, account for the influence of linguistic formulation on speech motor control. For example, as the phonetic representation for a specific semantic concept is formed, the rhythm programmer needs to account for lexical stress. At the same time, modifications might be made because of sentence intonation contour constraints as syntactic formulation continues. In like manner, as phonetic representation for certain lexical items is being activated, so is the motor program for the activation of particular muscle groups. As modifications might be made in phonetic representation, continuous modification needs to be made in motor assembly.

In this view, then, linguistic constraints operate primarily because of the simultaneous activation of formulation and control processes. Linguistic constraint may also operate at peripheral feedback monitoring levels. Verification of intent and verification that the correct lexical and syntactic constructs were used may influence motor control processes, especially if there is unfamiliarity with topic, confusion regarding listener reaction, and so forth. These influences on control processes may be seen in rhythm effects, hesitations, or changes in mid-utterance and in speech errors.

In summary, then, Child Talk assumes an interactive association of language formulation and motor speech processes. The model posits that parallel, simultaneous, and interactive systems of semantic, syntactic, phonological, and phonetic processes exist. Systems of rhythm or temporal programs are also simultaneously activated, as are motor programs. Temporal planning is dominant and less prone to breakdown. These claims are a move away from a serial type of hierarchy and toward a dominance or salience type of hierarchy. These assumptions constitute only a beginning, of course, to the construction of a detailed model.

Implications for Development

The claims just presented not only relate to explanations of utterance production at any one point in time during development but also yield explanation for acquisition as it proceeds. For example, evidence was presented to illustrate the influence of biomechanical constraints and motor skill on emerging phonology and lexical acquisition. Conversely, the production of early words influences continued development and refinement of motor skill. Not only does motor control, then, influence emerging language but production of early utterances facilitates continued development of speech motor control.

Explanations of how the development of early utterances proceeds is greatly enhanced through the study of controlled vs. automatic processing. The child's limited capacity requires that initially he or she use much attention and effort in both linguistic and motor performance. This greatly reduces the amount of language formulation or motor output that can occur. As the child practices language and motor control skills, aspects of performance become increasingly more automatic and less controlled. This allows more attention and effort to be directed toward increasingly complex language and motor skill. Therefore, development proceeds, and the child continues to exhibit qualitative and quantitive changes in competence and performance.

From this point of view, future research should be focused less on specific competencies and more on the interaction of language and motor control and the influence of processing demands on that interaction. If we are to determine the relative influences of such interactions on acquisition, longitudinal research is essential. The examination of linguistic and speech motor control performance over time will yield better explanations of early variability, regression and delay in acquisition, and how processing capacity facilitates or hinders acquisition as it proceeds. Specific issues to examine include (1) examination of temporal structure in early word acquisition to determine the influence of rhythmic structure on early utterances, (2) identification of variability in production attributable to motoric aspects vs. language parameters, (3) specific longitudinal study of the biomechanical constraints of the changing vocal tract on early sound production, (4) longitudinal examination of speech errors in early acquisition of utterances, and (5) longitudinal examination of variability in production accuracy across linguistic contexts.

IMPLICATIONS FOR CLINICAL PRACTICE

A process model that focuses on the integrated mental and physical activity that occurs in utterance production yields specific implications for clinical practice. A model such as Child Talk and, specifically, those claims that relate to the interaction of motor control and language formulation, provide a different theoretical perspective from which clinical decisions may be derived. Specifically, such a perspective dictates that the clinician's attention should be focused on performance—and those parameters that influence performance—rather than particular competencies. For example, traditional approaches to language modeling may suggest that clinicians measure the mean number of words per utterance to assess an aspect of language development at that point in time. The perspective described in this chapter would suggest that the clinician vary the context in which the series of utterances are elicited to determine what influences the number of words produced in an utterance.

It is imperative that clinicians approach diagnosis with the understanding that language formulation and speech processes make *relative* contributions to communicative deficits. The interaction between and among levels may provide some explanation for the variable, sometimes unpredictable behavior observed in language-delayed and -disordered children. One must consider the interactive influences of both in determining to what degree language and speech may be influencing a deficit in utterance production. Diagnosis, then, would not relate simply to developmental *level* of phonology or syntax but would address the *interactive influences* of those levels. For example, the role that phonological selectivity plays in early vocabulary inventories should be considered.

In both diagnosis and treatment, decisions regarding stimuli selection and context variables should reflect the interactive effects of speech and language processes. For example, it may be quite facilitative to control for linguistic complexity when one is targeting improvement in motor speech planning or fluency. Hierarchies of linguistic demands may be continually varied to reduce the resource allocation demands, allowing improved motor control for speech. In like manner, simplifying motor speech demands may reduce the "performance load" for the child, allowing for more effort and attention in language skills.

The influence of controlled vs. automatic processing is perhaps the most salient clinical implication of the perspective posited in this chapter. It is difficult to identify a particular "linguistic" deficit without accounting for limitations imposed by the capacity of the child to perform linguistic and motor skills concurrently. In addition, the clinician must account for the influence of attention and effort required for other aspects of the ongoing communication, such as verification of intent, evaluating listener reaction, and ongoing refinement of the communicative goal.

The influence of processing capacity requires that the clinician set up task requirements that vary in *demand* for processing capacity to determine the nature of the linguistic or speech motor control deficit. Evaluation of treatment efficacy also involves examination of changes in ability to perform increasingly complex language and motor skills concurrently.

The issues surrounding the integration of language formulation and speech motor control in general are complex. In early language acquisition, they are even more complex. Therefore, the comments put forth in this chapter are speculative and incomplete. They do lead to suggestions for research that will provide supporting data and elaboration of a process model that emphasizes the integration of speech motor control and language formulation in early talk.

REFERENCES

Bock JK: Towards a cognitive psychology of syntax: Information processing contributions to sentence formulation. *Psychol Rev* 1982; 89:1–47.

Bock JK: Syntactic persistence in language production. *Cognit Psychol* 1986; 18:355–387.

Bock JK: An effect of the accessibility of word forms on sentence structures. *J Memory Lang* 1987; 26:119–137.

Bock JK, Warren RK: Conceptual accessibility and syntactic structure in sentence formulation. *Cognition* 1985; 21:47–67.

Boomer DS, Laver JD: Slips of the tongue. *Br J Disord Commun* 1968; 3:1–12.

Campbell TF, Shriberg LD: Associations among pragmatic functions, linguistic stress, and natural phonological processes in speech-delayed children. *J Speech Hear Res* 1982; 25:547–553.

Chafe WL: Creativity in verbalization and its implications for the nature of stored knowledge, in Freedle RO (ed): *Discourse Production and Comprehension.* Norwood, NJ, Albex, vol 1, 1977.

Cromer RF: The basis of childhood dysphasia: A linguistic approach, in Wyke M (ed): *Developmental Dysphasia.* New York, Academic Press, 1978.

Crystal D: Towards a "bucket" theory of language disability: Taking account of interaction between linguistic levels. *Clin Linguist Phonetics* 1987; 1:7–22.

Dell GS: Positive feedback in hierarchial connectionist models: Applications to language production. *Cognit Sci* 1985; 9:3–23.

Dell GS: *A Spreading Activation Theory of Retrieval in Sentence Production.* Cognitive Science Tech Rep no 21, Rochester, NY, University of Rochester, 1986.

Dell GS: The retrieval of phonological forms in production: Tests of predictions from a connectionist model. *J Memory Lang* 1988; 27:124–142.

Fowler C: Coarticulation and theories of extrinsic timing. *J Phonetics* 1980; 8:113–133.

Fowler C, Rubin P, Remez RE, et al: Implications for speech production of a general theory of action, in Butterworth B (ed): *Speech Production.* New York, Academic Press, vol 1, 1980.

Fromkin VA: The non-anomalous nature of anomalous utterances. *Language* 1971; 47:27–52.

Garrett M: The analysis of sentence production, in Bower B (ed): *Psychology of Learning and Motivation.* New York, Academic Press, vol 9, 1975.

Garrett M: Levels of processing in sentence production, in Butterworth B (ed): *Language Production.* New York, Academic Press, vol 1, 1980.

Hawkins S: On the development of motor control in speech: Evidence from studies of temporal coordination. *Speech and Language: Advances in Basic Research and Practice,* 1984, vol 11, pp 317–374.

Kahneman D: *Attention and Effort.* Englewood Cliffs, NJ, Prentice-Hall, 1973.

Kamhi AG, Catts HW, Davis MK: Management of sentence production demands. *J Speech Hear Res* 1984; 27:329–338.

Kelso JS, Saltzman EL, Tuller B: The dynamical perspective on speech production: Data and theory. *J Phonetics* 1986; 14:29–59.

Kelso J, Tuller B: Converging evidence in support of common dynamical principles for speech and movement coordination. *Am J Physiol* 1984; 246:R928–R935.

Kent RD: Models of speech production, in Lass N (ed): *Contemporary Issues in Experimental Phonetics.* New York, Academic Press, 1976.

Kent RD: Sensorimotor aspects of speech development, in Aslin R, Alberts J, Peterson M (eds): *Development of Perception: Psychological Factors.* New York, Academic Press, 1981.

Kent RD: Psychobiology of speech development: Coemergence of language and a movement system. *Am J Physiol* 1984; 246:R888–R894.

Kent RD: The biology of phonological development, in Ferguson C, Menn L, Stoel-Gammon C (eds): *Phonological Development: Models, Research, Implications.* Parkton, Md, York Press (in press).

Kent RD, Minifie FD: Coarticulation in recent speech production models. *J Phonetics* 1977; 5:115–133.

Lashley KS: The problem of serial order in behavior, in Jeffress LA (ed): *Cerebral Mechanisms in Behavior.* New York, John Wiley & Sons, 1951.

Leopold W: *Speech Development in a Bilingual Child: A Linguistic Record.* Evanston, Ill, Northwestern University Press, vol II, 1947.

Levelt WM: *Speaking: From Intention to Articulation.* Cambridge, Mass, MIT Press, 1989.

MacNeilage PF: The motor control of serial ordering of speech. *Psychol Rev* 1970; 77:182–196.

MacNeilage P, Hutchinson J, Lasater S: The production of speech: Development and dissolution of motoric and premotoric processes, in Long J, Baddeley A (eds): *Attention and Performance IX.* Hillsdale, NJ, Lawrence Erlbaum Associates, 1981.

Martin JG: Rhythmic (hierarchial) versus serial structure in speech and other behavior. *Psychol Rev* 1972; 79:487–509.

McClelland JL: Connectionist models and psychological evidence. *J Memory Lang* 1988; 27:107–123.

McClelland JL, Rumelhart DE: An interactive activation model of context effects in letter perception: part 1. An account of basic findings. *Psychol Rev* 1981; 88:375–407.

Menn L: Development of articulatory, phonetic and phonological capabilities, in Butterworth B (ed): *Language Production.* New York, Academic Press, vol 2, 1983.

Molfese VJ, Betz JD: Language and motor development in infancy: Three views with neuropsychological implications. *Dev Neuropsychol* 1987; 3:255–275.

Nolan FJ: The role of action theory in the description of speech production. *Linguistics* 1982; 20:287–308.

Ostry DJ, Cooke JD: Kinematic patterns in speech and limb movements, in Keller E, Gopnick E (eds): *Motor and Sensory Processing of Language.* Hillsdale, NJ, Lawrence Erlbaum Associates, 1987.

Panagos JM, Prelock PA: Phonological constraints on the sentence productions of language-disordered children. *J Speech Hear Res* 1982; 25:171–177.

Panagos JM, Quine ME, Klich RJ: Syntactic and phonological influences on children's articulation. *J Speech Hear Res* 1979; 22:841–848.

Schneider W, Shiffrin R: Controlled and automatic human information processing: I. Detection, search, and attention. *Psychol Rev* 1977; 84:1–66.

Schwartz RG, Leonard LB: Do children pick and choose? An examination of phonological selection and avoidance in early lexical acquisition. *J Child Lang* 1981; 9:319–336.

Shaffer LH: Rhythm and timing in skill. *Psychol Rev* 1982; 89:109–122.

Shattuck-Hufnagel S: Speech errors as evidence for a serial-ordering mechanism in speech production, in Cooper W, Walker E (eds): *Sentence Processing.* Hillsdale, NJ, Lawrence Erlbaum Associates, 1979.

Smith BL: The emergent lexicon from a phonetic perspective, in Smith M, Locke J (eds): *The Emergent Lexicon.* New York, Academic Press, 1988.

Smolensky P: On proper treatment of connectionism. *Behav Brain Sci* 1988; 11:1–74.

Stark RE: Prespeech segmental feature development, in Fletcher P, Garman M (eds): *Language Acquisition,* ed 2. New York, Cambridge University Press, 1986.

Stemberger J: An interactive activation model of language production, in Ellis A (ed): *Progress in the Psychology of Language.* Hillsdale, NJ, Lawrence Erlbaum Associates, 1985.

Stemberger JP: A connectionist view of child phonology: Phonological processing without phonological processes, in Ferguson C, Menn L, Stoel-Gammon C (eds): *Phonological Development: Models, Research, Implications.* Parkton, Md, York Press (in press).

Sternberg S, Monsell S, Knoll RL, et al: The latency and duration of rapid movement sequences: Comparison of speech and typewriting, in Stelmach GE (ed): *Information Processing in Motor Control and Learning.* New York, Academic Press, 1978.

Studdert-Kennedy M: Sources of variability in early speech development, in Perkell J, Klatt D (eds): *Invariance and Variability in Speech Processes.* Hillsdale, NJ, Lawrence Erlbaum Associates, 1986.

Thelan E: Rhythmical behavior in infancy: An ethological perspective. *Dev Psychol* 1981; 17:237–257.

6 Nonlinear Phonology as a Framework for Phonological Acquisition*

Richard G. Schwartz, Ph.D.

I've always been more comfortable sinking while clutching a good theory than swimming with an ugly fact.
David Mamet

Vision is the art of seeing the invisible.
Jonathan Swift

These two quotations define the perspective and scope of this chapter. The overall goal is to consider current and emerging theories of phonology and phonological acquisition as they relate to the general framework of Child Talk. A secondary goal is to consider the current methodologies or alternatives that might be applied to infer the invisible knowledge a child has about the phonology of his or her language at any given time and the invisible processes of phonological acquisition.

Acquiring a phonology involves mapping the speech input of the environment to the perception and storage of that input and, in turn, mapping that to the output. The end result is a fully developed system of phonologically represented linguistic units, organized hierarchically, and a set of regularities reflecting language specific and language universal characteristics that can be invoked in the service of perception and production. The child brings to this a biological envelope that provides an important set of constraints on the initial state, the general course and speed of acquisition, and the end state (Gould, 1984; Gould and Marler, 1987; Locke, 1990). Thus, the child comes to this task with a set of predispositions to acquire the sound system of his or her language in a general way, allowing for a range of crosslinguistic and intralinguistic variation. Without question, the last 20 years of research provide us with a great many facts concerning development (some ugly and some not). However, the development of theoretical frameworks in this area has been much slower.

LINGUISTIC THEORY

Part of the difficulty may be that we need more than a single theory. First, we need a theory that, in some formal computational (e.g., algebraic) fashion, describes the abstract knowledge inherent in the developed system. This is the traditional role played by linguistic theory. Though it is not obligatory, such theories often strive for some degree of psychological reality. In recent years far greater attention has been paid to acquisition issues. Theories have been designed to meet learnability criteria, and in some cases, learning mechanisms have been proposed. As indicated in Chapter 2,

*Preparation of this chapter was supported by Public Health Service Grant RO1 DC 00583-04, Input-ouput relationships in speech and language impairments, from the National Institute of Deafness and Other Communication Disorders.

il be-
re not
', see
where
agree-
been
uacies
y and
hortly
d Pat-
umber
Nota-
trical,
hough
ive in
ules to
senta-
ve" ex-
utlined
dition,
esenta-
have
(1990)
f these

LEARNING THEORY

A second important piece that we need is a learning theory. This is a theory that describes the nature and cause of change over the course of development. Essentially three theoretical strings have remained active. I will pigeonhole them simply for the sake of discussion. First is a *constructivist* perspective, in which the child actively constructs a phonology through interaction with and observation of the environment. This is an interactionist perspective in which language domains are seen to influence each other and interact with other aspects of knowledge acquisition. Second is what has been characterized as a newer version of an *associationist* perspective. It is similar to traditional associationist perspectives in the importance attributed to environment but different in some versions in the need for feedback and the ultimate availability of knowledge representations and rule-based behavior. Finally, a *nativist* perspective is still very much alive. The importance of some type of hypothesis testing is retained, and its core remains an innately endowed universal grammar. The new wrinkles are parameters that specify basic language characteristics having innately specified settings that may be modified by triggers in the environment. Though these and alternative views are addressed in other chapters, I will consider them with respect to phonology and, in particular, to the goal of the establishment of the mapping and the internal structure of a phonology.

PROCESSING THEORY

Finally, a theory of processing is necessary. In particular, the nature of perception, production, storage, access, and retrieval needs to be specified. Ideally this should correspond to the units and their manipulation described by the linguistic theory and to the available developmental evidence.

To fully specify all of these is certainly beyond the scope of the present chapter; however, I will try to say something about each and the potential candidates, focusing on a linguistic theory of phonology and a potential theory of development and processing.

One other introductory comment concerns the nature of models of development and processing (or any human activity involving cognition). Several very general frameworks can be used as scaffolding within which to examine and to build such models. One such framework is David Marr's (1982) description of levels in cognitive science. He views them as hierarchically interrelated: beginning at the top with a computational level (e.g., a linguistic theory of competence), then an intermediate representational and algorithmical level (e.g., a psycholinguistic theory including representations of input and output and computational implementation), and finally, a level of hardware implementation, representing some physical reality. I will focus on two levels: the computational level, using nonlinear phonology, and an algorithmical level, using a connectionist framework with which to examine development.

COMPUTATIONAL LEVEL: PHONOLOGICAL THEORY

Generative Phonology

Even as *The Sound Pattern of English* (Chomsky and Halle, 1968) was published, it was apparent that this theory was lacking in its power to describe a number of aspects of phonology. Two central problems have been the focus of most of the criticism. First, the theory was linear. The prototypical description involved a bundle of features that changed in one or more of their values in a certain context (e.g., word final devoicing). This meant that stress had to be treated as a feature in the same way as the features of segments were treated and that larger units could not be related in a hierarchical fashion (e.g., syllables and segments). As a result, describing certain rules (e.g., why New Yorkers are "r-less" before consonants and at the ends of words) becomes problematic. To elaborate on the New York dialect example, generative phonology can only describe this phenomenon with unusual contortions and a generally unacceptable solution using curly brackets that contain a list without constraints of situations in which a phonological change might occur. The problem is that anything could go in these brackets, and so from a linguistic standpoint, the solution is unacceptable; the whole advantage of the formalism is lost. As a side note, the curly bracket notation and the more general description of rules means that anything could be a rule. An important point is that without a somewhat more constrained formalism, if this does indeed represent phonological knowledge, a child would be in real danger of taking wrong turns in learning a phonology. And it seems pointless to have a theory that allows for rules never evidenced in children's phonologies.

The linear nature of generative phonology has one further limitation: temporal and hierachical relationships among features cannot be represented because features are used in bundles to describe phonemes. Related to this is one final piece to the New York "r" story. In cases where an */r/* occurs before a consonant, it is omitted only when it occurs at the end of a syllable. A further constraint that some cases (like the word *bark* produced as *bak*) require depends on the notion of dividing a syllable structurally into an onset and rhyme. Then we can say that */r/* is omitted when it occurs in the rhyme slot in a syllable. Such structural descriptions are absent from generative phonology.

The second major problem is that like many linguistic theories, generative phonology employs a simplicity metric based on the number of feature changes to determine the relative likelihood of a rule. The difficulty has to do with the apparent conflict between simplicity and the relative naturalness or likelihood of a given rule. However, in the last chapter of *The Sound Pattern of English,* Chomsky and Halle (1968) invoke the notion of markedness so that not all feature changes are considered equal in the count of changes. In fact, some changes are viewed as involving no cost. Though this represents an improvement over the original metric, the bases for marking conventions are often intuitively motivated rather than data based.

To sum up, generative phonology fails as an adequate theory primarily because it does not account for the relationships among linguistic units of various sizes. As such, it fails to fit the Child Talk framework. The alternative is a nonlinear approach that deals not only with segments as we traditionally think of them but with larger units of speech. Furthermore, it is more suitable for both processing and learning models.

NONLINEAR PHONOLOGIES

Autosegmental Phonology

Autosegmental phonology was developed in response to these weaknesses and, in particular, to account for tone languages, in which there is a hierarchical relationship between tones and other units. Autosegmental phonology is composed of representations including separable and independent levels called *tiers*. On each tier are units that are termed *autosegments*. Each tier is defined by a single autosegment that may be realized in one or more ways. For example, the tonal tier may include high, middle, and low tones. Though independent, autosegments on different tiers are connected by association lines. Furthermore, there are a small number of conditions such as (1) the association convention—unassociated autosegments on the same side of an association line are associated in a one-to-one fashion radiating out from the existing association line; (2) the linkage condition—if a segment is not linked to a position on the skeletal tier (see later discussion), it will not be phonetically realized, which precludes association lines from crossing. Association lines are precluded from crossing by a well-formedness convention. Beyond these universal characteristics, there are language specific variations that add or delete an association line, delete a segment or change their order, or change the features of a segment on a tier.

One of the most important aspects of the theory is the identification of tiers. The initial specification of the theory used the following as the basis for proposing tiers. The first consideration is that what may appear to be atomic prosodic units (e.g., contour tones) seem more appropriately characterized as sequences of simpler units that are part of a representation that is lexical or larger. The second is what Goldsmith (1990) calls *stability*. This refers to the possibility that there may be changes to the autosegments of one tier that affect only that tier. This does not preclude interaction but does mean that there the tiers are independent. Finally, there can be patterns that recur on a given tier that are associated with different elements on another tier (e.g., a sequence of tones or a syllable structure that may be associated with different sets of segments on another tier).

Goldsmith (1990) and others have described tonal, segmental, and skeletal (also referred to as CV, or timing) tiers. It is important to note that the segmental tier is connected to other tiers in an n-dimensional fashion. These tiers therefore exist in at least a three-dimensional space. I have provided some general notion of what might be represented on each of the first two. Now I want to turn briefly to the skeletal tier, which contains a representation that includes slots labeled as C slots, V slots, or undifferentiated slots, represented by x. The skeletal tier is important because it provides a formal mechanism characterizing timing (e.g., compensatory lengthening), metathesis (changing the order of segments), epenthesis, and other phenomena.

The syllable is the most notable structure represented on the skeletal tier. It is important because it directly addresses a significant deficiency of generative phonology and because it provides an important link to the metrical structure discussed later on. This level includes a representation of syllable and its hierarchically related components, onset and rhyme. The rhyme can be subdivided into a nucleus (the vowel element) and the coda, which may or may not have a segmental realization. Syllables are linked to segments through language-specific rules that are conditioned to occur only with certain syllable structures. Certain segmental changes are conditioned by the syllabic positions in which they occur. Syllables are also linked to prosodic features in that syllables are categorized as heavy and light, which can determine stress assignment. There are language-specific constraints on permissible syllable structures, on stress assignment, and on the distribution of segments across syllable type and position. Another important aspect of syllable structure concerns two types of licensing, prosodic and autosegmental, which in somewhat different ways provide another connection between segments and larger, hierarchically related units. Prosodic licensing refers to a thread that ties segments to larger representational structure up through units of discourse. Autosegmental licensing is similar in that it proscribes connections between a primary licensing agent such as a syllable or a secondary licensing (e.g., a coda) agent and a segment. It is through this linkage that there can be a direct connection to the level that determines the stress pattern.

Metrical Phonology

Another piece of the integrated picture that Goldsmith (1990) presents is metrical phonology, which was originally proposed as an independent theory (Liberman, 1979; Liberman and Prince, 1977). There are two versions of this theory, differing in the formal nature of the representation, with one involving a metrical grid and one involving a tree structure. The differences are not critical for this discussion, and, in fact, they share many characteristics. Metrical phonology has as its focus the relative prominence of syllables, feet, words, and larger units in the hierarchical representation. Unlike generative phonology, stress is treated as something very different from other aspects of phonology. Stress patterns are determined by rhythm (alternating prominence) and syllable weight. The levels of representation, syllable components (only the rhyme in the tree structure version) marked alternatingly as strong or weak, are organized into units at the next level termed *feet,* also marked strong and weak. At the next level these are organized to form phonological words, which are not necessarily equivalent to our standard notion of word. The unit boundaries for a phonological word are specified for a given language in terms of the meter or foot structure.

Some other characteristics of metrical phonology that should be noted are the mechanisms and constraints responsible for ensuring a well-formed metrical structure. For example, the syllable integrity principle prevents prosodic structures from conflicting with syllable structure. Grid structure generation is governed by three rules. The first is called the *end rule.* It marks the left or right end of the unit at the level on which it is operating (e.g., foot). The *perfect grid rule* moves across a word, assigning grid marks to every other slot. Finally, there is a rule for grid construction that corrects the results of the preceding rule to ensure that the first portion of a heavy syllable is stressed.

Lexical Phonology

The last major piece of the synthesized formalism is lexical phonology. Lexical phonology includes a lexical component and a postlexical component. Postlexical, or phrasal, phonology is concerned with filling in the nondistinctive or underspecified features that are not present in phonological representations. It also contains rules that operate across word boundaries or are conditioned by syntactic or phrasal characteristics. The lexical component deals only with distinctive features of phonology (e.g., voicing for vowels). It also includes two rule types. The first are those that occur when two morphemes are combined (e.g., the velar softening when *electric* becomes *electricity*). The other type of lexical rule changes an underlying form, so that a segmental structure will not violate phototactic well-formedness conditions. This is one of the points of overlap with autosegmental phonology. The general structure also involves a further division into strata, or levels. Each contains a set of affixation processes and phonological rules. Rules may be applied cyclically, which serves as a mechanism of stress assignment. The theory adds three important notions: (1) underspecification, (2) phrasal phonology, and (3) the link between phonology and morphology that is provided (inflectional morphology).

There are two versions of underspecification theory. In the first, the representation is assumed to contain only nonredundant, nonpredictable features (e.g., height of a vowel). In the other version, the representation contains only marked features, so that the redundancy is only relative to the other value of the feature. Phrasal phonology provides an important link across words in phonological conditioning. For example, rules governing syllabification (where the syllable boundaries within a word change because of the influence of a phrasal context), fusion (where consonants are fused into a single articulatory gesture across word boundaries), and assimilation may have an effect across some words. These effects may provide important information about planning and perceptual units in performance and about the reality of such units in representation.

Feature Geometry

A final aspect of recent theoretical work in phonology concerns not what features are represented as in underspecification or the relationship of features to other levels of representation but the relationship of features to each other. In the traditional approach, features, with the exception of some major class features, are represented as a simultaneous bundle of segment characteristics. The goal was simply description and classification of observable events (i.e., positivism). There are two such general approaches. The first is based on information categories (e.g., position of the articulators, which can be achieved by any one or grouping of articulators), and the second is a view in which articulators are viewed as independent. These characterizations have three limitations: (1) they fail to describe relationships among features (e.g., stress is not realized directly phonetically but is realized as a set of features), (2) there may be a feature that is classificatory (e.g., vowels) that has only a temporal and not a discrete articulatory realization, and (3) there may be more abstract characteristics (e.g., inflectional changes that affect some words but not others that are phonologically similar, e.g., *wolf/wolves* vs *cliff/cliffs;* Goldsmith, 1990).

The alternatives are varying types of feature geometries, each of which places each feature on a separate tier. The two primary types differ in that one (Mohanan, 1983) represents hierarchical relationships using *class nodes* (e.g., place), which are then connected to features at lower levels (e.g., labial, coronal, dorsal, tongue root) and at a higher level (e.g., supralaryngeal). The other alternative represents features equivalently rather than hierarchically. Because of its graphical representation, this model has been called a *Rolodex,* bottle-brush, or spiral notebook model. Briefly, the timing unit of the skeletal tier is at the center, and the individual features radiate out from this central core. The features can be connected at the periphery, and ultimately, with sufficient connections, they can be higher-order features. The primary difference between the two versions is that in the first version the nature of multiple feature assimilation is highly restricted, whereas assimilation in the Rolodex model is minimally restricted. At least conceptually, it is also easier to envision how the latter model would accommodate assimilation across unit boundaries, along the skeleton.

I have provided an outline of only the major characteristics of these theoretical advances (Table 6–1). A great deal of detail has been omitted. Goldsmith (1990) provides a far more detailed discussion of many features of these theories and a more extensive reference list.

To summarize, we have a theory that provides a representational structure and a framework of rules, conventions, conditions, and units in which it may be easier to characterize many of the phenomena of adult phonology and, perhaps, some of the characteristics of young children's phonologies. Importantly, it is a theory that is more readily linked to other aspects of language, particularly syntax, morphology, and the lexicon. It also is not restricted to units of word, phrase, or even sentence length. However, in most respects the theory may have descriptive but not explanatory adequacy with respect to normal or disordered development. That is consistent with the goal of presenting a theory of how abstract phonological information is

TABLE 6–1.
Summary of Nonlinear Phonologies

Theory	Primary Structures	Conventions
Autosegmental	Hierarchically related but independent levels with autosegments. Tiers include, segmental, skeletal (timing and syllable structure), tonal. Association lines link tiers.	Association lines cannot cross. Association and linkage conventions govern association lines.
Metrical	Grid or tree structure, including syllables, feet, words, and larger units.	End rule, perfect grid, syllable integrity all work to create sequences of weak/strong, stressed/unstressed units.
Lexical	Phonology separated into lexical and postlexical rules and further division into strata (levels). Each level includes affixation processes and phonological rules. Underspecification theory provides for minimal representations. Phrasal phonology is provided.	Structure preservation and filters constrain structures. Rules are applied in cycles.
Feature geometry		
Type 1	Class nodes connected to features at lower levels and at a higher level.	Highly restricted multiple feature assimilation.
Type 2	Rolodex model with timing tier at center.	Minimally restricted assimilation.

stored and manipulated. To attain Goldsmith's (1990) goal of being able to use this theory to specify the underpinnings of perception, processing, and production, it needs to be compatible with a theory of processing and a theory of development. Though the phonological theory is still somewhat fragmented, it does provide a representation of phonological knowledge that may well be far more compatible with processing and learning theories than generative phonology.

REPRESENTATIONAL AND ALGORITHMIC LEVEL: DEVELOPMENTAL THEORY

Current Versions of Nativist Theories

What is available to us as a developmental theory? One notion that has been popular in generative theory was that the child selects the simplest available grammar that is compatible with the characteristics of the input and the universal grammar. Important assumptions of this view are that the child constructs and tests hypotheses against the data of the input and that adequate theories place sufficient constraints on the problem space so that it contains an accessible and correct solution. Formal simplicity is a primary guiding metric in this version. However, we have already seen that simplicity metrics may conflict with naturalness. In fact, it is relatively easy to find examples in children's phonologies that suggest that simplicity is not always the guiding principle. Another perspective is that there is a core grammar that cannot be deduced from available data. From this perspective, the child comes to the task with a group of parameters set in default positions. The settings can be changed, however, with the appropriate environmental triggers. The task is to select (i.e., deduce) the correct core from the grammars specified by the universal grammar. Underlying this formulation are the assumptions that grammars are not different across individuals exposed to the same input and that there is an algorithm that will yield the adult grammar when provided with the appropriate input (i.e., the language is learnable).

Inherent in this view is that the final grammar cannot be more complex than the input in combination with the child's initial state. It is really on this point that the current nativist view rests. Because the input is assumed to be limited (i.e., impoverished) and corrupted by noise and errors, a large portion of the grammar must be innately specified. However, this means that the system is entropic (Mohanan, 1989a). The notion is that one cannot create complexity out of simplicity (Fodor, 1981). Though this is an appealing notion, there are several problems. Often children appear to create systems more complex than that of the environment (Leonard, 1985). Furthermore, the invocation of formal simplicity as the guiding principle is a rather strange one in light of the apparent complexities in rules and constraints across languages. Across generations, the complexity does not seem to decrease (Mohanan, 1989a). Surely the solution is to attribute any such complexity to the core grammar. However, at best, that begs the question rather than provides an hypothesis that is falsifiable. The acquisition mechanisms proposed to date (e.g., morphological paradigms in Pinker, 1984) do not have much to offer. They are vague at best, offering an arraylike checklist that is not theoretically motivated. Nor does it provide any description of the process by which the array is either filled in or a control mechanism that determines when the paradigm has been filled. Despite the extent to which biology is viewed as the source of development, this view seems to have little to offer in terms of a specific algorithm for the acquisition of phonology.

Connectionist Models

I have been interested for some time in computer models of human cognition. There are two things that interest me. The first is the use of simulations as models for heuristic purposes. The goal of any kind of model making is to take a piece of the real world and recreate it in a way that preserves its basic character (or even a metaphor of its characteristics) in such a way that two things are accomplished. The model permits a level of control over a natural phenomenon that might otherwise not be possible. It forces an understanding of the workings of the system that might not be present in more passive observation. The most important issue is that a model must provide accurate predictions of reality. Without a reasonably high level of accuracy, a model will easily lose its credibility. The second reason for my interest is that I have become quite convinced that some recent models are capable of providing a plausible model of certain aspects of human language learning.

My interest began with traditional artificial intelligence (AI) models such as production systems. However interesting and important these were, they proved to be unsuccessful as developmental models. They simply did not develop but were better at modeling a single point in developmental time. In addition to traditional AI models, or in their place (depending on the author), a resurrected and enhanced approach has emerged. The paradigm has been varyingly termed *connectionist networks,* parallel distributed processing, or neural networks. There are several general reasons for the appeal of these networks as potential models of certain cognitive processes, most centering on their differences from traditional AI architecture. Briefly, connectionist networks seem more representative of certain aspects of brain structure and of what some view as a subsymbolic or microstructure level of cognition. They are composed of relatively similar, highly connected units that operate in a parallel rather than a serial fashion. However, I should note that the issue of level at which the model is aimed is an important one (Smolensky, 1988). They have activation levels that are determined by the sum of weights of the excitatory connections to the unit minus the weights of any inhibitory connections. Representations are generally distributed over a number of units rather than localized in single location. Perhaps the greatest appeal is that these networks are, using various procedures, adaptive; AI architectures are not. It is most certainly this feature that interests industry and the defense department. One can create an architecture and a learning algorithm and provide some input and the network "learns." Finally, connectionist networks do not have explicit rules provided to them. Instead, their "rule behavior" results from pattern extraction from input and probabilistic or frequency-based output behavior. They thus can begin with a structure and can readily discover structure in the input.

It is certainly interesting and important to consider what might go into the construction of such a model and what its output might be (Stemberger, in press). However, it is limiting in the same way that conducting a thought experiment about language acquisition might be. One simply is not able to see the reality of the outcome. Also, having data seems to promote a level of understanding of reality that is impossible to attain in either a thought experiment or in a box and line representation of such a model. Consequently, a few years ago some engineering colleagues and I embarked on a collaboration to create various forms of connectionist network simulations (Tenorio et al., 1989).

We decided to begin by examining

one particular network, termed *NETtalk,* designed by Sejnowski and Rosenberg (1986). This network is designed to learn to convert text to speech, like a number of now-available hardware devices, except that it does this with a neural network. In some commercially available devices, the conversion is made using a look-up dictionary and a set of preprogrammed pronunciation rules. NETtalk has units at three levels: input, hidden, and output. These units are massively interconnected, and all weights are initially set randomly. Each unit has a variable threshold. Thereafter, the network is provided with input of orthographic symbols (29 units plus punctuation and word boundary markers) and a corresponding broad phonetic transcription (in the features to be described). The orthographic input is moved through the network in windows of seven units, with the central unit being the target; this allows the network to learn some minimal context information. The hidden units never receive direct input or output. Instead they serve as internal representations of the text-to-phoneme mapping. As indicated earlier, the representation is not contained in a single location but instead is distributed. It is contained in the weights of the connections from the input units to the hidden units and from the hidden units to the output units. The output units are phonological features (21 features, primary stress, syllable boundaries, and word boundaries). Outside the actual network is a program that converts the output unit activations (features) to a phoneme and, in turn, can be connected to a speech synthesizer to produce speech.

The letters are moved through the center window one at a time. The window is coded for the input units in a binary code (a word including a 0 or a 1 for each orthographic possibility). A letter unit with the highest activation (closest word to the input; errors can be made) reaches threshold and "fires." Depending on the strength of connections to the hidden units, one of the hidden units will fire and will, in turn, activate a set of three feature units (e.g., place, manner, and voicing). This yields an output vector. This vector is then compared to a set of vectors provided by the programmer, and the program is designed to choose the closest match (called a "best guess") or to look for a perfect match. (If a match is not found, there is no output.) During training, the differences between the phoneme vector chosen and the output are back-propagated through the network to adjust the weights in a way that improves subsequent performance. The procedure was to provide an input set (e.g., a dictionary of 1,000 words or a connected speech sample of about 1,000 words) in both orthographic and phonetic symbols for a set number of times (e.g., 50) and then to present new text (without phonetic symbols and without back propagation adjustments) as a test of the network.

We undertook this work knowing that it was a strange architecture with which to examine speech development, but there were some appealing features: there was some notion of temporal relationships, the potential for representing larger units (syllables and words), multiple layers, and a two-level input. As it was structured, the network could be viewed as a crude metaphor of phonological acquisition. The network begins with a structure (units, connections, weights, thresholds that control output from one level to the next). It is provided with an input that is coded (possibly represented of perception) and a set of output units. So in a very general fashion, the network experiments might be considered a model of the input-perception-output mapping. We were also motivated by Sejnowski and Rosenberg's (1986) characterization of early stages of learning as babbling and their claim that the errors made in the course of learning were comparable with those made by young children in the course of early speech learning.

We made some technical modifications in the network but most notably added features to represent phonemes that would allow us to examine another language mapping. We chose Spanish because of its contrast with English in its orthographic transparency. In addition, we conducted a number of experiments in which we used different input sets, varying window sizes, and some other modifications to explore the general properties of the network. I will summarize the major findings and then turn to the general nature of such networks and their implications for models of processing and development.

As Sejnowski and Rosenberg (1986) found, the network, in fact, learns to translate text to speech. By the 50th pass of the English input set, the network performs at a level of accuracy of more than 90%. New text is converted to phonemes at a level of accuracy approaching 90%. The Spanish simulation is even more convincing. By the tenth pass through the input set, the network surpasses the English network at the end of its training. We also attempted to extend the training of these networks in two ways. The first was to continue training, which caused some interesting fluctuations, decreases in accuracy, and then a return to more accurate performance with some minimal gains. The second was to train each of the networks in the other language. The transition from English to Spanish seemed to be quite easy (i.e., rapidly successful). However, the Spanish to English transition was more difficult. The network never achieved a high level of accuracy or stability. In both cases it is important to note that the original text-to-phoneme mapping was not retained. Testing with the first language mapping never yielded the same level of accuracy as it did before the second mapping was trained.

The findings regarding the general characteristics of the network output and the pattern of learning are also interesting to consider. In its early stages of learning, the network's output did not sound like any babbling I have ever heard. However, it should be remembered that we really did not do a very good job with the initial state of the network; it was set randomly. The initial state might have been set more realistically. The errors later in the learning phase were in some respects very much like those that are made by both typically developing and atypically developing children. We found consonant omissions and errors involving consonant substitutions. In some cases the errors reflected connected speech simplifications (e.g., omitted consonants and neutralized vowels) that were present in the phonetic transcription of the input set. However, the output was not simply a reflection of the input. Such patterns were generalized beyond their scope in the input. Furthermore, in some cases substitutions not present in the input were generalized to other targets in the output.

There were, however, a number of characteristics of the learning and the output that were not comparable with the patterns seen in young children. For example, despite the architecture, the network did not adequately represent contextual or temporal information. As a result, there was no differentiation of the beginnings and ends of words (omissions occurred with equal frequency), nor were there any instances of assimilation. There were also some unexpected substitutions that may reflect differences in the initial state of the network or errors in coding of the input that reflect our failure to create a coding system that might have been a more accurate representation of a child's perception of speech. Notably, because strength in the network is based on frequency, the marking of primary stress that was included did not have the impact (saliency, duration, etc.) that it normally has in speech production or perception. Perhaps most important in light of the earlier theoretical discussion is the absence of hierarchically related levels of units. Despite its multiple levels, this network functions as a linear model.

We are currently exploring alternative architectures that will address some of these limitations. A final issue concerns the initial state and the input to such models. In our earlier experiments we employed connected speech (with simplifications), a dictionary (with no errors), and a child's speech (with errors) on different occasions. The input a child has comes from a combination of sources. We certainly have to do better in the network representation of the units and their structural relationships. The network does not need to be preformed, but the potential for hierarchical relationships and constraints needs to be included. The idea of a random set of weights seems an obvious misrepresentation. As I indicated at the beginning of the chapter, the child clearly comes with some set structure and predispositions to such a task, certainly not a random state.

Until we can find a way to construct a network with those possibilities, it might be useful to begin with a network "trained to babble." In cases where the goal is to simulate a particular aspect of phonology, it might be useful to provide input so that a network converging to the desired state is achieved. For example, a network can be created in which final consonant omission or a flapping rule is established in some predetermined fashion. The scope of errors or rules can then be examined. The advantage is that with the network the input characteristics can be reconfigured and presented anew to create a different condition. To date, networks like this have not been treated in this more constrained fashion. Usually more general questions have been asked of such networks (e.g., learning to provide a past tense of a large pool of verbs, when presented with the present tense). Perhaps at this point in the development of such models and in our knowledge of language acquisition, such models are being overdriven.

It seems to me that connectionism is at a dangerous point in its development. It has come under strong criticism from theoreticians and empirical researchers who cling strongly to traditional symbolic accounts. A number of researchers who have been actively involved in designing and exploring connectionist models have not been careful to ensure that their models are accurate in their representations of reality. Examples include characterizing comprehension and production as simply going in and out of a single network or claiming that a network has modeled the stages of past tense acquisition by simply manipulating the input over stages, in a way not representative of normal development. Placing such networks in opposition to rule-based systems proposed by linguists by claiming that such systems operate without rules also has placed connectionism at risk. In our own work we have found evidence from cluster analyses of connection weights that rules are formed based on patterns present in the input and, on occasion, by the network if it becomes "stuck" in some output pattern (i.e., a local minimum). Unfortunately, connectionist models have generated such excitement in cognitive science and in other areas that it takes on the feel of a cult (Smolensky, 1988). A new methodology and theoretical framework need to have the same opportunity to grow, and perhaps prove to be inadequate, as traditional AI architectures.

Dynamical System Model

I want to leave this computational implementation that fits Marr's middle algorithmic level (in Smolensky's characterization this might actually be considered to be a model at the level of hardware implementation) and consider a more general view of this level, the framework of initial state, growth, and structure that underlies many such architectures. This is the notion of a dynamical system in which structure emerges through self-organization of apparent chaos. A number of individuals (Goldsmith, 1990; Kent and Hodge, 1990; Mohanan, 1989b) have suggested the application of principles underlying such models from physics and biology. If we were to adopt such a framework, we would still view the child as coming to the language learning task with genetic or biological predispositions realized in the structure and relationships among the speech-motor, auditory, and visual mechanisms. Furthermore, I would assume that the environment places constraints on the child's linguistic growth without assuming the rigid imposition of environmental features. As Mohanan (1989b) points out, the developmental question of interest becomes how a grammar emerges in an individual through interaction with the environment. This is not qualitatively different from the emergence of other patterns in nature, such as the learning of cues to the location of pollen in honey bees, where biological predisposition interacts with the environment and the experience of the organism (Locke, 1990; Mohanan, 1989b). It is important to note that the grammar would then be assumed to be a representation of an individual's knowledge, not the knowledge of the community. The two would certainly correspond in important ways but underlyingly the representation of the individual's knowledge would allow substantial room for individual variation. As such, it is somewhat easier to conceive of phonological development that reflects limitations of the auditory or articulatory mechanisms (whether normal or impaired), communicative needs (perhaps best exemplified by children with articulatory abilities that do not coincide with their communicative abilities). It is apparent that a phonology that develops under conditions of limitation (e.g., a cleft palate) is different from one that develops under normal conditions. Even when the structural limitation is eliminated, the phonology may remain intact.

Mohanan (1989b) has outlined some of the initial details of such a model. The primary mechanism of structure is an attractor. In a physical system (as well as in parts of a larger system) the state may be characterized in terms of temperature or an energy level. At a macro level, as energy (heat to use the temperature metaphor) is introduced to a system, the system is chaotic. At a certain point, however, there may be a phase transition (e.g., the example of cold water coming to a boil and changing to steam). At a micro level, structures called attractors are formed, or existing attractors may be strengthened. These attractors represent structures (segments or features, as Kent and Hodge, 1990, suggest). Mohanan (1989b) has suggested some preliminaries in the application of such a notion to phonological acquisition and phenomena of phonologies across languages (e.g., variation in assimilation rules, vowel reduction). Because of the nature of such emergent structures, they are necessarily gradient rather than binary in nature. If the rule system is reconceptualized within such a structure, it would then permit variation that may remain or disappear gradually over time with the increasing or decreasing strength of such a structure. Furthermore, attractors may be considered to interact in a variety of ways (reinforcing, inhibiting, dominating, etc.). It is possible to imagine all sorts of differing paths to development, normal as well as disordered, some arising from the child's own misperceptions or misproductions (Leonard, 1985, 1989). Finally, the stronger role given to the environment more readily allows us to take into account the interaction of other aspects of language and knowledge on the acquisition phonology.

If indeed a paradigm shift occurs that turns toward nonlinear phonology and toward a dynamical systems view of phonological acquisition, we will need to be concerned with the nature of our data. For the most part, we impose a good many assumptions on children's phonologies as we look at them for either research or clinical purposes. To name a few, we assume that adults provide children with access to citation forms of words, we assume that children perceive and store this input accurately, we assume that the level of the segment is primary, we assume that other aspects of language are not directly relevant to phonology (and that phonology is not directly relevant to other aspects of language), and we assume that children's phonologies are simpler than those of the environment and any complexity that emerges must be present at the outset. Many of these may be wrong. Certainly all of these are open to empirical examination.

IMPLICATIONS FOR PROCESS MODELS

To return briefly to the topic of this chapter, it is interesting to consider what these frameworks of dynamical systems and nonlinear phonology might mean for process models. First, when a dynamical systems model is used, there are different degrees of organization across development, with a general trend from lack of organization to greater organization. As the strength of attractors develops, they tend to become more fixed (i.e., they have more inertia) and leave less opportunity for changes in overall organization. Thus, there is a general trend toward an adultlike state. However, along the way the child's system will reach points of equilibrium (or a series of local minima) that require some push (from the child or from the environment) to overcome the inertia. At these equilibrium points we might be able to find empirical approaches that will reveal the nature of the child's knowledge structure. We would need data of a different nature than we have typically collected. For the most part, we tend to collect data that is somehow dichotomous in nature (e.g., phoneme discrimination in syllables) rather than the gradient behaviors that might reflect the relationships among attractors characterized earlier. It is important to note that though there is a trend toward increasing organization, this model does not entail an assumption of an endpoint. Organization is a continuing process.

A second point concerning this dynamical system approach is the assumed relationships between the child and the environment. In each of the developmental frameworks discussed in the introduction to this chapter there is some commitment to either the environment or to the child as the prime mover of development. In a dynamical system (Mohanan, 1989a), both play active roles. The environment certainly imposes structure. In turn, the child's linguistic and biological potential and existing structure (which varies from individual to individual) impose structure on the environment. In this way the individual can be seen as source of linguistic change (Mohanan, 1989).

Finally, both nonlinear phonologies and dynamical systems provide a representational and developmental framework that has the potential for being highly interactive with respect to other aspects of language. It does not seem to me that within these frameworks it is reasonable to assume the modular encapsulation of various components of language (e.g., syntax, phonology, lexicon).

Instead, under some circumstances these components of language are bidirectionally interactive. Furthermore, the nature of environmental impact might imply a structure of phonology or a lexicon that is, at least in part, influenced by the events in which language is embedded.

IMPLICATIONS FOR DEVELOPMENTAL PHONOLOGICAL DISORDERS

I have alluded to some clinical considerations in my discussion of these theoretical frameworks, but they are worth considering more directly. The first general consideration is what the frameworks offer in terms of descriptive vs. explanatory adequacy. Clinicians have been presented with a number of linguistic frameworks that have claimed to describe and explain phonological disorders. To date, actual achievements in either area have been particularly limited. Generative phonology fails on both counts for reasons I addressed earlier. Natural phonology (phonological processes), which has gained great acceptance, actually has had limited success in describing some children's error patterns and has limitations in explaining why disorders might occur. Though it certainly is too early to evaluate either the theoretical or developmental frameworks I have presented here, they have some features that suggest advantages over earlier frameworks.

Three clinical issues come to mind. The first has to do with the interaction between phonology and other aspects of language in children with phonological disorders. Commonly, children seen in clinics exhibit errors that go beyond word boundaries (see Stemberger, 1988, for a review of patterns in normally developing children). Current frameworks do not describe such patterns. Variability within and across children also poses a descriptive problem for frameworks that do not allow for gradient rule application or gradient learning.

One of the characteristics of phonologically disordered children is that they appear to be variable not only in their own behavior but also in their characteristics across the population. Nonlinear phonologies include constraints (licensing, hierarchical relationships, etc.) that will reveal the bases for some of these patterns. A dynamical systems model, with its assumption that behaviors are gradient and that grammars are representations of individual knowledge, may, describe and possibly explain variability and individual variation.

Another issue that I raised earlier concerns situations in which children seem to have phonologies that are, in some respects, more complex than that of the target language (Leonard, 1985). To date there is no model of normal or disordered development that would predict the types of phonological systems that emerge and persist in some children. Because of the mechanisms of structure formation in the dynamical systems model, it is possible to imagine how a child might fall into patterns not present in the environment of the child. Furthermore, it is possible to understand the way in which a child's own productions might lead to the establishment of phonological organization, sometimes in a direction away from that of the target phonology (Leonard, 1989).

Finally, the theories I have presented may have important implications for the inference of underlying representation in phonologically disordered children. Recently, McGregor and Schwartz, in press, have examined the phonology of a 4-year-old child who appeared to produce all fricative and affricate targets as voiced or voiceless. In some frameworks it might have been assumed that this child had limited knowledge of a separable set of fricatives and a differentiated pair of affricates. On closer examination, there was convincing acoustic and perceptual evidence of far more knowledge than our first look revealed. Furthermore, some aspects of the data suggested a hierarchical organization of features within this child's fricative class consistent with the type of description provided by Goldsmith (1990).

A great deal of work remains before we see clinical applications. However, from both a descriptive and an explanatory standpoint, nonlinear phonology and dynamical systems seem to offer more than previous proposals. Providing the necessary details for such applications may be a valuable addition to our clinical procedures and may reveal critical strengths and weaknesses of the theories themselves.

If we can shift the focus of our experimental questions and our data analysis to reflect the kind of detail needed to explore hierarchical, self-organizing systems of phonology, perhaps we will have an opportunity to swim awhile with a more attractive theory.

REFERENCES

Chomsky N, Halle M: *The sound pattern of English.* New York, Harper & Row, Publishers, 1968.

Fodor J: *Representations.* Cambridge, MA, MIT Press, 1981.

Goldsmith J: *Autosegmental and Metrical Phonology.* Cambridge, Mass, Basil Blackwell, 1990.

Gould J: Natural history of honey bee learning, in Marler P, Terrace H (eds): *The Biology of Learning.* New York, Springer-Verlag New York, 1984, pp 149–180.

Gould J, Marler P: Learning by instinct. *Am Scientist* 1987; 255:74–85.

Grimshaw J: *Argument Structure.* Cambridge, Mass, MIT Press, 1990.

Ingram D: Underspecification theory and phonological acquisition. Vancouver, University of British Columbia, 1989 (unpublished).

Kent R, Hodge M: The biogenesis of speech: Continuity and process in early speech and language development, in Miller J (ed): *Research on Child Language Disorders.* Austin, Tex, Pro-Ed, 1990, pp 25–54.

Leonard L: Unusual and subtle phonological behavior in the speech of phonologically disordered children. *J Speech Hear Disord* 1985; 50:4–13.

Leonard L: Children with phonological disorders. Paper presented at the International Conference on Developmental Phonology, Stanford, Calif, Stanford University, 1989.

Liberman M: *The Intonation of English.* New York, Garland Press, 1979.

Liberman M, Prince A: On stress and linguistic rhythm. *Linguist Inquiry* 1977; 8:249–336.

Locke J: Structure and ontogeny of spoken language. *Dev Psychobiol* 1990; 23:621–643.

Marr D: *Vision.* New York, WH Freeman & Co, 1982.

McGregor K, Schwartz R: Converging evidence for underlying phonological representation. *J Speech Hearing Res* (in press).

Mohanan K: The structure of the melody. Cambridge, Mass, Massachusetts Institute of Technology, 1983 (unpublished).

Mohanan K: Universal attractors in phonology. Stanford, Calif. Stanford University, 1989a (unpublished).

Mohanan K: Emergence of complexity in phonological systems. Paper presented at the International Conference on Phonological Development, Stanford, Calif, Stanford University, 1989b.

Pinker S: *Language Learnability and Language Development.* Cambridge, MA, Harvard University Press, 1984.

Sejnowski T, Rosenberg C: Parallel networks that learn to pronounce English text. *Complex Systems* 1986; 1:145–168.

Smolensky P: On the proper treatment of connectionism. *Behav Brain Sci* 1988; 11:1–74.

Stemberger J: Between word processes in child phonology. *J Child Lang* 1988; 15:39–61.

Stemberger J: A connectionist view of child phonology: Phonological processing without the processes, in Ferguson C, Menn L, and Stoel-Gammon C (eds): *Developmental Phonology*. Parkton, Md: York Press (in press).

Tenorio M, Tom D, Schwartz RG: Adaptive networks as a model for human speech development. Lafayette, Ind, Purdue University, 1989 (unpublished).

7 The Role of Prosodic Variables in Language Processing by Children With Specific Language Impairment

Susan Ellis Weismer, Ph.D.

The purpose of this chapter is to consider the role of certain prosodic variables in language processing and acquisition by children with specific language impairment (SLI) (Lahey, 1988). These children experience difficulties in oral language abilities that cannot be attributed to emotional disturbance, hearing loss, deficits in oral motor function, or general intelligence. Recently the focus of researchers' attention has been shifting from sole concern with SLI children's linguistic knowledge and competence as the basis of language disorders to consideration of the impact of processing skills on linguistic knowledge (Tallal, 1988). This perspective was clearly reflected in the topics of researchers at the recent symposium on research on child language disorders (Curtiss, 1991; Johnston, 1991; Schwartz, 1991).

It is well documented that SLI children demonstrate various types of information processing deficits, including auditory perceptual deficits (see comprehensive reviews by Johnston, 1988; Tallal, 1988). Yet there is a paucity of research investigating how the manner in which the linguistic signal is presented affects language-impaired children's ability to process linguistic information and learn the rules of the language. Prosodic characteristics of linguistic input are easily manipulated and have the potential to influence various levels of linguistic processing (McNeil and Kimelman, 1986). It can be hypothesized that input manipulations of this type could offer a means of reducing the processing demands of the language learning task such that SLI children could allocate more attentional resources to the new target form being acquired.

Prosodic or suprasegmental features of the language extend across the phonetic segments of utterances and include rhythm, pauses, length, stress, and intonation (Bolinger, 1972; Crystal, 1975). The particular prosodic features of interest for this discussion are stress and speaking rate. The primary acoustic cues for prosodic features of utterances consist of fundamental frequency, intensity, and temporal pattern (duration and rate) (Freeman, 1982); however, the relation between the acoustic and perceptual attributes of prosody are often complex (as in the case of stress). The term "stress" is used in the literature to refer to both emphatic (or contrastive) stress and unemphatic lexical or sentential stress. The concern in this chapter is primarily with emphatic stress. Emphatic stress serves as a focusing device, and its placement within the utterance is more dependent on situational or pragmatic factors than grammatical or semantic factors (Bean et al., 1989).

As will be discussed, there is evidence from the normal acquisition literature that stress and rate are modified in speech addressed to young children (Chapman, 1981). In experimental studies, stress and rate manipulations have been demonstrated to affect linguistic processing in normal language (NL) individuals (Bean et al., 1989; Schmitt and Moore, 1989) and individuals with various types of language and learning deficits (Campbell and McNeil, 1985; Kimelman and McNeil, 1987; McNutt and Chia-Yen Li, 1980; Pashek and Brookshire, 1982). These studies have focused primarily on adults rather than SLI children and have not addressed language learning issues, that is, the effects of stress and rate modifications have been assessed only in terms of comprehension and use of known language forms. A preliminary investigation by Ellis Weismer et al. (1990) indicates that prosodic manipulations of the linguistic models provided to SLI children can facilitate their lexical learning.

The organization of this chapter is as follows: Evidence of processing deficits in SLI children will first be summarized, followed by a review of investigations of prosodic variables. Theoretical assumptions underlying this line of inquiry will then be considered, and implications for clinical intervention will be discussed.

PROCESSING DEFICITS IN LANGUAGE-IMPAIRED CHILDREN

Research has documented deficits in various aspects of SLI children's cognitive functioning from lower-level perceptual skills to higher-level representational and problem-solving abilities. Difficulties at any point in the processing stream are likely to result in learning problems. The conceptual knowledge base and global representational skills a child possesses will impact on the ability to process new input, that is, what the child knows will shape what can be learned and remembered (Chi, 1983; Keil, 1984). Conversely, dynamic on-line processing constraints at the attentional, perceptual, or short-term memory level will limit the encoding and storage of information in terms of some type of useful long-term representation. Various nonlinguistic information processing deficits have been found in SLI children, including limitations in visual imagery (Savich, 1984; Johnston and Ellis Weismer, 1983), hypothesis testing and analogical reasoning (Ellis Weismer, 1991; Ellis Weismer, et al., 1989; Kamhi et al., 1990; Nelson et al., 1987; Nippold et al., 1988), inference construction (Ellis Weismer, 1985), and dimensional thinking (Johnston and Smith, 1989). Children with SLI also exhibit limitations in verbal memory. Kirchner and Klatzky (1985) found that SLI children were deficient across various components of memory compared with age-matched peers and interpreted this in terms of limited resource capacity (Norman and Bobrow, 1975).

Numerous investigations by Tallal and colleagues have consistently demonstrated that SLI children are impaired in their ability to discriminate and sequence (and therefore remember) rapidly presented nonverbal stimuli (Johnston et al., 1981; Tallal and Piercy, 1973, 1974; Tallal et al., 1981, 1985). This finding has been replicated across studies using nonverbal auditory, visual, tactile, and cross-modal stimuli. Results indicate that the amount of time SLI children require for sensory information processing is orders of magnitude greater than that of NL children and that there is no significant difference between SLI and NL children on tasks of temporal integration when stimuli are presented more slowly. Investigations by Tallal and associates have also addressed the relationship between nonverbal processing deficits and language disorders. It has been found that SLI children have specific difficulty processing speech sounds characterized by rapidly changing acoustic spectra (Tallal and Piercy, 1974, 1975; Tallal and Stark, 1981) and that their speech production errors follow the same pattern as speech perception (Tallal et al., 1980). Tallal et al. (1985) also have found that the degree of temporal perceptual impairment is highly predictive of receptive language deficits in SLI children.

There is an extensive literature on central auditory processing (CAP) disorders in children (Keith, 1981; Levinson and Sloan, 1980; Singer and Hurley, 1985). Broad-based definitions of CAP have been proposed that encompass all central processes operating on auditory stimuli. For instance, CAP has been defined by Lasky and Katz (1983, p. 4) as "the manipulation and utilization of sound signals by the central nervous system—what we do with what we hear." Varying criteria have been employed in identifying children with CAP disorders, including definitions that would include many children with specific language impairment. Debates exist as to whether the nature of these children's difficulties is primarily auditory perceptual or linguistic, with some researchers urging consideration of the interactive influences of perceptual, linguistic, and cognitive factors (Duchan and Katz, 1983; Lasky, 1983). Because of the range of criteria used to identify CAP disorders and the fact that some children with no evident language or learning problems also experience difficulty on various CAP tasks (Keith, 1984), certain investigators have questioned the usefulness of the construct of central auditory processing disorders (Kamhi and Baesley, 1985).

INVESTIGATIONS OF PROSODIC VARIABLES

Observations of Normal Language Development

The "Motherese" (or child-directed speech) literature indicates that various prosodic modifications occur in the input provided during the early stages of normal language development. Mothers speak at a slower rate to 2-year-olds than to older children and adults (Broen, 1972; Cross, 1977). They stress more than one element in a sentence and produce longer durations of content words in commands, as well as using exaggerated intonational contours (Garnica, 1977). In child directed speech, pauses more predictably mark utterance boundaries than they do in adult conversations, occurring after each sentence or single word (Broen, 1972). It has been hypothesized that these types of modifications in the speech directed to young children facilitate comprehension in some way by aiding in the segmentation process and increasing the saliency of certain linguistic constructions.

Research on normal language acquisition in English-speaking children and cross-linguistic research both point to the importance of stress in particular as a factor in language learning. For example, Slobin's (1982) data on acquisition of relational roles indicate that children comprehend Turkish inflectional cues to relational roles earlier in life than children learning Serbo-Croatian. The inflectional cues in Turkish are stressed, a full syllable long, and do not deform surrounding elements phonetically (designated as "open class," Kean, 1977) in contrast to those in Serbo-Croatian, which are unstressed, subsyllabic, and phonetically deformed by adjacent material ("closed class"). Gleitman and Wanner (1982) have interpreted these different rates in the emergence of relational roles as supporting the principle that stressed material enjoys an advantage over unstressed material in language development.

EXPERIMENTAL STUDIES

Rate

A number of experimental studies have examined the effects of manipulating speaking rate on normal and language-disordered individuals' linguistic processing. Investigations of rate modifications have used either electronically altered (time-compressed or time-expanded) speech (Lass et al., 1984) or natural, speaker-generated alterations in rate. There is considerable variability in what are considered to be fast, normal, and slow rates of speech. A standard for "normal" rate that has been used in a number of investigations of rate manipulation is roughly 175 words/min or approximately 4 syllables/sec (McNutt and Chia-Yen Li, 1980; Schmitt and Moore, 1989). "Fast" and "slow" rates have been associated with varying percentages of the normal rate such that slow rates, for example, may correspond to 60% expansion ($\geq$2 syllables/sec) and fast rates to 60% compression ($\geq$6 syllables/sec).

Elderly adult listeners have been shown to demonstrate significantly reduced auditory comprehension of passages presented at fast speaking rates compared with normal rates (Schmitt, 1983; Schmitt and Carroll, 1985; Schmitt and Moore, 1989). There is evidence that slower rates of speech lead to improved auditory comprehension for adult aphasics (Lasky et al., 1976; Pashek and Brookshire, 1982; Weidner and Lasky, 1976). Other investigations with this population, however, have questioned the positive effects of rate reduction (Blumstein et al., 1985; Brookshire and Nicholas, 1984). As suggested by McNeil and Kimelman (1986), the effects of speech rate manipulations on adult aphasics' auditory comprehension abilities appear to be unresolved. Careful subject description and attempts to predict which subjects are likely to benefit from rate manipulations may be the key to future studies in this area.

Investigations of speech rate manipulations with children have demonstrated beneficial effects of reduced speaking rate for learning disabled children (McCroskey and Thompson, 1973) and children with acquired aphasia (Campbell and McNeil, 1985). Using a divided-attention paradigm, Campbell and McNeil (1985) found that slowing the rate of the primary sentence improved comprehension of a secondary sentence presented at normal rate. They interpreted these findings within the framework of a limited-capacity model of attention (Kahneman, 1973), suggesting that the slower rate of presentation of the primary sentence allowed more attentional resources to be allocated to the processing of the secondary sentence. With respect to increased speaking rates, studies have shown that children with auditory perceptual and language problems have more difficulty perceiving speech presented at a fast rate than do their age peers (Manning et al., 1977), and learning disabled children are less accurate than age-matched controls at repeating sentences presented at fast rate (McNutt and Chi-Yen Li, 1980).

In a preliminary investigation of the ways in which linguistic input can be modified to facilitate language learning by SLI children, acquisition of invented lexemes was assessed under linguistic input conditions that varied with respect to rate of speech, vocal stress, and use of visual cues accompanying spoken language (Ellis Weismer et al., 1990). Sixteen kindergartners participated in this study, including eight SLI children and eight age-matched children who were developing language normally (NL controls). Subjects participated in a game in which they were taught labels for three unusual objects (which were the names of an outerspace creature's toys). In the rate condition, the three invented lexemes (*/don/*, */pId/*, */kub/*) were presented within 5-syllable sentence frames at slow (2.8 syllables/sec), normal (4.4 syllables/sec), or fast (5.9 syllables/sec) rates such that each lexical item was consistently presented at a certain rate for a given subject. Stimuli consisted of tape recorded, natural speech involving speaker-generated rate alterations. An examination of the rate manipulations revealed different patterns of performance for the two groups of subjects. The NL control subjects displayed equivalent comprehension of all rates, with poorer production of lexemes presented at fast rates. The SLI subjects demonstrated increasing levels of accuracy from fast to normal to slow rates of presentation on comprehension and production items. We might speculate that the distinction between input presented at normal vs. slow rates would become even more apparent beyond the individual sentence level (i.e., in connected discourse contexts). For example, there may be an appreciable difference in SLI children's ability to answer questions about paragraphs read aloud at slow speaking rates compared with normal rates because of cumulative effects of increased processing time and reduced processing load.

Stress

Various studies have investigated the impact of emphatic stress on auditory comprehension in adult aphasics (Baum et al., 1982; Blumstein and Goodglass, 1972; Kimelman and McNeil, 1987; Pashek and Brookshire, 1982; Solomon, 1983; Solomon and Aronson, 1977; Turco, 1986). With the exception of the Baum et al. (1982) and Solomon and Aronson (1977) studies, emphatic stress has been reported to enhance aphasics' comprehension. Positive effects of emphatic stress on passage comprehension by normal adults was also found in a recent investigation by Bean et al. (1989). Evidence from reaction time studies indicates that normal adult listeners process stressed words faster than unstressed (Bock and Mazzella, 1983; Cutler, 1976; Cutler and Foss, 1977; Shields et al., 1974) and that acoustic modifications in the utterance before the stressed word serve as cues to predict the upcoming presence of the stressed targets (Cutler, 1976; Shields et al., 1974). These acoustic differences in the context preceding a stressed word include changes in duration (Kimelman and McNeil, 1989; Weismer and Ingrisano, 1979) and fundamental frequency (Cooper et al., 1983). Kimelman and McNeil (1989) investigated aphasics' ability to use cues that preceded stressed segments. They found that auditory comprehension of normally stressed target words was significantly better when preceded by emphatically stressed context than by normally stressed context.

To date, the only study that has examined the effects of emphatic stress on SLI children's linguistic processing is the preliminary investigation by Ellis Weismer et al. (1990) described previously. In the stress condition, invented lexemes were either presented with normal stress or emphatic stress within the stimulus sentences. There was no stress effect for the SLI group on comprehension items, but production of emphatic stress lexemes was considerably better than production of normal stress items. Normal language subjects evidenced improved comprehension and slightly better production of lexemes presented with normal compared with emphatic stress. The unexpected findings for the comprehension probes may be explained on the basis of pragmatic considerations pertaining to given vs. new information (Haviland and Clark, 1974). The word "Sam" rather than the target lexeme could have been interpreted as new information in the comprehension probe, "Put Sam by the /*kub*/." If that were the case, the placement of emphatic stress on *kub* would be incongruent with the structural marking of new information within the utterance. Violation of the control children's linguistic expectations may have resulted in their poorer performance on the items with emphatic stress. Although this factor may have also confounded the findings for the SLI children, it would not necessarily be assumed that they had developed a full understanding of structural marking of given vs. new information that would have interfered with their processing of the stressed items because this knowledge is acquired relatively late (Paul, 1981). The fact that Ellis Weismer et al. (1990) observed different patterns of response to the stress (and rate) manipulations for the two groups of subjects is consistent with the assumption that NL children, unlike the SLI children, are not operating at the limits of their processing capacity on these tasks and have more efficient means of encoding and accessing phonetic representations; therefore, input modifications of this type are less likely to enhance their performance.

IMPLICATIONS FOR PROCESS MODELS OF LANGUAGE

Prosodic characteristics of speech have received relatively little consideration in models of speech perception, word recognition and lexical access, and language comprehension (Lemme and Hedberg, 1988; Pisoni and Luce, 1986). However, it is clear that prosodic features carry useful information about lexical, syntactic, and pragmatic aspects of the message. Research suggests that prosody functions in two interrelated ways: (1) as a "chunking" device for segmenting the flow of speech into structures appropriate for further processing and (2) as a predictive device that signals potentially important information (Freeman, 1982). Within various active models of speech perception, prosody has been hypothesized to serve as an interface between acoustic representation and cognitive representation (Haggard, 1975; Pisoni and Sawusch, 1975). Haggard (1975) contends that prosody carries direct phonetic cues to particular semantic and grammatical classes, thereby restricting the search and integrative processes between the acoustic representation of a segment and the various cognitive operations acting on it. Similarly, prosodic information may limit listeners' focused search and aid in establishing "islands of reliability" in the stimulus input, which can be used to access various sources of knowledge (Pisoni and Luce, 1986). Cutler (1976) has concluded that the prediction of stress focuses attention and facilitates the location of a word in the mental lexicon, thus reducing the demands of the decoding process.

The logic underlying this area of investigation rests on the assumption that prosodic manipulations of input can serve to reduce the demands of linguistic processing in various ways. The model of auditory comprehension and processing proposed by McNeil and Kimelman (1986) is useful in considering possible effects that stress and rate manipulations would have on linguistic processing. Reduced rates of speech result in increased processing time, which may allow more efficient allocation of attention to new forms within the utterance (Campbell and McNeil, 1985). Use of emphatic stress on target forms can similarly be hypothesized to reduce processing demands by cuing the listener as to important information to which they should allocate attentional resources. The increased efficiency in allocation of resources may help SLI children overcome capacity limitations, thereby leading to improved processing of new linguistic material.

The nature of the relationship between the documented processing deficits exhibited by SLI children and their language impairment remains controversial (Johnston, 1988; Lahey, 1988; Leonard, 1987; Tallal, 1988). Intervention attempts aimed at directly modifying auditory perceptual skills (Lasky and Cox, 1983; Tallal, 1988) or higher-level representational skills (Leonard, 1987) are apparently based on the assumption that these processing deficits play a causal role in language disorders. No such assumption regarding causality is made here. Rather, it is suggested that the manner in which linguistic input is presented be manipulated in ways posited to reduce information processing demands such that more attentional resources are directed toward the acquisition of new target forms. Manipulation of performance variables may provide a needed boost in SLI children's ability to establish and employ linguistic representations, regardless of the nature of the factors that contributed to their difficulties in language development.

Pinker's (1984) theory of language learnability, which is set within an information processing framework, has recently been applied to SLI children's performance (Leonard, 1989). This model may offer some specific predictions with respect to the effects of prosodic manipulations of linguistic input. It can be hypothesized that the impact of prosodic input manipulations will be most evident for language targets, which are typically characterized by low phonetic substance and tend to pose the greatest difficulty in terms of language learning. Low phonetic substance morphemes are defined as nonsyllablic consonant segments and unstressed syllables, characterized by shorter duration than adjacent morphemes and often low fundamental frequency and amplitude (Leonard, 1989, p. 186). Traditional views of information processing involving sequential symbol manipulation have been challenged by more recent connectionist or parallel distributed processing (PDP) models (Rumelhart and McClelland, 1986). Theorists have begun to examine the relationships between information processing and connectionist models to consider ways in which these models might coexist in the field of cognitive science as viable frameworks of mental architecture (Estes, 1988; Pinker and Prince, 1988). Within an information processing account, beneficial effects of prosodic manipulations of the linguistic input would be assumed to be caused by factors related to increased processing time and allocation of attentional resources that facilitate acquisition of the linguistic form or rule. Alternately, a connectionist view, such as that proposed by the competition model of language learning (Bates and MacWhinney, 1987), might suggest that prosodic manipulations impact upon the "detectability" of cues (as opposed to rules) (MacWhinney et al.,

1989) such that cue strength and acquisition is enhanced.

Though investigation of prosodic modifications of the linguistic signal focuses on bottom-up processing that most directly impacts on perceptual abilities, interactions at various levels of processing are assumed to occur in language comprehension and use, and the importance of top-down processing involving world knowledge, situational expectations, and linguistic and nonlinguistic symbolic knowledge is certainly acknowledged (McNeil and Kimelman, 1986). From an information processing perspective, the Child Talk model (Chapman et al., Chapter 1) emphasizes top-down processing, such that the knowledge structures that support talk are posited to be embedded within the child's network of world knowledge. Although the focus is quite different, claims regarding potential influences of prosodic manipulations of input on linguistic processing are not incompatible with the Child Talk model. To the extent that language learning is viewed as context-specific according to the Child Talk framework, it can be assumed that part of the information that is encapsulated pertains to the physical (acoustic) characteristics of the talk. Thus, manipulation of the prosodic cues in utterances may lead to differential activation of knowledge schemas underlying language comprehension and use.

Further, for SLI children, prosodic characteristics of input may contribute to less frequent acquisition of language within event representations, and hence fewer lexical entries or fewer event contexts associated with a word.

IMPLICATIONS FOR CLINICAL INTERVENTION

There is a pressing need for research addressing the issue of facilitation of language learning by language-impaired children (Ellis Weismer, 1991; Vetter, 1991). One widely used language teaching technique is modeling (Cole and Dale, 1986; Connell, 1987; Leonard, 1981). However, scant information is available as to how the manner in which the linguistic input is provided might affect children's processing and acquisition of language. Manipulations in the manner of presentation of the linguistic signal in terms of stress and rate adjustments can be hypothesized to impact on auditory perception and comprehension of language, and thereby language use. This approach offers a potential means of mitigating the well-documented auditory processing constraints of SLI children through the nature of the input cues provided during training. In a sense, the clinician serves as a "preprocessor" of information for language-impaired children within this approach (Ellis Weismer and Dollaghan, 1989) by adapting the linguistic input in ways that have been shown to facilitate processing. Numerous questions remain concerning the impact of prosodic manipulations across various linguistic forms, phases of learning, and their interaction with subject variables that affect linguistic processing for individual language-impaired children. The value of experimental, group data is that it can serve as a guidepost to help identify important parameters to manipulate, as well as indicating the nature of the modifications that might be attempted as a first try. However, it is important to underscore the extent of individual variation that is likely to be encountered and the need to anticipate considerable trial therapy to fine-tune the match between the input provided and the child's processing abilities.

REFERENCES

Bates E, and MacWhinney B: Competition, variation, and language learning, in

MacWhinney B (ed): *Mechanisms of Language Acquisition.* Hillsdale, NJ, Lawrence Erlbaum Associates, 1987.

Baum S, Daniloff J, Daniloff R, et al: Sentence comprehension by Broca's aphasics: Effect of some suprasegmental variables. *Brain Lang* 1982; 17:262–271.

Bean C, Folkins J, Cooper W: The effects of emphasis on passage comprehension. J Speech Hear Res 1989; 32:707–712.

Blumstein S, Goodglass J: The perception of stress as a semantic cue in aphasia. *J Speech Hear Res* 1972; 15:800–808.

Blumstein S, Katz B, Goodglass J, et al: The effects of slowed speech on auditory comprehension in aphasia. *Brain Lang* 1985; 24:246–265.

Bock J, Mazzella J: Intonational marking of given and new information: Some consequences for comprehension. *Memory Cognit* 1983; 11:64–76.

Bolinger D (ed): *Intonation.* Baltimore, Md, Penguin Books, 1972.

Broen P: The verbal environment of the language-learning child. *American Speech and Hearing Association Monograph,* no 17. Washington, DC, American Speech and Hearing Association, 1972.

Brookshire R, Nicholas L: Consistency of effects of slow rate and pauses on aphasic listeners' comprehension of spoken sentences. *J Speech Hear Res* 1984; 27:323–328.

Campbell T, McNeil M: Effects of presentation rate and divided attention on auditory comprehension in children with an acquired language disorder. *J Speech Hear Res* 1985; 28:513–520.

Chapman R: Mother-child interaction in the second year of life, in Schiefelbusch R, Bricker D (eds): *Early language: Acquisition and intervention.* Baltimore, Md, University Park Press, 1981, pp 201–250.

Chi M (ed): *Trends in Memory Development Research.* New York, Karger, 1983.

Cole K, Dale P: Direct language instruction and interactive language instruction with language delayed preschool children: A comparison study. *J Speech Hear Res* 1986; 29:206–217.

Connell P: An effect of modeling and imitation teaching procedures on children with and without specific language impairment. *J Speech Hear Res* 1987; 30:105–113.

Cooper W, Soares C, Ham A, et al: The influence of inter- and intra-speaker tempo in fundamental frequency and palatalization. *J Acoust Soc Am* 1983; 73:1723–1730.

Cross T: Mother's speech adjustments: The contribution of selected child listener variables, in Snow C, Ferguson C (eds): *Talking to Children.* New York, Cambridge University Press, 1977, pp 151–183.

Curtiss S: On the nature of the impairment in language impaired children, in Miller J (ed): *Research on Child Language Disorders.* Austin, Tex, Pro-Ed, 1991, pp 189–210.

Cutler A: Phoneme-monitoring reaction time as a function of preceding intonation contour. *Percept Psychophys* 1976; 20:55–60.

Cutler A, Foss D: On the role of sentence stress in sentence processing. *Language Speech* 1977; 20:1–10.

Crystal D: *The English Tone of Voice.* New York, St Martin's Press, 1975.

Duchan J, Katz J: Language and auditory processing: Top down plus bottom up, in Lasky E, Katz J (eds): *Central Auditory Processing Disorders.* Baltimore, Md, University Park Press, 1983, pp 31–48.

Ellis Weismer S: Constructive comprehension abilities exhibited by language-disordered children. *J Speech Hear Res* 1985; 28:175–184.

Ellis Weismer S: Child language intervention: Research issues on the horizon, in Miller J (ed): *Research on Child Language Disorders*. Austin, Tex, Pro-Ed, 1991, pp 233–241.

Ellis Weismer S: Hypothesis testing abilities of language impaired children. *J Speech Hear Res* 1991; 34:1329–1338.

Ellis Weismer S, Digney K, Krueger W, et al: Linguistic input manipulations during lexical training. Paper presented at the Annual Convention of the American Speech-Language-Hearing Association, Seattle, 1990.

Ellis Weismer S, Dollaghan C: Jigsaw: Processing constraints and input modification in language intervention. Miniseminar presented at the Annual Convention of the American Speech-Language-Hearing Association, St Louis, 1989.

Ellis Weismer S, Erickson J, Soderberg L, et al: Problem solving abilities of language-impaired children. Paper presented at the Annual Convention of the American Speech-Language-Hearing Association, St Louis, 1989.

Estes W: Toward a framework for combining connectionist and symbol-processing models. *J Memory Lang* 1988; 27:196–212.

Freeman F: Prosody in perception, production, and pathologies, in Lass N, McReynolds L, Northern J, et al (eds): *Speech, Language, and Hearing*. Philadelphia, WB Sanders Co, 1982, vol II, pp 652–672.

Garnica O: Some prosodic and paralinguistic features of speech to young children, in Snow C, Ferguson C (eds): *Talking to Children*. New York, Cambridge University Press, 1977, pp 63–68.

Gleitman L, Wanner E: Language acquisition, in Wanner E, Gleitman L (eds): *Language Acquisition: The State of the Art*. New York, Cambridge University Press, 1982, pp 3–48.

Haggard M: Understanding speech understanding, in Cohen A, Nooteboom S (eds): *Structure and Process in Speech Perception*. New York, Springer-Verlag New York, 1975, pp 3–15.

Haviland S, Clark H: What's new: Acquiring new information as a process in comprehension. *J Verbal Learn Verbal Behav* 1974; 13:512–521.

Johnston J: Specific language disorders in the child, in Lass N, McReynolds L, Northern J, et al (eds): *Handbook of Speech-Language Pathology and Audiology*. Philadelphia, BC Decker, 1988, pp 685–715.

Johnston J: Questions about cognition in children with specific language impairment, in Miller J (ed): *Research on Child Language Disorders*. Austin, Tex, Pro-Ed, 1991, pp 299–307.

Johnston J, Ellis Weismer S: Mental rotation abilities in language-disordered children. *J Speech Hear Res* 1983; 26:397–403.

Johnston J, Smith L: Dimensional thinking in language impaired children. *J Speech Hear Res* 1989; 32:33–38.

Johnston R, Stark R, Mellits D, et al: Neurological status of language-impaired and normal children. *Ann Neurol* 1981; 10:159–163.

Kahneman D: *Attention and Effort*. Englewood Cliffs, NJ, Prentice-Hall, 1973.

Kamhi A, Beasley D: Central auditory processing disorders: Is it a meaningful construct or a twentieth century unicorn? *J Child Commun Disord* 1985; 9:5–14.

Kamhi A, Gentry B, Mauer D, et al: Analogical learning and transfer in language-impaired children. *J Speech Hear Disord* 1990; 55:140–148.

Kean M: The linguistic interpretation of aphasic syndromes: Agrammatism in Broca's aphasia, an example. *Cognition* 1977; 5:9–46.

Keil F: Mechanisms of cognitive development and the structure of knowledge, in Sternberg R (ed): *Mechanisms of Cognitive Development.* New York, WH Freeman & Co Publishers, 1984.

Keith R (ed): *Central Auditory and Language Disorders in Children.* Houston, College-Hill Press, 1981.

Keith R: Central auditory dysfunction: A language disorder? *Topics Lang Disord* 1984; 4:48–56.

Kimelman M, McNeil M: Emphatic stress comprehension in adult aphasia. *J Speech Hear Res* 1987; 30:295–300.

Kimelman M, McNeil M: Contextual influences on the auditory comprehension of normally stressed targets by aphasic listeners, in Prescott T (ed): *Clinical Aphasiology Conference Proceedings.* Boston, College–Hill, 1989, vol 18, pp 407–420.

Kirchner D, Klatzky R: Verbal rehearsal and memory in language disordered children. *J Speech Hear Res* 1985; 28:556–564.

Lahey M: *Language Disorders and Language Development.* New York, Macmillan, 1988.

Lasky E: Parameters affecting auditory processing, in Lasky E, Katz J (eds): *Central Auditory Processing Disorders.* Baltimore, University Park Press, 1983, pp 11–30.

Lasky E, Cox L: Auditory processing and language interaction, in Lasky E, Katz J (eds): *Central Auditory Processing Disorders.* Baltimore, University Park Press, 1983, pp 243–268.

Lasky E, Katz J (eds): *Central Auditory Processing Disorders.* Baltimore, University Park Press, 1983.

Lasky E, Weidner W, Johnson J: Influence of linguistic complexity, rate of presentation, and interphrase pause time on auditory-verbal comprehension of adult aphasic patients. *Brain Lang* 1976; 3:386–395.

Lass N, Riensche L, Beasley D: Applications of time-altered speech in speech-language pathology and audiology. *Commun Disord* 1984; 9:19–31.

Lemme M, Hedberg N: Auditory linguistic processing, in Lass N, McReynolds L, Northern J, et al (eds): *Handbook of Speech Pathology and Audiology.* Philadelphia, BC Decker, 1988, pp 277–308.

Leonard L: Facilitating linguistic skills in children with specific language impairment. *Appl Psycholinguist* 1981; 2:89–118.

Leonard L: Is specific language impairment a useful construct? in Rosenberg S (ed): *Advances in Applied Psycholinguistics.* New York, Cambridge University Press, 1987, vol 1, pp 1–39.

Leonard L: Language learnability and specific language impairment in children. *Appl Psycholinguist* 1989; 10:179–202.

Levinson P, Sloan C (eds): *Auditory Processing and Language.* New York, Grune & Stratton, 1980.

MacWhinney B, Leinbach J, Taraban R, et al: Language learning: Cues or rules? *J Memory Lang* 1989; 28:255–277.

Manning W, Johnston K, Beasley D: The performance of children with auditory perceptual disorders on a time-compressed speech discrimination measure. *J Speech Hear Disord* 1977; 42:77–84.

McCroskey R, Thompson N: Comprehension of rate controlled speech by children with specific learning disabilities. *J Learn Disabil* 1973; 6:621–628.

McNeil M, Kimelman M: Toward an integrative information-processing structure of auditory comprehension and processing in adult aphasia. *Semin Speech Lang* 1986; 7:123–146.

McNutt J, Chia-Yen Li J: Repetition of time-altered sentences by normal and learning disabled children. *J Learn Disabil* 1980; 13:25–29.

Nelson L, Kamhi A, Apel K: Cognitive strengths and weaknesses in language-impaired children: One more look. *J Speech Hear Disord* 1987; 52:36–43.

Nippold M, Erskine B, Freed D: Proportional and analogical reasoning in normal and language-impaired children. *J Speech Hear Disord* 1988; 53:440–449.

Norman D, Bobrow D: On data-limited and resource-limited processes. *Cognit Psychol* 1975; 7:44–64.

Pashek G, Brookshire R: Effects of rate of speech and linguistic stress on auditory paragraph comprehension of aphasic individuals. *J Speech Hear Res* 1982; 25:377–383.

Paul R: Children's understanding of surface structure cues to given/new information in sentences. Doctoral dissertation, Madison, University of Wisconsin, 1981.

Pinker S: *Language Learnability and Language Development.* Cambridge, Mass, Harvard University Press, 1984.

Pinker S, Prince A: On language connectionism: Analysis of a parallel distributed processing model of language acquisition. *Cognition* 1988; 28:73–193.

Pisoni D, Luce P: Speech perception: Research, theory, and the principal issues, in Schwab E, Nusbaum H (eds): *Pattern Recognition by Humans and Machines.* New York, Academic Press, 1986, pp 1–50.

Pisoni D, Sawusch J: Some stages of processing in speech perception, in Cohen A, Nooteboom S (eds): *Structure and Process in Speech Perception.* New York, Springer-Verlag New York, 1975, pp 16–35.

Rumelhart D, McClelland J (eds): *Parallel Distributed Processing: Explorations in the Microstructure of Cognition.* Cambridge, Mass, MIT Press, 1986.

Savich P: Anticipatory imagery ability in normal and language-disabled children. *J Speech Hear Res* 1984; 27:494–501.

Schmitt J: The effects of time compression and time expansion on passage comprehension by elderly listeners. *J Speech Hear Res* 1983; 26:373–377.

Schmitt J, Carroll M: Older listeners' ability to comprehend speaker-generated rate alteration of passages. *J Speech Hear Res* 1985; 28:309–312.

Schmitt J, Moore J: Natural alteration of speaking rate: The effect on passage comprehension by listeners over 75 years of age. *J Speech Hear Res* 1989; 32:445–450.

Schwartz R: Lexical acquisition and processing in specific language impairment, in Miller J (ed): *Research on Child Language Disorders.* Austin, Tex, Pro-Ed, 1991, pp 339–347.

Shields J, McHugh A, Martin J: Reaction time to phoneme targets as a function of rhythmic cues in continuous speech. *J Exp Psychol* 1974; 102:250–255.

Singer J, Hurley R (eds): *Central auditory processing disorders in children. J Child Commun Disord* 1985; 9(1).

Slobin D. Universal and particular in the acquisition of language, in Wanner E, Gleitman L (eds): *Language Acquisition: The State of the Art.* New York, Cambridge University Press, 1982; pp 128–170.

Solomon J: Prosodic factors in auditory comprehension in aphasia. Paper presented at the 19th Congress of International Association of Logopedics and Phoniatrics, Edinburgh, Scotland, 1983.

Solomon J, Aronson A: The Token Test *senza intonazioni particulari:* Does it make any difference? In Brookshire R (ed): *Clinical Aphasiology.* Minneapolis, BRK Publishers, 1977, vol 17.

Tallal P: Developmental language disorders, in J. Kavanagh J, Truss T Jr (eds): *Learning Disabilities: Proceedings From the National Conference.* Parkton, Md, York Press, 1988, pp 181–272.

Tallal P, Piercy M: Developmental aphasia: Impaired rate of non-verbal processing as a function of sensory modality. *Neuropsychologia* 1973; 11:389–398.

Tallal P, Piercy M: Developmental aphasia: Rate of auditory processing and selective impairment of consonant perception. *Neuropsychologia* 1974; 12:83–93.

Tallal P, Piercy M: Developmental aphasia: The perception of brief vowels and extended stop consonants. *Neuropsychologia* 1975; 13:69–74.

Tallal P, Stark R: Speech acoustic-cue discrimination abilities of normally developing and language-impaired children. *J Acoust Soc Am* 1981; 69:568–574.

Tallal P, Stark R, Kallman C, et al: Developmental aphasia: The relation between acoustic processing deficits and verbal processing. *Neuropsychologia* 1980; 18:273–284.

Tallal P, Stark R, Kallman C, et al: A reexamination of some non-verbal perceptual abilities of language-impaired and normal children as a function of age and sensory modality. *J Speech Hear Res* 1981; 24:351–357.

Tallal P, Stark R, Mellits D: The relationship between auditory temporal analysis and receptive language development. *Neuropsychologia* 1985; 23:314–322.

Turco T: Some effects of linguistic stress on auditory comprehension of aphasic adults. Master's thesis, Madison, University of Wisconsin, 1986.

Vetter D: Needed: Intervention research, in Miller J (ed): *Research on Child Language Disorders*. Austin, Tex, Pro-Ed, 1991, pp 243–252.

Weidner W, Lasky E: Interaction of rate and complexity of stimulus on the performance of adult aphasic subjects. *Brain Lang* 1976; 3:34–70.

Weismer G, Ingrisano D: Phrase-level timing patterns in English: Effects of emphatic stress location and speaking rate. *J Speech Hear Res* 1979; 22:516–533.

SECTION III

Interactive Processes in Lexical Acquisition

8 Adult-Based Models of the Lexical Long-Term Store: Issues for Language Acquisition and Disorders

Christine A. Dollaghan, Ph.D.

Questions about the nature of the representational system for linguistic information are not new, but recent years have seen a dramatic increase in both the number and specificity of proposals concerning the characteristics of the mental lexicon. The emergence of psycholinguistic and developmental psycholinguistic theories (Bresnan, 1982; Pinker, 1984), which assign the lexicon a central role not just in semantic processing but also in morphological and syntactic processing, in conjunction with an expanding body of theoretical and empirical work on lexical memory in cognitive psychology, have resulted in a literature with a variety of implications for efforts to develop process-based accounts of children's lexical (and language) acquisition.

The Child Talk model (Chapman et al., Chapter 1), however, explicitly questions the classical metaphor of the lexicon as a dictionary organized around abstract semantic features and categories, such as "animal." Indeed, Chapman et al. (see Chapter 1) appear to want to throw out the notion of a lexicon altogether in favor of an "event-based encyclopedia" to emphasize the extent to which the child's early representations for linguistic units are likely to contain much more than simply abstract semantic information. They argue that the proper organizing dimensions for the earliest phases of language comprehension and production are to be found in the child's memory representations for specific events or experiences, with their collocations of many and varied types of information: visual, auditory, tactile, emotional, and, at some point, linguistic.

It turns out that this less "classical" conception of the ways in which young children's lexical entries are structured and associated bears more than a passing resemblance to a number of recent proposals concerning the lexical representations of adult language users. Although not developed to address acquisition issues, these approaches to the organization and accessing of lexical information in adults may provide some inroads to further specifying Child Talk with respect to early lexical processing.

In this chapter, I will examine some of the features of several recent psycholinguistic models of the adult's lexicon, paying particular attention to hypotheses about its organization and its role in on-line language comprehension and production. I will then briefly consider how these hypotheses relate to efforts to develop a process-based account of children's lexical development. Finally, I will examine some of the ways in which these conceptions of the lexical long-term store might contribute to understanding the language processing deficits observed in language-impaired children.

Before beginning, a terminological clarification and two disclaimers are necessary. Child Talk's proponents explicitly eschew the term "lexicon" because of its historic association with various formal linguistic approaches to lexical information, with their nearly complete emphasis on abstract, decontextualized semantic features. In the adult psycholinguistic literature, by contrast, the meaning of the word lexicon has been greatly expanded from this narrower sense. To acknowledge the broader, more contextualized orientation to lexical information emphasized by the Child Talk model, I will use the phrase "lexical long-term store" (LLTS) to refer to the system for representing lexical information in memory. However, this phrase is interchangeable with the word lexicon as it is used in many adult psycholinguistic models.

The two disclaimers are as follows: First, the descriptions of adult-oriented LLTS constructs and models will be cursory and will not do justice to their richness and complexity or to the body of empirical evidence on which many of them rest. Second, a comprehensive review of the processing implications of the existing literature on children's lexical acquisition is not among the objectives of this chapter. It is a relatively simple matter to recast existing studies of lexical development in processing terminology. What appears to be more urgently needed are new studies, designed to contribute to more detailed processing accounts or to provide evidence sufficient to enable choices among existing accounts. This chapter is intended to provide an entry into the literature on adult lexical processing, identifying some of its more interesting constructs and questions and suggesting how these may bear on efforts to understand children's lexical processing.

THE ADULT'S LEXICAL LONG-TERM STORE

Basic Assumptions

Most language processing models share the premise that there exists a long-term memory system for lexical entries; this system, often referred to as the mental lexicon or LLTS, is envisioned as the ultimate repository of lexical information in memory. In many models, the LLTS is taken to consist of a complex network of interconnected nodes or information units that can vary in activation or state (Anderson, 1983; Collins and Loftus, 1975; Marslen-Wilson, 1989; McClelland and Rumelhart, 1987; Norman and Rumelhart, 1975, and many others). Connections between nodes are assumed to reflect relationships among the information represented by each node, with nodes representing similar or related information (e.g., "table" and "chair") presumed to share more or closer links than nodes representing dissimilar information (e.g., "table" and "cloud"), although the mechanisms by which such effects are accounted for vary from model to model (Schvaneveldt and Meyer, 1973). Activation of a node is assumed to "spread" automatically to connected nodes, with the probability that activation will spread from one node to the next determined largely by the number and closeness of their links (Anderson, 1983).

The automatic activation of related

nodes is invoked to provide one account of priming effects (McNamara and Healy, 1988) in which a subject's processing of a lexical item is speeded by prior processing of a related lexical item. For example, a subject who has recently encountered the word "robber" is more likely to interpret the ambiguous word "bank" as referring to a financial institution than would otherwise be the case (Swinney, 1979). Processing the word "robber," even in isolation, is presumed to have activated semantically related nodes such as "thief," "hold-up," and "bank" such that they are more rapidly activated in subsequent tasks.

Beyond these basic assumptions, models of the LLTS can be distinguished according to their views concerning such issues as the manner in which information associated with lexical entries is represented in the network and the scope and characteristics of the basic organizational unit of the LLTS, the lexical entry. We turn now to consider some of these views.

Representation of Information

Localist and Distributed Models

One major dimension along which models of the LLTS diverge concerns the manner in which the information associated with a lexical entry is represented in the system. If the LLTS is viewed as a network of information nodes or units, it is a logical step to envision each node as corresponding to a single lexical entry. This is the view implied by local, or *localist,* models, in which each node represents the nexus of the particular set of information associated with a given lexical entry. In such models, the individual node assumes a role of great importance, being independently and uniquely responsible for representing some units of information. The phrase "one lexical entry, one node" captures the flavor of localist approaches.

In *distributed* models, by contrast, a lexical entry is not represented by a single node; rather, each lexical entry is associated with a unique pattern of activation distributed over multiple nodes. In distributed models, individual nodes are content-free; it is only by virtue of their participation as parts of an aggregate pattern of activation that they play a role in representing information unique to a lexical entry. The phrase "one lexical entry, one set of nodes" roughly reflects the distributed approach to lexical representation.

An example may help to clarify this distinction. As shown in Figure 8–1, in a localist approach to representing the phonemic characteristics of the lexical entry for "baseball," the entire ordered set of phonemes *[beIsbal]* would be associated with a single node. A different node would contain all of the phonemic information about the entry for "football," and so on. By contrast, in a distributed approach to representing the phonemic characteristics of the word "baseball," each of the six phonemes might be associated with its own separate node. The lexical entry for "baseball" would be recognized only when the individual nodes for *[b] [eI] [s] [b] [a] [l]* were activated in the appropriate temporal sequence. The representation of the lexical entry thus would arise from a complex pattern of activation distributed over a number of nodes; a different set of nodes would be activated for an entry consisting of a different sequence of phonemes.

These examples are intended only to convey a very basic sense of the distinction between distributed and localist approaches to representing information, because they ignore a number of crucial questions about how content-free the individual nodes actually are in distributed approaches. The example of a distributed representation given earlier can be thought of as localist with respect to representing sublexical (phonemic) informa-

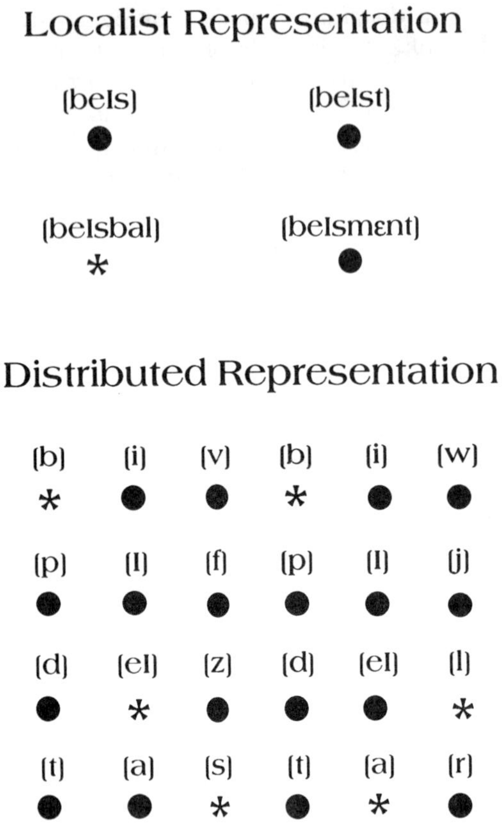

FIG 8–1.
Localist and distributed representations of phonemic information associated with the lexical entry "baseball" ([beIsbal]). Filled circles indicate nodes; asterisks indicate activated nodes. In the localist representation, a single node represents all phonemic information for the entry. In the distributed representation, individual nodes are associated with individual phonemes; a set of ordered phoneme nodes is necessary to represent the entry's phonemic characteristics.

tion, because although the lexical entry "baseball" is not to be found in a single node, individual phonemes are. A completely distributed network would not even associate individual phonemes with individual nodes but would define them too as patterns of activation distributed across content-free units.

As noted by Rumelhart and McClelland (1986), there currently are no compelling reasons to prefer either a local or a distributed representational model, and it is conceivable that both types of representation may be involved in language processing, depending on the nature of the information to be represented and the type of processing involved. According to these investigators, one striking and appealing property of distributed models is their ability to continue to function, albeit at reduced levels of accuracy and efficiency, under conditions of incomplete input or damage to the system. If information is distributed across multiple nodes, malfunctioning of any single node is relatively less crucial than if a great deal of information is associated with the defective node. To continue with the earlier example, in a localist network the entry for "baseball" would be associated with a single node; damage to this node could prevent its activation, making all information associated with the entry unavailable. In a distributed network, damage to a single node (e.g., *[s]*) would prevent its activation but not that of the remaining nodes *[b] [eI] [b] [a] [l]*. The activation of these nodes might be sufficient to activate the entry for "baseball," making its information accessible even in the absence of the activation of the node for *[s]*. The term "graceful degradation" of information (Elman, 1989; Rumelhart and McClelland, 1986) has been applied to this property of distributed networks to capture their ability to recover at least partially from many processing difficulties that would shut down a locally organized representation system altogether.

Characteristics of Lexical Entries

Independent of questions about the means by which information associated with a lexical entry is represented are questions about the defining characteristics of lexical entries. Here two general sets of issues can be discerned. First, what linguistic units qualify as lexical entries in the LLTS? Second, what types of information are associated with individual lexical entries?

Scope

At least for high-frequency content or open class words (typically defined as nouns, verbs, adjectives, and adverbs) (Crystal, 1980), lexical entries in the LLTS are often assumed to correspond to word-length units, "written dictionary words" (Grosjean and Gee, 1987), or root morphemes (i.e., uninflected or bare word stems, e.g., the word "smile"). However, it has long been recognized that this is an oversimplification. The meanings of idioms or other "fixed phrases" (Hankamer, 1989) such as "spill the beans" (to use an example from Chafe, 1970), cannot be determined by combining the meanings of their individual words; they must each be represented by a distinct lexical entry.

Considerably more controversy exists over the question of whether and how other meaningful linguistic units are represented in the LLTS. These include (1) morphologically complex words (i.e., words consisting of a root morpheme plus inflectional and/or derivational affixes, e.g., the words "smiles," "smiling," and "unsmiling"), (2) functors or closed class items (i.e., words with less semantic content that appear to function more as syntactic operators, e.g., articles "a," "an," and "the" and auxiliary verbs "do," "have," and "be"), (3) inflectional affixes (i.e., bound morphemes that are attached to word stems to code such notions as plurality *[−s, −z,* or *−Iz]* or progressive aspect *[-ing]*), and (4) derivational affixes (i.e., bound morphemes, e.g., *[-ly]* or *[un−]*, which often alter both the semantic and syntactic characteristics of a root word, changing the adjectival form "happy" to the adverbial "happily," for example).

Some investigators (Hankamer, 1989; Pinker, 1984) argue that affixes and roots are stored as separate lexical entries within the LLTS, so that, for example, the root verb "smile" and the affix "third person singular present tense" would each be represented in a distinct lexical entry. According to this view, producing the morphologically complex word "smiles" requires that the speaker retrieve the root form and the affix independently and combine them through some subsequent process. Similarly, to comprehend the word "smiles," the listener first must separate (or parse) the root word from the affix before retrieving the information associated with their entries and assigning an interpretation.

Other investigators have discussed the possibility that sublexical units such as affixes are cross-listed in the LLTS, being stored both as independent lexical entries and as part of the lexical entries for the morphologically complex words in which they appear (Hankamer, 1989; Stemberger and MacWhinney, 1986). Using the previous example, the root word "smile" and the affix "third person singular present tense" would each have its own independent lexical entry; in addition, however, the lexical entry for "smile" would contain the morphologically complex words consisting of the root word plus the relevant affixes, such as "smiles," smiling," and "unsmiling." Grosjean and Gee (1987) mention a third possibility that has been discussed with reference to adult aphasia for some time (Zurif, 1980): functors may be stored in a distinct part of the LLTS or in a separate functor lexicon.

As noted by Stemberger and MacWhinney (1986), the design of empirical investigations into these questions is complex at best. Hankamer (1989) pointed out that languages differ tremendously with respect to their morphological complexity. He suggested that models of the LLTS developed to account for the processing of morphologically simple languages such as English may be seriously inadequate with respect to morphologically complex, agglutinative languages such as Turkish. In agglutinative languages, morphologically complex words, often containing multiple affixes, are the rule rather than the exception. Hankamer (1989) suggested that lexical processing in such languages may well differ from processing in languages having fewer complex lexical forms. His conclusion that it is conceivable that the scope of lexical entries may vary from language to language raises the intriguing possibility that lexical entries may also vary across individuals, across phases of language acquisition, or across the histories of individual lexical entries.

Unified or Stratified?

In addition to different views about the eligibility of linguistic units for storage as lexical entries, models of the LLTS diverge according to the amounts and types of information that are believed to be represented in a single lexical entry, whether this entry is conceptualized as a single node or a single pattern of activation distributed across more than one node. In most accounts, each lexical entry is conceptualized as a single, complex locus for a number of diverse types of information; these might be termed *unified* node models. The most basic unified node view requires that each lexical entry contain semantic and acoustic information, but in many models (Fig 8–2) the lexical entry also specifies a number of additional types of information, such as its syntactic characteristics (Bresnan, 1982; Komisarjevsky Tyler, 1989; Marslen-Wilson, 1987) and its orthographic form (Donnenwerth-Nolan et al., 1981; Vellutino and Scanlon, 1987). In Bresnan's (1982) lexical-functional grammar, for example, each lexical entry includes a great deal of information relevant to its syntactic properties, including its predicate-argument structure and the grammatical functions associated with each of its arguments. Jackendoff (1987) went beyond the semantic feature or componential approach to representing information about the meaning of lexical entries by suggesting that lexical representations also contain what he termed a partial three-dimensional model structure, corresponding roughly to the key spatial and visual (and accordingly, nonpropositional) information associated with their referents.

In *stratified* node models, by contrast, the different domains of information associated with a lexical entry are not represented together; rather, each distinct modality of information is represented in a different, specialized layer of nodes (see Fig 8–2). For example, the acoustic-phonetic information about a lexical entry would not be stored together with its conceptual-semantic information; instead, these different forms of information would be represented in two separate networks or layers of nodes. Collins and Loftus (1975), for example, suggested that conceptual information is stored in one long-term memory network, which is distinct from the network of lexical entries encoding these concepts. Van Wijk and Kempen (1987) proposed separate conceptual, lexicosyntactic, morphophonological, and articulatory modules for the representation of these types of information.

Extensive multiple connections between these strata are required to ensure the bundling of the various forms of information into a single coherent lexical entry (Dell, 1986). Extensive multiple connections within each layer are also required to reflect the relative similarities among nodes at that level. For example, nodes representing similar conceptual-semantic information (e.g., "red" and "pink") would be presumed to share more connections than nodes representing information with fewer conceptual

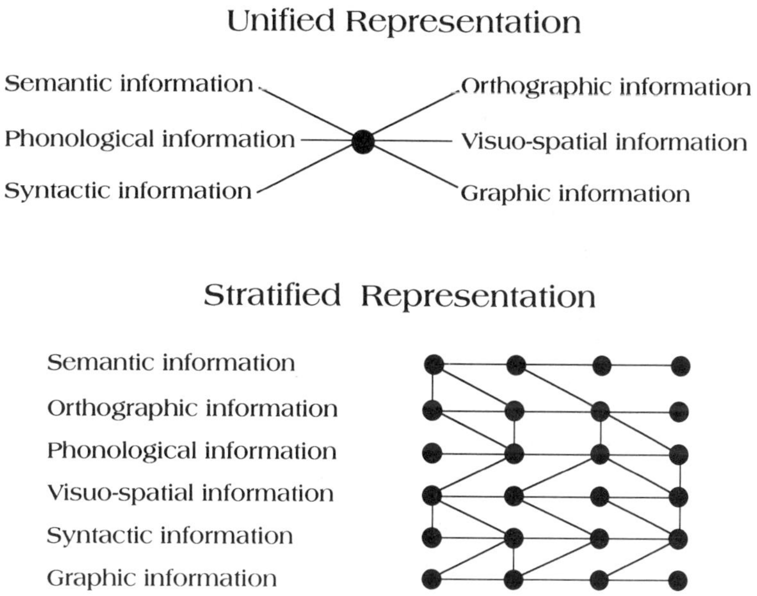

FIG 8–2.
Unified and stratified formats for representing information in the lexical store. In the unified approach, a single node represents many types of information associated with a lexical entry. In a stratified approach, the various forms of information associated with the entry are represented by modality-specific layers of nodes. Connections among layers enable activation to spread among different modalities.

similarities (e.g., "red" and "watch"). Similarly, Butterworth (1989) proposed a separate network for phonological information about lexical entries, organized such that nodes for phonologically similar information (which could be defined as narrowly as words that rhyme or as broadly as words with the same initial consonant) share more, or tighter, connections than nodes for phonologically dissimilar information.

As is true for choosing between distributed and local models of representation, it is difficult to conceive of ways to subject the unified vs. stratified node models to empirical test. The extensive and virtually instantaneous interconnections that must be assumed to exist between the different layers of information in stratified node models would appear to imply processing outcomes indistinguishable from those resulting from the operation of unified nodes. Domain-specific deficits after brain damage are sometimes taken as evidence of selective damage to different representational strata (Caramazza and Sloan Berndt, 1985), and it is certainly clear that there are differences in the relative vulnerability of various forms of lexical information (e.g., morphosyntactic vs. conceptual-semantic) to disruption after brain damage. However, the existence of such domain-specific effects could also be accounted for by positing that the damage differentially affects the processing routes by which the different forms of information associated within a single, unified lexical entry become available (Goodglass and Menn, 1985). Hence, efforts to interpret the linguistic sequelae of brain damage as evidence for a unified or stratified mode of representation have yielded equivocal results to date.

Activating Lexical Entries: Cues and Contact Representations

Questions about the types of information associated with each lexical entry have important implications for descriptions of the process by which information in the LLTS becomes available during language (or other) processing tasks. Most descriptions of this process refer to the construct of cues, which are defined roughly as information units bearing one of many potential relationships to a stored lexical entry (Gillund and Shiffrin, 1984). Cues may be thought of as pathways, or routes, into the LLTS, and a variety of cues (acoustic-phonetic, conceptual, syntactic, phonological, episodic, etc.) may be linked to a given lexical entry such that activation of the cue during processing results in activation, or "contacting" (Frauenfelder and Komisarjevsky Tyler, 1987) of the lexical entry. For example, the lexical entry for a long-lost friend may be activated by the acoustic-phonetic cue of hearing her name, making available the variety of forms of information associated with that entry (her appearance, her last-known whereabouts, the events in which she was a coparticipant, etc.). The same lexical entry also could be activated by other cues, such as viewing the picture and name of the national park in which the last contact with this friend occurred; processing this information might be sufficient to activate the acoustic-phonetic representation of her name along with all the other forms of information associated in her lexical entry. Activation of a lexical entry could also occur in a more top-down fashion if, for example, internal emotional or cognitive processing involved information sufficiently similar to that stored in the lexical entry.

The idea that multiple cues can be used to access a lexical entry is an extremely appealing one in attempting to account for the rapidity, flexibility, and interactive nature apparent in much lexical processing. However, for any cue to provide a route to a lexical entry, the information in the cue and the entry must be represented in a similar format. Specifying the nature of these formats (or contact representations) for different types of information is a difficult task. Adult processing models have focused primarily on the representational format problem with respect to speech perception, and a brief overview of the varying solutions proposed will illustrate the complexity of this issue.

Contact Representations in Adult Speech Perception

Models of adult language input processing vary considerably with respect to their descriptions of the representational format shared by the bottom-up information (or cues) entering the processing system and the information in the LLTS with which it must make contact (the contact representation). In some models of speech perception, for example, acoustic information from the speech waveform is assumed to undergo multiple transformations or encodings before it is stored in the LLTS (Pisoni and Luce, 1987). Perceptual processing of the acoustic signal is presumed to transform or encode it to varying degrees, yielding a more abstract representation to serve as the basis for contacting an entry in the LLTS. Contact representations consisting of distinctive feature matrices (Elman, 1989; McClelland and Elman, 1986), phonemes (Marslen-Wilson, 1987; Marslen-Wilson and Zwitserlood, 1989), syllables (Dupoux and Mehler, 1990), and stressed syllables (Grosjean and Gee, 1987) are among those that have been proposed.

In other models, it is assumed that acoustic information is stored in the LLTS in a relatively untransformed state, implying that activation can occur in a more direct fashion because both the cues for the acoustic information in the environment and its representation in the LLTS are much closer to the "raw" acoustic waveform. Klatt's (1979; 1989) lexical access from spectra model falls toward this end of the continuum. In this model, acoustic spectra encountered in the speech waveform are presumed to make contact with nearly identical (i.e., untransformed) acoustic spectra or "spectral templates" stored with individual lexical entries in the LLTS.

The possibility that different contact representations might be used for different processing tasks must also be countenanced, as pointed out by Pisoni and Luce (1987). It is also reasonable to speculate that contact representations may change with development. In any event, it should be clear that a multitude of potential cues could be associated with a lexical entry. Taking the approach that cues and contact representations are relatively untransformed raises questions about how the system can deal with partial or variable information. On the other hand, taking the approach that cues and contact representations consist of more highly encoded information raises questions about how the critical features guiding the transformation to the more abstract form are identified and implemented.

On-line Language Processing

Terms such as "activation," "access," and "retrieval" have often been used interchangeably to refer to the process by which information from the LLTS becomes available during the course of online language processing for purposes of either production or comprehension. However, recent work suggests that there are distinct components of this process. Marslen-Wilson's (1987, 1989) *cohort model* of language comprehension explicitly differentiates among the three constructs of *lexical activation, lexical access* (or *lexical retrieval*), and *lexical integration,* and it is within the context of the cohort model that the distinctions among them will be described.

Lexical Activation, Selection, and Integration in the Cohort Model

In the cohort model, speech input processing is assumed to take place in an essentially left-to-right, phoneme-by-phoneme fashion (Marslen-Wilson, 1987; 1989; Marslen-Wilson and Zwitserlood, 1989). In this model, processing of the initial segment of a word results in the simultaneous activation of all the lexical entries sharing that segment; this set of entries is known as the cohort.

Lexical activation is the term used to refer to this automatic and unconscious* spread of activation to entries having a segment (e.g., a phoneme) in common. The cohort could consist of a single entry if its initial segment were sufficient to distinguish it from all other entries in the lexicon. However, because so many lexical entries share similar word-initial sequences (for adults at least), the candidate set, or cohort, typically contains more than one lexical entry.

As additional acoustic segments from the speech stream are processed, some members of the cohort are found to be incompatible with the input, and the number of activated lexical entries decreases until a single entry with the "best fit" to the input data is identified or recognized. It is at this recognition point (Marslen-Wilson, 1989) or isolation point (Grosjean and Gee, 1987) that lexical access, lexical retrieval, or lexical selection (Andrews, 1989; Frauenfelder and Komisarjevsky Tyler, 1987) is said to occur; the processor has now identified the incoming input with a single lexical entry.

Consider an example in which a lis-

*Data from a number of studies (Carr et al., 1982; Eich, 1984; MacLeod, 1988) reveal the effects of lexical activation occurring below the threshold of conscious awareness. For example, MacLeod (1988) showed that subjects who had been exposed to a word on a list recall task but were unable to recall or recognize it. Nonetheless they relearned it more quickly on a subsequent task than words they had not encountered previously.

tener hears the word "ball" spoken in isolation. When enough acoustic information has been processed to identify the first phoneme as *[b]*, all *[b]*-initial lexical entries in his or her LLTS ("bagel," "buoyant," "bell," "bomb," "ball," "bake," "Bermuda," etc.) would be activated automatically. However, as the next phoneme *[a]* is identified, activation would cease for all members of the initial candidate set except those beginning with the sequence *[ba]* ("bomb," "ball," etc.). When the phoneme *[l]* is identified, along with a pause indicating word juncture, the cohort would be reduced to the single entry "ball"; this entry would now be said to be accessed or retrieved.

In the cohort model, it is at the point of lexical access that all of the other types of information associated with a lexical entry (e.g., its semantic, syntactic, orthographic, and episodic characteristics) become available for a final process known as lexical integration. In lexical integration, the information made available by lexical access is evaluated with reference to the processor's efforts to build representations of larger chunks of the input stream (e.g., syntactic or phonological phrases, utterances, text, or discourse units). In the example given earlier, the processor's task was to identify a word in isolation, so lexical integration was not required. However, if the listener had identified the lexical entry for ball as it occurred in the utterance "I can't believe he dropped the ball," syntactic information associated with the entry (e.g., its syntactic role as a concrete noun with the potential to occur following a determiner) would have been evaluated with reference to the syntactic and semantic characteristics of the input sentence for additional evidence concerning its precise identification.

The ease with which lexical activation, access, and integration can be separated in theory should not obscure the extent to which they are likely entwined during psycholinguistic processing or the difficulties inherent in efforts to specify the nature and timing of their interactions (Andrews, 1989; Eimas et al., 1990; Massaro, 1989). Controversies abound concerning the manner and time course of the process by which bottom-up cues from the acoustic waveform and top-down cues from such factors as prior discourse contexts and world knowledge interact to enable the emergence of a single best-fitting lexical entry from among the set of possibilities (Burton et al., 1989; Frauenfelder et al., 1990; Frauenfelder and Komisarjevsky Tyler, 1987; Marslen-Wilson, 1987, 1989). It seems likely that such interactions must involve rapid shifts between rapid parallel computations and decision points at which processing briefly takes a more serial turn, but this conjecture is much easier to make than to support with empirical evidence.

Creating Entries in the LLTS: Questions and Issues for a Process Model of Children's Lexical Acquisition

A crucial question for developmental and clinical psycholinguists concerns the process by which lexical entries become represented in LLTS in the first place. Unfortunately, little has been written concerning this process by psycholinguists and cognitive scientists. Work on lexical activation, access, and integration has typically involved processing of familiar words at a given point in time by adults (Craig and Kim, 1990; Marslen-Wilson, 1987) and children (Elliott et al., 1990) rather than the changes in processing that occur as an unfamiliar word becomes part of the LLTS (but see Dagenbach et al., 1990, concerning semantic priming from words newly learned by adults).

Until rather recently, even the child language acquisition literature has focused almost exclusively on the semantic and conceptual components of children's lexical entries (Carey, 1978, 1982). Questions about the changes in word meanings over time (Clark, 1973) and the abstract organizational relationships implied by children's word errors (Bowerman, 1982) have taken precedence over questions about the conditions under which a lexical entry is established initially and activated, accessed, and integrated subsequently. The brief review of the adult-based literature earlier suggests an almost unlimited number of possibilities for adapting constructs derived from work on adults' lexical processing to enrich future investigations of its development in children.

To take one example, the adult-based literature suggests the importance of specifying the extent to which information from different modalities is related or segregated in children's lexical representations at differing points in development. It may be possible to trace changes in the content of individual lexical entries with child-adapted variants of cross-modal priming paradigms, such as presenting the child with a visual cue to an existing LLTS entry and determining whether the acoustic-phonetic information associated with the entry is activated automatically, which would be expected to facilitate performance on phonetically similar items.

Similarly, the adult-based literature highlights a number of questions about the influence of the child's existing network of entries on his or her representation of new information, across or within modalities. For example, is the amount of acoustic-phonetic information represented during an exposure to a new word affected by the conceptual or visual similarity of its referent to others already in the child's network? Does the prior existence of a phonetically similar entry in the child's LLTS force a more detailed initial representation of the new word's acoustic-phonetic characteristics than if the new word has few acoustic-phonetic neighbors (Charles-Luce and Luce, 1990; Goldinger et al., 1989)?

As a final example, the trichotomy of lexical activation, access, and integration raises a number of questions concerning the time course and results of children's on-line lexical processing. Questions about the number and types of cues sufficient to create a new lexical entry or to activate an existing entry, as well as questions about the types and amounts of information available in lexical entries for words with which the child has had varying amounts of experience, are among the most obvious avenues for future explorations guided by the adult-based work.

THE CHILD TALK MODEL AND THE LLTS

With the emphasis of Chapman et al. (see Chapter 1) on an expanded view of the child's lexicon as "multiply cued" and containing more than simply "abstract core semantic, syntactic and phonological features associated with words," the Child Talk model suggests several points of contact between the adult-based proposals concerning the LLTS discussed earlier and efforts to develop a process-based account of lexical acquisition. However, by its focus on event-based representations and nonlinguistic information, Child Talk raises the questions of whether, and when, the young child can actually be said to have a lexical long-term store at all.

As noted by Chapman et al. (see Chapter 1), a number of developmental psycholinguists (Barrett, 1986; Bruner, 1975; Nelson, 1986) have proposed that the child's first representations of specifically linguistic information evolve out of more general representations of nonlinguistic information associated with the events, situations, or episodes that the child has encountered. As the child experiences a situation or event repeatedly over time, the memory representation for that event is presumed to become more detailed and more differentiated along some dimensions (Clark, 1987) and more generalized and schematic along others (MacWhinney, 1987; Pinker, 1989). Child Talk suggests that the child's memory is organized initially by associations among the situation-specific, nonlinguistic components of these events; rather than lexical entries in an LLTS, it appears that the representations are of event or situational entries in what might be described as an "episodic long-term store." The "experiential links" among these episodes discussed by Chapman et al. (see Chapter 1) appear to be directly analogous to the notion of cues discussed earlier, serving to activate the current representation of the event in memory.

Unfortunately, very little evidence currently exists concerning the nature of children's representations for events in memory or the cues by which these can be activated. To date, event representations have been described in quite general terms, more by excluding their linguistic components than by specifying the types of nonlinguistic information that they actually contain. As pointed out by Pinker (1989) it is not a trivial problem to make this sort of specification. Discovering how the child processes the myriad sets of co-occurring information in even a simple situation such that the relevant pieces (which might include who did what to whom and where) are represented while the irrelevant pieces (e.g., color of the participants' shoes) are ignored is a problem that should not be underestimated (McClelland and Rumelhart, 1987). The possibility that the child initially represents situations in formats unlike those of adults and correspondingly accesses these representations with nonadult cues is a very real one. Work addressing these issues would seem to be a crucial prerequisite to further progress in process-oriented accounts of language development.

Similarly, Child Talk's emphasis on the early primacy of nonlinguistic forms of information creates a pressing need for work aimed at determining when and how linguistic forms of information become represented in the child's event entries. The Child Talk model appears to imply that it is only after certain types of nonlinguistic information (e.g., the people, objects, and state changes typical of an event) are represented in memory that the child's processing begins to yield representations of other linguistically relevant information, such as the acoustic-phonetic waveforms occurring in conjunction with the event.

However, the early ability of infants to distinguish speech from nonspeech stimuli suggests that some acoustic information, albeit poorly specified, may well be represented in the child's earliest event entries. Just as children must identify and represent the key nonlinguistic components of situations in their event entries, so must they conduct similarly complex processes of differentiation and abstraction to represent crucial acoustic-phonetic information. And at some point, when the child's representation of a situation, event, or object does have some independently represented acoustic-phonetic components, the acoustic-phonetic information must begin to function as a solo cue, providing a new pathway for activating the representation for either comprehension or production purposes. At this point, the child should be able to access the information in an entry without benefit of episodic or situational cues; it may be at this point that it becomes reasonable to use the term LLTS (rather than episodic long-term store).

A pressing need exists for explicit

proposals concerning *when* and *how* children make the transition from event-based representations relatively devoid of acoustic-phonetic detail, to phonologically organized networks that can be activated, accessed, and integrated without benefit of nonlinguistic cues. The young child need not be capable of adultlike speech perceptual analyses to begin to tag lexical entries with phonological information. Successfully creating a phonologically specified entry for a linguistic unit requires only that the child's representation of acoustic-phonetic information be sufficiently detailed to enable the new entry to be distinguished from others in the network. A young child with few lexical entries may initially need to store very little acoustic-phonetic detail to differentiate them. It seems reasonable to suppose that the child's ability to make finer distinctions in entering acoustic-phonetic information into his or her lexical entries develops in tandem with the expansion in the number of entries in his or her LLTS. The interplay between the development of the child's auditory perceptual skills and the need to create distinct representations for a burgeoning number of LLTS entries is one of a number of questions facing process-oriented child language investigators.

VIEWS OF CHILD LANGUAGE IMPAIRMENT AND THE LLTS

One objective of this chapter has been to suggest that work in adult lexical processing can and should be mined for ideas and experimental paradigms in the quest for a defensible process-oriented model of lexical acquisition in normally developing children. In this final section, I suggest that adult-based LLTS models may also contribute to developing informative models of child language impairment. If speed and efficiency in activating, accessing, and integrating information in the LLTS are important determinants of verbal skill, as suggested by many investigators (Bock, 1982; Dell, 1986), it appears reasonable to consider how these processes might go awry and what the outward symptoms of such disruptions might be in light of the characteristics associated with language-impaired children. The scope of this chapter precludes a comprehensive exploration of such questions, and efforts to study them are clearly in their infancy. However, in the following section I will illustrate how constructs from adult-based LLTS models could be used to develop and test hypotheses concerning the structural characteristics of the LLTS in language-impaired children.

THE STRUCTURE OF THE LLTS IN NORMALLY DEVELOPING AND LANGUAGE-IMPAIRED CHILDREN: THREE HYPOTHESES

It is possible to imagine at least three general ways in which the structural features of the LLTSs of normal and language-impaired children could differ (if we ignore the possibility that such differences could occur synergistically). First, the LLTS of a language-impaired child might simply contain fewer entries than that of his or her normally developing peers, with existing entries containing equivalent amounts of information and appropriate connections to related entries. Second, the language-impaired child might have the same number of lexical entries but have less, or less detailed, information associated with any given entry than his or her normal peers. Third, the language-impaired child might have as many lexical entries, with as much information, as his or her normal peers but fail to have established the appropriate connections to related lexical entries. Each of these possibilities yields different predictions concerning these children's performance characteristics, as shall be described with reference to a hypothetical female language-impaired child.

Hypothesis 1: Fewer Lexical Entries

If the first possibility were the case, and the language-impaired child simply had fewer lexical entries in her LLTS, we would expect her to have a smaller vocabulary than her peers, with no unusual differences between comprehension and production vocabulary. No differences would be expected between the performances of the normal and language-impaired child on either explicit and implicit memory tasks involving existing LLTS entries, but the normal child should obviously perform much better on any tasks involving entries in her LLTS that are not represented in the LLTS of the language impaired child.

If the language-impaired child simply had fewer lexical entries, we would also expect her to perform as rapidly and efficiently as her peers in activating, selecting, and integrating her existing lexical entries in such tasks as the gating and priming paradigms that have been used with adults. According to the cohort model (Marslen-Wilson, 1987, 1989), in fact, having a smaller LLTS might actually lead to faster identification of familiar words on gating tasks under some conditions, because the first segments of the target word would activate a smaller candidate set, allowing the competition for a "winner" to be resolved sooner. This could be tested, of course, by comparing gating task speed and accuracy when the target words are chosen to manipulate their frequency and the number of entries with which they share initial segments. For example, a language-impaired child and normal child should perform at similar rates on familiar, high-frequency words that do not share initial segments with other entries; the initial segments of such words should activate a similar, small cohort for both of them. However, the language-impaired child might have an advantage in identifying high-frequency target words that share initial segments with low-frequency entries that exist in the LLTS of the normal, but not the language-impaired, child, because of the additional time required by the normal child to wait for additional information to distinguish the winner from among the candidate set. The normal child would be expected to have an accuracy advantage in identifying less frequent words that activate a large cohort containing both frequent and less frequent entries; in this case, the language-impaired child should have fewer entries in competition and should therefore make faster but more erroneous responses, being limited to selections from among her small number of existing entries.

Hypothesis 2: Informationally Impoverished Lexical Entries

Consider now the second possibility, in which the LLTS of the language-impaired child contains the same number of lexical entries as her normal peer but less information is associated with these entries. Such a child might be expected to perform as well as her normal peers on lexical tasks requiring certain domains of information but more poorly on others, depending on the information missing from her lexical entries. To test this possibility, one would have to thoroughly explore such children's performances on tasks tapping different forms of information associated with lexical entries, comparing, for example, skill in identifying or recalling the visual features associated with an entry's referent with skill in recognizing its phonological, syntactic, or orthographic characteristics. Investigators of reading disability have demonstrated how such experiments can be constructed (Vellutino and Scanlon, 1987); the need for similar examinations of language-impaired children is evident. If future investigations do suggest that language-impaired children show consistent patterns in the vulnerability of information associated with their LLTS entries, there are clear clinical implications for intervening to make such information more salient to such children as they attempt to establish lexical entries.

Hypothesis 3: Inadequate Connections Among Lexical Entries

What of the third possibility, that language-impaired children might actually suffer from difficulties in establishing links among related lexical entries? Priming experiments might profitably be used to explore this hypothesis, providing evidence on the extent to which language-impaired subjects show priming effects for unrelated or marginally related entries after an encounter with a new lexical form under controlled conditions.

This brief description of three possible ways in which the structural features of the LLTSs of language-impaired children might differ from those of their normally developing peers has been included only to illustrate how models of the LLTS might be used to design experiments providing a clearer picture of such children's deficits. Even if structural LLTS differences such as those described earlier are found, they will be only part of the story. A complete account will have to include studies of the specifics of lexical processing in language-impaired children; investigators such as Gathercole and Baddeley (1989, 1990), Kail et al. (1984), and Sininger et al. (1989), among others, have taken important steps toward this goal.

CONCLUSION

The intent of this chapter has been to suggest that future investigations into the language processing skills of both language-impaired children and their normally developing peers will profit by capitalizing on models of lexical processing developed with adults in mind. There is an obvious need for caution in applying constructs and findings derived from adults to accounts of children's lexical processing, and each adult-based assumption must be tested for its relevance to children. However, the large body of literature on the structure and processes of the adult's LLTS suggests a number of questions and investigations with the potential to contribute to well-specified, process-oriented models of child language development.

REFERENCES

Anderson JR: *The Architecture of Cognition.* Cambridge, Mass, Harvard University Press, 1983.

Andrews S: Frequency and neighborhood effects on lexical access: Activation or search? *J Exp Psychol Learn Memory Cognit* 1989; 15:802–814.

Barrett MD: Early semantic representations and early word-usage, in Kuczaj SA, Barrett MD (eds): *The Development of Word Meaning.* New York, Springer-Verlag New York, 1986, pp 39–67.

Bock JK: Toward a cognitive psychology of syntax: Information processing contributions to sentence formulation. *Psychol Rev* 1982; 89:1–45.

Bowerman M: Reorganizational processes in lexical and syntactic development, in Wanner E, Gleitman LR (eds): *Language Acquisition.* New York, Cambridge University Press, 1982, pp 319–346.

Bresnan J (ed): *The Mental Representation of Grammatical Relations.* Cambridge, Mass, MIT press, 1982.

Bruner J: The ontogenesis of speech acts. *J Child Lang* 1975; 2:1–19.

Burton MW, Baum SR, Blumstein SE: Lexical effects on the phonetic categorization of speech: The role of acoustic structure. *J Exp Psychol (Hum Percept)* 1989; 15:567–575.

Butterworth B: Lexical access in speech production, in Marslen-Wilson W (ed): *Lexical Representation and Process.* Cambridge, Mass, MIT Press, 1989, pp 108–135.

Caramazza A, Sloan Berndt R: A multicomponent deficit view of agrammatic Broca's aphasia, in Kean ML (ed): *Agrammatism.* New York, Academic Press, 1985, pp 27–63.

Carey S: The child as word learner, in Halle M, Bresnan J, Miller GA (eds): *Linguistic Theory and Psychological Reality.* Cambridge, Mass, MIT Press, 1978, pp 264–293.

Carey S: (1982). Semantic development: The state of the art, in Wanner E, Gleitman LR (eds): *Language Acquisition.* Cambridge, Mass, Cambridge University Press, 1982, pp 347–389.

Carr TH, McCauley C, Sperber RD, et al: Words, pictures and priming: On semantic activation, conscious identification, and the automaticity of information processing. *J Exp Psychol (Hum Percept)* 1982; 8:757–777.

Chafe WL: *Meaning and the Structure of Language.* Chicago, University of Chicago Press, 1970.

Charles-Luce J, Luce PA: Similarity neighborhoods of words in young children's lexicons. *J Child Lang* 1990; 17:205–215.

Clark EV: What's in a word? On the child's acquisition of semantics in his first language, in Moore TE (ed): *Cognitive Development and the Acquisition of Language.* New York, Academic Press, 1973, pp 65–110.

Clark EV: The principle of contrast: A constraint on language acquisition, in MacWhinney B (ed): *Mechanisms of Language Acquisition.* Hillsdale, NJ, Lawrence Erlbaum Associates, 1987, pp 1–33.

Collins A, Loftus E: A spreading activation theory of semantic processing. *Psychol Rev* 1975; 82:407–428.

Craig CH, Kim BW: Effects of time gating and word length on isolated word-recognition performance. *J Speech Hear Res* 1990; 33:808–815.

Crystal D: *A First Dictionary of Linguistics and Phonetics.* Boulder, Colo, Westview Press, 1980.

Dagenbach D, Carr TH, Barnhardt TM: Inhibitory semantic priming of lexical decisions due to failure to retrieve weakly activated codes. *J Exp Psychol (Learn Mem Cogn)* 1990; 16:328–340.

Dell GS: A spreading activation theory of retrieval in sentence production. *Psychol Rev* 1986; 93:283–321.

Donnenwerth-Nolan S, Tanenhaus MK, Seidenberg MS: Multiple code activation in word recognition: Evidence from rhyme monitoring. *J Exp Psychol (Hum Learn)* 1981; 7:170–180.

Dupoux E, Mehler J: Monitoring the lexicon with normal and compressed speech: Frequency effects and the prelexical code. *J Memory Lang* 1990; 29:316–355.

Eich E: Memory for unattended events: Remembering with and without awareness. *Memory Cognit* 1984; 12:105–111.

Eimas PD, Marcovitz Hornstein SB, Payton P: Attention and the role of dual codes in phoneme monitoring. *J Memory Lang* 1990; 29:160–180.

Elliott L, Scholl ME, Grant JO, et al: Perception of gated, highly familiar spoken monosyllabic nouns by children with and without learning disabilities. *J Learn Disabil* 1990; 23:248–252.

Elman JL: Connectionist approaches to acoustic/phonetic processing, in Marslen-Wilson W (ed): *Lexical Representation and Process*. Cambridge, Mass, MIT Press, 1989, pp 227–260.

Frauenfelder UH, Komisarjevsky Tyler L: The process of spoken word recognition: An introduction. *Cognition* 1987; 25:1–20.

Frauenfelder UH, Segui J, Dijkstra T: Lexical effects in phonemic processing: Facilitatory or inhibitory? *J Exp Psychol (Hum Percept)* 1990; 16:77–91.

Gathercole SE, Baddeley AD: Evaluation of the role of phonological STM in the development of vocabulary in children: A longitudinal study. *J Memory Lang* 1989; 28:200–213.

Gathercole SE, Baddeley AD: Phonological memory deficits in language disordered children: Is there a causal connection? *J Memory Lang* 1990; 29:336–360.

Gillund G, Shiffrin RM: A retrieval model for both recognition and recall. *Psychol Rev* 1984; 91:1–67.

Goldinger SD, Luce PA, Pisoni DB: Priming lexical neighbors of spoken words: Effects of competition and inhibition. *J Memory Lang* 1989; 28:501–518.

Goodglass H, Menn L: Is agrammatism a unitary phenomenon? in Kean ML (ed): *Agrammatism*. New York, Academic Press, 1985, pp 1–26.

Grosjean F, Gee JP: Prosodic structure and spoken word recognition. *Cognition* 1987; 25:135–155.

Hankamer J: Morphological parsing and the lexicon, in Marslen-Wilson W (ed): *Lexical Representation and Process*. Cambridge, Mass, MIT Press, 1989, pp 392–408.

Jackendoff R: *Consciousness and the Computational Mind*. Cambridge, Mass, MIT Press, 1987.

Kail R, Hale CA, Leonard LB, et al: Lexical storage and retrieval in language-impaired children. *Appl Psycholinguist* 1984; 5: 37–49.

Klatt DH: Speech perception: A model of acoustic-phonetic analysis and lexical access, in Cole RA (ed): *Perception and Production of Fluent Speech*. Hillsdale, NJ, Lawrence Erlbaum Associates, 1979.

Klatt DH: Review of selected models of speech perception, in Marslen-Wilson W (ed): *Lexical Representation and Process*. Cambridge, Mass, MIT Press, 1989, pp 169–226.

Komisarjevsky Tyler L: The role of lexical representations in language comprehension, in Marslen-Wilson W (ed): *Lexical Representation and Process*. Cambridge, Mass, MIT Press, 1989, pp 439–462.

MacLeod CM: Forgotten but not gone: Savings for pictures and words in long-term memory. *J Exp Psychol (Learn Mem Cogn)* 1988; 14:195–212.

MacWhinney B: The competition model, in MacWhinney B (ed): *Mechanisms of Language Acquisition*. Hillsdale, NJ, Lawrence Erlbaum Associates, 1987, pp 249–308.

Marslen-Wilson W: Functional parallelism in spoken word recognition. *Cognition* 1987; 25:71–102.

Marslen-Wilson W (ed): *Lexical Representation and Process*. Cambridge, Mass, MIT Press, 1989.

Marslen-Wilson W, Zwitserlood P: Accessing spoken words: The importance of word onsets. *J Exp Psychol (Hum Percept)* 1989; 15:576–585.

Massaro D: Testing between the TRACE model and the fuzzy logical model of speech perception. *Cognit Psychol* 1989; 21:398–421.

McClelland JL, Elman JL: The TRACE model of speech perception. *Cognit Psychol* 1986; 18:1–86.

McClelland JL, Rumelhart DE: A distributed model of human learning and memory, in McClelland JL, Rumelhart DE (eds): *Parallel Distributed Processing*. Cambridge, Mass, MIT Press, 1986, vol 2, pp 170–215.

McNamara TP, Healy AF: Semantic, phonological and mediated priming in reading and lexical decisions. *J Exp Psychol (Learn Mem Cogn)* 1988; 14:398–409.

Nelson K: *Event Knowledge*. Hillsdale, NJ, Lawrence Erlbaum Associates, 1986.

Norman DA, Rumelhart DE: *Explorations in Cognition*. New York, WH Freeman, & Co, Publishers, 1975.

Pinker S: *Language Learnability and Language Development*. Cambridge, Mass, Harvard University Press, 1984.

Pinker S: *Learnability and Cognition*. Cambridge, Mass, MIT Press, 1989.

Pisoni DB, Luce PA: Acoustic-phonetic representations in word recognition. *Cognition* 1987; 25:21–52.

Rumelhart DE, McClelland JL: *Parallel Distributed Processing*. Cambridge, Mass, MIT Press, 1986.

Schvaneveldt R, Meyer D: Retrieval and comparison processes in semantic memory, in Kornblum S (ed): *Attention and Performance*. New York, Academic Press, 1973, pp 395–409.

Sininger YS, Klatzky RL, Kirchner DM: Memory scanning speed in language-disordered children. *J Speech Hearing Res* 1989; 32:289–297.

Stemberger JP, MacWhinney B: Frequency and the lexical storage of regularly inflected forms. *Memory Cognit* 1986; 14: 17–26.

Swinney D: Lexical access during sentence comprehension: (Re)consideration of context effects. *J Verbal Learn Verbal Behav* 1979; 14:645–660.

Van Wijk C, Kempen G: A dual system for producing self-repairs in spontaneous speech: Evidence from experimentally elicited corrections. *Cognit Psychol* 1987; 19:403–440.

Vellutino FR, Scanlon DM: Linguistic coding and reading ability, in Rosenberg S (ed): *Advances in Applied Psycholinguistics*. Cambridge University Press, 1987, pp 1–69.

Zurif EB: Language mechanisms: A neuropsychological perspective. *Am Sci* 1980; 68:305.

9 Fast Mapping: A New Look at Word Learning

Elizabeth R. Crais, Ph.D.

In recent years to investigate how children acquire new words, researchers have used methodologies employing the introduction of novel words. The term *novel* in most instances implies either nonsense words created by the examiner or real, but unfamiliar, words. When encountering a novel word, children have been shown to use a strategy called *fast mapping* to help them infer the meaning of the word. Fast mapping is the term coined by Carey and Bartlett (1978) to refer to the rapid acquisition of information about a word during the first few encounters with it. During this phase, only a small portion of the information available to the child is actually mapped into long-term memory. Later, as suggested by Carey (1978a), during the extended mapping phase, which includes several more encounters, the remainder of the available information is mapped.

The availability and use of a fast mapping strategy has significant implications for vocabulary acquisition in young children. Children are reported to learn an average of nine new words per day, reaching 14,000 words in their comprehension vocabularies by age 6 years (Carey, 1978a). The use of a fast mapping strategy may help explain this amazing acquisition feat. If a child is able to enter some information about a word into long-term memory, hold the initial representation while continuing to add further information from similar experiences, then representations of many words can evolve simultaneously. Indeed, Carey (1978a) hypothesizes that at any one time a child may be working out the meanings of more than 1,600 words.

HISTORICAL VIEW OF FAST MAPPING STUDIES

Over the years the focus of fast mapping studies has varied, with the early studies asking whether children could use surface syntactic cues to infer a word's meaning (Berko, 1958; Brown, 1957; Katz et al., 1974). Later studies looked at such issues as referential vs. nonreferential children's acquisition (Leonard et al., 1979, 1981; Nelson et al., 1985) or the acquisition of object vs. action words (Leonard et al., 1979, 1981, 1982; Rice and Woodsmall, 1988; Schwartz and Leonard, 1984). Other studies have examined the effect on learning of varied conditions or contexts (Au and Markman, 1987; Crais, 1987a; Dickinson, 1984; Dockrell and Campbell, 1986; Heibeck and Markman, 1987; Holdgrafer and Sorenson, 1984; Leonard et al., 1979, 1981, 1982; Nelson and Bonvillian, 1973; Streim and Chapman, 1987) and the acquisition of a new word over time (Bates et al., 1988; Carey and Bartlett, 1978; Dockrell and Campbell, 1986; Tomasello et al., 1988). More recent studies have compared the fast mapping skills of children who are normally developing with those who have language impairments (Dollaghan, 1987;

Leonard et al., 1982; Meline, 1988; Rice et al., 1990).

The study cited most frequently as representing the fast mapping paradigm is that of Carey and Bartlett (1978), in which the new word "chromium" was introduced to 3- to 4-year-old preschool children in a naturalistic setting. The teacher, when setting up for a snack, individually asked each child, "See those two trays? Bring me the chromium one, not the red one, the chromium one." The use of an explicit contrast, red vs. chromium, indicated chromium as a color word and was intended to allow the child to identify readily the referent (the olive-colored tray). With comprehension and production tasks administered 1 week later, Carey and Bartlett (1978) found that one to two encounters with the word had allowed at least one half of the children to map something about the word in long-term memory. Of particular significance were the pretask and posttask probes for partial knowledge acquired about chromium in which the children were asked to match colors, recognize and produce color names, and recognize whether various "words" were colors. As noted by Carey and Bartlett (1978), the children's partial mappings of chromium were quite variable and highly dependent on the child's preexisting color lexicon and the name the child used for olive during the pretests.

Other fast mapping studies with children as young as 15 to 24 months (Bates et al., 1988; Dollaghan, 1985; Ross et al., 1986; Schwartz and Leonard, 1984) have indicated that young children are able to map various aspects of a new word such as the designated referent, its color, texture, or function, its semantic category, its location or actions performed on the referent, or its phonetic shape (at least for recognition). Conclusions drawn by Crais (1987b) when reviewing recent fast mapping studies include: (1) even one encounter with a new word is sufficient for very young children (12–15 months) to map something in long-term memory (Schwartz and Leonard, 1984); (2) as predicted by Carey and Bartlett (1978), the more exposures to a word, the more complete is the map; (3) comprehension and phonetic production of the word are achieved separately, and as noted by Dollaghan (1985), the production of the new word is the most vulnerable aspect; and (4) the type of presentation context (conversation, story, definition) differentially affects the acquisition process at different ages (Dickinson, 1984).

Although many similarities exist in the studies' results regarding children's recognition and comprehension of new words under fast mapping conditions, less agreement is evident about the number of presentations and the conditions necessary before children *produce* newly introduced words. For example, the question of how readily children can learn to produce new words receives a variable answer relative to the production task (spontaneous vs. elicited), the number of repetitions presented, and also the number of other novel words concurrently introduced. The number of repeated presentations necessary for correct *spontaneous* production in infants (Leonard et al., 1979) and preschoolers (Holdgrafer and Sorenson, 1984) has ranged from 10 to 40. Whereas, under *elicited* conditions, only one to two presentations were necessary for correct production in almost half of Dollaghan's (1985) 2- to 5-year-olds. In addition, studies that have introduced one or only a few words (Dollaghan, 1985; Somers, 1991; Streim and Chapman, 1987) typically report more favorable production results than do those presenting several or more words concurrently (Crais, 1987a; Holdgrafer and Sorenson, 1984; Leonard et al., 1979). In a recent study examining 4-year-olds' abilities to acquire information about a new word in a story context, Somers (1991) concluded that the number of repetitions of the word within the story was a key factor in whether the children could produce, identify the referent for, and recognize the word during follow-up testing. On all three measures, the children who received five presentations of the word performed significantly better than those receiving only one presentation. These results can be contrasted with those from Somers' story comprehension task in which the children were asked questions about the referent and its actions during the story. On this task, there were no differences between the children receiving one vs. five presentations. Thus, although number of presentations was an important element affecting the production results, it differentially affected the children's ability to respond to some comprehension tasks.

Inconsistencies between studies also arise when the studies consider whether or not age-related changes exist in fast mapping skills, and if so, which age ranges and tasks reveal differences. For example, Heibeck and Markman (1987) reported no age differences between groups of 2-, 3-, and 4-year-olds on the comprehension or production of new shape, color, or texture words. They did note differences between the groups on a hyponym task, in which the child was asked, "See this? It's not fibrous because it's ______________," to determine if he or she had inferred the novel word's semantic domain. In contrast, in a study with first, third, and fifth grade children and adults, Crais (1987a) reported differences between all groups (except the third and fifth graders) on both comprehension and production tasks. Thus, when one is attempting to compare results among fast mapping studies and to account for the inconsistencies that exist, it is first useful to examine a number of methodological issues that affect the generalizability of these studies (Table 9–1).

TABLE 9–1.
Important Methodological Issues Related to Fast Mapping Studies

1. Developmental level of the subjects
2. Dependent measures used to indicate acquisition (e.g., comprehension, production, recognition, hyponym)
3. Relationship of the novel word, the concept represented, and the knowledge the subject has about similar words or concepts
4. Ecological validity of the presentation context (e.g., training paradigm vs. naturalistic setting)

METHODOLOGICAL ISSUES RELATED TO FAST MAPPING STUDIES

Developmental Level

The first methodolgical issue crucial to understanding the variations reported in the speed and amount of word learning across studies concerns the differing developmental levels of the subjects studied and the effects these levels may have on word acquisition. Nelson (1988) suggests that word learning takes place in at least three developmental periods, each with its own problems to be solved and distinct strategies for lexical acquisition. The first period, identified by the phrase "learning what words do," represents the child's efforts at figuring out what a word is, what it does, and how a word is used to refer to things or events. This period, as noted by Nelson (1988), lasts approximately 6 to 12 months from the time when a child first becomes sensitive to language forms and responds consistently to them (as early as 9 months) until the production of 30 or more words and the first two-word combinations (as late as 24 months). Characteristics of this period are comprehension better than production, restricted use and infrequent production of words, and emphasis on one or a few functions.

The second period, beginning when children have approximately 30 productive words, is evidenced by a naming explosion and by children finding words for the conceptual categories for things, peoples, actions, and events in their worlds. Nelson (1988) suggests that the period may last several years and is particularly characterized by the fast mapping of words onto meanings. The final period, which begins in the early preschool years and extends into the early school years, is characterized by revision, reorganization, and consolidation of words into the semantic network. As noted by Nelson (1988), Bowerman (1982) has documented the occurrence of reorganization within different domains during this time period.

Nelson (1988) argues that distinct problems are encountered within each period and, therefore, differing processes of acquisition should be expected at each developmental level. If Nelson (1988) is correct, the presence or absence of developmental differences within an age range relative to other age ranges may not be surprising. However, little empirical information is available regarding different processes used at differing age levels, because no one study has yet attempted to span all three of Nelson's developmental periods, and, in fact, very few studies span even two periods.

Dependent Measures

A second important issue when results from acquisition studies are compared is that of describing what constitutes "learning," or "acquiring," a word. Both theoretical and methodological issues arise. Bierwisch (1981) argues that there are two aspects of meaning, the semantic and conceptual structures involved, and presents a complex framework for distinguishing the principles guiding each aspect. Carey (1978a) describes learning as, at least minimally, entering the word into the mental lexicon, and thus recognizing that a word is a word. She also notes that the child must learn its properties (syntactic, semantic, referential), its relation to other words, its role in determining entailments, and its conceptual underpinnings. Dockrell and Campbell (1986), following the work of Lyons (1977), use the terms reference, denotation, and sense to provide an operational definition of what is acquired. In using this framework, they are concerned primarily with the semantic information that determines the meaning of words across different situations. Accordingly, *reference* refers to the relationship between an object and an expression used on a particular occasion; therefore, an object can be referred to in many ways dependent on the situation. *Denotation* describes the knowledge of the range of objects or instances to which a word can be applied; thus, "cup" denotes a set of objects that are used for drinking. Finally, *sense* refers to the ways that words are joined or separated from each other within the language system (e.g., "red" is a color word but not a size word).

Methodologic differences in the definition of word learning or acquisition also arise. The type of task used to test for learning within each study constitutes how word learning is viewed. Many word learning studies have employed comprehension tasks that require responses such as choosing objects or pictures representing the objects or actions (Brown, 1957; Carey and Bartlett, 1978; Dollaghan, 1985; Katz et al., 1974; Leonard et al., 1982; Somers, 1991; Tomikawa and Dodd, 1980; Wykes and Johnson-Laird, 1977), performing specified actions on objects (Bates et al., 1988; Leonard et al., 1982), distinguishing some aspect of the word such as that it represents a color or material term (Au and Markman, 1987; Dickinson, 1984; Heibeck and Markman, 1987), providing a response based on the comprehension of the word in a story (Crais, 1987a; Dickinson, 1984; Somers, 1991; Wykes and Johnson-Laird,

1977), answering questions about the word (Keil, 1983), and recognizing the novel words as "real" or "silly" words or determining correct syntactical usage (Dickinson, 1984).

Information on the production of novel words has also been gained by varied means, from counting spontaneous productions of novel words (Bates et al., 1988; Leonard et al., 1979; Nelson and Bonvillian, 1973) or spontaneous imitations (Bates et al., 1988; Leonard et al., 1979) to requiring labeling of objects or actions (Au and Markman, 1987; Heibeck and Markman, 1987; Holdgrafer and Sorenson, 1984; Leonard et al., 1981, 1982, 1984; Schwartz and Leonard, 1984; Somers, 1991), asking "what is an 'X' or what do you remember about 'X'?" (Crais, 1987a; Keil, 1983), requiring definitions (Dickinson, 1984), noting the spontaneous use of novel words during story retellings (Crais, 1987a), and using hyponym tasks (Au and Markman, 1987; Heibeck and Markman, 1987).

Although a variety of measures to test word learning have been used, few studies have employed multiple measures focusing on aspects of both comprehension and production. In addition, few studies have examined the word learning process over time or differing developmental levels or have attempted generalization of learning across settings or exemplars.

Relationship of Word, Concept Represented, and Child's Knowledge

A third important issue when results from word learning studies are compared is to examine the relationship of the novel word to the concept it represents and the knowledge that the child has about similar words or concepts. Jenkins and Dixon (1983) suggest that prior knowledge regarding a word differs markedly from prior knowledge about the concept it represents. In describing vocabulary development in reading, Jenkins and Dixon (1983) note four word-to-knowledge-base conditions, each representing a different relation the novel word may have to the child's prior knowledge. The first two conditions involve the learning of new words for old concepts: (1) "relabeling" the known item or concept (e.g., "purse" = "pocketbook") and (2) learning the name for a known but previously unlabeled concept (e.g., "speedometer" = "the dial on the dashboard"). Jenkins and Dixon (1986) suggest that this type of "known concept" word learning is much easier than the remaining two conditions in which the child must learn both a new word and a new concept.

Learning Words For Known Concepts

Several studies have examined word learning of known concepts in young children, with particular interest on which words would be learned faster, words for objects with existing labels or words for objects with no known labels. One such study is Dockrell's (1981), in which children had to identify the referent in a picture when an unknown word was used. When children already had a name for an object, they had more difficulty indicating that object as the new word. As suggested by Dockrell and Campbell (1986), the children used a "preemption strategy" and preempted use of the novel word with the known word. (This would be an instance of the principle of contrast that Clark, 1987, proposed.)

In later work, however, Dockrell and Campbell (1986) compared the introduction of new words and objects using perceptual and lexical contrasts (e.g., "Pass me the gombe block, not the red or green one."). In this study, preemption did not preclude the children learning a synonym for known terms, and Dockrell and Campbell (1986) suggest that preemption may be a significant variable only at particular stages and in particular circumstances. Crais (1987a) documented this age-related variability in the use of preemption by first, third, and fifth grade children and adults when novel words with common referents were introduced in stories. In their storytellings, although the groups varied in the number of novel words they used within their stories, the first graders used many more synonyms than novel words, the third and fifth graders used equal amounts of each, and the adults used primarily novel words with few synonyms. Thus, in spite of the synonyms available to the adults, they were more able to override the use of a preemption strategy, whereas the children were less likely to do so.

Learning Words for Unknown Concepts

Studies presenting children or adults with unknown words and concepts have indicated the extreme difficulty encountered in this type of learning. In a study with 9- to 13-year-old children, Werner and Kaplan (1952) introduced new words in sets of six sentences and asked the students to figure out the meaning of each imaginary word after reading each sentence (e.g., "People with bordicks are often unhappy. A person who has many bordicks is not well liked."). Werner and Kaplan (1952) noted that even the oldest students were incorrect on more than half of the items, particularly the more abstract items. Without information available about the students' underlying conceptual knowledge of the words, however, it can only be surmised that many of the words were unknown both lexically and conceptually to the students. Similar results were reported by Carey (1978a) from a study by Klatzky et al. (1973), in which children experienced difficulty learning comparative terms that had no English equivalency, indicating the children's problems in mapping new words with unknown concepts. Finally, learning new words with unknown concepts is a difficult task even for adults, as evidenced by Daalen-Kapteijns and Elshout-Mohr's (1981) adult subjects, who had difficulty learning new words referring to realistic but nonexistent items. Daalen-Kapteijns and Elshout-Mohr (1981) also noted different strategies of word learning used by their subjects, dependent on the subjects' verbal skills (e.g., whether high or low verbal).

Ecological Validity of Presentation Context

The fourth and final methodological issue relates to the ecological validity of the experimental tasks and the contexts within which word learning in children has been examined. Two primary types of presentation contexts can be identified in fast mapping studies: those that attempt to represent the natural environment within which new words are learned and those that use a training paradigm to teach new words to some set criteria. In addition, some methodologies use aspects of both types within one study, for example, studies in which children are taught a series of new words within a naturalistic setting (e.g., during play with objects). Although positive results have generally been documented within both naturalistic and training presentation contexts, differences in methodologies (e.g., number of words presented within any one context, number of exemplars, dependent measures) make direct comparison difficult. As noted by Carey (1978a), Dockrell and Campbell (1986), and Nelson (1988), many experimental word learning tasks do not represent the typical ways in which young children interact with adults or the ways in which they typically learn new words. For example, how often do children encounter 12 to 16 new words within one play session, and how likely is it that an adult would name each item 22 times? Similarly, the use of conceptual terms that violate English lexical constraints creates undue difficulty for children and adults in acquiring new terms. Although some early studies may have used less ecologically realistic presentation contexts, more recent work has focused primarily on naturally occurring contexts for the introduction of new words.

All four of these sources of methodological variation have contributed to the differences noted in the amount and manner of learning achieved by children within word learning studies. When findings across studies are compared, it is critical to hold in mind these methodological differences in developmental level of child, measures of word learning used, relation of the new word to other knowledge, and ecological validity of the task.

The remainder of this chapter will focus on factors noted to affect the word learning process and the strategies used by children when encountering a new word. A variety of factors have been shown to influence the acquisition process; they are as diverse as the methodologies used to document their effects. The factors have a direct impact on the strategies used by children. The following discussion will first highlight factors known to influence word learning and then present a sampling of strategies. The factors have been categorized into four sets of characteristics, those representative of (1) the child, (2) the new word, (3) the referent, and (4) the introducing event (Table 9–2).

TABLE 9–2.
Examples of Factors Affecting Word Learning

Characteristics of the child
Learning style
Phonological skills
Existing lexicon
Language skills
Characteristics of the word
Sound components
Syllabic shape
Characteristics of the referent
Object vs. action
Number of possible actions on object
Perceptual features
Relationships within semantic system
Characteristics of the introducing event
Sentential variation
Syntactic structure
Use of linguistic contrast
Number, type, and timing of exemplars
Single vs. multiple
Number of overlapping features
Temporal contiguity of word and referent
Clearness of referent
Physically present object vs. novel words presented in oral stories
Number of words presented concurrently
Discourse context
Conversation
Story
Definition

FACTORS AFFECTING WORD LEARNING

Characteristics of the Child

Although the results of all of the studies using a fast mapping paradigm are dependent on the individual characteristics of the children studied, several researchers (Leonard et al., 1979; 1981; Carey and Bartlett, 1978; Markman and Wachtel, 1988; Nelson et al., 1985) have specifically chosen to document differences in word learning relative to individual characteristics present in children. In Leonard et al. (1979), children identified as referential in their early vocabulary development (more than 50% nominals in first 50 words) were more likely than nonreferential children to imitate newly introduced words. Referential children also acquired a greater number of object words; however no differences were seen between the groups on action words (Leonard et al., 1981). Similar findings of a word learning advantage for imitative-referential children over personal-social children at 22 and 27 months of age were reported by Nelson et al. (1985). These same groups of children, however, showed the reverse trend at 54 months of age, at which time the personal-social children gained more of the presented concepts. Nelson et al. (1985, p. 448) suggest that perhaps heavy reliance on imitation after 27 months by the imitative-referential children may "no longer be developmentally appropriate or advantageous."

As for the impact of a child's individual phonological inventory of sounds, the work of Leonard and his colleagues (Leonard et al., 1979, 1981) has indicated that new words composed of consonant sounds already present in a child's speech are easier to learn than those composed of sounds absent from the child's speech.

The child's existing lexicon also has been shown to have an effect on the word learning process (Carey and Bartlett, 1978; Heibeck and Markman, 1987; Markman and Wachtel, 1988). For Carey and Bartlett's (1978) subjects, the properties of the child's existing color lexicon often predicted which color label would be used by the child for the new word "chromium." Heibeck and Markman (1987) also found modest correlations between the prior lexical knowledge held by their subjects and the fast mapping of color, shape, and texture words. In Markman and Wachtel (1988), when the children had existing labels for the items presented, they assumed the novel terms referred to something other than the name of the object.

Finally, for those children with language impairments, the child's language abilities have been shown to be a factor in word learning (Dollaghan, 1987; Leonard et al., 1982; Meline, 1988; Rice et al., 1990). Although only a few studies have examined the skills of these children compared with those developing language normally, both similarities and differences between the groups have been reported. In a study of children with language impairment (LI) and age-matched normally developing (ND) preschool children, Dollaghan (1987) found no differences between the groups in their ability to associate a single new word and its referent, to comprehend the new word, or to store nonlinguistic information about the word. The groups differed, however, on their abilities to produce the novel word, with the children with LI performing more poorly than their ND peers. As noted by Dollaghan (1987), a determination could not be made as to whether the difficulty for the subjects with LI was caused by storage or retrieval deficits, although Dollaghan suggested that it was more likely retrieval, in that four out of five children who did not name the object were able to recognize the novel word from among other nonsense words.

In an attempt to examine LI children's word learning skills compared with children with similar language skills, Leonard et al. (1982) matched children with LI between the ages of 2:8 (year:months) and 4:2 with younger ND children aged 1:5 to 1:10, whose expressive vocabularies matched those of the LI children. The LI children's overall performance was similar to the ND children, although the children with LI did not show the same bias as the ND children for object vs. action words in either comprehension or production. Leonard et al. (1982) hypothesized that both the LI subjects' increased age and intellectual functioning may have been a factor in the LI children's increased ability with action words.

Using both age- and language-matched ND children, Rice et al. (1990) examined 5-year-old LI children's abilities to comprehend 20 novel words incorporated into a narrative presented by video. In contrast to the comprehension findings of Dollaghan (1987), Rice et al. (1990) found significant differences between all three groups' comprehension of the new words, with the group performances in descending order: age-matched, language-matched, and children with LI. Rice et al. (1990) hypothesized that the contrasting results reflect the methodological differences between the studies (i.e., the introduction of 1 vs. 20 words and a referent that was physically present and clearly indicated vs. auditorily presented words embedded in an ongoing narrative). Rice et al. (1990) also suggested that although their task was more difficult, it more closely approximates the linguistic and referential information available to children in their daily interactions and therefore may more aptly reflect the fast mapping abilities of children with language impairments. They further noted that the restricted abilities of these children in comprehending new words may be a causal factor in their limited vocabularies.

A final study that examined LI children's abilities when confronting novel items was that of Meline (1988), in which novel referents were presented in a referential communication task. Meline examined 8-year-old LI children and two groups of normally developing (age- and language-matched) children's abilities to communicate verbally about the novel referents. Although Meline (1988) did not present novel words associated with the referents, and thus the study would not be classified as a "traditional" fast mapping study, the results can be informative as to the strategies used by children when describing novel objects. All three groups typically attempted to associate the novel item with a known referent, describe it, or use a combination of the two strategies. Although the groups used the same strategies in the same proportions to communicate about the referents, they differed in their communicative effectiveness. The LI children were less successful verbally than their age-matched peers and generally performed similarly to the language-matched children.

Taken together, these studies argue for the powerful influence of the child's own lexical orientation, existing lexicon, phonological system, and current language abilities on the word learning process. Further delineation of these individual characteristics, especially those influencing word learning in special populations, may lead to a heightened awareness of the need to manipulate the acquisition process for some children.

Characteristics of the New Word

Although several studies have noted attempts to introduce words "easy" for children to learn, few studies have systematically varied the phonological or syllabic components of newly introduced words. Among them is the work of Leonard et al. (1979, 1981) cited previously, noting children's preferences for words composed of sounds within their phonological repertoires. The Leonard et al. (1979, 1981) studies, however, were not designed to compare the same words across children and therefore provide no information regarding the relative ease or difficulty of learning particular words. One study that examined the learning of specific words across children and adults was that of Crais (1987a), in which monosyllabic (e.g., "tash"), bisyllabic reduplicated (e.g., "kiki") and bisyllabic nonreduplicated (e.g., "fepo") nonsense words were introduced in stories. Crais (1978a) found significant differences between the production of reduplicated and nonreduplicated words. In this context, the reduplicated words proved easier to produce, with monosyllabics falling between the reduplicated and the nonreduplicated words but not significantly different from either. Further studies focusing on the phonological and syllabic composition of newly acquired words may prove to be useful when word types are selected for introduction to young children and for those with language difficulties. As suggested by Crais (1987a), other factors for study could include variation in phonological encoding such as rhyming or the use of similar phoneme or syllable structure.

Characteristics of the Referent

A variety of referent characteristics have been shown to affect the word learning process. Work by Leonard and his colleagues (Leonard et al., 1979, 1981; Schwartz and Leonard, 1984) have indicated that object words are more readily learned than action words. Between objects, Ross et al. (1986) found improved naming for the objects that potentially had more specific actions that could be performed on them than objects with fewer potential actions. Nelson (1982) reported improved word learning for objects that could be manipulated vs. flat, two-dimensional pictures and suggested that this action-defined quality could be an additional defining characteristic for the child. When looking at children's knowledge about word meaning gained from listening to sentences, Keil (1983) found differences between the words representing physical and nonphysical objects. The children were more likely to choose the correct category for physical objects.

Perceptual characteristics also play an important role in word learning, as evidenced by a series of studies in which Markman and her colleagues (Au and Markman, 1987; Heibeck and Markman, 1987) documented the effect that perceptual characteristics of the referent have on both comprehension and production. By using perceptual and linguistic contrasts, Heibeck and Markman (1987) found that shape terms (e.g., "Bring me the hexagon one, not the square one.") were easier to learn than those with color or texture contrasts. Au and Markman (1987) similarly found a preference for material over color terms in the hypotheses children made about the new words. Dockrell and Campbell (1986) found similar results in that shape terms were easier than pattern terms.

Arguing that perceptual features play a more important role in word learning than functional features, Tomikawa and Dodd (1980) reported their 2- and 3-year-old children learned the names of blocks with similar shapes and differing functions more readily than those with different shapes and similar functions. They suggested that when perceptual and functional features are independently available, children will base both their early conceptualizations and word meanings on perceptual features. In contrast, Schwartz and Leonard (1984) found no differences between their subject's acquisition of perceptually based vs. functionally based object concepts. Schwartz and Leonard (1984) suggest that there may be a progression in the relative use of form and function information from equal use of form and function to predominant use of form at a later time. Whether form or function predominates, from the work of Tomasello et al. (1988), it is clear that when objects have both visual and functional similarities (e.g., "hook" and "clip"), the labels of these objects are easier to learn than those of objects without similarities (e.g., "hook" and "horn").

Focusing further on children's preferences for some objects over others, Whitehurst et al. (1982) reported that both forced choice preference of a novel object and amount of time spent playing with the object were positively correlated with later comprehension and production of the names of the objects. However, Nelson and Bonvillian (1978) reported an inverse relation between concept naming and the number of actions on the objects.

An additional characteristic of a referent is its relationship with other elements within its semantic domain. Focusing on children's abilities to infer semantic properties, Harris (1975) presented preschoolers with nonsense words while revealing their semantic category (e.g., "A mib is a man."). The children were then asked questions about the new words (e.g., "What is a mib?" "Is a mib alive?"). The results indicated that the children were readily able to ascribe the properties of the original entity to the nonsense words. In another experiment, Harris (1975) presented children with nonsense words paired with superordinate categories plus an attribute (e.g., "A mib is a red bird."). The children were able to infer subordinate category membership from the attributes and to infer the presence or absence of other attributes. Examining further the relationship that a referent has with other superordinate vs. subordinate terms, Gelman et al. (1989) documented that compound names (e.g., "zav-tree") were easier to learn than single nouns (e.g., "zav"). This finding was especially true for subordinates because of the explicitness of the relation established by the compounding (e.g., "Zav is a kind of tree."). In this study, both the linguistic form and the conceptual level of the new terms influenced the word learning process. Finally, Keil (1983) examined the abilities of children to infer ontological characteristics of new words given predicate information (e.g., "The hyrax is sleepy."). The children were often able to choose the correct category for the words representing physical objects and to answer correctly copredication questions such as, "Could a hyrax be hungry?"

It is evident from the previous studies that the characteristics of a referent are highly influential as to which words are more easily learned by children and therefore as to which features of the referent are more salient. Using this information to guide decisions about both conceptual and perceptual information provided in the introduction of new words may facilitate learning by children.

Characteristics of the Introducing Event

A variety of factors related to the introducing event have been shown to influence the word learning process. The factors range from the kind of information provided at the phrase or sentence level to the broader context within which the word is introduced, such as presence of a referent or use of conversational, narrational, or definitional presentations. Several of these factors will be outlined.

Sentential Variation

As for information provided at the sentential level, studies by Brown (1957) and Katz et al. (1974) have indicated the ease with which young children are able to identify the syntactic category of a new word from surface syntactic indicators. Brown (1957) revealed 4-year-olds' abilities to recognize the differences between verbs and count and mass nouns (e.g., "to sib," "a sib," and "some sib"). Katz et al. (1974) found that 17-month-old girls were able to distinguish between common and proper nouns by the presence or absence of an article (e.g., "There's a Corgi." vs. "There's Corgi."). Indeed, many researchers using a variety of presentation formats have noted the ease with which children recognize the syntactic and semantic properties of newly presented words (Carey, 1978a; Crais, 1987a; Keil, 1983).

The use of linguistic contrast has also been shown to affect the word learning process but only in certain situations and especially when it is consistent with children's preferences for semantic domain choices (Au and Markman, 1987).

Indicating domain preferences, Dockrell (1981) noted preschooler's interpretations of novel words as shape terms in spite of the linguistic contrast with a color term (i.e., "Pass me the gombe block, not the red or green one."). Au (1985) similarly found shape preferences over color terms with both children and adults even with linguistic contrasts using a color term. Au and Markman (1987) suggest that perhaps in both studies the shapes of the objects were so salient that color seemed a less likely choice for the new word meanings, and therefore the linguistic color contrast was ignored. Or alternately, Au and Markman (1987) hypothesize that the subjects could have been using the contrast to pick out the correct object (e.g., the particular block) rather than inferring information about the semantic domain of the objects (e.g., color). However, in follow-up work, Au and Markman (1987) and Heibeck and Markman (1987) found no differences between using explicit (e.g., "Bring me the chartreuse one, not the green one.") and implicit contrast (e.g., "Bring me the chartreuse one, not the other one."). Au and Markman (1987) concluded that when both the linguistic and nonlinguistic information converge, or when children or adults have strong preferences, linguistic contrast is not necessary. However, when more than one hypothesis is available, linguistic contrast can be useful as long as it mirrors the child's preferences. Finally, linguistic contrast appears more helpful in some domains than others. Au and Markman (1987) presented single objects (e.g., a rattan cup) and used linguistic contrasts consisting of material or color terms (e.g., "This is not wood or cloth; this is rattan." "This is not red or green; it is ecru."). The linguistic contrast helped the preschool children assign consistent meaning to the material terms but was not helpful in mapping the color terms (see Au and Markman, 1987, for further discussion of linguistic contrast).

Number, Type, and Timing of Exemplars

Other types of variations influential in the word learning process have included the number, type, and timing of exemplars. In a study using multiple exemplars, Nelson and Bonvillian (1978) reported that although the 2½-year-old children could learn the new concepts with only one exemplar, learning was more likely and faster with two or four exemplars. In another study with multiple exemplars, Ross et al., (1986) found differences between their 20-month-old subjects in the number of exemplars necessary for generalization to occur to new examples of the referents. One exemplar was sufficient for the fast learners to generalize, whereas the slower learners were more likely to generalize with three exemplars. Beyond exhibiting interesting differences in introducing events, the Ross et al. (1986) study also points out some very real individual differences among children who are ND and their abilities to use differing amounts of information.

Further work with multiple exemplars by Nelson and others (Kogan, 1976; Nelson and Nelson, 1978; Nelson, 1982) has indicated that the more closely the exemplars represent the original concept (defined by Nelson as the number of defining features held in common), the better the generalization to new exemplars. Similarly, Holdgrafer and Sorenson (1984) found improved labeling of nonsense forms when the same exemplar was used as additional input vs. transformations of the figure. In an effort to look at the effect of contrasting the presentations of new objects, Nelson and Bonvillian (1973) presented unfamiliar exemplar objects in sets of six, either consecutively (caboose$_1$, caboose$_2$, caboose$_3$, etc.) or in alternated pairs (e.g., $caboose_1$, $caboose_2$, $handcuff_1$, $handcuff_2$). In addition, three objects in each set were named, whereas the other three were not named. They reported no differences between contrasts in the children's later abilities to label the objects. However, they did find that the children were more likely to label the exemplar objects that had been named for them.

Whitehurst et al. (1982) found temporal contiguity of the presentation of a new word and its referent to be an important factor in word learning. When looking at either simultaneous presentation or 10-second delays between the label and presentation of an object, Whitehurst et al. (1982) reported that for both comprehension and production, the contiguous condition was the most effective. In a second study, they examined the effect that different word/referent ratios would have on comprehension and production. The words and referents were either paired exactly (e.g., five words and five referents) or with extra words or referents presented (e.g., five words, five referents, two extra presentations of each word; or five words, five referents, two extra presentations of each referent). Whitehurst et al. (1982) noted that the "exact" pairing condition promoted the best word-referent associations; thus, the children found it harder to learn when extra presentations of the referents without the words or words without the referents were available.

Clearness of Referent

Markman and Wachtel (1988, p. 121) note that "the learning of words can be viewed as an inductive process, where from a limited amount of information, children must figure out the meaning of a novel term." Word learning is particularly difficult when there are a number of possible word meanings that can be developed by the child. Clearly some situations appear to represent this type of word learning, such as children listening to stories with multiple novel words or for preschoolers, new words presented without objects or other nonlinguistic contextual support. In contrast to this situation, there are instances where the context, either linguistic or nonlinguistic, is quite clear as to a word's meaning, and thus the child's word learning may be narrowly constrained. Indeed, when examining experimental paradigms used to introduce novel words, one can see marked differences in the introducing event, necessitating different types of processing, and, therefore, marked differences in the success of the word learning process.

Several studies in particular represent the "limited word meanings," or what can be termed "clear referent" methodologies, for example, Dockrell and Campbell's (1986) "novel animal term" experiment and Dollaghan's (1985) "koob" study. Dockrell and Campbell (1986) asked preschool children for a novel animal (e.g., "tapir") while having the children put away a small set of familiar animals (e.g., "Pass me the patas, not the pig, sheep, or cow, but the patas."). Similarly, Dollaghan (1985) asked 2- to 5-year-old children to hide a "koob" (a novel plastic object), after they had hidden three familiar objects. In both studies, the intention was to facilitate the linking of the referent and the new word, and both studies were quite successful. From these few encounters with the new words, 13 of 16 of Dockrell and Campbell's (1986) and 32 of 35 of Dollaghan's (1985) children responded correctly by giving or hiding the object. Crais (1987a) similarly had a hint of the effect of having a clear referent in a study that introduced 16 novel words within 4 stories to first, third, and fifth graders and adults. Although the children had difficulty in using the novel words in their own retellings of the experimental stories, most were successful in doing so in the practice story, which contained only one novel word with a very clear referent. It is evident that in contexts where the referent for the new word is obvious, children are easily able to connect the referent and the new word and therefore to respond successfully to recognition or comprehension tasks.

Other studies in which difficulty in word learning was associated with less clear referents and, therefore, more available word meanings are exemplified by Crais (1987a), Werner and Kaplan (1952), Klatzky et al. (1973, cited in Carey, 1978a), and Daalen-Kapteijns and Elshout-Mohr (1981). Crais (1987a) introduced novel words to first, third, and fifth grade children and adults through stories. The subjects were asked to retell the stories and to answer questions about familiar and novel words in the stories. Variations of both the distance between the three repetitions of each novel word and the specificity of propositional information associated with each word were incorporated into the design. For the distance variable, the word repetitions were either very close (within one sentence of each other) or were farther apart (three or more sentences and a topic shift between them). For the specificity variable, either very specific or very nonspecific propositional information accompanied the new words. The results of the study indicated difficulties for all the subjects (including the adults) in direct relation to the level of specificity provided about each referent. On measures of phonological production of the words and recalling propositional information about the words, significant differences were noted between three of the four groups studied; however, no differences were found between the third and fifth graders. The two factors (distance between repetitions and the type of propositional information) had differing effects on the dependent measures relative to the type of information to be acquired and recalled. When the repetitions of the words were close together and the information about the words was specific, the listeners were more likely to choose a referent for the novel word and were therefore less dependent on the novel word itself. Indeed, in these cases, the listeners had difficulty remembering the phonological form of the new words, although they performed well on the recall of information about the word. When the words were farther apart and less specific propositional information was provided, the listeners had difficulty figuring out the meaning of the word and choosing a referent, and, therefore, the phonological form of the words was more important to retain. In these cases, the phonological forms were recalled better and the propositional information was less well recalled. In Werner and Kaplan (1952), Klatzky et al. (1973, cited in Carey, 1978a), and Daalen-Kapteijns and Elshout-Mohr (1981), the abstractness, and therefore the unclearness of the referent, was a major difficulty for children and adults.

Discourse Variation

Three types of contextual discourse for word learning in an oral context were examined by Dickinson (1984) in a study in which novel words were introduced to first and sixth grade children through conversation, stories, and definitions. The conversational context was patterned after Carey and Bartlett's (1978) "chromium" task (e.g., "Give me the chromium tray, not the blue one."), the stories were composed of a few sentences setting up a problem for which the children created a solution, and the definition task presented the children with the meanings of four words (one of which was the experimental word). The children were exposed to only one word in each condition, and their performance on several dependent measures was compared. Dickinson (1984) reported that presentation mode had differing effects at the two ages. The sixth grade children profited more from the definitional context than from the story, whereas the first grade children did poorly on both tasks. There were no age differences noted on the word introduced in the conversational task. These findings should be seen as preliminary, however, because of important methodological limitations (e.g., lack of counterbalancing of words across conditions, one dependent measure that was collected for only some children, and an absence of comprehension and production tasks for all three novel words). Further studies into the effects that different discourse types have on children's word learning should prove beneficial in understanding the factors that are influential in this process.

In summary, a number of factors have been shown to affect the word learning process. As will be indicated in the next section, these factors also influence the strategies used by children to determine word meaning. Several researchers (Carey, 1978a; Chapman, 1978; Markman and Wachtell, 1988; Dockrell and Campbell, 1986) have commented on and documented various strategies that children use to help constrain the possible meanings of new words (Table 9–3). The use of comprehension strategies seems to guide children not only in which word meanings to entertain but also in the order in which the meanings should be examined. The final portion of the chapter will highlight a few of these strategies, followed by some reference to the order of preference that children adhere to in using one strategy over another.

COMPREHENSION STRATEGIES USED BY CHILDREN IN WORD LEARNING

Odd Name = Odd Referent

This strategy is typically employed when either a single new referent is presented and named or a new element is contrasted with one or more known items. In these situations, the child need only link the new referent with the new word. As noted by Carey (1978a) and further documented by Dockrell and Camp-

TABLE 9–3.
Strategies Used by Children When Determining Word Meanings for Novel Words

Comprehension strategies
Odd name = odd referent (i.e., assign novel word to novel referent)
Mutual exclusivity (i.e., assign only one name per referent)
Taxonomic organization (i.e., assign object labels to novel words)
What is present at the time (i.e., link novel word to nonlinguistic context of introducing event)
Phonetic association (e.g., identify "letter" as "ladder")
Monitoring a speaker's gaze
Production strategies
Provide familiar name for novel referent within same category (e.g., "dog" for "beaver")
Provide familiar name for novel referent with similar shape (e.g., "ball" for "round fishing cork")
Name a part of an object (e.g., "leg" for "lobsterlike animal")
Produce a phonological attempt (e.g., "kiki" for "keke")
Use an indefinite referent (e.g., "it," "thing")
Include content about referent but omit label (e.g., "There was this {um I don't know} by the river.")
Produce or attempt phonological production of other novel words
Produce phonological production not close to any of the novel words introduced

bell (1986), this strategy is one that simplifies the word learning process by limiting the number of word meanings available to the child. In several studies (Bates et al., 1988; Carey and Bartlett, 1978; Dockrell and Campbell, 1986; Dollaghan, 1987; Markman and Wachtel, 1988; Somers, 1991), young children have frequently been shown to choose a novel object when provided a novel label. Some might suggest that this tendency is purely in response to children's interests in novel objects and does not necessarily reflect an association between the new word and the object. However, in two studies conducted by Hutchinson (1986) and Markman and Wachtel (1988), when children were given the opportunity to choose between familiar and novel objects (e.g., "Select one."), they did not always choose the novel object and, in fact, did so only at a chance level. In both cases, when the children were presented with a novel word, they reliably chose the novel object.

The child's ability to know anything more than that the new word refers to the immediate referent, however, may be a factor of both the child's semantic network and the context of the introducing event. For example, although Carey and Bartlett's (1978) subjects were able to respond immediately by giving the chromium tray when asked, "Give me the chromium tray, not the red one," their overall performance on the comprehension and production tasks 1 week later was poor. In contrast, Dockrell and Campbell's (1986) findings showed good comprehension and reasonable production attempts, even with a time delay, using a similar lexical contrast task to introduce a new animal. As suggested by Dockrell and Campbell (1986), for a child to make use of a lexical contrast, the child must be able to identify the correct semantic field and to differentiate items in the field. For young children, the semantic field of color terms appears to be both more complex and less well established than animal names, which may explain Carey and Bartlett's (1978) subjects' relative difficulties on later testing. In addition, some introducing contexts such as orally presented stories (Crais, 1987a) or video narration (Rice and Woodsmall, 1988) may not so clearly indicate the correct referents for novel words. Therefore, although the odd name and odd referent strategy can be useful, for certain semantic categories and contexts, it may prove ineffectual and an alternative strategy may be needed.

Mutual Exclusivity

A second strategy used by children when learning new words is to assume that terms are mutually exclusive, and, therefore, each object can have only one name and each name can refer to only one object (Hutchinson, 1986; Markman, 1987; Markman and Wachtel, 1988). This assumption fares well for children with basic level categories and helps explain why children have great difficulty with class inclusion relations, such as a dog is also a pet (Markman, 1987). Mutual exclusivity is also used in conjunction with the odd name, odd referent strategy when a novel term is contrasted with known terms. In this case, the child needs only to recognize that all the referents have known labels except one, and therefore it must be the referent for the novel word. Using lexical contrasts, Markman and Wachtel (1988) demonstrated children's strong preferences for the mutual exclusivity principle, except (as will be discussed later) when the item introduced with a novel label is already known to the child by another name.

Clark (1983, 1987, 1988), in discussing a related strategy, the contrastive principle, argues that different words have different meanings, and that to acquire new words, children must assume that word meanings are contrastive. Although there is disagreement over whether Clark's principle of contrast is tenable (Clark, 1988; Gathercole, 1987; Merriman, 1986a), Markman and Wachtel (1988) suggest that Clark's argument may be supported by assuming that mutual exclusivity is a preferred way of following the principle of contrast. They argue that mutual exclusivity can be seen as a stronger and more specific constraint than the principle of contrast, and that although there are many other ways in which words can contrast, mutual exclusivity is a very specific one. Thus, children may initially try to use mutual exclusivity, but if that fails, they may use an interpretation that violates mutual exclusivity and yet maintains some type of contrast.

Nelson (1988), in citing the work of others (Merriman, 1986b; Mervis, 1984), has suggested that mutual exclusivity may be developmental in nature and may not be evidenced until the age of 3 years. Merriman's subjects less than three years old, when given novel names for familiar objects with known labels along with unfamiliar objects, did not systematically apply the novel words to the novel objects. Mervis (1984) demonstrated that 1-year-olds simultaneously use basic terms (e.g., "kitty") and adult terms (e.g., "tiger") to apply to the same object and therefore are not yet using the principle of mutual exclusivity. Merriman's (1986b) 4- and 6-year-olds, however, did apply the principle of mutual exclusivity. But as indicated by Harris (1975), older children do not always treat new words contrastively. Nelson (1988) suggests that because much of the work on mutual exclusivity has been performed with preschool children, it obscures the fact that this principle may develop in the course of language acquisition and may not be present in early word learning. In addition, little work of this nature has been performed with adults to determine if mutual exclusivity is routinely employed by older age groups.

Taxonomic Organization

As argued by Markman and her colleagues (Hutchinson, 1986; Markman and Hutchinson, 1984; Markman and Wachtel, 1988), the presence of a novel word and a novel object causes preschool children to look for a taxonomic relationship between the word and the object and thus to interpret the term as a label for the object. In cases where both the linguistic and nonlinguistic information converge on the same word meaning (e.g., "This is a dax," said while holding a novel object), a taxonomic strategy helps the child determine the new object is a "dax."

In using a taxonomic strategy, children often combine it with the mutual exclusivity and the odd name = odd referent strategies. If there are no competing word meanings, a novel word and novel object are mapped onto one another, the word is assumed to be a category label, and both word and referent function mutually exclusively. However, when the taxonomic and mutual exclusivity assumptions are in competition (e.g., new label for known referent), the choice of a strategy often depends on the features of the referent. In a series of studies by Markman and Wachtel (1988), in which children were presented a novel word for an already labeled object, the children were more likely to interpret the new word as referring to a salient part of the object rather than the name of the object. Thus, with already labeled objects, mutual exclusivity was the dominant strategy. If, however, there was not a clear alternative (e.g., no salient part), the children rejected the mutual exclusivity principle and used the taxonomic one in assuming the new word was a second object label. Even when the linguistic information was inconsistent with a taxonomic relationship (e.g., use of a substance term, "It's pewter."), the children displayed a clear preference for taxonomic organization as long as the object did not have a known label. As suggested by Markman and Wachtel (1988), children first apply the taxonomic principle and use the mutual exclusivity principle only when they already have a label for the object. In addition, they argue that children eventually learn to override mutual exclusivity, in a case-by-case fashion, if there is enough evidence to do so.

What Is Present at the Time

A fourth strategy in determining word meaning, proposed by Dockrell and Campbell (1986), involves children's use of the nonlinguistic context in which the word first occurred. Barrett's (1983) results with early action-related words and Carey's (1978b) with spatial adjectives illustrate this strategy. In both cases, children understood certain words only in relation to other words present during acquisition. Dollaghan (1985) also documented the salience of contextual information to her young subjects in noting their ability to recall the location in which they had hidden the new object during the exposure task.

Other Strategies

Dockrell and Campbell (1986) suggest two additional strategies that may be used by children as default mechanisms for comprehending new words. The first, phonetic association, although used by Dockrell's (1981) subjects, was reported to be highly unsatisfactory in identifying the referent in a picture when an unknown word was provided. The second, monitoring a speaker's gaze, may prove to be beneficial in some situations in helping eliminate alternatives. Finally, Dockrell and Campbell (1986) suggest that comprehension strategies used by children during word learning may be different from strategies used for production and that comprehension and production are not simply opposites. Little information, however, is available concerning production strategies and consists mainly of anecdotal reports from studies focusing primarily on whether or not children produced the newly introduced words.

PRODUCTION STRATEGIES USED BY CHILDREN

Although a number of studies have examined whether children could produce new words during fast mapping tasks, few have categorized the types of responses made by children when the novel words are not correctly produced. One of the few, Nelson and Bonvillian (1978), presents detailed information on the frequencies and types of nonexperimental words used by children when mislabeling novel objects. The most frequent category of mislabelings (34%) was for "animal names" where the children called a new animal by a familiar name (e.g., "dog" for "beaver"). The second most frequent category (24%) was the result of similarity of shape (e.g., "ball" for "bobber"). The third largest category (16%) included parts of objects (body parts or parts of inanimate objects). The remaining categories were vehicle names, family terms, foods, superordinate terms, clothing, and liquids, or container names. As noted by Nelson and Bonvillian (1978), the children were quite selective in their misnamings in that they often misnamed only certain of the experimental objects. The children who were most successful in learning and naming the concepts tended to have the largest number of extensions to nonexperimental words.

In a study that introduced novel words in oral stories to first, third, and fifth grade children and adults, Crais (1987a) examined the groups' abilities to use the novel words in their own story retellings. The groups differed in both their ability to produce the novel words and their relative use of various response strategies. A significant age effect was seen across the groups, except between the third and fifth graders, on the overall ability to produce the novel words. Of the 16 novel words introduced (four each within four stories), the first graders produced a mean of 1.45 (0.94 S.D.) words, with the third and fifth graders, and adults producing, respectively, 3.36 (2.18), 3.15 (2.48), and 10.35 (3.15) words.

If, during the story retelling, a subject did not produce a particular novel word correctly (all phonemes present and in the correct order), the examiner looked through the retold story for evidence of any reference to that novel word. The references made by the subject were then categorized by type of response, a hierarchy of responses was established, and the subject received credit for the highest response type achieved for each word (for detailed information on scoring, see Crais, 1987a). The categories in descending order were (1) phonological attempt, (2) synonym (any common word used in place of the novel word), (3) an indefinite response (e.g., thing, it, somebody), (4) content included but phonological production omitted (e.g., "There was this {uh, oh I don't remember} by the river."), (5) production or phonological attempt of another novel word, (6) phonological production not close to any of the novel words, and (7) complete omission of both the content and phonological production of the novel word.

Although the overall number of categories used by the children and adults was the same, the proportion of use between the groups differed. The categories used most frequently by the adults were the phonological attempt (65%) and synonym (18%), with no other category greater than 6%. If unable to recall the novel words, the adults worked very hard to produce a close approximation of the words and often made multiple attempts for each word. If this failed, they typically resorted to a synonym. The categories were more evenly distributed among the children, and the five most frequently used were synonym (28%), content and phonological production omitted (24%), phonological attempt (17%), wrong novel word (11%), and indefinite referent (10%). The first, third, and fifth graders were similar in their distribution, although the first graders rarely used phonological attempts (6%), and the highest proportion of their responses (33%) involved leaving out both the content and the phonological production. Thus, the children depended less on a particular strategy and were much less likely than the adults to attempt phonological production of the words.

When both the poor performance of the children and the less than perfect performance of the adults in this study are considered, it is important to note that 16 novel words were introduced in 4 orally presented stories, thus increasing the task complexity over other studies. In addition, because of the ages of the subjects, the criterion for correct production was defined as all phonemes present and in the correct order, which is more stringent than some studies, where phonological approximation is accepted as correct. Yet, in the Crais (1987a) study, even when the phonological approximations were added to the correct productions, out of 16 words possible, the means were 2.32, 7.02, 6.06, 14.02, respectively, for the first grade through adult groups. Thus, it can be seen that even with a less stringent criterion, the children had great difficulty producing multiple novel words after hearing them in stories.

Dockrell and Campbell (1986) make

note of two other production strategies that could be used by children. The first is using general purpose words where a lexical gap exists and the second is extending words whose denotational boundaries are vague. Both of these strategies were observed in Crais' (1987a) subjects through their use of indefinite referents and synonyms. Crais also noted the use of real words that were phonologically similar to the novel words (e.g., "mumu" for the novel word "momo"). These words were categorized as phonological attempts and were generally more frequently produced by the adults. In these cases, the subjects typically noted that they were producing a word that "sounds like" the novel word.

IMPLICATIONS FOR PROCESS MODELS OF CHILDREN'S LANGUAGE

The fast mapping literature provides significant information about young children's acquisition of new words and thus can be a critical element in the discussion of models of children's language. This literature can be seen as providing support for a number of the assumptions of the Child Talk model of children's language production and disconfirming several arguments made by the classical account. When describing the Child Talk model and arguing against a classical view of child language, Chapman et al. (see Chapter 1) suggest that early language formulation appears to be formulaic and narrowly restricted to use within the introducing event. Clear support for this nonclassical position comes from the results of a number of fast mapping studies that indicate that although comprehension of new words may occur very rapidly, the early mapping process for production is a slow and arduous one and highly dependent on the context surrounding the introduction of the new word. The fast mapping literature has shown that multiple repetitions of words are necessary before children spontaneously use new words and that the retention of a new word over time is quite fragile and will diminish rapidly without repeated instances. In addition, the fast mapping results indicate the importance of a clearly specified referent and an uncomplicated context for successful mapping of a new word. When the context is clear and the child can readily identify the referent, the mapping process is facilitated.

In examining differences in children's word learning abilities, Nelson (1988) suggests different developmental levels as crucial to the mapping process and highlights a demarcation somewhere between 18 and 24 months as significant to a child's mapping ability. According to Nelson (1988), the child could be considered a very slow mapper before 18 months of age, whereas afterward, the mapping process occurs more rapidly. As noted previously by Chapman et al. (see Chapter 1), children by 18 months have had many encounters with the objects, actions, and routines within their environments and, therefore, through past experiences, are able to map new information onto existing schemas. Just as young children have been shown to need contextual cues to recall the content of recently heard stories (Fivush, 1981), young word learners need some aspects of the physical and conversational contexts previously experienced to provide support for their productive word use. In addition to the facilitation provided by the increasing familiarity of the contexts for word learning, the improvement in children's abilities to produce new words may also be related to their improved retrieval skills. As noted by Merriman (1986b), improved retrieval skills in preschoolers are evidenced by the greater improvement in recall skills than recognition skills (Perlmutter and Lange, 1978; Ratner and Myers, 1981). The ability to recall information has long been associated with the ability to develop schemas and to associate relevant information within those schemas. Thus, repeated experiences provide both the content and the words to use productively, as well as the schemas for embedding that information.

Following these notions and in an attempt to describe children's productive abilities, the Child Talk model argues for the importance of the development of "lexical scripts" that include the conversational and physical contexts present during word learning. The fast mapping literature, rather than arguing for "fast" mapping in very young children (before 18–24 months) and creative productive use, tends to support the Child Talk notion of productive use that is based on much repetition requiring high levels of contextual and schematic support.

In regard to the classical account's claim that rules are acquired through the process of hypothesis generation and testing, three issues from the fast mapping literature related to word learning need to be highlighted. The first issue regards negative evidence and the possibility that this type of correction may be more accessible during the initial word learning phase. As suggested by Markman and Wachtel (1988), although there is little evidence for negative correction related to grammatical forms, the frequency of correction for single words during vocabulary acquisition may be greater. They suggest that children's use of the wrong labels for objects and their mistaken use of other terms are often corrected (e.g., "It looks like a dog, but it is a wolf."), however, little information on the frequency of this type of correction is available. In addition, young children may initially ignore this type of correction, as evidenced by their refusal to accept new names for already labeled objects (Merriman, 1986b). Evidence of this initial refusal appears to refute Barrett's (1978) and Clark's (1983) claim that toddlers' acquisition of new names results in immediate correction of overextensions. And, as suggested by Chapman et al. (see Chapter 1), even if negative evidence is available to children learning new words, it is not necessary that hypothesis generation and testing be attributed to the child. Consequently, the second issue of importance is whether the Child Talk alternative to hypothesis generation, the summation of experiences, is supported by the fast mapping literature.

In looking again at the results indicating children's refusals to apply new words to already labeled objects, some have found both evidence of resistance to "correction" and support for summation of experiences. In thinking of the process necessary for children to override the principle of mutual exclusivity, and therefore, to allow an object to have two names (e.g., "dog" and "pet"), children must have multiple exposures to the "new" name and do not readily override the "rule" with a single instance. The repeated experiences necessary for the child to counter such a principle as mutual exclusivity may be provided during the extended mapping phase, noted by Carey (1978a) to be necessary for children to map most of a word's aspects. Thus, what appears to be the generation of two rules (e.g., the dog is a dog and the dog is an animal), may, in fact, be the summation of distinct experiences introducing two labels for the same referent.

The third issue for discussion relates to the innatist argument that hypotheses are innately constrained. The Child Talk model, supported by the fast mapping literature, argues alternatively that the child's decisions related to new words are driven jointly by the input available to the child at the time of exposure and the ways in which that information relates to previous experiences. From the earlier discussion of the factors affecting word learning and the comprehension strategies used by children, it is evident that the use of particular strategies is highly dependent on the presence or absence of certain factors. For example, the use of a strategy such as the taxonomic principle is highly influenced by the input received by the child (Hutchinson, 1986; Markman and Hutchinson, 1987; Markman and Wachtel, 1988). Given that a high proportion of words used by caretakers are labels for objects and people, the Child Talk model suggests that it is not surprising that children associate new words and their referents by presuming the relationship is taxonomic. Assuming that some caretakers may consciously avoid the use of overlapping or confusing terms for young children, the principle of mutual exclusivity may also be strategically applied. The Child Talk model further suggests that because of the caretakers' knowledge of the interactive histories of many of the child's words, new and salient features of the words will successively be highlighted by the caretakers. In this way, then, the child's experiences are shaped by the repeated instances of the routines, the caretakers' input, and the caretakers' shaping of the strategies available to the child (e.g., taxonomic principle). The combination of these features provides highly predictable and readable cues to the child about the new content introduced. Thus, each individual child and his or her caretakers direct the flow of the child's word learning. As noted by Chapman et al. (see Chapter 1) in relation to the connectionist models, the strength of these models is their ability to direct and predict a child's output dependent on the weights of connections acquired through both past experience and the current input.

The final implication of the fast mapping literature for process models comes from the evidence of the distinction between comprehension and production skills of children. Numerous fast mapping studies have indicated the separation of these processes in development (Carey and Bartlett, 1978; Crais, 1987; Dollaghan, 1985; Somers, 1991), arguing against the notions of information encapsulation and domain specificity held by modular or classical accounts. In recognizing these distinctions, Child Talk proposes that it is the summed representations of events that create modularity and that these representations are composed of the linguistic and nonlinguistic information available at the multiple occasions of input. Although the first representations contain much information, rarely is this information available for productive use by young children. As children become more experienced with events and as the structure of those repeated events supports and requires production, the child is able to move from a comprehension-only status to one of productive participation. The Child Talk model thus predicts that the child's early productions will certainly be tied to the comprehension of information provided by others but will be even more directly tied to the number of productions modeled by others within those summed representations. Indeed, in the recent work by Somers (1991) in presenting a novel word to children within a story, although there were no differences in story comprehension between those receiving one vs. five presentations of the word, multiple representations of the word resulted in significant production differences.

Finally, across several issues related to children's language production, the assumptions made by the Child Talk model have been supported by the fast mapping literature, whereas those of the classical models have not. Although many questions remain concerning which of the various models of children's language production are most likely, the fast mapping literature has contributed significantly to finding answers.

IMPLICATIONS FOR CLINICAL PRACTICE

The fast mapping literature has added enormously to the understanding of the word learning process in children, primarily in those children who are developing language normally, but increasingly for those who are not. In spite of the wealth of information available, however, this literature has not traditionally been used to guide teaching or clinical practices with either group of children. Without overstating the case, it would appear that much of the current chapter related to the methodologies and results of fast mapping studies is relevant to working with any child (or adult) learning new words. The factors related to word learning, such as the characteristics of the child, word, referent, and introducing event, have strong implications for the teaching of new words. As was indicated throughout the chapter, the introducing context surrounding the word (including the sentential and discourse variation, the clearness of the referent, and the number of exemplars) often determines the child's representation of the word in memory. The importance of the individual history of each word and the mutual influences of the child, caretaker, and linguistic and nonlinguistic *events* surrounding word learning all are critical to understanding the child's knowledge and use of words.

The proposed strategies, if available to and used by children, can help them identify possible meanings or reject those that will not fit a particular situation. For example, because of the high proportion of object names used by caretakers, the child can be quite successful in early word learning when applying the taxonomic strategy. When the referent already has a label, the child is led by the mutual exclusivity principle to other possibilities such as identifying a salient part of an object, its substance, or other attributes. Markman and Wachtel (1988) suggest that the use of these two primary principles should help children learn the color or shape terms of the objects that they have already labeled. By observing the strategies that are used by a child, professionals can be guided as to what new terms related to a word a child might be able to achieve.

As indicated by the proposed developmental levels in children's mapping abilities, professionals need also to recognize the strengths and limitations exhibited by children at different levels and to plan their activities accordingly. In addition, the fast mapping literature indicates that the performance of a child depends on both the introducing event and the particular dependent measure used and therefore careful examination of methodologies for introducing and testing new words is warranted. The overall implications related to the number of words introduced simultaneously and the clearness of the referent may also indicate preferred methods for professionals presenting new words and concepts. The fast mapping literature has also highlighted the early disassociation between production and comprehension, therefore indicating the need for professionals to plan for the acquisition of and testing of both processes.

For children with language difficulties, the results of the few available fast mapping studies suggest clear production difficulties for these children (Dollaghan, 1987; Rice et al., 1990) but also indicate comprehension difficulties as well (Rice et al., 1990). As suggested by Dollaghan (1987), an important issue in production is whether the child's difficulties can be attributed to storage or retrieval deficits; Dollaghan's (1987) recognition results indicated retrieval deficits as more likely. In explaining LI children's difficulties, Rice et al. (1990) contend that a significant factor in their limited vocabularies may be their poor mapping skills. Finally, although there were differences between the groups of children with and without LI, similarities between the groups also existed in comprehension (Dollaghan, 1987) and overall performance (Leonard et al., 1982). Therefore, use of the results of fast mapping studies performed with children whose language skills are normally developing can be beneficial in working with children with language impairments.

CONCLUSION

Using a fast mapping paradigm to introduce new words and to observe which aspects of the words are stored and recalled can be illuminating when working to discover what and how a child learns from context. The use of fast mapping techniques has proved to be informative across a wide developmental range, has provided a natural context for word acquisition, has motivated the subjects to attend to the tasks, and has permitted the systematic manipulation of variables affecting the fast mapping process. Further investigation into the factors affecting the word learning process and the strategies used by children to decipher new words will allow a much richer base from which to argue for particular theories of word learning and from which to teach new words to children who are normally developing and those with special needs.

REFERENCES

Au TK: Children's word-learning strategies. *Pap Rep Child Lang Dev* 1985; 24:22–29.

Au TK, Markman EM: Acquiring word meanings via linguistic contrast. *Cognit Dev* 1987; 58:1021–1034.

Barrett MD: Lexical development and overextension in child language. *J Child Lang* 1978; 5:205–219.

Barrett MD: The course of early lexical development: A review and an interpretation. *Early Child Dev Care* 1983; 11:19–32.

Bates E, Bretherton I, Snyder L: Study 5: Acquisition of a novel concept at 20 months, in *From First Words to Grammar.* New York, Cambridge University Press, 1988, pp 124–134.

Berko J: The child's learning of English morphology. *Word* 1958; 14:150–177.

Bierwisch M: Basic issues in the development of word meaning, in Deutsch W (ed): *The Child's Construction of Language.* New York, Academic Press, 1981, pp 341–387.

Bowerman M: Reorganizational processes in lexical and syntactic development, in Wanner E, Gleitman LR (eds): *Language Acquisition: The State of the Art.* New York, Cambridge University Press, 1982, pp 319–346.

Brown R: Linguistic determinism and the part of speech. *J Abnorm Soc Psychol* 1957; 55:1–5.

Carey S: The child as word learner, in Halle M, Bresnan J, Miller G (eds): *Linguistic Theory and Psychological Reality.* Cambridge, Mass, MIT Press, 1978a, pp 264–293.

Carey S: Acquiring a single new word. *Pap Rep Child Lang* 1978b; 15:17–29.

Carey S, Bartlett E: Acquiring a single new word. *Pap Rep Child Lang Dev* 1978; 15:17–29.

Chapman RS: Comprehension strategies in children, in Kavanagh JF, Strange W (eds): *Speech and Language in the Laboratory, Schools, and Clinic.* Cambridge, Mass, MIT Press, 1978, pp 308–327.

Clark EV: Meanings and concepts, in Flavell JH, Markman EM (eds): *Handbook of Child Psychology.* New York, John Wiley & Sons, 1983, vol 3, pp 787–840.

Clark EV: The principle of contrast: A constraint on language acquisition, in MacWhinney B (ed): *The 20th Annual Carnegie Symposium.* Hillsdale, NJ, Lawrence Erlbaum Associates, 1987.

Clark EV: On the logic of contrast. *J Child Lang* 1988; 15:317–335.

Crais E: (1987a). Fast mapping of novel words in oral story context. *Diss Abstr Int* 48 (part 3b): 724 (University Microfilms no AAC8711019).

Crais E: Fast mapping of novel words in oral story context. *Pap Rep Child Lang Dev* 1987b; 26:40–47.

Daalen-Kapteijns MM van, Elshout-Mohr M: The acquisition of word meanings as a cognitive learning process. *J Verbal Learn Verbal Behav* 1981; 20:386–399.

Dickinson D: First impressions: Children's knowledge of words gained from a single exposure. *Appl Psycholinguis* 1984; 5:359–373.

Dockrell J: The child's acquisition of unfamiliar words. Doctoral dissertation, 1981, Stirling, Scotland, University of Stirling.

Dockrell J, Campbell R: Lexical acquisition strategies in the preschool child, in Kuczaj SA II, Barrett MD (ed): *The Development of Word Meaning, Progress in Cognitive Development Research.* New York, Springer-Verlag New York, 1986, pp 121–154.

Dollaghan C: Child meets word: "Fast mapping" in preschool children. *J Speech Hear Res* 1985; 28:449–454.

Dollaghan C: Fast mapping in normal and language impaired children. *J Speech Hear Disorders* 1987; 52:218–222.

Fivush R: Learning about school: The development of kindergartener's school scripts. *Child Dev* 1981; 55:1697–1709.

Gathercole V: The contrastive hypothesis for the acquisition of word meaning: A reconsideration of the theory. *J Child Lang* 1987; 14:493–531.

Gelman SA, Wilcox SA, Clark EV: Conceptual and lexical hierarchies in young children. *Cognit Dev* 1989; 4:309–326.

Harris P: Inferences and semantic development. *J Child Lang* 1975; 2:143–152.

Heibeck TH, Markman EM: Word learning in children: An examination of fast mapping. *Child Dev* 1987; 58:1021–1034.

Holdgrafer G, Sorensen P: Informativeness and lexical learning. *Psychol Rep* 1984; 54:75–80.

Hutchinson JE: Children's sensitivity to the contrastive use of object category terms. *Pap Rep Child Lang Dev* 1986; 25:49–56.

Jenkins J, Dixon R: Vocabulary learning. *Contemp Ed Psychol* 1983; 8:237–260.

Katz B, Baker G, MacNamara J: What's in a name? On the child's acquisition of proper and common nouns. *Child Dev* 1974; 45:269–273.

Keil F: Semantic inferences and the acquisition of word meaning, in Seiler TH, Wannenmacher W (eds): *Concept Development and the Development of Word Meaning.*

New York, Springer-Verlag New York, 1983, pp 103–124.

Kogan N: *Cognitive Styles in Infancy and Early Childhood.* Hillsdale, NJ, Lawrence Erlbaum Associates, 1976.

Klatzky R, Clark E, Macken M: Asymmetries in the acquisition of polar adjectives: Linguistic or conceptual? *J Exp Child Psych* 1973; 16:32–46.

Leonard LB, Schwartz RG, Chapman K, et al: Early lexical acquisition in children with specific language impairment. *J Speech Hear Res* 1982; 25:554–564.

Leonard LB, Schwartz RG, Folger MK, et al: Children's imitations of lexical items. *Child Dev* 1979; 50:19–27.

Leonard LB, Schwartz RG, Morris B, et al: Lexical orientation and phonological composition. *Child Dev* 1981; 52:882–887.

Lyons J: *Semantics 1.* New York, Cambridge University Press, 1977.

Markman EM: How children constrain the possible meanings of words, in Neisser U (ed): *Concepts and Conceptual Development: Ecological and Intellectual Factors in Categorization.* New York, Cambridge University Press, 1987.

Markman EM, Hutchinson JE: Children's sensitivity to constraints on word meaning: Taxonomic vs thematic relations. *Cognit Psychol* 1984; 16:1–27.

Markman EM, Wachtel GF: Children's use of mutual exclusivity to constrain the meanings of words. *Cognit Psychol* 1988; 20:121–157.

Meline TJ: The encoding of novel referents by language-impaired children. *Lang Speech Hear Services Sch* 1988; 19:119–127.

Merriman WE: How children learn the reference of concrete nouns: A critique of current hypotheses, in Kuczaj SA, Barrett MD (eds): *The Development of Word Meaning.* New York, Springer-Verlag. New York, 1986a, pp 1–38.

Merriman WE: Some reasons for the occurrence and eventual correction of children's naming errors. *Child Dev* 1986b; 57:942–952.

Mervis CB: Early lexical development: The contributions of mother and child, in Sophian C (ed): *Origins of Cognitive Skills: The 18th Annual Carnegie Symposium on Cognition.* Hillsdale, NJ, Lawrence Erlbaum Associates, 1984, pp 339–370.

Nelson K: Constraints on word learning? *Cognitive Dev* 1988; 3:221–246.

Nelson KE: Experimental gambits in the service of language-acquisition theory: From the fiffin project to operation input swap, in Kuczaj SA (ed): *Language Development.* Hillsdale, NJ, Lawrence Erlbaum Associates, 1982, vol 1, pp 159–199.

Nelson KE, Baker ND, Denninger M, et al: *Cookie* versus *Do-it-again:* Imitative-referential and personal-social-syntactic-initiating language styles in young children. *Linguistics* 1985; 23:433–454.

Nelson KE, Bonvillian JD, Kaplan BJ: Concepts and words in the 18-month-old: Acquiring concept names under controlled conditions. *Cognition* 1973; 2:435–450.

Nelson KE, Bonvillian JD: Early language development: Conceptual growth and related processes between 2 and 4½ years of age, in Nelson KE (ed): *Children's Language.* New York, Gardner Press, 1978, vol 1.

Nelson KE, Nelson K: Cognitive pendulums and their linguistic realization, in Nelson KE (ed): *Children's Language.* New York, Gardner Press, 1978, vol 1.

Perlmutter M, Lange G: A developmental analysis of recall-recognition distinctions, in Ornstein PA (ed): *Memory Development in Children*. Hillsdale, NJ, Lawrence Erlbaum Associates, 1978, pp 243–258.

Ratner HH, Myers NA: Long-term memory and retrieval at ages 2, 3, 4. *J Exp Child Psychol* 1981; 31:365–386.

Rice ML, Buhr JC, Nemeth M: Fast mapping word-learning abilities of language-delayed preschoolers. *J Speech Hear Disord* 1990; 55:33–42.

Rice ML, Woodsmall L: Lessons from television: Children's word learning when viewing. *Child Dev* 1988; 59:420–429.

Ross G, Nelson K, Wetstone H, et al: Acquisition and generalization of novel object concepts by young language learners. *J Child Lang* 1986; 13:67–83.

Schwartz R, Leonard L: Words, objects, and actions in early lexical acquisition. *J Speech Hear Res* 1984; 27:119–127.

Somers AD: Preschool children's fast mapping skills in stories. Master's thesis, Chapel Hill, University of North Carolina, 1991.

Streim N, Chapman R: The effects of discourse support on the organization and production of children's utterances. *Appl Psycholinguist* 1987; 8:55–66.

Tomasello M, Mannie S, Werdenschlag L: The effect of previously learned words on the child's acquisition of words for similar referents. *J Child Lang* 1988; 15:505–515.

Tomikawa SA, Dodd DH: Early word meanings: Perceptually or functionally based? *Child Dev* 1980; 51:1103–1109.

Werner H, Kaplan E: The acquisition of word meanings: A developmental study. Monogr Soc Res Child Devel 1952; 15(51).

Whitehurst GJ, Kedesdy J, White TG: A functional analysis of meaning, in Kuczaj SA (ed): *Language Development*. Hillsdale, NJ, Lawrence Erlbaum Associates, 1982, vol 1, pp 397–427.

Wykes T, Johnson-Laird PN: How do children learn the meanings of verbs? *Nature* 1977; 28:326–327.

10 The Use of Morphology by Children With Specific Language Impairment: Evidence From Three Languages

Laurence B. Leonard, Ph.D.

The acquisition of English morphology is a daunting task for young children. In contrast to the early and relatively error-free development of morphology seen in languages such as Turkish and Tamil, young children learning English initially go through a telegraphic stage in which grammatical inflections (e.g., *-s, -ed*) and function words (e.g., *the, is*) are missing. Only gradually do these grammatical morphemes make their way into children's sentences.

For English-speaking children with language disorders, one might expect the same telegraphic look, though with significantly slower development overall. However, for at least one group of children with language disorders, this telegraphic pattern is actually exaggerated. These are children who are given the clinical label of "specifically language impaired" (SLI). As the label implies, although these children show deficits in language ability, their hearing, nonverbal intelligence, emotional functioning, and motor development fall within normal limits.

These children do not constitute a homogeneous group. Nevertheless, they often show a common profile: a mild to moderate limitation in a range of language areas and a more serious deficit in morphology (Leonard, 1989). This is typically revealed when SLI children are compared to a group of younger children who are matched according to a general measure of language development such as mean length of utterance (MLU). Studies of this type usually report that despite the similar length of sentences in the two groups of children, the SLI children show less use of inflections and function words.

The purpose of this chapter is to discuss possible reasons for the extraordinary difficulty that morphology seems to present to SLI children who are learning English. A cross-linguistic approach is taken, because the natural confounds that exist in English would severely limit the hypotheses that could be entertained if this language were the sole source of evidence. I shall rely on evidence from Italian, as well as some preliminary data from Hebrew.

The chapter is organized in the following way. First, I shall review several alternative hypotheses that might account for English-speaking (E) SLI children's special problems with morphology. In doing so, I will at the same time note how the study of Italian-speaking (I) SLI children can assist in the evaluation of each hypothesis. A summary of the available evidence from ESLI and ISLI children will then be presented. The alternative hypotheses will receive a final evaluation using preliminary data obtained from SLI children acquiring Hebrew.

SOME HYPOTHESES

Sparse Morphology

Languages can be divided into those with a uniform morphology and those with a nonuniform morphology (Hyams, 1987). English has a nonuniform morphology, because although inflections occur, nouns, verbs, and adjectives frequently appear as bare stems. It seems possible that the paucity of inflections in English might contribute to ESLI children's lack of attention to grammatical morphemes in favor of more dependable cues, such as word order. That is, if ESLI children have limited resources, it may be more adaptive to focus on those aspects of the grammar that are more reliable. Hereafter, this hypothesis shall be termed the sparse morphology hypothesis.

In contrast to English, Italian is a morphologically rich and uniform language; nouns, verbs, and adjectives can never appear as bare stems. One can say *dormo* "I sleep," *dormi* "you sleep," and *dorme* "he or she sleeps" but never **dorm*. Consequently, when an Italian-speaking child hears a noun, verb, or adjective, the word is always accompanied by an inflection that modulates its meaning. If a child acquiring this language were faced with limited resources, as presumably is the case for ISLI children, inflections would be the place to focus attention.

The sparse morphology hypothesis can be tested through a two-step process. Initial support for this hypothesis would be seen if ISLI children show greater use of grammatical inflections than ESLI children. However, the advantages of an inflectionally rich morphology over an inflectionally sparse morphology can be seen even in normally developing (ND) children (Bates et al., 1984). Therefore, to account for ESLI children's especially weak morphology, we must also find that the differences between ESLI children and their MLU-matched English-speaking controls are greater than the differences between ISLI children and MLU-matched Italian-speaking controls.

It should be pointed out that other hypotheses that point to the sparseness of English morphology can be proposed. One such hypothesis has already been tested and found to be inadequate. That hypothesis employed the framework of government-binding theory (Chomsky, 1981), in which it is assumed that the language faculty contains parameters that can assume one of two (or more) possible values, thus permitting languages to vary in principled ways. The initial value of a parameter, in place before evidence from language input, is the unmarked setting. This is changed to the marked setting if evidence from the input is incompatible with the initial setting.

According to Hyams (1987), there is a parameter whose unmarked setting is

*Throughout this chapter, an asterisk that precedes a word indicates an ungrammatical form or sentence.

compatible with a uniform morphology in which inflections always appear or never appear. The same setting allows grammatical subjects to be optional. Presumably a change to the marked setting is rather late in English because young English-speaking children, noting many bare stems in the ambient language, treat the language as if it did not employ inflections. Because morphologically uniform languages of this type do not require subjects, these are treated as optional. When the presence of inflections is finally noted, the parameter is changed to the marked setting. At this point, the acquisition of English inflections proceeds, and grammatical subjects are treated as obligatory.

Loeb and Leonard (1988) explored the possibility that ESLI children's especially poor morphology might be traced to an unusually late resetting of this parameter. Unfortunately, evidence from a group of ESLI children did not support this view. One problem for this view (among others) was that there was no relationship between the children's use or nonuse of grammatical inflections and their treatment of grammatical subjects as optional or obligatory. Loeb and Leonard (1988) concluded that if the sparse morphology of English has an especially detrimental effect on ESLI children, it must be for reasons that are unrelated to parameter setting. Because the sparse morphology hypothesis to be explored in this chapter makes no use of the notion of parameters, it remains viable.

Surface Properties

A second possible explanation for ESLI children's poor morphology is that many of the grammatical morphemes of English might present perceptual and articulatory obstacles that are too difficult for these children to overcome. Even ND children acquiring English are faced with a challenge. English grammatical morphemes are difficult perceptually because, as nonsyllabic consonant segments and unstressed syllables, they are shorter in duration than adjacent morphemes. From the standpoint of production, they are vulnerable to final consonant deletion and weak syllable deletion.

In light of earlier reports of SLI children's difficulties with perceptual stimuli involving rapid acoustic events (Tallal and Piercy, 1973; Tallal and Stark, 1981), it seems reasonable that SLI children's problems with morphology could be related to these surface characteristics of English grammatical morphemes. However, an adequate explanation cannot be based on perceptual and articulatory factors alone, because SLI children show greater use of the same phonetic forms when these forms appear in nonmorphophonemic contexts. For example, higher percentages of use of */s/* are seen in *fix* than in *kicks*.

A more reasonable proposal is that the perceptual and articulatory characteristics of English grammatical morphemes make ESLI children's task of morphological paradigm building especially difficult. For example, although the perception of */t/* in a word such as *wrist* may be difficult for ESLI children, the acquisition of */t/* in a word such as *kissed* might be even more problematic. In the latter case, the children must not only perceive */t/*, they must relate *kissed* to *kiss* and place *kissed* in the appropriate cell of a morphological paradigm (Pinker, 1984). It is possible that these operations severely tax the resources of SLI children when coupled with the already greater perceptual demands placed on them by the surface properties of these morphemes. As a result, the demanding morphemes would be slow in entering and becoming established in the paradigm of each word, yielding the findings of less frequent use of grammatical morphemes by ESLI children than by ND children matched for MLU. Hereafter, the hypothesis that the perceptual and articulatory characteristics of morphemes contribute to ESLI children's extraordinary problems with morphology shall be referred to as the surface hypothesis.

Unlike English, many grammatical morphemes in Italian take the form of word-final vowels or word-final multisyllabic morphemes ending in vowels. For such morphemes, of course, final consonant deletion is not a concern. Most of these morphemes do not receive primary stress. However, because Italian has relatively flexible word order, all of these word-final morphemes can appear in clause-final position and hence benefit from clause-final vowel lengthening. According to the surface hypothesis, then, ISLI children should use these morphemes to the same degree as their MLU-matched compatriots. An additional test of this hypothesis is permitted because there are also several morphemes in Italian that resemble those seen in English, taking the form of unstressed syllables whose vowels are not in a position to receive lengthening. These particular morphemes should be more difficult for the ISLI children than for the control children.

Missing Features

According to Gopnik (1990a, 1990b), some SLI children's extraordinary difficulties with grammatical morphology might be because of the absence of "syntactico-semantic" features in their grammars. Because these features are absent, both morphophonemic rules and rules that match features in the syntax will be missing. The ramifications of such a problem would be striking. For example, there would be no feature marking for number, person, tense, and aspect. This is not to say that the phonetic form that ordinarily represents the feature will always be absent. Rather, there will be no evidence that the form, when it appears, is actually functioning in a manner that reflects the feature. For example, Gopnik noted that *-s* and *a* sometimes co-occurred in inappropriate contexts (e.g., **You got a tape recorders)*.

This proposal, which shall be termed the missing feature hypothesis, can be tested quite easily in Italian. There are several grammatical morphemes in the language whose appropriate use clearly requires the presence of features in the underlying grammar, yet they pose no special difficulty in terms of their perceptual and articulatory characteristics. These include verb inflections that must agree with the subject in person and number and adjective endings that must agree with the noun in number and gender, among others. According to the missing feature hypothesis, all morphemes of this type should be more difficult for ISLI children than for MLU-matched controls.

EVALUATING THE HYPOTHESES: EVIDENCE FROM ITALIAN

What does the available evidence say about these three hypotheses? Let us turn first to the findings from Italian.

Data from Leonard et al. (1987, 1988)

Two different groups of ISLI children have been studied in a manner permitting an evaluation of these hypotheses. The first group participated in a study by Leonard et al. (1987, 1988). There were eight ISLI children in this group, who ranged in age from 4:1 (year: months) to 6:11. The children's MLU in words ranged from 2.0 to 3.5. A comparison group of ESLI children also participated in the study; these children ranged in age from 3:6 to 6:9 and in MLU in words from 2.0 to 3.5.

A spontaneous speech sample was obtained from each child. To ensure a sufficient number of obligatory contexts for all of the grammatical morphemes under study, Leonard et al. (1987, 1988) presented preselected pictures, and the child was asked to describe them. The Italian grammatical morphemes to be discussed here are those that have approximate English equivalents. These are the inflections (1) noun plural, (2) third person singular verb inflection, and (3) past participle; and the function words (4) article and (5) third person singular copula. These morphemes are exemplified in Table 10–1. The English counterparts explored in the speech of the ESLI children were (1) noun plural, (2) third person singular inflection, (3) regular past inflection, (4) article, and (5) uncontractible third person singular copula. These, too, are provided in Table 10–1. A summary of the ISLI and ESLI children's use of the grammatical morphemes in obligatory contexts appears in Table 10–2.

It is clear from Table 10–2 that most of the percentages of use in obligatory contexts were higher for the ISLI children, dramatically so for the third person singular and regular past verb inflections. We consider now what these data tell us about the three hypotheses.

TABLE 10–1.
Some English and Italian Grammatical Morphemes Examined by Leonard et al. (1987, 1988)

Grammatical Morpheme	Example
Italian	
Plural	libr*i* "books"
Third singular	dorm*e* "sleeps"
Past participle	mangi*ato* "ate"
Article	*il* libro "the book"
Third singular copula	Brenda *è* di Memphis "Brenda is from Memphis"
English	
Plural	dog*s*
Third singular	like*s*
Regular past	walk*ed*
Article	*the* ball
Uncontractible third singular copula	The bus *is* blue

TABLE 10–2.
Summary of the English- and Italian-Speaking Children's Production of Grammatical Morphemes in Obligatory Contexts

	ESLI*	ISLI*
Articles	45	46
Plurals	79	94
Third singular	8	92
Past	7	63
Copula	52	77

*All values are mean percentages.

Sparse Morphology Hypothesis

The data from Leonard et al. (1987, 1988) can provide only a partial evaluation of the sparse morphology hypothesis. It can be recalled that this hypothesis requires not only that ISLI children show greater use of inflections than ESLI children but also that the gap between ESLI children and ND English controls be greater than the gap between ISLI children and their Italian controls. Because ND children were not included in the study, only the first step in the evaluation can be performed. Here it can be seen that all three inflections studied—noun plural, third person singular, and past participle/regular past—showed differences favoring the ISLI children. As the hypothesis was framed (dealing only with inflections), the results for the function words are not relevant.

Surface Hypothesis

The surface hypothesis requires that the two groups of children show comparable use of the article and third person singular copula, because these morphemes are unstressed syllables in both languages. For the remaining morphemes, the ISLI children would be expected to have the edge, because the Italian morphemes are word-final vowels or multisyllablic morphemes ending in vowels that often receive vowel lengthening. For four of the five comparisons, the results were consistent with this hypothesis. However, the greater use of the copula by the ISLI children cannot be explained on the basis of surface characteristics.

Missing Feature Hypothesis

According to the missing feature hypothesis, morphemes requiring features such as number, person, and tense should be absent from the grammars of both the ESLI and ISLI children. Clearly this hypothesis would have difficulty handling the data summarized in Table 10–2. As noted earlier, the complete absence of forms such as *-s,* and *-ed* is not required by the hypothesis if it can be shown that these forms are not used contrastively. Indeed, a few errors of commission were observed (e.g., **They is big.*), though they were very infrequent. The results from the ISLI children seem especially thorny for the hypothesis. Both the noun plural and third person singular verb inflections were used appropriately in more than 90% of their obligatory contexts.

Data From Leonard et al. (in press)

Although the earlier study of Leonard et al. (1987, 1988) provided informative data, it had a few shortcomings. Chief among these was the fact that ND comparison groups were not employed. A second sample of children, studied by Leonard et al. (in press), remedied this problem. (The Leonard et al. study that is in press also included comprehension tasks. In the interest of space; only production data are reviewed here.) In this two-part study, a total of six subject groups participated. Three of the groups were English speaking: (1) ten ESLI children ranging in age from 3:8 to 5:7 and in MLU in words from 2.7 to 4.2; (2) ten ND children matched with the ESLI children according to MLU (hereafter, END-MLU children) who ranged in age from 2:11 to 3:4; and (3) ten ND children matched with the ESLI children according to chronological age (hereafter, END-A children). The three Italian-speaking groups were (1) 15 ISLI children ranging in age from 4:0 to 6:0 and in MLU in words from 1.9 to 4.3; (2) 15 ND children matched with the ISLI children according to MLU (the IND-MLU children) and ranging in age from 2:6 to 3:6; and (6) 15 ND children matched with the ISLI children according to chronological age (the IND-A children).

The data collection procedures were similar to those used by Leonard et al. (1987, 1988). Spontaneous speech samples were obtained, and preselected pictures designed to create obligatory contexts for particular grammatical morphemes were presented. Although some of the grammatical morphemes selected for study in each language had counterparts in the other language, the principal concern in this investigation involved the ESLI vs. END-MLU and ISLI vs. IND-MLU comparisons.

The English grammatical morphemes examined were (1) article, (2) noun plural, (3) third person singular verb inflection, (4) regular past verb inflection, (5) irregular past (e.g., *caught, threw*), and (6) copula. A summary of the three English-speaking subject groups' use of these morphemes can be seen in Table 10–3.

As expected, high percentages were seen for the END-A children, with one

TABLE 10–3.

Summary of the English-Speaking Children's Production of Grammatical Morphemes in Obligatory Contexts

	ESLI*	END-MLU*	END-A*
Articles	52	62	95
Plurals	69	96	97
Third singular	34	59	91
Regular past	32	65	98
Irregular past	65	77	64
Copula	41	71	97

*All values are mean percentages.

exception: the percentage for irregular past was no higher for these children than for the other two subject groups. However, the similar percentages are masking a difference among the three groups of children. For the ESLI and END-MLU children, the clear majority of errors involved the use of the present instead of the irregular past (e.g., *fall* for *fell, throw* for *threw*), whereas the great majority of errors by the END-A children were overregularizations (e.g., **falled*, **throwed*). Overregularizations represented 21.6%, 15.3%, and 81.9% of the errors by the ESLI, END-MLU, and END-A children, respectively.

Because age-matched ND children typically perform at much higher levels than SLI children, the comparisons between the ESLI and END-MLU children were more telling. Differences favoring the END-MLU children were seen for the noun plural, third person singular inflection, regular past inflection, and the copula.

The data were also examined for evidence of unsystematic use by calculating the percentage of grammatical morpheme productions that occurred in inappropriate contexts. A summary is provided in Table 10–4. As can be seen from this table, the ESLI children usually restricted their use of a grammatical morpheme to an appropriate context and in this regard were highly similar to the END-MLU children.

The Italian grammatical morphemes of interest were (1) article, (2) noun plural, (3) third person singular verb inflection, (4) third person plural verb inflection, (5) adjective-noun gender agreement, and (6) clitic pronouns. Examples of the last three are provided in Table 10–5; examples of the others can be found in Table 10–1.

From the standpoint of the surface hypothesis, articles and clitics are expected to be difficult for ISLI children because they are unstressed syllables that do not receive vowel lengthening (clitics were assessed only in clause-medial position). The third person plural inflection (e.g., *-ano*) should also be difficult according to this hypothesis because the first syllable of this two-syllable inflection is unstressed and primary stress occurs in the stem (e.g., *cómprano*). Consequently, the penultimate syllable is likely to be difficult to perceive, produce, or both. Furthermore, because a production with the syllable missing (e.g., **comprno*) violates the phonotactic structure of Italian words and bare stems are impermissible, the child is likely to use a different, incorrect inflection with the verb. The remaining grammatical morphemes should be relatively easy for the ISLI children, because they involve word-final vowels that can be lengthened. According to the missing feature hypothesis, the ISLI children should have greater difficulty than the IND-MLU children with all of these grammatical morphemes, because each requires a feature presumed missing from the children's grammars. Finally, the sparse morphology hypothesis pre-

TABLE 10–4.
Percentage of Grammatical Morpheme Productions That Occurred in Inappropriate Contexts

	ESLI*	END-MLU*
Articles	0.2	1.1
Plurals	1.6	1.9
Third singular	8.0	7.5
Copula	4.3	4.5

*All values are mean percentages.

TABLE 10–5.
Some Italian Grammatical Morphemes Examined by Leonard et al. (in Press)

Grammatical Morpheme	Example
Third plural	dorm*ono* "(they) sleep"
Adjective-noun gender agreement	pettin*e* giall*o* "yellow comb"
	nav*e* giall*a* "yellow ship"
Clitic pronouns	Cristina *lo* vede. "Cristina sees him."

dicts that those grammatical inflections occurring in both Italian and English will be produced with higher percentages by the Italian children and that the differences between SLI and ND-MLU children will be larger in English. A summary of the three Italian-speaking groups' use of the grammatical morphemes can be seen in Table 10–6.

The high percentages of use by the IND-A children were expected; the more informative findings pertain to the ISLI and IND-MLU groups. The ISLI children showed lower percentages than the IND-MLU children only on the article, third person plural inflection, and clitics.

We turn now to how these data fit the three hypotheses of interest. It will be seen that the Italian data, taken singly and together with the English data, offer considerable insight into the relative adequacy of these hypotheses.

Sparse Morphology Hypothesis

Two of the grammatical morphemes—the noun plural and the third person singular verb inflection—were examined in both English and Italian and can be used to evaluate the sparse morphology hypothesis. Two steps are involved in this evaluation. First, the ISLI children should show greater use of these two morphemes than the ESLI children. Second, the difference between the ESLI and END-MLU children in the use of these morphemes should be greater than the difference between the ISLI and IND-MLU children.

TABLE 10–6.
Summary of the Italian-Speaking Children's Production of Grammatical Morphemes

	ISLI*	IND-MLU*	IND-A*
Articles	41	83	97
Plurals	87	89	98
Third singular	93	93	93
Third plural	50	82	91
Adjective-noun	97	99	100
Clitics	26	66	92

*All values are mean percentages.

The first of these comparisons is complicated somewhat by the fact that the MLU range for the 15 ISLI children was 1.9 to 4.3 words, whereas for the 10 ESLI children this range was 2.7 to 4.2 words. Accordingly, I made a comparison that included only the ten ISLI children with the highest MLUs (range = 2.6 to 4.3 words). The mean percentage of plural use in obligatory contexts was 90 for the ISLI children and 69 for the ESLI children. For the third person singular inflection, the mean percentages for the ISLI and ESLI children were 95 and 34, respectively. Given that the ISLI children showed higher percentages of use, we can turn to the question of whether the differences between the ISLI and IND-MLU children were smaller than those between the ESLI and END-MLU children. An inspection of Table 10–3 and 10–6 reveals that this was clearly the case.

Surface Hypothesis

The differences between the ESLI and END-MLU children on the noun plural, third person singular inflection, regular past inflection, and the copula were consistent with the surface hypothesis, because all of these forms are bound morphemes involving word-final consonants or unstressed syllables. However, the results for the English article confounded the predictions of this hypothesis. The ESLI children were expected to have more difficulty than the END-MLU children on this morpheme, yet the difference observed (see Table 10–3) did not achieve statistical significance. The remaining nonsignificant difference was in accord with the surface hypothesis: ESLI children produced the irregular past with percentages as high as their controls. According to the surface hypothesis, the irregular past should not be especially difficult because this type of morpheme can be distinguished from its present tense form by (at least) a vowel whose duration exceeds that of function words.

The data from Italian were especially helpful in evaluating the surface hypothesis. The ISLI children showed lower percentages than the IND-MLU children only on the article, third person plural inflection, and clitics. This finding is entirely consistent with the surface hypothesis predictions.*

Missing Feature Hypothesis

The English data reflected in Table 10–3 fit the predictions of the missing feature hypothesis, as well as those of the surface hypothesis. Because all of the grammatical morphemes except the irregular past presumably require a feature such as tense, number, and/or person, the hypothesis correctly predicted the group differences seen for the noun plural, third person singular inflection, regular past inflection, and the copula and incorrectly predicted that a difference would be seen for the article as well. A difference was not expected for the irregular past, because this form can be learned as part of the lexicon.

On the other hand, even though the ESLI children were limited in their use of most of the grammatical morphemes involving features, the percentages of use seen in Table 10–3 are well above zero, suggesting that features were not altogether absent. Two other findings lend support to this view. First, as seen in Table 10–4, when the ESLI children did produce these morphemes, they usually did so in appropriate contexts. This suggests that the grammatical morphemes were not applied in a random way. Second, the instances of overregularization of the past (e.g., **drawed picture*) observed in the ESLI children's speech were sufficiently frequent (constituting approximately 20% of their errors on irregular past) to suggest that the use of *-ed,* at least, was not simply the product of rote learning.

The Italian data were also problematic for the missing feature hypothesis. In particular, for three of the grammatical morphemes that seemingly required features—noun plurals, third person singular verb inflections, and adjective-noun gender agreement—the ISLI children's use did not differ from that of the IND-MLU children. Furthermore, the fact that the percentages for these particular morphemes were so high makes it unlikely that they were the result of the memorization of individual lexical items. Even in one case of a low percentage of use there was evidence incompatible with the position that observed productions were simply memorized lexical items. The stems of certain verbs change when the third person plural form is used. Yet several ISLI children (with relatively low percentages of use of this inflection) overregularized the stems. For example, *leggono* [leg:ono] "they read" was pronounced [ledʒono] such that the consonant matched that seen in *legge* [ledʒe] "he or she reads." Such productions were scored as correct and therefore do not alter the conclusion that the ISLI children's percentage of use for this inflection was well below that of the IND-MLU children. Yet productions of this type suggest that even in the face of limited ability, some degree of creativity is involved.

In summary, the data from Leonard

*There are a few Italian verbs that consist of only two syllables when expressed in the third person plural. Examples include *danno* "they give," *fanno* "they make," and *stanno* "they stay." In verbs of this type, the first syllable of the third person inflection receives primary stress, and the final syllable of the inflection can receive vowel lengthening. Consequently, for these particular verbs, the surface hypothesis predicts that the ISLI children will perform as well as the IND-MLU children. This proved true. The ISLI children's percentage of use of the third person plural inflection with these verbs was 80.5 (in contrast to 45.1 for verbs of more typical length), which was comparable with the IND-MLU children's percentage of 85.4 for the same verbs.

et al. (in press) were consistent with and extended the findings of Leonard et al. (1987, 1988). Considerable support was seen for the surface hypothesis, and to the extent that it was tested, the sparse morphology hypothesis, too, appears viable. On the other hand, the missing feature hypothesis does not seem consistent with the data from these children.

EVALUATING THE HYPOTHESES: PRELIMINARY EVIDENCE FROM HEBREW

Hebrew offers a somewhat different means of assessing the three hypotheses. Like Italian, Hebrew has a rich morphology, in which nouns, adjectives, and verbs are always inflected. However, unlike Italian, in which the stem is almost always readily identifiable, the base unit in Hebrew is a triconsonantal root. In some cases grammatical distinctions are made by the addition of a suffix, in others they are made by word-internal vowel changes, and in the bulk of cases they are made by changes in both a suffix and a vowel. For example, the verb "go" has the root *h-l-x*. "He goes" has the form *holex,* "she goes" has the form *holexet,* "he went" has the form *halax,* and "they (masculine) go" has the form *holxim.**

Given the fact that nouns, verbs, and adjectives are always inflected, the sparse morphology hypothesis would predict that Hebrew-speaking (H) SLI children would show greater use of bound grammatical morphemes than their English-speaking counterparts, and the difference between HSLI children and HND-MLU children would be smaller than the difference between ESLI and END-MLU children. Because most of the grammatical morphemes in Hebrew are syllabic and receive either primary stress or vowel lengthening in clause-final position, according to the surface hypothesis they would not be expected to be any more difficult for HSLI children than for their MLU controls. On the other hand, certain Hebrew morphemes are unstressed syllables that never benefit from vowel lengthening. For these morphemes, HSLI children should show percentages of use below those of HND-MLU children. The predictions of the missing feature hypothesis are quite different. Because all of these morphemes can be presumed to require features such as number, gender, and definiteness in the underlying grammar, they should be especially difficult for HSLI children.

At this point, only preliminary evidence from Hebrew can be provided. These data come from a study by Rom and Leonard (1990). The subjects were (1) seven HSLI children ranging in age from 4:4 to 5:3 and in MLU in words from 1.8 to 3.4; (2) seven HND children who served as MLU controls and ranged in age from 2:4 to 3:3, and (3) seven ESLI children from the study of Leonard et al. (1987, 1988) who were matched to the HSLI children in MLU in words and ranged in age from 3:6 to 6:9.

Spontaneous speech samples served as the source of data. Because these samples were relatively short, it was necessary to collapse some of the specific grammatical morphemes (e.g., third person masculine singular past inflection) into a single category (e.g., past inflections). In other respects, the procedure was similar to the one used with the English- and Italian-speaking children. The grammatical morphemes of interest included (1) noun plural, (2) present verb inflections, (3) past verb inflections, (4) adjective-noun agreement, and (5) the case marker *et.* Examples of these morphemes are provided in Table 10–7. The case marker requires comment. This morpheme marks the accusative case

*Hebrew examples are written in phonemic notation rather than Hebrew script for clarity of presentation.

TABLE 10–7.
Some Hebrew Grammatical Morphemes Examined by Rom and Leonard (1990)

Grammatical Morpheme	Example
Plural	iton*im* "newspapers"
Present inflections	holex "(masc sing I/you/he) go"
	holxot "(fem plur we/you/they) go"
Past inflections	halax "(he) went"
	halxa "(she) went"
	halaxnu "(we) went"
Adjective-noun agreement	sefer gadol "large book"
	mexonit gdola "large car"
Case marker *et*	Etti rotsa lirot *et* Kansas "Etti wants to see Kansas"

when the noun is definite. It is used with both common noun direct objects (e.g., *hu kotev et ha-mixtav* "he writes the letter") and proper noun direct objects (e.g., *hi ohevet et Oliver* "she loves Oliver").

A summary of the HSLI and HND-MLU children's percentages of use in obligatory contexts appears in Table 10–8. As can be seen, group differences were found only for the case marker *et.*

These findings were entirely consistent with the surface hypothesis, though at odds with the missing feature hypothesis. The sparse morphology hypothesis also receives support from these findings in that all of the grammatical morphemes that show similar percentages of use by the HSLI and HND-MLU children are inflections. As can be seen from the eight ESLI children in Table 10–2 (seven of whom formed the comparison group for the HSLI children), verb and noun inflections show much lower percentages of use in English. From Table 10–3 it can be seen that the differences between ESLI and END-MLU children in the use of these inflections is much larger than the (nonexistent) differences between the HSLI and HND-MLU children.

TABLE 10–8.
Summary of the Hebrew-Speaking Children's Production of Grammatical Morphemes

	HSLI*	HND-MLU*
Present inflections	94	97
Past inflections	93	89
Plurals	100	100
Adjective-noun	74	75
Case marker	64	94

*All values are mean percentages.

INTERPRETING THE DATA

We have examined three hypotheses in an attempt to uncover possible reasons for the extraordinary morphological difficulties experienced by SLI children acquiring English. These hypotheses—the missing feature hypothesis, the surface hypothesis, and the sparse morphology hypothesis—were evaluated in light of data from three different languages.

Collectively, the data reviewed suggest that features such as number, person, tense, and gender were probably not missing from the grammars of these SLI subjects. If one could in some way discount the occasional use of overregularized past forms by the ESLI children and overregularized stems in the third person plural forms by the ISLI children, it might be possible to argue that the limited grammatical morpheme use by these children reflected mere memorization. However, there were too many Italian and Hebrew morphemes showing high percentages of use by the SLI children to permit such a conclusion. Furthermore, because these morphemes were produced by the SLI children with percentages as high as those of the MLU controls, one would have to conclude that the grammatical morpheme use of the ND children also was the product of memorization.

In spite of the negative findings regarding the missing feature hypothesis, it is quite possible that the characterization of a featureless grammar may be appropriate for the child studied by Gopnik (1990b) and possibly for other individual cases. The heterogeneity seen in the population of children with specific language impairment certainly allows for the possibility of varying sources of difficulty. However, for the children selected as subjects in the studies reviewed here, a different type of account is needed.

A more likely possibility is that the surface characteristics of certain grammatical morphemes contributed to the SLI subjects' poor performance relative to that of MLU controls. Of the 22 comparisons that tested predictions of the surface hypothesis (see Tables 10–2, 10–3, 10–6, and 10–8), only 2 produced disconfirming evidence: (1) the ISLI children in the Leonard et al. (1987, 1988) study showed higher percentages for the third person singular copula than the ESLI children, and (2) the ESLI children of the Leonard et al. (in press) investigation produced the article with percentages comparable with those shown by the END-MLU children. The latter finding is somewhat surprising, given that differences in article use between ESLI and END-MLU children have been reported in earlier studies (e.g., Beastrom and Rice, 1986).

Although it is unlikely that the surface hypothesis will ever be capable of providing a complete account of the problems of SLI children, when incorporated into a comprehensive theory of language learning, the assumption of problems with surface characteristics of language can go a surprisingly long way in accounting for the errors of these children. For example, Leonard (1989) and Leonard et al. (in press) have found that given this assumption, Pinker's (1984) learnability theory permits a range of errors that have been observed in ESLI children. These include telegraphic versions of complementation and relativization, problems with the passive, and case errors such as *her* for *she* in subject position.

The third hypothesis evaluated in this chapter holds that ESLI children do especially poorly in morphology because their limited resources are not directed toward the relatively sparse morphological information that is available in the ambient language. This hypothesis was not tested as thoroughly as the other two hypotheses, because in some cases only one of the two steps required in its evaluation could be performed. Furthermore, the hypothesis as framed concerned only grammatical inflections. Hence, the free-standing morphemes that were included to examine the other hypotheses had no bearing on this one.* Nevertheless, it is noteworthy that this hypothesis was supported by every comparison that was designed to test it.

Given the viability of both the surface and sparse morphology hypotheses, it will be necessary for future research to eliminate those confounds that still remain. This might be accomplished by (1) comparing two languages in which inflections are obligatory and ensuring

*It is certainly conceivable that children learning a language with obligatory inflections might be drawn to morphological information in general, such that they also identify the functions of free-standing grammatical morphemes at an earlier age than children acquiring a language such as English. Such a possibility provides a plausible account of the differences between the ISLI and ESLI children of the Leonard et al. (1987, 1988) study in the use of the third person singular copula. On the other hand, the finding that the ISLI and ESLI children in both Leonard et al. (1987, 1988) and Leonard et al. (in press) showed similar percentages of article use serves as counterevidence for such an extended interpretation of the sparse morphology hypothesis. On balance, it appears more prudent to anchor this hypothesis to the known structural distinction between languages in which nouns, verbs, and adjectives are always inflected and languages in which these words are often not inflected.

that the inflections of one language are more difficult than those of the other in their surface characteristics, (2) performing a similar comparison using two languages in which inflections are less abundant, and (3) comparing a language with a sparse but highly perceptible and pronounceable morphology with a language containing obligatory inflections that are challenging in their perceptual and articulatory characteristics.

IMPLICATIONS FOR PROCESS MODELS OF CHILDREN'S LANGUAGE

As is clear from the data reviewed here, even after particular forms emerge in SLI children's speech, the subsequent development of these forms toward mastery is often protracted. Hence, one finds percentages of use by these children that are safely above 0 yet well below 100. Because the instances of use are usually in appropriate contexts and occasional evidence for invention is found, these productions must be interpreted as reflecting some type of intermediate level of development. But how does one characterize such a level?

This question is especially difficult for all-or-none rule- or principle-based models, such as those proposed within the general framework of government-binding theory. In government-binding theory, language acquisition is treated as an instantaneous process. Of course, investigators of child language working within this framework recognize that the instantaneousness assumption is only an ideal and that factors must be proposed to account for the more gradual process that actually occurs. For example, it has been noted that verbs and prepositions must be learned one at a time, and because each verb and preposition carries its own subcategorization frame (e.g., the preposition *before* can be followed by a noun phrase such as *the race* or a full sentence such as *the stranger arrived*), some details of grammar will necessarily be acquired after others. However, something more must be proposed to account for the gradual development of closed-class grammatical morphemes such as articles.

The framework within which the surface hypothesis was considered earlier, that of Pinker (1984), is rule based but allows for more gradual acquisition. Specifically, grammatical morphemes are first placed in word-specific paradigms, such that the entry in, say, the third person singular cell for *jump* might be *jumps,* the entry in the definiteness cell for *car* might be *the car,* and so on. These word-specific paradigms persist in the grammar, and for each word the child learns thereafter, a new word-specific paradigm is created. However, at some point, the child begins to show productive use of the grammatical morphemes. That is, hearing, for example, a new noun in a nondefinite context, the child can add the appropriate article in the definite context. For this to be possible, the word-specific paradigms contribute to the development of general paradigms. The latter are paradigms in which the grammatical morphemes are free of open-class words.

The creation of even a word-specific paradigm is not instantaneous. Each entry in the paradigm becomes more firmly established with each encounter of the form, and other morphemes can compete for the same cell. Furthermore, because general paradigms are formed before all word-specific paradigms are filled out, the general paradigms also become stronger over time.

This particular learnability model can accommodate either the surface or sparse morphology hypothesis. That is, whether SLI children's limited resources were taxed because of added perceptual and articulatory demands placed on them by the surface properties of grammatical morphemes (surface hypothesis) or because of the necessity to attend to both sporadic grammatical morphemes and more prevalent cues such as word order (sparse morphology hypothesis), entries would be slow in entering and becoming established in the paradigm of each word. Furthermore, because each successful application of the procedure strengthens the general paradigm, the children's difficulty with word-specific paradigms would also leave the children with relatively weak general paradigms. The net effect of these word-specific and general paradigm limitations would be the well-documented finding of less frequent use of grammatical morphemes by SLI children than by their MLU-matched controls.

However, the property of permitting the gradual development of grammatical morphemes is not unique to models of this type. In a model such as Child Talk (Chapman et al., see Chapter 1), gradual development of grammatical morphemes is also assumed but, in this case, characterized as a product of the child's event-based conversational history. This model dispenses with rules and instead describes systematic use as a reflection of organized networks that are the result of the pattern and frequency of input in interpretable contexts and the child's pragmatic need to convey information.

In principle, Child Talk also has no difficulty with the assumptions behind the surface and sparse morphology hypotheses. It readily admits factors such as perceptual salience, frequency of occurrence, and reliability of use in interpretable contexts, all factors that are implicated in one or both of the hypotheses. Given this general fit, it would seem worthwhile to use data from SLI children as a catalyst for additional exploration of this model.

IMPLICATIONS FOR CLINICAL PRACTICE

Because neither of the two hypotheses showing the most promise has been put to a thorough test, alterations in current clinical practice as a result of the findings to date would be premature. However, we can consider the types of changes that might be appropriate if either of these hypotheses proves correct.

If the surface characteristics of grammatical morphemes prove important, treatment procedures designed to facilitate SLI children's acquisition of these morphemes should make provisions for presenting the morphemes in salient contexts. For example, grammatical inflections should probably be introduced in sentence-final positions (e.g., "There she go*es*.") and subsequently presented in clause-final position (e.g., "When she come*s*, we'll eat dinner.") to take advantage of pauses and other facilitative prosodic cues. Similarly, contractible function words might be presented first in uncontractible contexts (e.g., "There he *is!*"). Where possible, syllabic allomorphs could be used, especially in clause-final position to increase their duration. Thus, when one is teaching regular past verb inflections and noun plurals, an abundance of forms such as "plant*ed*" and "dish*es*" could be put on display.

The SLI children's production of grammatical morphemes might be assisted if inflections were first presented in contexts in which they immediately follow a vowel (e.g., "play*ed*," "play*s*") rather than a consonant (e.g., "jump*ed*," "jump*s*"). A function word's vulnerability to weak syllable deletion might be reduced by first presenting it in sentences serving as self-corrections of false assertions (Fey, 1986), as in "I don't think this one will be tall, let's see. Oh, it *is* tall."

If SLI children's difficulty with morphology relates to the relative sparseness of English grammatical morphemes, the clinical procedures adopted might be those that emphasize the communicative contribution of these morphemes. For example, activities might be designed that contrast, say, "The fish see the boat," and "The fish see*s* the boat," or "I want the mommy cat," and "I want the mommy'*s* cat." Examples of this type might highlight the fact that although some grammatical morphemes are infrequent, their appearance can sometimes affect the interpretation of the message.

CONCLUSIONS

Of the three hypotheses considered in this chapter, the surface and sparse morphology hypotheses appear most consistent with the available evidence on SLI children's morphological limitations. Both of these hypotheses can be incorporated into existing models and carry important clinical implications. To be sure, many questions remain, and it is not clear that either of these hypotheses will survive future scrutiny. What does seem certain is that the eventual discovery of a satisfactory account of SLI children's morphological difficulties will be aided significantly if languages in addition to English are regularly consulted.

Acknowledgments

The research reviewed in this chapter was supported by NIH grant no. DC00458. I express my thanks to the many colleagues who provided comments during presentations of this work at McGill University, University of Oslo, University of Kansas, the meeting of the European Group on Child Language Disorders, the meeting of the Italian Group on Child Language Research, and the University of Wisconsin Symposium on Research in Child Language Disorders.

REFERENCES

Bates E, MacWhinney B, Caselli MC, et al: A cross-linguistic study of the development of sentence interpretation strategies. *Child Dev* 1984; 55:341–354.

Beastrom S, Rice M: Comprehension and production of the articles *a* and *the*. Paper presented at the Convention of the American Speech-Language-Hearing Association, Detroit, 1986.

Chomsky N: *Lectures on Government and Binding*. Dordrecht, The Netherlands, D Reidel, 1981.

Fey M: *Language Intervention With Young Children*. San Diego, College-Hill Press, 1986.

Gopnik M: Feature-blind grammar and dysphasia. *Nature* 1990a; 344:715.

Gopnik M: Feature blindness: A case study. *Lang Acquisit* 1990b; 1:139–164.

Hyams N: The setting of the null subject parameter: A reanalysis. Paper presented at the Boston University Conference on Language Development, Boston, 1987.

Leonard L: Language learnability and specific language impairment in children. *Appl Psycholinguist* 1989; 10:179–202.

Leonard L, Bortolini U, Caselli MC, et al: Morphological deficits in children with specific language impairment: The status of features in the underlying grammar. *Language Acquisition* (in press).

Leonard L, Sabbadini L, Leonard J, et al: Specific language impairment in children: A crosslinguistic study. *Brain Lang* 1987; 32:233–252.

Leonard L, Sabbadini L, Volterra V, et al: Some influences on the grammar of English- and Italian-speaking children with specific language impairment. *Appl Psycholinguist* 1988; 9:39–57.

Loeb D, Leonard L: Specific language impairment and parameter theory. *Clin Linguistics Phonetics* 1988; 2:317–327.

Pinker S: *Language Learnability and Language Development.* Cambridge, Mass, Harvard University Press, 1984.

Rom A, Leonard L: Interpreting deficits in grammatical morphology in specifically language-impaired children: Preliminary evidence from Hebrew. *Clin Linguistics Phonetics* 1990; 4:93–105.

Tallal P, Piercy M: Defects of non-verbal auditory perception in children with developmental aphasia. *Nature* 1973; 241:468–469.

Tallal P, Stark R: Speech acoustic-cue discrimination abilities of normally developing and language-impaired children. *J Acoust Soc Am* 1981; 69:568–574.

11 Lexical Development in Young Children With Down Syndrome*

Jon F. Miller, Ph.D.

Research documenting the development of lexical skills in children with Down syndrome (DS) has focused on a single issue: Does the development of lexical skills in children with DS differ from typically developing children? This issue has been addressed from several different perspectives examining vocabulary size, type/token ratios, and lexical categorization (form class). The results of this work pose some interesting paradoxes, both methodological and theoretical. The methodological difficulties of this research offer some insight into the conflicting outcomes of a number of vocabulary studies with these children. The theoretical concerns have to do with mental retardation first and language learning second. This is not the usual order of theoretical concerns for child language research because it is assumed that we have a firm grasp on population definition and classification.

MENTAL RETARDATION THEORY

The concept of mental retardation is undergoing revision as the result of advances in theories of intelligence (Campion and Brown, 1984; Gardner, 1983; Sternberg, 1985; 1986). In addition, our understanding of the specific cognitive deficits associated with mental retardation has broadened to include the full range of skills; for example, now we ask, What are the intellectual skills that set the gifted child apart from the normal child and from the child with mental retardation (Day and Borkowski, 1987; Robinson and Janos, 1987)? Even a cursory examination of literature on the measurement of intelligence reveals that vocabulary measures have been a part of almost every intelligence test since the first efforts at measuring intelligence began in this country after Binet's work (Terman, 1916). Aspects of vocabulary knowledge have become central to what we consider to be intelligent behavior: vocabulary size, definitions for infrequently used words, and knowledge of words representing complex concepts.

The fact that language skills are a central part of the skills we think of as "intelligent" requires a distinction be made between "verbal" and "nonverbal" tasks on intelligence tests when investigating language performance. This distinction allows investigators the opportunity to document mental abilities not confounded by language skills required to perform the task. This distinction turns out to be important in another way

*The work reported in this chapter was supported by research grant 12–192 from the National March of Dimes (Jon Miller and Lewis Leavitt, principal investigators) and research grant RO1–HD22393 from the National Institutes of Health (Jon Miller, principal investigator).

because it provides the criteria for language performance expectations in children who have cognitive deficits. In practice, investigators use nonverbal mental age (MA) rather than chronological age (CA) to match subjects with controls. This practice incorporates the assumption that mental age (MA) is a better predictor of language development than chronological age (CA). There is a large body of literature supporting this view (Miller and Yoder, 1974; Miller, 1978; 1981) for populations with mental retardation. There is growing concern that this practice oversimplifies the language-cognition relationship (Cole et al., 1991) and may be used inappropriately for making decisions about developmental status. The operationalization of nonverbal intelligence is further complicated by variability in the tests of nonverbal MA available through the developmental period and the range of "mental constructs" tested. In summary, MA, although clearly flawed, is still the best predictor of language performance in children with mental retardation and will be used in this chapter to organize research for review to attempt to equate development across studies.

VOCABULARY LEARNING AND MENTAL RETARDATION

Words provide us with the most direct example of the representation of our knowledge of the world (objects, acts and relations) through language. That is, the knowledge being represented is relatively clear compared with that conveyed by larger linguistic units, for example, utterances. Vocabulary acquisition may provide a unique window into the cognitive processes of mentally retarded children if language learning is a product of cognition. The outcomes of this view might be two. Mental retardation might result in a general delay in vocabulary acquisition, reflecting a slower rate of verbal information processing associated with a general cognitive deficit. Or, mental retardation as a behavioral classification associated with a variety of etiological conditions may affect language learning in unique ways related to the specific etiology. Different brain syndromes should result in unique language learning patterns, as revealed by rates of progress in vocabulary, syntax, semantics, and pragmatics for both comprehension and production. The first view predicts language learning to be a slow-motion version of normal development. The alternative view predicts unique language profiles associated with each of the more than 200 specific etiologies that may cause mental retardation, including genetic, metabolic, trauma prenatally or postnatally, and disease processes. Although the majority of research on mental retardation in the past has supported the first view (Yoder and Miller, 1972), recent research supports the latter view (Miller, 1988; Miller et al., 1981). Vocabulary learning provides a window to explore the development of representational skills and perhaps gain some insight into the impact that cognitive deficits have on this aspect of language performance. This chapter will review the research on vocabulary development of children with DS as a specific etiology associated with mental retardation, discuss the methodological issues, review several paradoxes in the literature, and discuss how mental retardation theory relates to the acquisition of language and communication skills.

LEXICAL ACQUISITION RESEARCH: METHODOLOGICAL ISSUES

The literature on lexical acquisition in children with mental retardation is variable in methodology and outcome.

For the most part, vocabulary development and use has received very little attention from investigators in the field. A review paper by Barrett and Diniz (1989) reports only 23 articles from 1954 to the present. Nine of these studies investigated children with DS only, and five studies contrasted performance of retarded children with DS and without DS. Barrett and Diniz (1989) summarize the results of these studies as follows: (1) children with DS do not differ from retarded children with other etiologies on vocabulary skills, (2) all children with mental retardation acquire vocabulary at a rate different from typically developing children, and (3) the actual words acquired by retarded and nonretarded children seem to be very similar. These conclusions must be viewed with caution for a number of methodological and conceptual reasons. However, it is important to note that the prediction of equivalent vocabulary performance for MA-matched groups is not generally supported by the studies reviewed by Barrett and Diniz (1989); performance is poorer than one would expect. What are the issues we need to consider when attempting to interpret this literature?

At almost every level, questions can be raised about the existing literature on lexical acquisition in children with mental retardation. Probably the most basic has to do with the measures of intelligence used to calculate MA. Most of the older work did not match children on MA at all, using CA instead. Other studies, particularly those published in the 1960s and 1970s, did not use nonverbal measures in determining MA. The measures used to match children on MA are critical to the interpretation of the results of these studies. The "catch-22" here is that the use of verbal measures of MA will ensure equivalent performance between matched groups, and nonverbal measures may assess cognitive skills that have nothing to do with language acquisition and use. The ideal would be to measure the nonverbal cognitive skills associated with language acquisition directly. We have neither the theory nor the measurement tools to meet this need at present (Bates and Snyder, 1987). The second set of questions can be raised about what is measured across studies of vocabulary development in retarded children.

Cromer (1987) reminds us that there are two basic things that children must learn when learning a word, referential meaning and grammatical classification. The research to date deals exclusively with referential skill development. Cromer points out that without the acquisition of grammatical classification, form class, children will experience difficulty in producing well-formed multiword utterances. This is of particular concern for children with DS, where deficits in productive syntax are well documented (Miller, 1987). In fact, Fowler (1990) argues that a specific deficit in learning syntax is the basic language learning problem of children with DS. Barrett and Diniz (1989) reviewed the literature on the acquisition of semantic-syntactic classes of words. Their review focused on the retarded children's acquisition of object names, action names, adjectives, prepositions, demonstratives, and connectives. They conclude that retarded children acquire object names in the same manner as nonretarded children but experience difficulty in acquiring prepositions and proforms. They suggest that the lag in vocabulary acquisition may be associated with specific semantic-syntactic classes of words.

The types of referential notions that retarded children can represent with words may be more limited than for nonretarded children. To access the semantic knowledge, as well as the syntactic classification of vocabulary items, children have to code words for both the grammatical category and the referential meaning expressed. The efficiency of children with DS to use such dual systems has not been investigated to date. Fowler (1990) would predict that children with DS would code referential meaning but would fail to effectively code the grammatical category of new words.

REFERENTIAL VOCABULARY MEASURES

The research on referential vocabulary employs a variety of measures that code different aspects of lexical development. These differences make it impossible to generalize the data across studies and have produced a number of paradoxical results as well. Referential vocabulary measures have included vocabulary tests requiring recognition of words relative to pictures in comprehension and production: the Peabody Picture Vocabulary Test and the Expressive Single Word Picture Vocabulary Test, for example. These tests focus on picturable words that are primarily names of things. Picturability, of course, limits the range of vocabulary that can be tested. In addition, the difficulty level of these tests is not governed by the conceptual complexity of the words but by notions of what is easy and hard for children taking the tests. The resulting complexity constructs assessed may include the frequency of occurrence of the words in the language or the obscurity of the line drawings representing the words.

Several measures have been derived from language samples, including the number of different words produced in samples of specified length and type/token ratios of different words to total words in a sample of 50 utterances. These measures are frequency based and, although focusing on vocabulary diversity, deal only with samples of the child's language performance. They are not measures of total vocabulary size. Total vocabulary indices have been derived primarily from extensive experimental data (Bloom, 1973) or diaries (Weir, 1964; Nelson, 1973). Recent parent report vocabulary scales may provide investigators with reasonable measures of total vocabulary size for the first 24 to 30 months of development (Bates et al., 1984, 1989; Rescorla, 1989). The use of these different measures of vocabulary performance, as well as different subject matching strategies, have produced some interesting conflicts in the literature.

ARE THERE DELAYED OR ACCELERATED VOCABULARY SKILLS IN CHILDREN WITH DOWN SYNDROME?

Recent studies of lexical development in children with DS present conflicting results. Differences in their results and conclusions may be traced to differences in matching strategies, as well as dependent measures. Rondal (1978) found children with DS produced proportionally more different words in a language sample than typically developing (TD) children of the same linguistic stage, as defined by mean length of utterance. Rondal (1978) used the high type/token ratios of children with DS as evidence for their having larger vocabularies than younger TD children participating in conversations with their mothers in free play. He explains that advanced lexical development is present in the DS subjects because of their advanced CA, reflecting more linguistic and nonlinguistic experience.

Alternately, Cardoso-Martins et al. (1985) claim lexical acquisition on experimental tasks proceeds at a slower rate for children with DS than for normal children matched for language development and MA. They studied six TD children and six children with DS in a longitudinal study with subjects at a 10- to 12-month developmental level at the onset. Subjects were followed for 14 to 21 months. They found that the acquisition of object names proceeded at a significantly slower pace for the DS group than for the normal group. They argue that these results are caused by specific cognitive deficits for language learning in the group with DS. Given the delays in vocabulary acquisition, they predict further delays in the onset of syntactic acquisition. It is interesting to note that these investigators also found that the two groups produced the same number of different words in language samples at the end of the study when matched for MA. This apparent contradictory finding suggests that the two dependent measures, number of different words produced in a language sample and the number of words learned in an experimental task, assess different language abilities.

Calculating the number of different words involves gathering a language sample of a specified length in time, generally a conversation between a parent and child. The sample is transcribed, and the number of different words the child produced are counted. This is interpreted as an index of the child's vocabulary diversity and is often inappropriately generalized as an index of the child's total vocabulary size. The experimental method counts the number of trials or exposures required by the child to learn a new word under controlled conditions. This measure is interpreted as an index of learning potential and is generalized as an index of the child's rate of learning of new words in the natural environment. Apparently, children with DS require more trials to criterion to learn new words in experimental tasks but produce the same number of different words in a language sample as control children matched for MA. If slower learning equals smaller total vocabularies, perhaps the number of different words produced in a language sample is not an appropriate estimate of total vocabulary size.

Does vocabulary acquisition relate to the acquisition of syntax? The relationship between lexical and syntactic acquisition has not received much attention. Only one case study, reported by Fowler (1985), and a paper by Cromer (1987) have appeared. These papers suggest different mechanisms may operate for lexical vs. syntactic learning. Cromer (1983) argues that vocabulary learning involves both referential and grammatical aspects. Vocabulary measures, however, tend to focus on the referential aspect of words, which may be acquired gradually over time. Syntax, he argues, requires a reorganization process to accommodate new grammatical data. Fowler (1985) suggests that some retarded people may be unable to reorganize their grammar beyond a particular point, resulting in a plateauing of their syntactic skills. The construct of productivity was put forth by Ingram (1981) as an index of the combinatorial diversity of children's early lexicons. He argued that simple frequency was not sufficient to claim grammatical mastery. The word had to be used with two or more different words preceding it and following it to be considered productive on co-occurrence grounds. Differences in meanings encoded should also occur. Ingram's (1981) productivity index provides us with a mechanism to quantify the combinatorial properties of early vocabularies, providing opportunity to relate lexical skills to the emergence of syntax. Children with higher percentages of productive words in their lexicon, for example, would be viewed as having more advanced grammatical systems.

OUR RESEARCH ON THE EARLY LANGUAGE DEVELOPMENT OF CHILDREN WITH DOWN SYNDROME

Two questions remain unanswered from the research reviewed on early language development. (1) do children with

DS show lexical differences compared to MA-matched normal children, and (2) will children with DS show differences in early syntactic skills? A series of studies have been completed over the past 5 years that address these questions. First we will address the issue of lexical development.

Our first study addressed the issue of control group matching criteria. We were convinced that the method used in matching control subjects contributed to the nature of the results and the resulting explanation. In our initial work (Miller et al., 1987) we contrasted measures of lexical production in subjects matched on mean length of utterance (MLU) and MA. Mental age was measured by the Bayley ($\leq$30 months) and nonverbal subtests of the fourth edition of the Stanford-Binet ($\geq$30 months). The subjects included 73 children with DS ranging in age from 2 to 12.5 years of age and 100 TD children. These children were sorted into several MA and MLU groups to compare their lexical skills. Mental ages of the children with DS were compared with the CAs of the TD children. Ages ranged from 11 to 36 months and MLUs ranged from 1.2 to 1.7. The data were derived from 30-minute language samples recorded while children were conversing with a parent.

The results of analyzing the language samples for the number of different words produced revealed that when subjects are matched on MA, children with DS produce fewer different words than matched control subjects. But when they were matched on MLU, a general index of syntactic development, children with DS produce significantly more different words. The results of this study conflict with those of Cardoso-Martins et al. (1985) in one regard. They found that the number of different words produced in a language sample were not different for DS and TD control subjects matched on MA. It seems unlikely that our CA match for the TD subjects is the source of the variance, because MA must, by definition be within 2 S.D. of their CA. This conflicting result is serious, because both of the studies were well controlled. One major variable that was uncontrolled for both studies was socioeconomic status (SES). Socioeconomic status is a powerful predictor of developmental progress in all areas, including language. A second sample of subjects, matched for both SES and MA, will have to be studied to confirm which view is correct.

To investigate the potential contribution of SES to our original results, we examined the number of different words produced in experimental language samples in two additional samples of children with DS and a control group matched for MA and SES. The number of different words produced in 30-minute language samples was calculated for the first group of 44 children, grouped by mental age at 11, 14, 17, 20, 23, and 26 months. Analysis revealed no differences between the DS and TD groups except at 20 months of age (Fig 11–1). The reliability of these findings was tested by studying a second group of 30 DS subjects grouped at 17, 20, 23, and 26 months of MA. Analysis of the second group of DS subjects revealed that their performance was virtually the same as the first group, confirming the reliability of these data. Our conclusion is that adding the SES control reduced the variability between groups, improving the consistency of the result. We cannot, at this time, rule out sampling bias in the selection of our original sample, whose language was so much worse than the two samples controlled for both MA and SES.

ALTERNATIVE MEASURES OF LEXICAL ACQUISITION

Measuring early vocabulary knowledge in very young children poses special

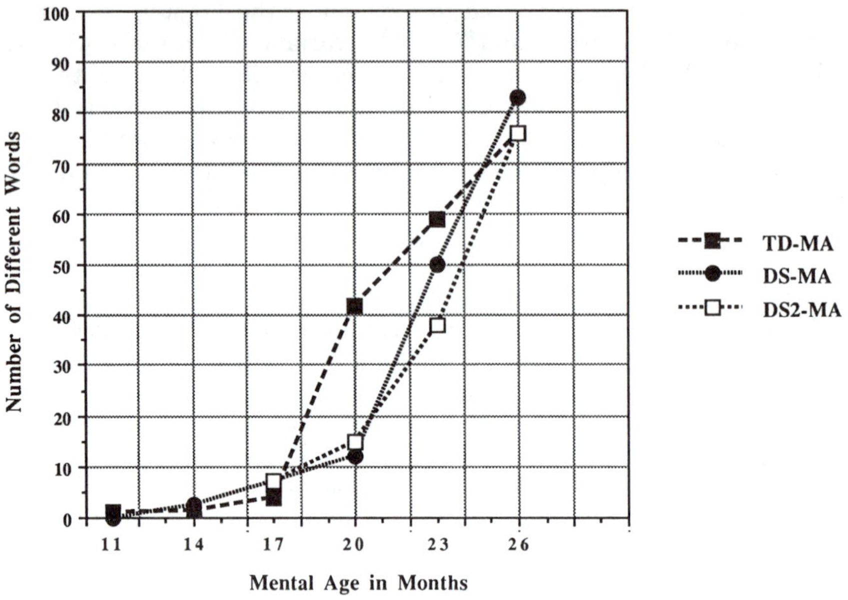

FIG 11–1.
Number of different words produced by three subject groups by mental age: typically developing (TD-MA), Down syndrome (DS-MA), and a second group of subjects with Down syndrome (DS2-MA).

problems. Children's overall linguistic skill is limited, eliminating direct assessment methods using verbal responses. Two measures have been used in the experimental literature, each measuring something different about the vocabulary acquisition process. The first involves gathering a language sample of a specified length in time, generally a conversation between a parent and child. The sample is transcribed, and the number of different words the child produced are counted. This is interpreted as an index of the child's vocabulary diversity and is often generalized as an indication of the child's total vocabulary size. The second method is to determine the number of trials or exposures required by the child to learn a new word under experimental conditions. This measure is interpreted as an index of learning potential and is generalized as an index of the child's rate of learning of new words in the natural environment. Both of these measures have been used to make inferences about the child's overall vocabulary learning.

The best index of vocabulary learning in natural conditions is the child's total vocabulary size. Researchers have been limited to indirect measures, as discussed previously, or to diary methods that require special dedication, usually found only in mothers who happen to be linguists. The task of writing down everything the child says throughout the day for months or years is particularly daunting. Recently an alternative approach has been developed using parent report as an index of child vocabulary knowledge (Bates et al., 1988). This procedure, the Macarthur index of communication development (Fenson et al., 1990), asks parents to check off words they have heard their children produce spontaneously from a list of more than 500 words grouped into major meaning categories, such as animal names, clothing, or transportation. This procedure can be completed in approximately 15 to 30 minutes and works quite effectively from the time of the child's first words until the child is about 2½ years of age.

The validity of parent report as an overall measure of language development, particularly for vocabulary, has been demonstrated in several recent research projects (Beeghly et al., 1989; Dale et al., 1989; Rescorla, 1989; Tomblin et al., 1989). Research on this index has demonstrated that parent report of the child's vocabulary size at 20 months of age predicts language achievement at 3 to 3½ years of age better than direct measures of language achievement at 20 months of age (Bates et al., 1988). Further, this measure of parent report has been demonstrated to be quite reliable over time and correlates very highly with vocabulary size as measured in a sample of language taken in conversation with parents. This method allows investigators, for the first time, direct access to the child's total vocabulary.

The Macarthur scale offered the opportunity to determine if families of children with DS performed as reliably as families of TD children in recording overall vocabulary size. If this proved to be the case, it would allow us the opportunity to compare total vocabulary development of children with DS with TD children at the same MA and family SES. It would also allow us to compare the child's vocabulary production in a language sample with the total vocabulary reported by families to get an idea of how the language sample measure performed as an index of vocabulary size.

CAN PARENTS OF CHILDREN WITH DOWN SYNDROME RELIABLY REPORT VOCABULARY PRODUCTION?

Our first task was to determine if families could reliably report their children's vocabulary production. To do this, we compared the number of different words produced in the language sample condition with the number of different words parents reported their child produced spontaneously for 44 DS children and 46 TD children matched for MA and SES. Correlations between the language sample vocabularies and the parent report vocabularies for the TD children were r = 0.78 and for the children with DS were r = 0.85. Both of these correlations are significant and quite robust in accounting for the overall variance of these measures. Our conclusion is that the families of children with DS perform as well or better than families of TD children in accurately reporting their children's vocabulary size. This finding is extremely important for two reasons. First, it documents that parents of children with DS have realistic views of their children's developmental progress. Second, the data support the use of the Macarthur scale to monitor vocabulary development in children with DS.

Having confirmed the reliability of the Macarthur scale for all of our families, we then went on to compare the total vocabularies of the two groups. As can be seen in Figure 11–2, the children performed similarly to one another until 17 months of age, at which time the TD children experienced a rapid acceleration in their acquisition of vocabulary that continued through 26 months of age. Children with DS progressed at a steady rate until 23 months of age, at which time they also experienced a period of rapid acceleration. Two things are important to note in Figure 11–2: (1) there is a significant difference in total vocabulary size between children with DS and TD children after 17 months of MA; and (2) although vocabularies remain smaller, the children with DS do demonstrate a period of rapid acceleration of vocabulary in the same way that TD children do. This period of rapid acceleration suggests that both groups have the same cognitive mechanisms for vocabulary acquisition, though they may be activated at differ-

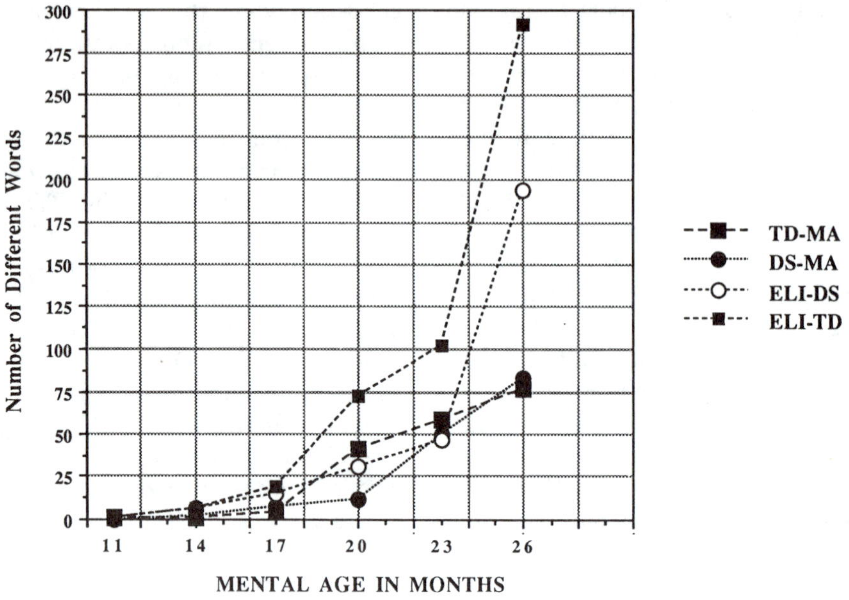

FIG 11–2.
Number of different words produced by typically developing subjects and subjects with Down syndrome on two vocabulary measures: language sample index (typically developing subjects [TD-MA] and subjects with Down syndrome [DS-MA]) and parent report measure (subjects with Down syndrome [ELI-DS] and typically developing subjects [ELT-TD]).

ent times and with a somewhat different overall efficiency. This research has documented that vocabulary size, when measured by the language sample method, does not yield differences between the two groups overall. But when measures of parent report of total vocabulary size are administered, the children with DS exhibit smaller overall vocabularies after 17 months of MA when compared with TD children. The question remains, why should children with DS (who are twice the age on average as the TD child) exhibit smaller vocabularies when presumably they have the same cognitive skills available to them to learn new words?

The results of the vocabulary studies suggest some reasons for conflicting outcomes of studies of the language characteristics of children with DS. Studies grouping subjects at MA levels would find productive language status different among normal and DS subjects, a fact that could confound the outcomes of paradigms assuming equivalent production status. Language input studies, for example, may be seriously compromised by MA matching, because maternal language is typically directed to production status rather than cognition or comprehension status (Brooks-Gunn and Lewis, 1984). The MLU matches, on the other hand, assume synchrony among language levels, an assumption not supported by the data from this study. New grouping strategies will have to be found, using variables relevant to the research question addressed. Vocabulary size as measured by parent report or the number of different words produced in a language sample of standard size may prove to be a better general index of early language development than MLU. Clearly the relationships among language levels assumed in normal children cannot be assumed to hold for biologically distinct populations.

WHAT FACTORS ARE ASSOCIATED WITH LEXICAL GROWTH?

Children with DS exhibit particular difficulty acquiring language and communication skills relative to other nonverbal cognitive skills (Miller, 1987, 1988). Cross-sectional research documents deficits in language production in 60% to 75% of subjects 18 to 60 months of age (Miller et al., 1987). Several causal constructs, including speech motor skills, cognitive skills, and SES have been proposed to account for these language production deficits. We examined the ability of two sets of variables: (1) speech motor skills and (2) cognitive skills and SES to predict change in lexical development over a period of 18 months in 45 children with DS. If language production was limited by speech motor control deficits, these variables, speech motor structure score, speech motor function score, mean syllable type, and phonetic inventory would be the best predictors of lexical change. If, on the other hand, progress in lexical acquisition is governed by cognitive factors or SES, the variables, SES, MA, symbolic play test score, or CA would be the best predictors of lexical progress. The ability of the speech motor and cognitive variables to predict the number of different words produced in a 30-minute language sample was analyzed in correlational and multiple regression studies.

The results indicated that symbolic play and MA were the best social-cognitive predictors of vocabulary diversity 18 months later. Speech motor function and phonetic inventory were the best speech predictors of vocabulary diversity 18 months later. Two speech production variables, phonetic inventory and speech motor function, are better predictors of vocabulary diversity in spontaneous speech than are nonverbal symbolic skills and general cognitive status. Thus, increases in the number of different words produced in language samples are associated with increasing phonetic diversity and improved function of the speech motor system. The study supports the view that the productive language deficits documented in children with DS are, in part, related to deficits in speech motor performance.

ARE LANGUAGE PROFILES STABLE?

Language profiles are a method of comparing the synchrony of development across language comprehension and language production. An initial study of language development profiles (Miller, 1988; Miller et al., 1987) was undertaken to determine if the language acquisition of children with DS was homogeneous or revealed wide individual differences in rate and synchrony of progress in comprehension and production relative to nonverbal cognitive status. The initial study found that two profiles of language performance relative to nonverbal cognitive status accounted for 95% of the children studied. Sixty percent to 75% of the subjects had deficits in language production. Twenty-five percent to 35% exhibited profiles where language comprehension and production were consistent with cognitive status. Only 5% had deficits in both comprehension and production. The present study is a longitudinal examination of profile consistency in a large group of children with DS. Examining profile types over time may provide insight into the forces that influence the language development of these children. Stable profiles may reflect the language learning abilities of the child. Alternately, changing profiles may be attributable to environmental or adaptive forces.

We evaluated the profiles of an additional group of subjects, 43 children with

TABLE 11–1.

Experimental Protocol, Age Scores, and Criteria Defining Profile Type for the Profile Study

Cognition: Bayley Scales of Infant Development—Mental Scale, the Symbolic Play Test, Lowe and Costello, 1976, Stanford Binet, ed 4, nonverbal subtests
Language comprehension: Sequenced Inventory of Communication Development, Miller-Chapman procedures, *JSHR* 1980, Test for the Auditory Comprehension of Language, revised, Peabody Picture Vocabulary Test.
Language production: Language samples in free play, 30 min total time (15 min with parent, 15 min with examiner); analysis: orthographic transcription—SALT format
Speech production: IPA transcription of language samples, PEPPER format, Weiss Articulation Test, Photo Articulation Test
Speech motor control: Perceptual index of speech motor structure and function, Robbins and Klee, *JSHD,* 1987
Socioeconomic status: Maternal education level—highest grade completed
Age scores: Age equivalent scores were derived for language comprehension and production.
Profile criteria: Each child's language comprehension and production age level performance was compared with his or her mental age. Criteria for determining accelerated, equivalent, or delayed language performance were established as follows:
Mental ages ≤24 mo: Language ± 3 mo
Mental ages ≥25 mo: Language ± 6 mo

DS, ages 11 to 58 months of CA at the time of initial testing. The mean CA was 37.2 months, and the mean MA was 22 months of age. The data for this study consist of four data points covering 24 months of development. The subjects were evaluated every 6 months for the first year and every 12 months thereafter.

An experimental protocol consisting of developmentally appropriate tests and procedures from each of the following categories was administered to each child at every visit (Table 11–1). Language profiles were calculated for each subject at each data point for a total of 172 profiles. Three profile types accounted for all 172 profiles out of a possible nine profile types for this analysis (Table 11–2). The three types were mental age = comprehension = production, mental age = comprehension > production, and mental age > comprehension > production. The number of subjects with each profile type at each data point can be found in Table 11–3. The most frequent profile type is profile type 2, MA equal to language comprehension with language production delayed. This profile type accounts for 64% of all the profiles. Table 11–3 documents the change in profile types (the change in language status relative to MA) over 24 months of development. These data clearly document a shift in language status for the subject sample from about 50% showing delays in language production at time 1 to 72% at time 4.

To explore the nature of the profile

TABLE 11–2.

Percent of Subjects With Each Profile Type

Profile Type	No. of Subjects	%
1. Mental age = comprehension = production	58	34
2. Mental age = comprehension > production	110	64
3. Mental age > comprehension > production	4	2

TABLE 11–3.
Number of Subjects With Each Profile Type at Each Data Point

Profile Type*	Time 1	Time 2	Time 3	Time 4
1	21	15	13	9
2	21	28	30	31
3	1	0	0	3

*Profile types: 1 = mental age = comprehension = production; 2 = mental age = comprehension > production; 3 = mental age > comprehension > production.

shift further relative to changes in mental age, we calculated a MA distribution table for the subjects with profile 2 at each data point. A summary of that data includes the following statements:

1. More than 60% of the total subject profiles reflect deficits in language production over language comprehension and cognitive skills measured by MA.
2. The percentage of subjects exhibiting language deficits profiles (profiles 2 and 3) increases at each data point: 51% at time 1, 65% at time 2, 69% at time 3, and 79% at time 4.
3. Children with profiles of productive language deficits at time 1 maintain those profiles through times 2 to 4.
4. Deficits in language production are associated with advances in MA: 54% to 61% of subjects less than 24 months of age have this profile, whereas 83% to 100% of the subjects older than 25 months have production deficits.

From this study we drew several conclusions. First, a profile of productive language deficit relative to language comprehension and cognitive skill characterizes the majority of children with DS in this study. Second, more than 90% of the profile changes were the result of language production skills failing to keep pace with advancing MA. Third, the subjects in this study appear to fall into two groups relative to their language learning progress. One group's production skills were impaired from the onset of first words. The second group's production skills were commensurate with their cognitive skills initially, but production ability failed to keep pace with cognitive skills as they grew older. Fourth, the two longitudinal profile types documented in this study, one stable and one changing, suggest that two different causes of language delay may be operating. Stable profiles may be attributable to learner characteristics, and changing profiles may be attributable to environmental or adaptive forces.

LANGUAGE LEARNING PROCESS MODELS

The data presented in this chapter are consistent with models of child language acquisition that predict interaction between linguistic levels, phonology, vocabulary, syntax, and semantics. These studies add to the growing body of evidence documenting the disassociation between language comprehension and production. Comprehension skills consistently exceed production skills in children with DS, and the gap appears to widen with increasing CA. These data are evidence against theoretical models that fail to distinguish lexical knowledge for comprehension and production independently. A model of language acquisition must permit at least minimal interaction among linguistic levels while allowing the relative independence of language comprehension and language production.

CLINICAL IMPLICATIONS

The research on vocabulary acquisition broadens our view of the language production skills of children with DS. First, this work confirms that language comprehension skills are more advanced than language production skills for vocabulary, as well as syntax. Parents and teachers should be advised that language production performance seriously underestimates language comprehension ability. If communication and continued language learning is to be optimized, the language addressed to the child with DS should be at or just above his or her language comprehension ability. Second, parent report vocabulary measures have been documented to be both reliable and valid for monitoring vocabulary growth in this population. This provides an additional important measure of language progress that is robust and cost effective. Parents can report vocabulary progress frequently without fear of overuse of standardized tests. Third, the results of these studies suggest that early intervention focusing on vocabulary production is necessary. Although vocabulary production skills are better than production of syntax, the rate of vocabulary learning is not keeping pace with the development of other cognitive skills.

SUMMARY

Children with DS offer an opportunity for investigators interested in cognition and language problems to study asynchronous development of various language levels in language production relative to comprehension and cognitive status. Our work to date has documented consistent deficits in language production. These deficits appear to be associated with advancing MA, because more subjects exhibit production deficits as their MA increases beyond 24 months. Longitudinal studies will be necessary to determine if production skills decline with age. We have not yet analyzed the data on the transition from single word production to syntax. We expect syntactic skills to be particularly difficult for these children. The difficulties these children exhibit in improving their productive language skills are likely to be the result of several factors operating simultaneously across the population. One or more factors may be affecting any individual child. The answers to the questions posed in this chapter have been answered for only a single data set. We must be particularly alert to sampling bias in studies using small numbers because the variability in performance in children with DS is quite large. The finding of significant differences in vocabulary size between DS and TD children suggests that despite the increased age and experience of the DS children, lexical acquisition mechanisms are less efficient than we have assumed from past research.

REFERENCES

Barrett M, Diniz F: Lexical development in mentally handicapped children, in Beveridge M, Conti-Ramsden G, Leudar I (eds): *Language and Communication in Mentally Handicapped People*. New York, Chapman and Hall, 1989, pp 2–32.

Bates E, Bretherton I, Snyder L: *From First Words to Grammar: Individual Differences and Dissociable Mechanisms*. New York, Cambridge University Press, 1988.

Bates E et al: *Early Language Inventory*. Unpublished procedure, Dept of Psychology, University of California at San Diego, 1984.

Bates E, Snyder L: The cognitive hypothesis in language development, in Uzgiris I, McV Hunt J (eds): *Infant Performance and Experience: New Findings With the Ordinal Scales*. Champaign, University of Illinois Press, 1987, pp 168–206.

Beeghly M, Jernberg E, Burrows E: Validity of the early language inventory for use with 25-month-olds. Presented at the Society for Research in Child Development, Kansas City, 1989.

Bloom L: *One Word at a Time: The Use of Single-Word Utterances Before Syntax*. The Hague, Mouton, 1973.

Brooks-Gunn J, Lewis M: Maternal responsivity with handicapped infants. *Child Dev* 1983; 3:782–793.

Campione J, Brown A: Toward a theory of intelligence: Contribution from research with retarded children. *Intelligence* 1978; 2:279–304.

Cardoso-Martins C, Mervis CB, Mervis CA: Early vocabulary acquisition by children with Down syndrome. *Am J Ment Defic* 1985; 90:177–184.

Cole K, Dale P, Mills P: Defining language delay in young children by cognitive referencing: Are we saying more than we know? *Appl Psycholinguistics* 1990; 11:291–302.

Cromer RF: Word knowledge acquisition in retarded children: A longitudinal study of acquisition of a complex linguistic structure. *J Speech Hear Disord* 1987; 52:324–334.

Dale P et al: The validity of a parent report instrument of a child language at twenty month. *J Child Lang* 1989; 16:239–250.

Day J, Borkowski J: *Intelligence and Exceptionality: New Directions for Theory, Assessment, and Instructional Practice*. Norwood, NJ, Ablex Publishing Corp, 1987.

Fenson L et al: *Technical Manual for the Macarthur Communicative Development Inventories*. Developmental Psychology Laboratory, San Diego State University, Calif, 1990.

Fowler A: Language acquisition in Down's syndrome children: Production and comprehension (unpublished doctoral dissertation, University of Pennsylvania). *Dissertation Abstracts Int* 1985; 46(1-B):324.

Fowler A: Language abilities of children with Down syndome: Evidence for a specific syntactic delay, in Cicchetti D, Beeghly M (eds): *Children With Down Syndrome: A Developmental Perspective*. Cambridge, Cambridge University Press, 1990.

Gardner H: *Frames of Mind: The Theory of Multiple Intelligences*. New York, Basic Books, 1983.

Ingram D: Early patterns of grammatical development, in Stark R (ed): *Language Behavior in Infancy and Early Childhood*. New York, Elsevier North-Holland, 1981.

Lowe M, Costello A: *The Symbolic Play Test*. Windser, Nfer Publishing Co, 1976.

Miller J: Assessing children's language behavior: A developmental process approach, in Schiefelbusch RL (ed): *The Basics of Language Intervention*. Baltimore, University Park Press, 1978.

Miller JF: *Analyzing Language Production in Children: Experimental Procedures*. Baltimore, University Park Press, 1981.

Miller JF: Language and communication characteristics of children with Down syndrome, in Paschel S, Tingey C, Rynders J, et al (eds): *New Perspectives on Down Syndrome*. Baltimore, Brooks Publishing Co, 1987, pp 233–262.

Miller JF: Developmental asynchrony of language development in children with Down syndrome, in Nadel L (ed): *Psychobiology of Down Syndrome*. New York, Academic Press, 1988.

Miller J, Budde M, Bashir A, et al: Lexical productivity in children with Down syndrome. Paper presented at the Annual Convention of the American Speech-Language-Hearing Association, New Orleans, November 1987.

Miller J, Chapman RS, Branston MB, et al: Language comprehension in sensorimotor stages V and VI. *J Speech Hear Res* 1980; 23:284–311.

Miller J, Streit G, Salmon D, et al: Developmental synchrony in the language of children with Down syndrome. Paper presented at the Annual Convention of the American Speech-Language-Hearing Association, New Orleans, November 1987.

Miller J, Yoder D: An ontogenetic language teaching strategy for retarded children, in Schiefelbusch R, Lloyd L (eds): *Language Perspectives—Acquisition, Retardation and Intervention.* Baltimore, University Park Press, 1974.

Nelson K: Structure and strategy in learning to talk. *Monogr Soc Child Dev* 1973; 38(1-2 serial no. 149).

Rescorla L: The language development survey: A screening tool for delayed language in toddlers. *J Speech Hear Dis* 1989; 29:394–399.

Robbins J, Klee T: Clinical assessment of oropharyngeal motor development in young children. *J Speech Hear Disord* 1987; 52:271–277.

Robinson N, Janos P: The contribution of intelligence tests to the understanding of special children, in Day J, Borkowski J (eds): *Intelligence and Exceptionality: New Directions for Theory, Assessment and Instructional Practices.* Norwood, NJ, Ablex Publishing Corp, 1987.

Rondal JA: Maternal speech to normal and Down's syndrome children matched for man length of utterance, in Meyers CE (ed): *Quality of Life in Severely and Profoundly Mentally Retarded People: Research Foundations for Improvement.* Washington, DC, American Association on Mental Deficiency, 1978, pp 193–266.

Sternberg R: Beyond IQ: *A Triarchic Theory of Human Intelligence.* New York, Cambridge University Press, 1985.

Sternberg R: *Intelligence Applied.* New York, Harcourt Brace & Jovanovich, 1986.

Terman L: *The Measurement of Intelligence.* Boston, Houghton-Mifflin, 1916.

Tomblin B, Shonrock C, Hardy J: The concurrent validity of the Minnesota Child Development Inventory as a measure of young children's language development. *J Speech Hear Dis* 1989; 54:101–105.

Weir R: *Language in the Crib.* The Hague, Mouton, 1964.

Yoder D, Miller J: What we may know and what we can do: Input toward a system, in McLean J, Yoder D, Schiefelbusch R (eds): *Language Intervention With the Retarded: Developing Strategies.* Baltimore, University Park Press, 1972.

SECTION IV

Interactive Processes in Syntactic Development

12 Context Priming of Sentence Structure

Nancy W. Streim, Ph.D.

Among child language researchers there is ongoing debate about the relative contributions of innate and environmental factors to children's syntactic performance. In support of a strong innatist position, it has been argued that the degenerate nature of the input provides inadequate guidance for the child mastering the syntactic rules of the language. As a result, the child must apply sets of genetically determined linguistic rules to create grammatical utterances. Typical of this approach to language learning is the assumption that the form of children's utterances directly reflects the current state of their syntactic rule system.

However, there is considerable evidence that the form of young children's utterances may be initially shaped not by rules but by the syntactic model provided in input, suggesting that learning syntactic rules may be significantly constrained by factors in the discourse environment. For example, it has been noted that children's one-word utterances are predictable in context and correlated with the linguistic forms modeled (Barrett, 1986; Harris et al., 1988; Streim and Chapman, 1990). It has also been shown that young children draw on aspects of the adult syntactic model as a scaffold for increasing levels of grammatical complexity in their spoken utterances (Nelson and Kamhi, 1985; Ninio and Bruner, 1978; Snow, 1981). These findings have led some researchers to look at the mental processes that underlie the formulation of grammatical speech as a way of determining how syntactic information may be stored and retrieved by children.

Recent advances in modeling spoken language processing have brought a new perspective to these efforts to explain contextual influences on grammatical development in children's speech. In process models of language production, we find descriptions of possible cognitive processing mechanisms by which conceptual, discourse, and linguistic information can be formulated into spoken language (Bock, 1982, 1986, 1989; Dell, 1985, 1989; Garrett, 1982; Levelt and Maasen, 1981; Stemberger, 1985). Examining the processes by which stored linguistic information is instantiated as spoken language allows us to investigate the nature of the developing linguistic rule system. To date, much of this work has focused on syntactic and lexical processing in the fluent adult speaker. However, process models hold promise as a way to account for the nature and consequences of linguistic and discourse context effects on children's syntactic development.

A plausible developmental process model of children's spoken language not only must explain how language production might occur in a stable linguistic planning system but must also account for changes in processing that might occur as children expand their linguistic knowledge and achieve increasing flexibility in creating spoken utterances.

Chapman et al. (see Chapter 1) are among the first child language researchers to provide a process framework within which we can account for relationships among children's language behavior, the discourse context in which language occurs, and children's underlying representation of production rules for spoken language. This chapter provides an argument for a developmental process model as an effective account of the role of context in shaping and constraining children's early syntactic utterances.

In this chapter I will present evidence for different types of context effects on the form of children's utterances. The chapter addresses three questions about context effects on syntactic structure:

1. How does event context, that is, the social situation in which language is produced, constrain early lexical production, and what are the implications of these situational constraints for modeling lexical representation and lexical accessibility?
2. How does the syntactic model in the adult input affect children's syntactic formulation?
3. Can the syntax of children's sentences be primed, and if so, what are the implications for describing the nature of the developing syntactic rule system?

By attempting to fit situational and linguistic context effects into a model of sentence planning for children, I will demonstrate the potential usefulness of a process approach for describing children's language use and development of spoken language skills.

INTERACTIVE PROCESS MODELS

The following discussion of context effects on children's language is based on several assumptions about utterance production found in recent interactive language process models (Dell, 1985, 1989; Stemberger, 1985). First, it is assumed that a speaker must start with a mental representation of some communicative goal and a particular message to convey. The message level representation must specify a number of linguistically relevant features such as illocutionary effect, topic, and perspective. It must also account for pragmatic considerations such as listener characteristics, discourse environment, and social context. The speaker must then retrieve from memory the necessary linguistic elements to translate this conceptual plan into an appropriately ordered string of words. The process of utterance formulation requires retrieval and assembly of syntactic forms, semantic concepts, lexical representations, phonological features, and phonetic instructions for instantiating message content.

In an interactive model of utterance production, the linguistic knowledge needed to create grammatical speech is distributed in a network of cognitive units, or nodes, connected by multiple pathways within the speaker's general store of world knowledge (see Dell, 1989, for a description of the possible architecture of a node-based system). Each node specifies a discrete unit of linguistic information. The units are unordered and may vary in scope. A unit may contain a lexical meaning, a phonetic representation, or the instructions for creating a commonly used syntactic structure. Pathways among conceptual, syntactic, semantic, and phonetic units transmit information throughout the network by means of automatic spreading activation, which measures the degree to which any unit is available for retrieval and execution at a given moment during production planning (Dell, 1989; Posner and Snyder, 1975). When one unit is activated, some degree of activation automatically spreads to all other units that are related. For example, Dell (1989) argues that activation of a lexical representation causes activation to spread to semantically and phonologically related words. In the Child Talk model described by Chapman et al. (see Chapter 1), it is further assumed that activation spreads to representations of events where the lexical item has appeared before. Strength of activation on a particular unit, or convergence of activation onto a single unit, determines the likelihood that it will reach threshold for production.

Not all nodes are equal in weight or value. Nodes, or the connections among them, acquire increasing amounts of strength through repeated experience and use. All else being equal, frequently practiced words, routines, or syntactic structures are more likely to be selected for production than infrequently used ones.

Feedback among units is the hallmark of the interactive models. Many types of interaction are permitted, some of which may affect the spoken output. It has been shown, for example, that strong activation of a phonological feature, or set of features, can bias lexical selection toward words that contain activated features (Dell, 1985). Others have shown that early activation of a lexical item can influence selection of utterance form by biasing the speaker to cast a message to accommodate its syntactic privileges (Streim, 1988). Still other investigators have demonstrated how lingering activation of previously used utterance forms can affect subsequent message specification (Bock, 1986). Speech error data are often cited as evidence of interactive, or "bottom-up," feedback from phonological, lexical, or syntactic processing units whose activation influences the product of utterance formulation (Dell, 1989; Stemberger, 1985).

The feedback mechanism in the interactive model suggests that the proc... of creating utterances is highly sensitive to contextual influences. In the Child Talk model, context effects on lexical production are attributed to connections that the child creates among (1) representations of the semantic representations that define an object or action word, (2) syntactic forms associated with past use, and (3) some representation of contextual features that have supported past production of particular words and phrases. According to the model, the probability of producing a word is directly affected by activation of the connections among related nodes.

Most cognitive scientists agree that utterance production requires some investment of cognitive resources. Under normal discourse conditions, the process of sentence planning moves quickly and automatically from message specification to linguistic representation with minimal investment of conscious attention. However, for adults, as well as children, unfamiliar settings, unusual discourse requirements, and retrieval of infrequently used words all affect the degree of automaticity with which speakers are able to formulate utterances (Levelt and Maasen, 1981; Streim and Chapman, 1987). It has been suggested that the highly formulaic syntax of routine, spontaneous discourse derives from a cognitive bias toward minimizing cognitive load during sentence formulation (Bock, 1982).

The interactive process models of language production suggest several interesting empirical questions about the process by which young children formulate spoken language. In the next section, I will examine one such question: What is the relationship between mental representation of event context and early language production? Here I will attempt to explain the data on contextual constraints on lexical production in light of the assumptions of an interactive language processing model.

WHAT IS THE ROLE OF EVENT CONTEXT IN CONSTRAINING EARLY WORD USE?

A number of investigations have shown that for young children, early word use is often context bound. In other words, for the young word learner lexical accessibility is influenced by the presence of a situational context in which an event or action schema has occurred in the past (Barrett, 1983, 1986; Barrett et al., 1991; Bloom, 1973; Cuvelier, 1986; Edwards and Goodwin, 1986). In one well-known example, Bloom (1973) reports that Allison, at age 2 years, produced the word *car* only when she watched cars pass below her window but not when she passed a car in the street or saw one in a book. In a similar vein, Barrett (1986) describes the behavior of a child who only produced the label *duck* when hitting a rubber duck off the edge of the bathtub despite repeated opportunities to label the same object in other contexts. Edwards and Goodwin (1986) cite the example of a child who at 18 months produced the verb *drop* only when an object fell from her own hands, although she saw others drop objects in her presence.

Contextual constraints on lexical access are typically attributed to a fusing of semantic, discourse, and situational features in the child's initial lexical entries for newly acquired words. Bloom (1973) suggests that Allison had undergeneralized the semantic features of her lexical representation for the word *car* to include only those cars encountered in a single event context.

Another view of constrained lexical production attributes context effects to the child's representation of events (Chapman et al., see Chapter 1; Nelson, 1985, 1986; Streim and Chapman, 1990). In this view of context-bound word use, the child forms mental representations of particular events that include language. In the extreme, event representation is characterized as a script (Nelson, 1986). Within the framework of scriptal models, the child's access to the lexicon is achieved by activating the representation of an event with which particular words have been associated.

Although the notion of script is useful for characterizing how children might encode language as part of action routines, in the Child Talk model, the event representation is more than a script. It recognizes that children are exposed to language in the context of events and that certain aspects of events are encoded in essentially nonlinguistic representations.

Early word use is often treated as a labeling activity. However, it has been suggested that contextually constrained single word utterances are better understood as ritualized responses to the enactment of a familiar event (Barrett, 1986; Cuvelier, 1986). According to Barrett's argument, recognition of a familiar action sequence elicits the child's typical response. This view is particularly appealing as an approach to understanding children's language use because it recognizes the role of communicative intentions in determining what children say.

The evidence of contextual constraints on early word use fits well with the assumptions of a process model of speech production such as Child Talk. The data suggest that the child's lexicon contains representations of semantic content and representations for events in which the words have been previously encountered. The strength of connections between words and events determines the probability that words will be retrieved for production. In the framework of a production process model, as the child adds event associations to his or her lexical representations for individual words and expressions, the nodes, or connections among nodes, become reweighted. With repeated exposure in multiple contexts, the child's constellation of representations that make up the lexical entry generalizes to highlight the features that are common to all the events in which the word is encountered. Representations of events merge, and representation of linguistically related features of words such as action category, object class, or syntactic privileges take on greater weight in the child's lexical network. As a result, over the course of early production history with particular words, context becomes a less central predictor of word use, although representations of events in which the words have appeared may remain.

These theories of constrained early word use prompt a number of additional questions about the ways event knowledge might figure into the process of lexical acquisition. For example, how and when do children disentangle the properties of events from the properties of actions or objects, and how much exposure to new words is required before a child generalizes its use to multiple contexts?

A case study by Streim and Chapman (1990) investigated these questions by charting the early production history for a set of novel verbs. The subject (2.0 years; mean length of utterance [MLU] = 2.0) was introduced to four novel actions and their labels every day for 2 weeks in a controlled experimental setting. The actions were modeled in two different event contexts. Each word was assigned a primary event context (C1) in which the actions were labeled during weeks 1 and 2 and a secondary event context (C2) in which the actions were labeled only during week 2. The actions, their labels, and their contexts are described in Table 12–1.

In the "breakfast" context, two actions, *meep* and *koob,* were demonstrated and labeled each day, and the subject was prompted to perform the actions and produce their labels. The other two actions, *ruck* and *tighe,* were demonstrated without labels for the first week and demonstrated and labeled during the second week. Similarly, in the "Lego-play" context, all four actions were demonstrated every day; however, labels were introduced for *ruck, tighe,* and *meep* during the first week and for *koob* only during the second week. One novel word, *meep* was labeled in both contexts throughout the investigation.

The child was prompted to carry out each action and provide its label each day in each context. The total record of novel word use, including imitations, prompted labeling, and spontaneous labeling, was recorded. The investigators analyzed the relationship between exposure to the actions and labels and word production within, between, and beyond the experimental event contexts.

Streim and Chapman (1990) report several interesting findings about the subject's early novel word use. First,

TABLE 12–1.
Novel Verbs With Event Contexts and Definitions*

Word	C1†	Definition	C2†	Definition
Koob	Breakfast	Scoop cereal from box to bowl	Legos	Scoop Legos from bucket to pile
Ruck	Legos	Insert straw through Lego or wall of Legos	Breakfast	Insert straw through piece of toast
Tighe	Legos	Twirl Lego on base plate	Breakfast	Twirl spoon on table
Meep‡	Breakfast	Stack toast pieces into pyramid	Legos	Stack Legos into pyramid

*From Streim N, Chapman RS: A case study of the acquisition of novel action verbs. 1990 (unpublished). Used by permission.
†C1-primary event context: labels provided days 1–14; C2-secondary event context: labels provided days 8–14.
‡*Meep* labeled in C1 days 1–14, and in C2 days 2–14.

each of the novel words was produced at least once during the first week in which it was labeled; however, with one exception, novel words were not produced in either context until the label was provided *in that context.* Second, for labels introduced in week 1, frequency of labeling increased during week 2 in the same context; however, for actions labeled during week 2, frequency of production was suppressed compared with the rate of production of the same word in the primary context. Third, novel words were consistently produced as labels for the experimenter's actions several days before they were produced to label self-initiated action. Fourth, though the child failed to generalize the action labels from one context to the other until the label was modeled in context, he did produce familiar general purpose verbs (e.g., *make, play*) to describe the novel actions in the new contexts. Finally, only the word modeled in both contexts throughout the study appeared as a spontaneous reference to a completely novel (but appropriate) action outside the experimental contexts.

Streim and Chapman (1990) hypothesize that the contextual constraints on the subject's use of new words arose from two sources. They propose that the child created lexical entries for the novel verbs that specified an obligatory actor, action, and object of action. In particular, it seems that the subject identified the experimenter as the necessary agent and associated the new label with the experimenter's predictable and unvarying daily demonstrations of the novel actions. This finding supports Barrett's (1986) argument that verbs are initially represented in the lexicon as action schemas.

Second, the authors suggest that the child's lexical acquisition strategy involved distinguishing between the semantic and discourse features of the new verbs and features of frequently used general purpose verbs. This finding is consistent with other accounts of children's reluctance to abandon already productive labels for objects in the environment when provided with new labels (Markman and Wachtel, 1988; Merriman and Bowman, 1989; Mervis and Canada, 1981).

As noted earlier, only the label *meep,* modeled in both contexts throughout the study, generalized beyond the event contexts provided by the experimenter. Analysis of the history of production for this label shows that there were approximately 30 exposures to the novel action and label in multiple contexts before the child disassociated the semantic properties of the novel word from the properties of the experimental event context. This pattern of behavior supports Carey's (1978) hypothesis that it may take several months of exposure for a child to completely "acquire" a novel word. It is, however, also pointed out that the subject seemed to treat the action associated with *meep* as a subset of his general purpose verb *make,* perhaps increasing his readiness to absorb its properties into a productive action category.

How does an interactive process model of language production account for the context effects reported by Streim and Chapman (1990)? In an interactive model, lexical representation for the four novel action words is characterized as a network of linkages among the child's representations of the event, the features and consequences of the action, the required agent, instrument and object of action, and his memory for past production history with the new word. It can be argued that specification of these features formed a minimal set of criteria for labeling the new action with the new verb.

The connection between the child's representation of events and the words associated with them was initially very strong, as seen in the fact that when prompted to label the novel actions in a new context, where no label had been modeled, the child selected "old" labels that were already linked to that context by previous history of production rather than use new labels linked to the same action labeled in a different context. If production of the novel label depends on convergence of activation from a set of nodes representing its criterial features, and if activation is also spreading to familiar labels previously used in the same context, the old word can be expected to win out over the new one, which is less well patterned, unless the input model sets up a new connection. This interpretation is similar to MacWhinney's (1987) argument for a "competition model" of production. Repeated production experience can be expected to strengthen the bonds between the new action and the new label, increasing the likelihood of its accessibility. In Streim and Chapman's (1990) study, the probability that the child would produce the new verbs depended on the length of their production history in a particular event context. His failure to generalize word use in the absence of linguistic modeling suggests that direct modeling may be a critical factor in establishing links between words and events in the lexicon (Bates et al., 1988; Gruendel, 1977; Mervis and Canada, 1981).

These data support a view of utterance formulation in which word selection can be controlled by pragmatic factors outside the normal bounds of linguistic planning. I have argued that event context effects can be attributed to the strength of connections among cognitive nodes representing nonlinguistic experiences with words. Because the interactive model describes lexical representation as a pattern of active associations among bits of knowledge and experience, event context can be thought to affect utterance production by influencing the direction and strength of spreading activation among these nodes. Activation of the event representation spreads to the child's mental representation of the typical linguistic response to that event, and activation of the lexical representation of the child's response influences the syntactic form, as well as illocutionary effect of the resulting utterance (Cuvelier, 1986).

WHAT IS THE EFFECT OF SYNTACTIC MODELING ON THE STRUCTURE OF CHILDREN'S UTTERANCES?

The literature on children's sentence production suggests that the syntactic model in the adult input plays a facilitative role in children's formulation of the syntax of their own utterances. Ninio and Bruner (1978) argue for a scaffolding effect where children build on the syntactic foundation provided in the prior adult utterance. In support of this view, Bloom et al. (1975) and Nelson and Kamhi (1985) show that children's utterances at age 2 years are longer and more syntactically complex when they share syntactic structure with the prior adult utterance than when they are constructed de novo. The literature on imitation also suggests that immediate or delayed use of some portion of the input allows the child to increase production capacity (Snow, 1981; Snow and Goldfield, 1983).

There are several implications of these findings for modeling child language production. First, they suggest a relationship between utterance complexity and cognitive processing complexity. When a child of limited syntactic means incorporates prior discourse into a new utterance, he or she lightens the cognitive burden required for syntactic formulation and frees cognitive resources that can be used to increase utterance complexity or length. For young speakers with limited processing capacity, the facilitative effects of syntactic modeling appear to be significant in expanding the child's communicative range. Important to this argument, however, is the assumption that utterances produced from the fragments of prior discourse reflect the surface effects of a processing strategy and do not necessarily represent the child's competence in constructing utterance syntax for completely novel speech.

The findings on syntactic modeling effects also suggest that children store portions of utterances heard in discourse as a single node and connect these nodes to representations of events. The phenomenon of reusing bits of prior discourse to build new utterances is consistent with Bowerman's (1985) notion of "unanalyzed wholes," according to which children may treat word forms, phrases, or even whole sentences as single lexical units (Bates et al., 1988; Peters, 1983).

Evidence for the effect of input structure on the form of children's utterances can also be seen in the early use of verb inflections. DeVilliers (1985), analyzing the relationship between use of verb inflections in the spontaneous speech of mothers and their 2-year-old children, reports that the range of inflections found in the children's speech mirrors the range of verb inflections found in maternal input for the same verbs. These findings provide strong support for a view of syntactic development in which children learn about syntactic privileges of individual verbs by encoding the lexical forms of the input.

Streim and Chapman (1990) report similar findings for a child's acquisition of grammatical privileges for a set of novel verbs. In their study of novel verb acquisition by a 2-year-old described earlier, the range of verb forms in the child's spontaneous utterances containing the novel verbs was similar to the inflections modelled in the input. In fact, the child's syntactic use of novel verbs looked more like the input model than the child's own utterances containing his frequently used "old" verbs. They argue that the subject formed a grammatically unanalyzed but inflected lexical entry for each new verb modeled, reflecting the syntactic form of the input, even when the form of the model varied from the child's typical use of verb inflections.

Streim and Chapman (1990) and de Villiers (1985) also report syntactic context effects on the sentence structure of utterances containing modeled verbs. In both studies the children's use of subject and object pronouns was predicted by the structure of the input. In Streim and Chapman (1990), the subject consistently produced a preferred sentence structure for each "new" and "old" verb studied. The distribution of sentence constituents in the novel verb utterances was usually similar to the form of the input and sometimes quite different from the syntactic patterns found in "old" verb utterances.

These data suggest that children may encode grammatical properties of newly acquired words directly from the input model. Similar to the connection seen earlier between words and event contexts, children may form sentence level representations for newly acquired verbs that incorporate the linguistic context in which the word was encountered in the input. The fact that Streim and Chapman's (1990) subject used sentence structures for the new verbs that never appeared in his old verb utterances highlights the extent to which syntactic modeling may constrain early syntactic formulation for newly acquired words. In terms of a model of utterance production, pathways of spreading activation between lexical and syntactic nodes can be seen to bias the formulation of sentence structure to accommodate the preferred form of a particular lexical item. The interactive process model explains the child's bias toward familiar modes of expression by allowing for increased automaticity and strength of activation to occur along pathways with a history of use.

CAN SENTENCE FORM BE PRIMED?

A key claim of an interactive process model is that any activated element in the production processing system can influence the course and outcome of utterance formulation by providing an independent source of activation (Bock, 1982, 1986; Dell, 1985, 1989; Stemberger, 1985). For example, a word or syntactic structure retrieved early in the utterance planning process can theoretically influence the speaker's conceptualization of the topic or perspective to be communicated. This claim seems somewhat counterintuitive, because it might be assumed that discourse planning must necessarily drive selection of linguistic elements, including syntactic forms and lexical items. However, there is evidence that such effects do, in fact, occur, with children, as well as adults, by means of linguistic priming. Bock (1986), for example, reports that words retrieved early in production planning are more likely to become sentence subjects even when the event representation biases against such an interpretation.

Priming is defined here, in accordance with the interactive models, as the partial activation of a unit of linguistic information. Priming effects are achieved when the level of activation of a linguistic unit (e.g., a word or syntactic form) is sufficiently high that the unit's strength influences subsequent utterance planning by serving as a source of further spreading activation.

Streim and Chapman (1987) demonstrate lexical priming effects on syntactic planning for children's sentences. In a study of lexical accessibility and the syntax of children's picture descriptions, the investigators compared the sentence form of picture descriptions produced by 4- to 8-year-olds in the presence or absence of lexical priming for a target word in each picture. Target words were concrete nouns, presented as pictures, that the child labeled immediately before describing an event picture containing the same target object (e.g., target word picture: rabbit; event picture: rabbit chasing a girl under a ladder). The length, form, complexity, and fluency of the picture descriptions were analyzed for effects of increased lexical accessibility of the target words. Findings show that priming an object label resulted in (1) earlier placement of the object label in the subsequent picture descriptions, (2) increased utterance length (for the older children), and (3) increased utterance fluency.

These findings suggest that syntactic formulation is sensitive to influences from several sources, including discourse effects such as focus or perspective, lexical accessibility of previously mentioned words, and cognitive processing constraints (as seen in the variations in utterance fluency for primed and unprimed event descriptions). It is often argued that earlier mention effects can be attributed to a tendency to topicalize previously introduced information, usually by pronominalizing the subject or object. However, in Streim and Chapman's (1990) study, the absence of increased pronominalization for target words suggests that topic manipulation alone cannot account for earlier mention of target words. Rather, their findings support an argument for linguistic interactions during production planning in which syntactic form can be made to vary to accommodate early placement of a lexical label already activated in working memory. The results are consistent with Bock's (1982) claim that the utterance planning system is sensitive to the order in which words are retrieved for production. Streim and Chapman's (1990) results, when considered in the context of an interactive process model, illustrate that children and adults are susceptible to effects of lexical availability on syntactic structure.

In most models of sentence formulation, sentence type is normally specified by message features, such as topic and perspective. However, interactive models permit syntactic priming to activate a sentence type before a message has been formulated. Bock (1986) demonstrated this effect by eliciting active and passive sentences from adult subjects with a syntactic priming manipulation. She reports that speakers produced more passive picture descriptions after reading a passive voice prime sentence than after an active voice prime sentence. Her results show that a speaker can be influenced, by priming sentence voice, to select a passive structure for a picture description even though the active voice is significantly more common and, in her study, equally suitable to describe common events.

Streim (1988) extended Bock's (1986) study to children in a developmental study of grammatical voice priming. Streim (1988) elicited active and passive picture descriptions from 6- and 9-year-olds and adults. The design of the study included three levels of priming for active and passive sentence structure to tap hypothesized developmental changes in the nature of the syntactic production rule for creating active and passive voice sentences. Table 12–2 describes the priming manipulations.

TABLE 12–2.

Sample of Passive Prime Sentences and Event Picture*

Event picture: Boy chasing girl
- Level 1 prime sentence: "The mouse is heard by the cat."
- Level 2 prime sentence: "The mouse is eaten by the cat."
- Level 3 prime sentence: "The mouse is chased by the cat."

*From Streim N: The effects of syntactic priming on the production of active and passive sentences. Doctoral dissertation, Madison, University of Wisconsin, 1988. Used by permission.

The prime sentences varied in their linguistic relationship to a set of event pictures to be described by each subject. Level 1 prime sentences shared no semantic or lexical relationship with the event picture, only the potential for reusing the activated active or passive sentence structure. It was hypothesized that children would respond to level 1 priming if they had an abstract grammatical voice production rule susceptible to independent activation. Level 2 prime sentences shared case structure with the event picture to be described. It was hypothesized that children would respond to level 2 priming if the active-passive production rule were based on a case grammar. Level 3 prime sentences shared case structure and action-verb with the event picture. It was hypothesized that children would respond to this level of priming if (1) the active-passive production rule is a lexical feature of the verb or (2) if convergence of activation from syntactic, semantic, and lexical representations overrode the strong tendency to produce only active sentences.

Streim (1988) reports that all subjects produced more passive picture descriptions in the prime conditions than in a control condition. However, children and adults responded to different types of linguistic priming. For the children, priming affected sentence structure at level 3, where the prime sentence shared syntactic, semantic, and lexical information with the event picture. The adults showed priming effects at all three prime levels.

Streim's (1988) data provide evidence that children can be influenced to select an infrequently used sentence structure by having a representation of the structure activated in memory. Furthermore, the results show that linguistic planning for sentence form can precede and influence the specification of message level representations of the topic, focus, and perspective to be communicated.

The evidence that children can be primed by a combination of syntactic, semantic, and lexical activation has several implications for modeling children's language production. First, it suggests that the young child's passive production rule may be a lexical formula activated when a verb, in its passive form, is selected for production. This claim is consistent with a lexicalist production grammar (Bresnan, 1978, 1982). Second, the results suggest that convergence of prime effects from the syntactic, semantic, and lexical domains of utterance planning may be necessary to attain prime effects for sentence voice in children. Third, it is possible to interpret the syntactic prime effect as an epiphenomenon of phonetic level priming for the verb and its associated verb phrase constituents (e.g., "is V-ed by"). This interpretation is consistent with earlier claims that children store unanalyzed portions of prior utterances and reuse them to boost their communicative capabilities.

The third alternative is particularly attractive for explaining these data. The children's production of passive voice picture descriptions showed a significantly higher proportion of the full grammatical passive and the "be" passive (as opposed to the more common truncated and "get" passive) in the prime conditions than in the control condition. This finding suggests that the children used a different mechanism for creating event picture descriptions in the control and experimental conditions. It appears that the children may have employed a storage and retrieval strategy for chunks of prior language, in this case, the passive voice verb phrase. The findings argue for an utterance production process in which highly activated bits of language that are consistent with the event representation may bias selection of a syntactic form that accommodates their reuse. In the vocabulary of an interactive process account of speech production, the lexical priming effects demonstrated by Streim (1988) illustrate the facilatory activation that can occur when a verb form appropriate to a communicative task is activated in the speaker's working memory during subsequent message formulation.

Syntactic priming effects achieved by Bock (1989), Streim (1988), and others suggest that there are multiple routes through the linguistic processing system leading to formulation of the surface structure of an utterance. Furthermore, the strength of activation emanating from a previously used syntactic form can affect how the speaker represents an event to be described. Thus, syntactic priming provides evidence for feedback effects from syntactic planning to discourse level message planning.

DEVELOPMENTAL IMPLICATIONS FOR PROCESS MODELS OF CHILDREN'S LANGUAGE

Any process model of child language production, including Child Talk, must be able to account for changes in the nature of children's linguistic representation, as well as changes in the relationships among its component parts. It has been widely argued that the units of linguistic information accessible to working memory during utterance formulation may change with age (Bowerman, 1982, 1985; Pinker, 1984). Therefore, we can assume that the nature of syntactic context effects may change with age as well. The very flexibility in organization and access that is characteristic of an interactive system make process models especially attractive for accommodating linguistic growth and change. Reported developmental differences in syntactic priming effects illustrate how the interactive language production processing model allows for activation of syntactic information in whatever form it is stored by the speaker. Streim (1988), for example, suggests that priming effects in young children may appear when the child encodes verbatim fragments of prior discourse into lexical memory, whereas syntactic priming in adults may result from activation of an abstract representation of a syntactic production algorithm used to generate a prior utterance. Child Talk can also account for data on decontextualization such as Barrett et al. (1991), who report that only the child's initial word use reflects contextual constraints deriving from maternal use. Subsequent usage of recently acquired words is shown to bear little resemblance to the input model, leading the researchers to claim that children quickly come to rely on an internal logic to induce appropriate word usage. These findings are entirely consistent with a process model of language production where decontextualization reflects reassignment of weights that connect linguistic and experiential aspects of word representation in the child's production vocabulary. Although interactive process models generally refrain from positing a particular grammar to account for the syntactic forms found in children's early talk, it is clear that this type of model can accommodate a number of different production grammars.

There are several drawbacks to an interactive process model as an account of how children create spoken utterances. First, in permitting multiple representations of linguistic information, the model fails to provide an isolable description of the child's grammar. The Child Talk model, for example, has been criticized as being so undifferentiated that it is difficult to represent the boundaries of the child's linguistic knowledge.

Second, because the linguistic units in an interactive process model may assume any number of characterizations and all experience is interconnected, the system has also been criticized as being unrealistically duplicative and complex. Finally, as a description of the utterance formulation process, Child Talk, along with other interactive models, can be criticized for permitting an unlimited range of linguistic and nonlinguistic interactions to occur at any point in utterance planning. As a result, it has been argued that the model does not permit one to limit its predictions and propose a critical test. Work by Bock (1989) has shed some light on this issue by demonstrating that once set in motion, syntactic processing proceeds automatically according to its own rules and procedures. Thus, although there may be myriad interactions among linguistic, message, and motor planning, the timing of these effects may be restricted.

Despite these drawbacks to interactive process models, it can be argued that the weakness of the process approach to language production is also its strength. Child language is both highly variable and often idiosyncratic. Many child language researchers have come to believe that language is acquired in lexical units and gradually analyzed into features, patterns, and rules (Bowerman, 1985; Braine, 1976; Maratsos, 1983; Peters, 1983; Roeper et al., 1981). The interactive model captures the lexical nature of early syntactic knowledge and ties it to features in the child's language learning environment. By connecting world knowledge and linguistic knowledge, the model allows us to achieve quite a satisfying justification for contextual constraints on the form of children's speech.

IMPLICATIONS FOR CLINICAL PRACTICE

In this chapter I have presented several arguments about the nature of the child's language production processing system. First, I have attempted to illustrate how syntactic and lexical representations are initially linked to the child's representations of events as a result of which early language production is dependent on access to event representation. Second, I have tried to show how the utterance formulation process accommodates natural cognitive biases, tendencies, and constraints on the creation of spoken utterances as seen in priming effects on the structure of children's utterances.

These findings have interesting clinical implications. For example, the process approach to linguistic representation suggests that clinical intervention in language production could focus on helping the child generate and strengthen connections between representations of events and predictable language associated with them. Events may be narrowly defined depending on the child and the clinical goals. An event may be an action schema with language (e.g., dropping a toy and responding with "Fall down") or a more complex event such as a build-and-bash game or joint reading of picture books. In keeping with the implications of the model, the focus of the clinician's efforts in these actititities would be on consistent mapping between a regular set or sequence of actions and predictable language to be elicited about the event.

The findings on the effects of syntactic modeling on children's early word use offer an additional rationale for consistent modeling of appropriate word use in the context of events or routines. Traditionally, much of the child language research hailed the importance of object labeling as a route to language growth. And yet, it is verbs that are central to predicate construction and utterance formulation. The evidence provided by Streim and Chapman (1990) and de Villiers (1985) about the effects of syntactic modeling of verb forms on children's word use illustrates the value of highlighting verbs in structured input. For example, the clinician might look for correlations between his or her own verb use and subsequent use of the same verb forms by the child as a means of understanding and strengthening the effect of lexical and syntactic modeling on the child's creative output.

The evidence for syntactic and lexical priming effects in language production also suggests possible clinical strategies. I showed earlier that speakers are inclined to use words and syntactic forms recently spoken. This tendency has been described as an effect of lingering activation in the processing system (Bock, 1986; Streim, 1988). However, reuse of activated fragments of language functions as a naturally occurring and unconscious means to reduce cognitive processing load during utterance formulation. According to Streim's (1988) findings about children's responses to linguistic primes, it is most likely that young children will incorporate primed language into novel utterances when there is a match between the lexical and syntactic aspects of the prime utterance and the subsequent linguistic task. The clinician can use this effect to prime language output. Through priming manipulations, language tasks can be set up to bias the child to create particular words and linguistic forms.

Many of these suggestions for clinical application are not new. However, it is hoped that the evidence for context effects on language production will provide the clinician with a new framework for understanding clinical strategies in current use and suggest new ones. To the extent that clinical intervention bridges the child's developing knowledge of events (and the expectancies they create) with specific language production goals, the cognitive processing mechanisms observed in the naturalistic language environment can be used in the clinical setting to foster language development.

CONCLUSIONS

In this chapter we have seen that context affects children's language production at several levels. First, there is strong evidence that event context plays a role in what young children learn about words and their uses. For the very young child, initial associations of language and events may constrain lexical representation as well as lexical accessibility. In the framework of a process model, these early event context effects arise because lexical knowledge is embedded in the child's mental representation of events. Lexical accessibility during utterance production planning is therefore stimulated, or thwarted, by the strength of activation between lexical representations and event representations. Over time, experience with words in multiple contexts generates more connections, and more general connections, between the representations of words and events. Ultimately, lexical representations come to assume an increasingly abstract relationship to the record of the history of word use. There is quite a bit of evidence that children may be conservative in their willingness to generalize word use beyond the event contexts within which words are initially encountered until the input model helps direct the child to the properties of word meaning that extend beyond a single exemplar or context.

It is also clear that children imitate the adult model not only to learn when to use new words but to learn the syntactic uses and privileges of new words as well. According to the assumptions of a process model of language production, these findings arise because word knowledge is initially encoded into units accessible to the child speaker as unanalyzed segments of speech. During the early phase of exposure to verbs, the child may glean from the input a dominant syntactic template for each one. This template may be accessed directly from the lexicon, eliminating the need for an abstract syntactic rule system (Bates et al., 1988; Roeper et al., 1981).

Evidence from the priming studies with children suggests that context effects can be understood not only in terms of constraints on availability of words for production (event and discourse context effects) but also as constraints on the utterance production process (linguistic processing effects). The syntactic form selected by a speaker can be influenced by the activated trace of a syntactic form or by a word lingering in working memory from a prior utterance. It is also possible that there is a priming component in the scaffolding effects reported in the speech of young children. The child's tendency to build utterances from prior discourse may be enhanced by the tendency of the language production system to reuse activated units of previously processed language.

REFERENCES

Barrett MD: Early acquisition and development of meanings of action related words, in Seller T, Wannenmacher W (eds): *Concept Development and the Development of Word Meaning*. New York, Springer-Verlag New York, 1983.

Barrett MD: Early semantic representations and early word usage, in Kuczaj SA, Barrett MD (eds): *The Acquisition of Word Meaning*. New York, Springer-Verlag New York, 1986.

Barrett M, Harris M, Chasin J: Early lexical development and maternal speech: a comparison of children's initial and subsequent uses of words. *J Child Lang* 1991; 18:21–40.

Bates E, Bretherton I, Snyder L: *From First Words to Grammar*. New York, Cambridge University Press, 1988.

Bloom L: *One Word at a Time*. The Hague, Mouton, 1973.

Bloom L, Miller P, Hood L: Variation and reduction as aspects of competence in language development, in Pick A (ed): *Minnesota Symposia on Child Psychology, 9*. Minneapolis; University of Minnesota Press, 1975.

Bock K: Toward a cognitive psychology of syntax: information processing contributions to sentence formulation. *Psychol Rev* 1982; 89:1–47.

Bock K: Syntactic persistence in language production. *Cognit Psychol* 1986; 18:355–387.

Bock K: Closed-class imminence in sentence production. *Cognition* 1989; 31:163–186.

Bowerman M: Reorganizational processes in lexical and syntactic development, in Wanner E, Gleitman LR (eds): *Language Acquisition: The State of the Art*. New York, Cambridge University Press, 1982.

Bowerman M: Beyond communicative adequacy: From piecemeal knowledge to an integrated system in the child's acquisition of language, in Nelson KE (ed): *Children's Language*. Hillsdale, NJ, Lawrence Erlbaum Associates, 1985, vol 5.

Braine M: Children's first word combinations. *Monogr Soc Res Child Dev* 1976; 41.

Bresnan J: A realistic transformational grammar, in Halle M, Bresnan J, Miller G (eds): *Linguistic Theory and Psychological Reality*. Cambridge, Mass, MIT Press, 1978.

Bresnan J: The passive in lexical theory, in Bresnan J (ed): *The Mental Representation of Grammatical Relations*. Cambridge, Mass, MIT Press, 1982.

Carey S: The child as word learner, in Halle M, Bresnan J, Miller G (eds): *Linguistic Theory and Psychological Reality*. Cambridge, Mass, MIT Press, 1978.

Cuvelier P: Situational properties of early verb meaning. *Pap Rep Child Lang Dev* 1986; 25:17–24.

de Villiers J: Learning how to use verbs: Lexical coding and the influence of the input. *J Child Lang* 1985; 12:587–595.

Dell GS: Positive feedback in hierarchical connectionist models: Applications to language production. *Cognit Sci* 1985; 9:3–23.

Dell GS: A connectionist model of speech production. *J Memory Lang* 1989; 27:124–142.

Edwards D, Goodwin R: Action words and pragmatic function in early language, in Kuczaj SA, Barrett MD (eds): *The Development of Word Meaning*. New York, Springer-Verlag New York, 1986.

Garrett, MF: A perspective on research in language production, in Mehler M, Walker ECT, Garrett M (eds): *Perspectives on Mental Representation*. Hillsdale, NJ, Lawrence Erlbaum Associates, 1982.

Gruendel JM: Referential extension in early child language. *Child Dev* 1977; 42:1567–1576.

Harris M, Barrett MD, Jones D, et al: Linguistic input and early word meaning. *J Child Lang* 1988; 15:77–94.

Levelt W, Maasen B: Lexical search and order of mention in sentence production, in Klein W, Levelt W (eds): *Crossing the Boundaries in Linguistics*. Dordrecht, Holland, Reidel, 1981.

MacWhinney B: The competition model, in MacWhinney B (ed): *Mechanisms of Language Acquisition*. Hillsdale, NJ, Lawrence Erlbaum Associates, 1987.

Maratsos M: Some current issues in the study of the acquisition of grammar, in Flavell J, Markman E (eds): *Handbook of Child Psychology*. New York, John Wiley & Sons, 1983, vol 3.

Markman EM, Wachtel GF: Children's use of mutual exclusivity to constrain the meaning of words. *Cognit Psychol* 1988; 20:121–157.

Merriman W, Bowman L: The mutual exclusivity bias in children's word learning. *Monogr Soc Res Child Dev* 1989; 54(serial 220).

Mervis CB, Canada K: Child-basic categories and early lexical development. Paper presented at the Biennial Meeting of the Society for Research in Child Development, Boston, 1981.

Nelson K: *Making sense: The acquisition of shared meaning*. New York, Academic Press, 1985.

Nelson K: *Event knowledge: Structure and function in development*. Hillsdale, NJ, Lawrence Erlbaum Associates, 1986.

Nelson K, Kamhi A: Discourse information as a factor in preschool children's sentence production. Paper presented at the Meeting of the Society for Research in Child Development, Toronto, April 1985.

Ninio A, Bruner J: The achievement and antecedents of labelling. *J Child Lang* 1978; 5:1–15.

Peters A: *The Units of Language Acquisition*. New York, Cambridge University Press, 1983.

Pinker S: *Language Learnability and Language Development*. Cambridge, Mass, Harvard University Press, 1984.

Posner MI, Snyder CR: Attention and cognitive control, in Solso RL (ed): *Information Processing and Cognition*. Hillsdale, NJ, Lawrence Erlbaum Associates, 1975.

Roeper T, Lapointe S, Bing J, et al: A lexical approach to language acquisition, in Tavakolian S (ed): *Language Acquisition and Linguistic Theory*. Cambridge, Mass, MIT Press, 1981.

Snow C: The uses of imitation. *J Child Lang* 1981; 8:205–212.

Snow C, Goldfield B: Turn the page please: Situation-specific language acquisition. *J Child Lang* 1983; 10:551–569.

Stemberger JP: An interactive activation model of language production, in Ellis AW (ed): *Progress in the psychology of language*. Hillsdale, NJ, Lawrence Erlbaum Associates, 1985, vol 1.

Streim N: The effects of syntactic priming on the production of active and passive sentences. Doctoral dissertation, Madison, University of Wisconsin, 1988.

Streim N, Chapman RS: The effects of discourse support on the organization and production of children's utterances. *Appl Psycholinguist* 1987; 8:55–66.

Streim N, Chapman RS: A case study of the acquisition of novel action verbs. 1990 (unpublished).

13 Speech-Language Interactions in the Talk of Young Children*

Rhea Paul, Ph.D.

A 3-year-old is brought to a communication disorders clinic by his mother. She explains that his problem is that no one can understand what he says. His hearing and receptive language are tested and found to be normal. When the clinician attempts to collect a speech sample, she finds that the child's speech is too unintelligible to compute a mean length of utterance (MLU) or look at sentence structural complexity. Does this child have a speech or language delay? Or both? Do "simple articulation disorders" arise from faulty motor patterns that are independent of higher level problems in encoding language? Are articulation management techniques different from the approaches used to remediate language formulation deficiency? Is speech separate from language? Can the Child Talk model help to answer these questions?

The Child Talk model grew out of a desire to explain the nature and organization of the knowledge the child brings to the task of producing language, to explain how that knowledge is used, and to explain how and why both knowledge and usage change with development. All of these are certainly worthy goals. My own desires have been, perhaps, somewhat more mundane. I have been interested for some time in understanding the consequences for development of a "slow start" in talking, that is, in looking at children who appear to be normal in every way but who fail to begin speaking at the expected time.

At the age at which late talking becomes worrisome, generally 18 to 30 months, it is clinically impossible to determine whether the delay is in phonology (execution) or in the more traditional realm of language (formulation of semantics and syntax). It has been assumed that the late talker's primary problem is in the realm of language formulation; "lower level" processes such as articulation have not been thought to be central enough to impede the emergence of talk. Yet recent studies (Paul and Jennings, in press; Paul and Shiffer, in press; Stoel-Gammon, 1991) show that phonological, lexical, and communicative development are very closely linked in the first stages of language acquisition. This finding seemed a provocative one. Why should it be the case such varied aspects of linguistic behavior are so highly correlated when it is not logically neces-

*Preparation of this chapter was supported by Public Health Service grant no. R01-DC00793 from the National Institute of Deafness and Other Communication Disorders.

sary? Child Talk, as a process model, seemed to be a useful way of thinking about such questions. In this chapter, I will outline what has been said in the literature about the relations, or "interactions," of speech and language in both normal development and in language disorders. I will also present some data from my longitudinal study of late-talking toddlers. I will then attempt to apply the Child Talk model to these data to see how the model might help us understand the ways in which the processes of language formulation and speech execution come together in both normal and delayed children.

SPEECH VS. LANGUAGE?

Traditionally, formulation and execution have been seen as distinct processes, the former "higher," or more cognitive, and the latter "lower," or more motoric. When children's linguistic development has been studied, it is frequently divided into realms or domains, such as syntax, semantics, pragmatics, and phonology. Although it is understood that these areas are not really separate entities but develop synergistically throughout the child's growth, the task of describing the child's acquisition of language has often been consciously simplified by investigators to highlight the domain of interest. However, recent models of language processing that make more ambitious attempts to describe linguistic development more richly (see Chapter 3) have emphasized the interactions among domains. Interactions of semantic and syntactic ability, for example, have frequently been the focus of discussion (Bloom and Lahey, 1978). When such studies have been carried out, phonology has often been considered to be more separate than the other domains for the reasons discussed earlier. Still, Leonard and his colleagues (Camarata and Leonard, 1986; Leonard et. al, 1981; Schwartz and Leonard, 1982) have done extensive research on the interactions between phonology and semantics in the earliest stages of language development, and Kamhi (see Chapter 3) has looked in detail at interactions between syntax and phonology.

Part of the reason for recent interest in interactions between phonology and other domains of language has to do with recent changes in theoretical perspectives on phonology. As phonologists began advocating such theories as Chomsky and Halle's (1968) generative phonology, Stampe's (1979) natural phonology, and, more recently, various nonlinear phonologies (see Chapter 6) that emphasized an underlying level of phonological representation, child language researchers and speech-language pathologists begin to apply these concepts to normal and disordered development. With this shift it became possible to consider questions about the ways in which underlying phonological knowledge interacted with other domains of language.

CASE STUDIES ON SPEECH-LANGUAGE INTERACTIONS IN NORMAL DEVELOPMENT

The ways in which children pronounce words in different lexical, syntactic, and conversational contexts and the extent to which these contexts influence phonological simplification or elaboration constitute the study of speech-language interactions. Attempts to address these phenomena in normal children have, for the most part, been carried out in case studies. The reason for this is primarily that the amount of data and level of detail necessary to address these questions is so great that group studies would require an inordinate allotment of resources. A second reason is that the extent of individual differences among subjects is expected to be considerable. Thus, group studies might overshadow the very effects of interest. Although case studies cannot provide the generalizable trends that group studies do, they can point out the possible ranges of behavior that are seen. In this sense, we know more about what is possible in speech-language interactions than what is typical.

One of the first attempts to assess the interaction of phonological and syntactic skills was presented by Scollon (1976), who showed that single-word productions were simplified when they were pronounced in successive one-word utterances rather than isolated one-word productions. DeVilliers and deVilliers (1978), in a diary study of their son, tracked use of phonological processes in single-word utterances and in the first multiword combinations the child produced. They found that when words were combined, the child made phonological simplifications in two-word sentences on words that were produced correctly in single-word utterances. They raised the possibility that the new context of a multiword utterance may add enough programming complexity to disrupt the established production of words.

Waterson (1978), in another diary study, looked at the number of phonological contrasts produced within syllables, within words, and within multiword utterances. She reported that the same contrasts that were seen in single-word utterances were also seen in the first-word combinations. The early multiword utterances were only as complex as the single-word utterances produced during the same period, and often less so. There appeared to be an interaction, or "tradeoff," in complexity, with the longer utterances containing fewer contrasts.

Donahue (1986) presented a diary study in which she argued that phonological selection and consonant assimilation operated not only within words but across word boundaries in the speech of her son between ages 11 and 24 months, to limit the production of two-word sentences. Although he used some two-word utterances at 15 months of age, they dropped out suddenly, not to reappear until his vocabulary size was more than 150 words, later than telegraphic utterances would normally emerge. The child appeared to select word combinations so that only those that contained his "favorite sounds" /*b*/ and /*p*/ were produced. Thus, the child's first two-word combination was "bye-bye poopie." Two word combinations with mostly bilabials would be produced with assimilation to the bilabials ("big book": *[bIbUp]*, "big ball": *[bIbau]*), but two-word utterances with other sounds ("big dog," "big cookie") would not be attempted, even on parental request. The child also used some pivot forms with primarily vocalic construction *(where, want, uh-oh)* to produce two-word utterances. Because they did not contain consonants, these were not prey to the assimilation process and provided a phonologically simple way to "ease the child into syntax," as Ramer (1976) discussed for semantic simplification. Thus, it appears that this child's phonological constraints may have delayed the production of two-word utterances and determined which words would be selected to appear in combinations.

In a diary study of a child from the age of 2:5 to 4:3 (years:months), Stemberger (1988) identified several phonological processes that operated not within words but between words. Here again it was found that words that had been produced correctly as single words for some time regressed in pronunciation to simpler forms or syllable structures in certain word combinations. The combinations that caused problems were those in which one word contained a new phonological structure, such as a final alveolar nasal. In this case, assimilation processes in the following word that had disappeared for several months were seen to operate again. Stemberger (1988) emphasized that cognitive load increases in utterances longer than a single word and that this increase is sometimes manifested in phonological regression.

Matthei (1989), in an observational study of a child from age 11 to 22 months, reported further evidence that phonological limitations that had ceased to operate when words appeared in simpler contexts were seen again in the production of words when they first appeared in two-word combinations. Matthei (1989) argued, though, that the forms were not regressions, because they were produced differently than the forms were produced at an earlier stage. For example, "baby's book" was pronounced *[be bU]*, even though both words were pronounced as CVCVs *([bebi], [bUkə])* in single-word utterances at the same time. However, when "baby" had been produced as a CV (consonant-vowel) earlier, it was pronounced *[bi]*, not *[be]*. Matthei (1989) suggested that the forms produced in two-word combinations were truncations rather than regressions. This interpretation implies that the ways in which words are simplified in early multiword utterances reflects strategies that the child uses for producing sounds in words rather than how the word is stored phonologically in the child's lexicon. He argued that it is not the case that "rules" are "leaking out" of the lexicon to operate on multiword combinations but that the processes that operate across word boundaries are relatively idiosyncratic mechanisms for overcoming articulatory difficulties until new articulatory programs are established to automatize pronunciation in more stressful contexts, such as multiword utterances.

What these case studies demonstrate is that new syntactic demands can interact with phonological simplification strategies, and even with selection and avoidance strategies, to reduce overall complexity of the speech execution task. This implies that speech execution is to some extent a unitary phenomenon, receiving input from several linguistic levels, including lexical, syntactic, and phonological. Further, it suggests something like a "limited processing capacity" model (see Chapter 3) for describing the encoding skills of children in the early stages of language acquisition. Such a model posits a capacity for handling complexity that is restricted by some constraint, such as memory as one example. When the system is stressed by demands for more resources than are available, "something's gotta give," and some aspect of the output is simplified. Because all of these data have come from case reports, it is not possible at this point to know to what extent the relatively middle class, academic sample of researchers' offspring represented in them is typical of children learning languages. It does appear, however, that as the child attempts to move beyond the one-word stage and produce more complex speech, compromises can be made in output accuracy that bridge the traditional barriers among linguistic domains.

THE LIMITED ENCODING CAPACITY MODEL

Normal children in the earlier stages of language encoding appear to operate in these studies as if their encoding capacity were somewhat limited. What is not clear is whether this limitation resides in articulatory constraints, as some have argued, or in higher-level memory or programming limitations that restrict the number of elements that can be incorporated into a motor plan. Either way, the normal child soon overcomes these limitations, perhaps through increased motor maturity or memory and planning capacity. Or, the ability to handle greater complexity in encoding may result from increased automaticity of some of the processes involved (Sternberg, 1985), such as motor programs for familiar words and often-used word sequences or the retrieval networks for sentence construction. Such automaticity would free up encoding resources for concentration on new levels of complexity.

Kamhi (see Chapter 3) discusses the limited processing capacity approach to understanding language processing. Traditionally this model has postulated a hierarchical system in which limited resources are allocated to some aspects of the encoding process, leaving others unserved, resulting in simplification. Because phonology is traditionally considered a lower-level process, this model predicts that phonology will be the "first to go" when the system is stressed in some way. Kamhi reviews a variety of studies undertaken by him and his colleagues and shows that several factors affect whether increasing linguistic complexity leads to phonological simplification, including the child's language-cognitive level, his or her tolerance for phonological variability, the sensitivity of the measures of phonological change (because changes may be happening at the phonetic level that are not detected by phonemic-level investigations), and the conversational context. For example, he points out that interactions were much more likely to be seen in elicited imitation tasks than in spontaneous productions, presumably because in spontaneous speech the child has more control over the macrolevel of complexity in the discourse. As Kamhi points out, the limited processing capacity model has been used more widely to conceptualize language disorders than to explain normal development. An examination of this attempt will be made here before returning to the question of the efficacy of this model for thinking about language development in general and about its relation to Child Talk.

SPEECH-LANGUAGE INTERACTIONS IN CHILDREN WITH DISORDERS

Schwartz et al. (1980), in a study of a small number of language-impaired individuals, found that these children's phonological behavior did not differ significantly on a number of phonological dimensions from that of normally developing children at similar levels of language acquisition. They concluded that these findings argued for a "synergistic view" of linguistic disorders in which an overall organizational deficit underlies problems that children have in encoding language. Although Schwartz et al. (1980) stress that the relationship is not one to one, suggesting that consistent predictions about specific points of simplification cannot be made, the relationship seemed in their view to be "quite close"—close enough to suggest the need for reconceptualizing expressive language deficits as perhaps more generalized encoding or output disorders.

The limited encoding capacity hypothesis was invoked by Panagos et al. (1979) in a series of studies of the phonemic accuracy of language-disordered children in elicited imitation tasks with sentences of varying syntactic complexity. They argued that children with speech delays are limited in their ability to manage complexity in encoding. This resulted in the loss of phonetic accuracy in new or complex productions because of competing demands for processing resources at higher linguistic levels. Their observations have been replicated in studies (Menyuk and Looney, 1972; Panagos, 1974; Schmauch et al., 1978) that ask children to repeat sentences and look for phonological simplifications in more vs. less complex versions (e.g., passive vs. active sentences).

Paul and Shriberg (1982), in a study using free speech samples, concluded that, even though one half of their sample of speech-delayed children showed performances that could be interpreted as consistent with a hierarchical limited encoding capacity model, one half did not. This remaining half showed interactions between phonological and syntactic abilities but not in the direction predicted by a hierarchical model. That is, some children in the sample, instead of showing poorer performance on sentences that were more morphophonemically complex, were able to "tune up" their phonology to the level of their overall syntactic competence rather than simplifying whenever a complex morphophoneme was encoded. Paul and Shriberg (1982, p. 545) argued, "Although their overall delay in syntactic production may be the result of a system limited in encoding capacity, the exact points at which the system will simplify output are not easily predicted in terms of sentence or word complexity in free speech." This study suggests that limited encoding as a concept is not sufficient to predict how speech will be simplified at any given point in time, even if it is correct in postulating some form of constraint on the number of bits of complexity that can be handled during encoding. The work of Kamhi (see Chapter 3) accords with these findings.

There may be other factors, such as social motivation, that play a role in determining when children make an extra effort to maximize the accuracy of their productions. Campbell and Shriberg (1982) showed, for example, that speech-delayed children were significantly more likely to use phonological simplification processes when producing old information than when commenting or presenting information not already referred to in the discourse. Speech-delayed children made a greater attempt to clarify their speech when new information was being conveyed. Kamhi (see Chapter 3) also reports that intelligibility in his studies was never traded off in spontaneous speech as a result of increased linguistic complexity, but such trade-offs did appear in elicited imitation. This finding is presumably attributable to the low information value and therefore the reduced communicative need for intelligibility present in elicited contexts. These data point out that pragmatic or social factors are also important in influencing the allocation of encoding resources.

These studies suggest that if a limited processing capacity model is appropriate in development, it cannot rely on hierarchical organization of processes, with lower-level processes such as phonology easily disrupted and higher-level ones such as syntax more buffered. This suggestion has implications for the Child Talk model, to which I will return later.

SPEECH AND LANGUAGE INTERACTIONS IN TODDLERS WHO "DO NOT TALK"

As mentioned earlier, recent studies of speech in 2-year-olds have shown very close connections among phonological, lexical, and communicative performance. Although toddlers could produce lots of communicative vocalization containing lots of different consonants and syllable shapes without producing intelligible words, generally they do not. Conversely, children could produce lots of approximations with different meanings with only a few consonants and canonical types available and rely on gestures to help adults infer their meaning from context. Again, they generally do not. Children who initiate communication more frequently tend to do so by means of meaningful vocalizations that tend to contain larger repertoires of sounds and syllable structures than children who initiate communication less frequently. Let me review briefly the evidence for these assertions.

A co-worker and I (Paul and Jennings, in press) examined phonological productions in both nonmeaningful vocalizations and words produced during unstructured mother-child play sessions collected from two groups of toddlers: late talkers, who produced fewer than 50 words and no two-word combinations at 24 to 34 months, and normally speaking toddlers, whose productions skills exceeded these criteria. The late talkers had significantly less mature syllable structures in terms of presence and heterogeneity of consonants, the frequency of any type of closed syllable, and the presence of consonant clusters of any kind. In addition, the late talkers produced only one half as many different consonant types as their normally speaking counterparts and tended to produce only the earliest developing consonant classes, such as glides, front stops, and nasals rather than a full range of place and manner of articulation. These findings, too, appeared in both meaningful and nonmeaningful vocalizations. Thus, it appears that even in their nonspeech vocalizations late-talking toddlers are showing signs of phonological deficits. In addition, late-talking toddlers produced significantly fewer utterances, either verbal or vocal, by a factor of 3 per 10-minute mother-child interaction, than did their age mates. Not only were their vocalizations less mature, but they were also less frequent.

A co-worker and I (Paul and Shiffer, 1991) also looked at expression of communicative intentions in the two groups during these same mother-child interactions. Here it was seen that late-talking toddlers produced significantly fewer expressions of intention, either gestural, vocal, or verbal, in a 10-minute mother-child interaction. However, one particular type of intention appeared to account entirely for the difference: late talkers produced as many regulatory intentions, including requests for objects, requests for actions, and protests, as did the normal speakers, but they produced significantly fewer comments, or joint attentional intentions. Although the late-talking children could produce the same range of intentions seen in the normal group, they appeared, at least on the basis of their frequency of attempts to initiate joint attention, less interested in engaging in social interaction for its own sake than for the attainment of environmental ends.

Testing of receptive language skill indicated that at age 2 years the children in this cohort could be considered to be primarily delayed in the acquisition of expressive language. Two-thirds showed no decrement in receptive performance, whereas those who were below the norm in comprehension had greater deficits in production.

A somewhat surprising finding was that when the toddlers were examined using the *Vineland Adaptive Behavior Scales* (Sparrow et al., 1984), 90% of those with slow speech acquisition were found to be more than 6 months below age level in terms of socialization skill even when verbal socialization items were partialed out (Paul et al., 1991). None of the normally speaking children fell below this level. This decrement in social skills persisted in some of the children (about 20%) to age 3 years, in some cases even when language skills had moved into the normal range. This large prevalence of social deficits in late talkers led to the hypothesis that some part of the explanation for their late acquisition of speech could lie in a decreased motivation to interact.

Data on maternal linguistic input to these children (Paul and Elwood, 1991) showed that mothers were providing very similar language stimulation to normal and late-talking toddlers, but we did find that the late talkers were giving their mothers fewer opportunities to expand and extend child utterances, processes known to be associated with accelerating language development (Scherer and Olswang, 1984). This suggests that children with a language delay may not be providing their interlocutors with optimal contexts for encouraging their language growth.

A CHILD TALK PERSPECTIVE

We have so far examined three sets of literature that pertain to the question of the ways in which the growth of speech and language skills intertwine in development. Case study data from young normal children suggested that in the early stages of language development children appear as if they are limited in their ability to encode the full range of linguistic output that they might shoot for and can be seen to sacrifice some aspect of production accuracy for the sake of greater complexity. Data from language-disordered preschoolers also suggested the possibility of trade-offs but showed that what gets traded is multiply determined and cannot be attributed to a simple hierarchical model of linguistic complexity. Research on late-talking toddlers pointed out the tight connections between speech, language, and communicative development in the third year of life, reinforcing the notion of the production system as a unitary module. How do these findings accord with the postulates of Child Talk?

Child Talk posits, first, that what is modular in development is not the traditional domains of language—syntax, semantics, pragmatics, and phonology—but the modalities of communication—comprehension and production. Child Talk sees these processes as to some extent separable in development. This implies that the task demands and mechanisms involved in accomplishing communication in each modality are somewhat different and that a child's development in each domain can proceed somewhat autonomously. Second, Child Talk asserts that automatization is a crucial process in language acquisition. In other words, practice makes perfect. The more the child is given, and (this is important) the more the child takes the opportunity to rehearse and overlearn scripts in reliable, routine interpersonal contexts, the sooner language progresses, and the more generalizable do the frames learned in these routines become. This claim is related to the data cited by Chapman et al. (see Chapter 1) regarding the dramatic increases in amount of talk as children get older. Not only are normal children learning more, they are practicing more. This practice increases the rapidity of automatization of learned material, which, in turn, makes acquisition of new material easier. Third, the Child Talk model suggests the child is not learning semantic relations and then learning syntactic rules but is, instead, learning integrated frames of various sizes from syllable to paragraph length. These frames, or scripts, are embedded in interpersonal contexts. Linguistic knowledge grows, in this view, not through the child's hypothesis testing of particular forms for corrective feedback, but in these larger chunks, or frames, that are acquired in repeated routine interactions primarily with adults. In development, the linguistic knowledge eventually becomes freed from the frame, but the frame serves as a bootstrap to help the child step up to a more sophisticated analysis of the language around him or her. Let us try to relate some of these postulates to the data reviewed thus far.

First, it seems clear that evidence from all of the sources cited supports the notion of a relatively unitary, relatively modular production system. The trade-offs from one domain to another, the prevalence of speech and language delays that co-occur in children, and the firm bond among speech, language, and communication development in the early stages of language acquisition all argue for an encoding process that functions as a sort of whole.

Second, the importance of practice in the development of automaticity can be seen in the strong relationship between dearth of output and lack of maturity in production. Data from late talkers at age 2 years showed reduced frequency of both verbal and nonverbal communication. In addition, follow-up assessments of these children, both at age 3 years and at age 4 years, showed that many children with a history of late talking produced fewer than 50 utterances during a 15-minute free play interaction with their mothers, although none of the normal children did. Again, it appears that these children are less inclined to talk.

Finally, the Child Talk model emphasizes the importance of participation in interactive routines in which children eventually memorize scripts that contain embedded world knowledge for encyclopedic storage. This means that to learn to talk, a child must have taken the opportunities afforded by adults in his or her world to play the game for the umpteenth time and to tune into its linguistic script and its interpersonal detail, as well as its more general affective color. The depressed social and interactive skills seen in the late talkers suggest that though their parents are providing normative opportunities for language growth, the children are less prepared to make the most of what they are being afforded.

Seeing the data discussed here from the Child Talk perspective suggests that two things might be operating simultaneously in children with delayed expressive language. First, they may start out with immaturity in their speech output system, which leads to less complex phonological behavior, more difficulty in producing intelligible words, and more powerful constraints on their encoding resources. Either as a result, or for some other reason, they find vocal interaction less satisfying or more onerous than other children, even in the prelinguistic stages. This also reduces their vocal and verbal output. The result is less practice routinizing neuromotor pathways for speech, less automatization of processes, and the maintenance of constraints on encoding resources.

Second, they are not initiating communication as frequently, so they get less interaction. Routine joint attention games will not last very long if the child does not fulfill his or her turn, and they will not happen as often if the child very seldom initiates them. Less exposure to these frames results in fewer opportunities to overlearn the scripts that are used within them.

The child with a language delay can be seen, in the Child Talk framework, as showing some initial limitation in encoding capacity, perhaps more powerful than that experienced by normal toddlers, that is complicated by a somewhat reduced drive to initiate communication. These two deficits coalesce to result in reduced number of opportunities to engage in the kinds of interactions in which language development flourishes. In addition, because they are talking and vocalizing less, poor speakers get less practice and are less able to routinize their encoding processes. The constraints with which they started continue to operate; resources are not rapidly freed up by automatization of production subunits as they are in children who are vocalizing and talking more frequently.

ANOTHER POSSIBILITY: PERCEPTUAL DYSFUNCTION

There is an alternative to this hypothesis. In discussing language learnability, Leonard (1989) attempted to apply current theories to the problem of the language-impaired child. He also argued that numerous studies of input to language-impaired children have shown that adults adjust their input to the language level of the child, so that language-impaired children are probably receiving an ideal form of input but are for some reason unable to take advantage of it. He suggests that the reason is that the input is distorted in the perceptual process. Leonard (1989) pointed out that one universal deficit seen in language-impaired children studied who were learning a variety of languages is a difficulty in acquiring grammatical morphemes and auxiliaries. He contrasts this difficulty to the children's generally MLU-appropriate usage of words (Leonard et al., 1982), semantic relations (Leonard et al., 1976), syntactic structures (Morehead & Ingram, 1973), and pragmatic conventions (Skarakis and Greenfield, 1982). Leonard (1989) hypothesized that the source of language-impaired children's difficulty with grammatical morphemes lies in the fact that they have low "phonetic substance." Leonard (1989, p. 186) defines this term as "nonsyllabic consonant segments and unstressed syllables, characterized by shorter duration than adjacent morphemes and, often, lower fundamental frequency and amplitude."

Leonard (1989) then refers to the work of Tallal and her colleagues (Tallal and Piercy, 1975; Tallal and Stark, 1981) that shows children with specific language disorders to have difficulty with auditory stimuli in which the duration of a contrastive feature of the signal is less than that of the rest of the signal. This difficulty corresponds to the definition for low phonetic substance. Leonard (1989) points out that these findings not only parallel those of Paul and Shriberg (1982) in explaining production difficulties with phonologically complex grammatical morphemes but also apply to phonological processes that are seen more frequently in the speech of language-impaired children than in those of normally developing children at similar articulation levels: final consonant deletion and unstressed syllable deletion. Leonard (1989) argues that according to Pinker's (1979) theory of language learnability, normal children use grammatical morphemes to decide how to parse sentences with unfamiliar forms in them. If children are unable to do this parsing because they have difficulty perceiving the auditory bits that carry the information, it could explain the observations Leonard (1989) lists.

This theory, then, is an alternative to the notions that I have discussed: that the child starts out with limited encoding capacity and fails to overcome the limitations as quickly as normal children do because of deficits in social motivation that lead to dearth of practice and reduction of automatization. Rather than hypothesizing a constraint on the execution side of the process, Leonard (1989) sees the deficit as being in the perception of the units with low auditory salience. This hypothesis makes very different predictions about the nature of language disorders and speech and language interactions. It implies that children with perceptual deficits will have primary receptive deficiencies in addition to their productive limitations.

Although the issue of subgrouping of language-disordered children on the basis of linguistic performance is a matter of debate among researchers in the field (see Rapin, 1988, for review), clinical experience, as well as a number of research studies (Tallal, 1988), suggest that even though some language-impaired children have primary receptive deficits, there are those for whom the expressive disorders are the sole problems or the major components. It seems reasonable to suggest that Leonard's (1989) perceptual disorder hypothesis would apply to children with primarily receptive disorders, whereas some form of a limited encoding capacity coupled with decreased social orientation hypothesis, consistent with the Child Talk model, could be explanatory for children with more restricted expressive problems.

SOME ADDITIONAL EVIDENCE: SPEECH-LANGUAGE INTERACTION IN NARRATIVES

Data from the late talkers provides some evidence for this position. As part of the follow-up evaluation of children originally seen at age 2 years because of slow language growth, the subjects were seen again at ages 3 and 4 years for a language assessment. At the 4-year-old visit, the children were given *The Bus Story Language Test* (Renfrew, 1969). This test consists of a story about a "naughty bus" told to the child with a series of pictures depicting each segment of the story (Fig 13–1). The child is then shown the pictures again immediately after hearing the story and is asked to retell it. Bishop and Edmundson (1987) have shown that the bus story is one of the best predictors of school achievement in a population of language-delayed preschoolers, suggesting a strong relationship between narrative skill and reading and writing ability.

Figures 13–2 and 13–3 are examples of story retellings given by a normal child and one with a history of slow language development, respectively. Several striking differences can be seen in these examples. Whereas Mike, the late talker, does show less use of copula and auxiliary *be* forms, both children use regular past tense correctly in some cases, and both overgeneralize the regular *-ed* ending. Mike also overgeneralizes plural /s/. Mike shows a lack of use of another higher phonetic substance morpheme, the article *the,* which is absent from sentences in which it should occur in initial position. Thus, Mike's use of grammatical morphemes does not appear to follow the predictions made by Leonard's (1989) perceptual disorder hypothesis. Similarly, 87% of the children with a history of slow language growth scored within the normal range on the grammatical completion subtest (which assesses productive morphology) of the *Test of Language Development-2* (Newcomer and Hammill, 1988), whereas only 47% of them scored within the normal range on the *Developmental Sentence Analysis* (Lee, 1974). These observations would suggest that children with primary expressive disorders can be distinguished on the basis of their morphophonemic usage from those whose problems reside in perceptual deficits and result in receptive delays.

Is there evidence in the children's stories to support the explanation of specific expressive language delay offered here? Can the delayed child, for example, be seen as showing continuing and more powerful limits in encoding capacity? Mike, the child with a history of slow language growth, certainly uses shorter sentences. On the sentence length measure of this test, his score was 6.8, whereas Phillip's was 11.8. But short sentences on their own do not speak directly to a limited encoding hypothesis, because they may be a result solely of a lack of grammatical knowledge or complexity.

Another way to look at this question is to examine the amount of information encoded in the stories. Whereas Mike's story contains more utterances than Phillip's, the normal child's contains significantly more information. Phillip's information score, according to Renfrew's (1969) criteria, is 20, whereas Mike's is 7. Why is it that Mike produces more sentences but tells the listener so much less? For one thing, many of Mike's utterances are direct repetitions or partial repetitions of his own previous statements. It appears that Mike is able to en-

FIG 13–1.
The bus story. (From Renfrew C: *The Bus Story Language Test.* Oxford, 1969. Used by permission.)

There was a, a, a little bad bus. He went, he, when, everytime the, the, the person tried to do something, he, the bus ran away. He, he w... knocked into a train. And they both make funny faces. But they look like mad faces to me. And they, and, and, and look like, and, and the bus was on his own now, 'cause the train goed into a tunnel. And, I, I'm tired of being on the road now. So he jumped up and onto the grass. He, he ma... he met a ca.. cow wh.. who said, "Moo, I, I can't believe my eyes." And, and then and when he saw the water, he falleded into the water. And, and the end.

FIG 13–2.
Retelling of the bus story (Fig 13–1) by Philip, age 4:1 (years:months), who has normal language development. (From Renfrew C: *The Bus Story Language Test.* Oxford, 1969. Used by permission.)

A bus. They crashed. They crashed. I see a crash one. A wheel falled. Train went into a tunnel. Train went over this truck. This, this, this, bus. Wheel went off. I can't find the water. Cow goes moo. Stucked [dʌkt] in the mud. He felled in the mud. He went boom. Then he went boom. Then he crashed. The the water went in the mouth. Went down in the...in the tunnel. Then went up here around this and in the water. That one out of the mud. It have to get out, it got out. He pulled out with his hook. He tried to pull this one out.

FIG 13–3.
Retelling of the bus story by Mike, age 4:11, who is a late talker. (From Renfrew C: *The Bus Story Language Test.* Oxford, 1969. Used by permission.)

code less information per unit time. Even if he is producing several utterances, the amount of information included in them is equal to only the amount produced by the normal child in one. Although the absolute length of sentences does not appear to be a limitation for Mike (one of his utterances contains ten words, though the majority do tend to be short), the amount of information they can encode does seem to be limited. It seems that limited encoding capacity, then, may also involve a constraint on the number of bits of information that can be expressed in a given utterance, so that information has to be encoded in a series of related utterances rather than in one concise production.

Compare Phillip's description of the bus falling in the water with Mike's:

Phillip: When he saw the water, he falled into the water.
Mike: Then he went boom.
Then he crashed.
The water went in the mouth.
Then went up here around this and in the water.

Mike appears to be unable to combine propositions to encode relationships among events, whereas Phillip does show the beginnings of this capacity. Although there could be several explanations for this difference, one possible reason is that propositional load adds cumulatively with syntactic and phonological load, resulting in a burden that is greater than Mike's encoding capacity can handle. Here, simplification takes the form of limiting propositional content.

In addition to looking at propositional content, complex sentence usage can also shed light on the limits of Mike's encoding capacity. Although Mike's grammatical morpheme usage is consistent with Brown's stage IV (Miller, 1981), his use of complex sentences, which encode more than one proposition per utterance, is not. Normal children who are at this stage would be expected to use 10% to 20% complex sentences (Paul, 1981). Although Phillip's proportion of complex sentences is 27% in the retelling of the bus story, Mike's is only 4%.

There is another piece to this puzzle, though. In reading both renditions of the story, one gets the feeling that, in fact, both children are having difficulty with the task, but they manifest their difficulty in different ways. Mike displays his problems with encoding multiple propositions by repeating short, single proposition sentences, using only contiguity rather than cohesive devices to relate them to each other. His articulation in the retelling, though, is quite clear. In fact, there is only one instance of a phonological process: *stucked* is pronounced *[d/\ kt]*. This simplification is striking in that other words containing consonant clusters with a fricative in which the cluster contains a grammatical morpheme, such as *crashed,* are produced accurately. Like subjects in the Paul and Shriberg (1982) study, Mike is able to tune up his phonological productions in the service of accurate syntax. Instead of sacrificing phonological accuracy, he keeps his sentences relatively short and simple to keep his narration intelligible. This is in contrast to his intelligibility in free play with his mother, which is rated as only fair and contains more use of simplification processes. Mike appears to have traded syntactic and propositional complexity for intelligibility in this task.

Phillip, on the other hand, shows a different response to the difficulty of the test. He has relatively consistent use of phonological process on a small number of phonemes, primarily /r/ and voiced and voiceless *th*. These processes have little effect on intelligibility but are used throughout the retelling. Instead of attempting to tune up phonological accuracy, which is not really necessary to get his message across, Phillip pushes his syntactic and propositional load limits, with the result of a decrease in fluency of speech. His level of fluency is much lower than Mike's and appears to represent the type of "formulation dysfluency" seen frequently in the speech of young children. Again, in his free speech sample, the level of dysfluency is much lower, suggesting that this task places a stress on his formulation capacity. But rather than meeting this stress with reduction in syntactic or propositional complexity, Phillip sacrifices fluency.

Although these choices on the part of these two children are obviously not conscious ones, what can be seen is that the children make different decisions about what to sacrifice to achieve their communicative ends. Although a comparison of two children can serve only as an example of some of the many possible differences that could exist in terms of encoding performance, these two boys do exemplify some of the varying ways in which children might deal with a difficult task. They also show how many levels of linguistic processing must be subserved by the encoding system, as well as the many potential points of simplification. Although it may not be possible to predict exactly how or where any given child will simplify output in a stressful situation, it may be plausible to forecast which situations will trigger some kind of simplification based on the child's typical and optimal performance. Such a prediction might help to determine goals for intervention by highlighting the kinds of linguistic contexts that are likely to stress the child's encoding capacity and attempting to provide additional practice with them to develop some routinization.

In summary, the anecdotal data from narrative samples presented here exemplify the way in which many levels of speech (articulation, fluency) and language (syntax, morphology, propositional content) can be seen to interact in a task that stresses encoding capacity. They also show that although a child with a language delay may have more powerful constraints on his or her encoding resources, a normal child also will make trade-offs in a difficult production task. Limited encoding capacity would appear to be a useful adjunct to our model of specific expressive language disorder and can be integrated with the Child Talk model of normal development to provide insights into the ways in which speech and language are unified in normal and disordered development.

CLINICAL IMPLICATIONS

The integrated model suggested earlier is also helpful for thinking about what kinds of intervention might be useful for children like the one in our initial vignette, the child with a specific expressive disorder that impacts both speech and language. Child Talk holds that teaching integrated frames containing routine scripts mimics the way in which language is learned normally. The advantage of this approach over more traditional language intervention techniques is that rather than using imitation or asking the child to induce rules from examples, the Child Talk approach would provide the child with a script to be internalized in an integrated way and then used for additional communicative purposes.

In addition, Child Talk implies that children need to be encouraged to talk more and communicate more. Toward this end, tasks that require the child to speak to participate and result in more turns on the part of the child than on that of the clinician would be important. Part of the task in setting up these activities would be to maximize the child's motivation to communicate, because Campbell and Shriberg (1982) have shown that pragmatic issues do impact on intelligibility. One way to encourage increased amounts of talking without increasing encoding load and to incorporate the principles of Child Talk into intervention is to use routine language activities. These involve teaching the child certain language routines, or overlearned sequences, that are either functional or particularly motivating and contain phonological and syntactic contexts that are targets for the child. These could include having the child "read" well-loved books, sing songs, do finger plays, recite poetry, or perform any other verbal activity that lends itself to repetition and overlearning. Contexts can be set up in which it makes sense for the child to produce the routine repeatedly. Then opportunities for the child to ring changes on the routine can be developed. In these ways, the child is allowed to practice a production until it can become an automatic encoding process. As changes are made on it, encoding resources for the changes are freed up by the automaticity of the rest. The child is encouraged to develop some well-known routines that can lay the basis for other speech acts he or she can use in everyday situations.

For example, if the child needs to increase the use of copula verbs, decrease final consonant deletion, and increase the propositional load of sentences, he or she might be taught a simple story to retell such as *Goldilocks and the Three Bears*. The activity can start out by having the clinician tell the client a simplified version of the story with copula verbs and simple CVC words emphasized in the telling ("This soup *is* too *hot;* this soup *is* too *cool;* this soup *is* just *right.*"). The client can be taught the story by having the clinician model it sentence by sentence using puppets the clinician and child make together from socks or paper plates to act it out. After several rehearsals in which the client is encouraged to tell increasingly longer portions of the story from the clinician's script, situations in which the client tells the story to several audiences can be arranged. The child could tell it to a younger client of the clinician's, his or her class, younger siblings, or neighbors and record it on an audiotape to send to grandparents and so forth. The object is to create motivating situations for the client to practice this routine. After the routine is well learned through these repeated rehearsals, the client and clinician can work together to modify the script to create a silly version of the story. The silly version can then be retold to several different audiences as well. This extended practice with relatively complex language in the context of an overlearned routine should be useful in reducing encoding stress through automatization while allowing for the production of more sophisticated structures and discourse forms in a motivating environment.

What about the young child or toddler who is talking very little? Seeing this child's problem also as related to limited encoding resources, coupled perhaps with decreased motivation to interact, would imply certain treatment strategies. For one thing, this view of the late-talking young child suggests, I think, that careful control of the linguistic stimuli presented to the child is necessary if he or she is expected to produce a verbal response. That is, if the child is limited in encoding capacity, any stress on this capacity may produce either a simplification or a refusal on the part of the child to respond at all. The principle that seems to apply is the idea of one new thing at a time, formalized by Slobin (1973) as "new forms encode old functions, new functions are encoded by old forms." This applies to the ability to use new phonological forms only in familiar syntactic contexts and to limit new phonological contexts when attempting to produce new syntactic forms. This principle suggests that when one is attempting to get children to produce new words, they must be carefully controlled for phonological shape to include only sound and syllable structures the child already produces in other words or vocalizations. Similarly, when one is asking the child to produce new multiword combinations the words included should be only those the child has already used with reasonable phonetic accuracy in single word utterances, and even then, some simplification is likely to take place. Also, because of the apparently decreased motivation to communicate seen in these youngsters, a strong pragmatic context needs to be present in any activities designed for them. Simple imitation activities are not likely to teach them the value of interactions and the need for language to facilitate them.

As Leonard (1989) and Paul and Elwood (1991) have shown, mothers of language-delayed children provide linguistic input similar to that provided to normally speaking youngsters. This implies that providing more "indirect language stimulation" to these youngsters will not be highly efficacious. A more structured form of input, controlled for syntactic complexity and phonological shape, will be required to make changes in the child's output. Also, because the children need to practice talking in a nonimitative, pragmatically motivating context, more contrived situations need to be constructed to elicit speech.

Kamhi (see Chapter 3) discusses the popularity and some of the problems of holist approaches to the study of language. Although I have argued that the implications of Child Talk would suggest the use of integrated frames (i.e., those containing not just words but gestures, interpersonal involvement, particularized topic, setting, and addressee), the activities I have outlined are by no means "whole language" approaches to intervention. On the contrary, the notions of limitation in encoding capacity and the need for automatization of production subunits are fundamental. Although Child Talk emphasizes the integrated nature of language production and its interpersonal underpinnings, the whole is, in some sense, the sum of the parts. That is, the child cannot produce a fluent whole unless the component pieces are accessible from working memory and encodable with the amount of resources available. If this is not the case, the "whole" will break down, and trade-offs will become necessary. The way to build toward the whole is to strengthen the parts of the system using integrated frames and concentrating on one aspect of the frame until trade-offs are no longer obligatory because each subunit has been sufficiently automatized to allow for production of the whole.

SPEECH-LANGUAGE INTEGRATION IN THE TALK OF YOUNG CHILDREN

The foregoing might, perhaps, have been a more appropriate title for this chapter. It has presented evidence from varying sources that supports two tenets of the Child Talk model that relate to the integration of speech and language development:

1. The production system is unitary, spanning a range of domains and levels, and can be thought of as modular. I have argued further that this system appears to have a limited capacity, although the limits normally relax with development.

2. Child Talk's assertion of the importance of practice and automaticity is supported by a range of data from young children with language disorders who do not practice or automatize as readily as normal children do. I have also proposed that the concept of "practice makes perfect" applies across all of the components of this module. That is, usage increases automatization, which frees up resources that become available for increasing ac-

curacy and complexity across the range of speech and language skills involved in the production system.

There is more to be learned about speech-language integration in development and disorders. Studies that attempted to control complexity by using imitation formats have been criticized as being too different from natural speech situations to reflect the processes that actually occur during normal encoding. On the other hand, studies involving free speech suffer from the researcher's inability to have any control over the complexity of the production. Natural language tasks vary in difficulty, from free speech during play, through story retelling, spontaneous narration, explanation, and exposition. Comparing syntactic, propositional, and phonological output in each of these contexts may be one way to address researchers' concerns.

Another question of interest is the extent to which some trade-offs are more normal than others. Although it appears that young children trade phonological for syntactic complexity and vice versa, there may be a stage at which these trade-offs (or some subset of them) are no longer typical. Similarly, it appears that some children with expressive language disorders trade propositional or syntactic complexity for intelligibility. Is this a route that normal children ever use, or are they more committed to expressing the full range of grammatical and ideational intricacy, with less regard for phonological accuracy? Can these different strategies be diagnostic cues? Can children's choice of trade-off be linked to other language style variables, such as referential vs. expressive or Gestalt vs. analytic approaches to language learning, and would these tendencies be similar in normal and language disordered children?

The Child Talk model provides a framework for looking at language production as a unitary system that functions in a social context. Such a framework will be useful for integrating emerging knowledge about the ways in which children manage the problem of increasing linguistic complexity in their talk.

REFERENCES

Bishop D, Edmundson A: Language-impaired 4-year-olds: Distinguishing transient from persistent impairment. *J Speech Hear Disorders* 1987; 52:156–173.

Bloom L, Lahey M: *Language Development and Language Disorders*. New York, John Wiley & Sons, 1978.

Camarata S, Leonard L: Young children pronounce object words more accurately than action words. *J Child Lang* 1986; 13:51–65.

Campbell T, Shriberg L: Associations among pragmatic functions, linguistic stress, and natural phonological processes in speech-delayed children. *J Speech Hear Res* 1982; 25:547–554.

Chomsky N, Halle M: *Sound Pattern of English*. New York, Harper & Row, Publishers, 1968.

DeVilliers P, deVilliers J: Simplifying phonological processes in the one- and two-word stage. Paper presented at the Boston University Conference on Child Language Development, Boston, 1978.

Donahue M: Phonological constraints on the emergence of two-word utterances. *J Child Lang* 1986; 13:209–218.

Lee L: *Developmental Sentence Analysis*. Evanston, Ill, Northwestern University Press, 1974.

Leonard L: Language learnability and specific language impairment in children. *Appl Psycholinguist* 1989; 10:179–202.

Leonard L, Boulders J, Miller J: An examination of the semantic relations reflected in the language usage of normal and language disordered children. *J Speech Hear Res* 1976; 19:371–392.

Leonard L, Camarata S, Rowan L, et al: The communicative function of lexical usage by language impaired children. *Appl Psycholinguist* 1982; 3:109–125.

Leonard L, Schwartz R, Morris B, et al: Factors influencing early lexical acquisition: Lexical orientation and phonological composition. *Child Dev* 1981; 52:882–887.

Matthei P: Crossing boundaries: More evidence for phonological constraints on early multi-word utterances. *J Child Lang* 1989; 16:41–54.

Menyuk P, Looney P: Relationships among components of the grammar in language disorders. *J Speech Hear Res* 1972; 15:395–407.

Miller J: *Assessing Language Production in Children: Experimental Procedures.* Baltimore, University Park Press, 1981.

Morehead D, Ingram D: The development of base syntax in normal and linguistically deviant children. *J Speech Hear Res* 1973; 16:330–352.

Newcomer P, Hammill D: *Test of Language Development-2.* Austin, Tex, Pro-Ed, 1988.

Panagos J: String complexity increases phonemic interference. *Percept Motor Skills* 1974; 38:1219–1222.

Panagos J, Quine M, Klich R: Syntactic and phonological influences on children's articulation. *J Speech Hear Res* 1979; 22:841–848.

Paul R: Complex sentence analysis, in Miller J (ed): *Assessing Language Production in Children: Experimental Procedures.* Baltimore, University Park Press, 1981.

Paul R, Elwood T: Maternal linguistic input to normal and expressively delayed toddlers. *J Speech Hear Res* 1991; 34:982–988.

Paul R, Jennings, P: Phonological behavior in late-talking toddlers. *J Speech Hear Res* (in press).

Paul R, Shiffer M: The expression of communicative intention and mean length of utterance in normal and late-talking young children. *Appl Psycholinguist* (in press).

Paul R, Shriberg L: Associations between phonology and syntax in speech-delayed children. *J Speech Hear Res* 1982; 25:536–547.

Paul R, Spangle-Looney S, Dahm P: Communication and socialization skills at ages two and three in late-talking young children. *J Speech Hear Res* 1991; 34:858–865.

Pinker S: Formal models of language learning. *Cognition* 1979; 7:217–283.

Ramer A: Syntactic styles in emerging language. *J Child Lang* 1976; 3:49–62.

Rapin I: Discussion of developmental language disorders, in Kavanaugh J, Truss T (eds): *Learning Disabilities: Proceedings of the National Conference.* Parkton, Md, York Press, 1988.

Renfrew C: *The Bus Story Language Test.* Oxford, 1969.

Scherer N, Olswang L: Role of mothers' expansions in stimulating children's language production. *J Speech Hear Res* 1984; 27:387–396.

Schmauch V, Panagos J, Klich R: Syntax influences the accuracy of consonant production in language-disordered children. *J Commun Disord* 1978; 11:315–323.

Schwartz R, Leonard L: Do children pick and choose? An examination of phonological selection and avoidance in early lexical acquisition. *J Child Lang* 1982; 9:319–336.

Schwartz R, Leonard L, Folger K, et al: Early phonological behavior in normal-speaking and language disordered children: Evidence for a synergistic view of linguistic disorders. *J Speech Hear Disord* 1980; 45:357–377.

Scollon R: *Conversations With a One-year-old: A Case Study of the Developmental Foundation of Syntax*. Honolulu, University of Hawaii Press, 1976.

Skarakis E, Greenfield P: The role of new and old information in the verbal expression of language disordered children. *J Speech Hear Res* 1982; 25:462–467.

Slobin D: Cognitive prerequisites for the development of grammar, in Ferguson C, Slobin D (eds): *Studies of Child Language Development*. New York, Holt, Rinehart, & Winston, 1973.

Sparrow S, Balla D, Ciccetti D: *The Vineland Adaptive Behavior Scales*. Circle Pines, Minn, American Guidance Service, 1984.

Stampe D: *A Dissertation on Natural Phonology*. New York, Garland Publishing, 1979.

Stemberger J: Between word processes in child phonology. *J Child Lang* 1988; 15:39–62.

Sternberg R: *Beyond IQ: A Triarchic Theory of Human Intelligence*. New York, Cambridge University Press, 1985.

Stoel-Gammon C: Normal and disordered phonology in 2-year-olds. *Topics in Language Disorders* 1991; 11:21–32.

Tallal P: Developmental language disorders, in Kavanaugh J, Truss T (eds): *Learning Disabilities: Proceedings of the National Conference*. Parkton, Md, York Press, 1988.

Tallal P, Piercy M: Developmental aphasia: The perception of brief vowels and extended stop consonants. *Neuropsychologia* 1975; 13:69–74.

Tallal P, Stark R: Speech acoustic-cue discrimination abilities of normally developing and language-impaired children. *J Acoust Soc Am* 1981; 69:568–574.

Waterson N: Growth of complexity in phonological development, in Waterson N, Snow C (eds): *The Development of Communication*. New York, John Wiley & Sons, 1978.

SECTION V Interactive Processes in Pragmatic Development

14 Speech Act Development in Nondisabled Children and Individuals With Mental Retardation*

Leonard Abbeduto, Ph.D.

Glenis Benson, M.Phil.

Language is a tool for social interaction, and the utterance of a linguistic expression by a participant in an interaction constitutes the performance of a social act. Austin (1962) introduced the term *speech act* to refer to the social acts people perform with their linguistic utterances. In this chapter, we will describe the developments that occur in the production and comprehension of speech acts by people acquiring a first language. We will also consider the ways in which those developments are linked to knowledge about communication (i.e., pragmatic knowledge) and to acquisitions in the domains of language (i.e., syntax, semantics, and phonology), cognition, and social cognition. We will discuss research on persons with mental retardation, as well as research on typically developing children. We do so because we believe that research on individuals with mental retardation can yield insights into the nature of development in nondisabled persons. Because problems in the area of speech acts will make everyday social interaction difficult, such research also has the advantage of yielding insights into the adaptive functioning of individuals with mental retardation. We will conclude with a consideration of the implications of research on speech acts for (1) the Child Talk model of Chapman et al. (see Chapter 1) and (2) clinical practice.

*Preparation of this manuscript was supported by grant HD24356 awarded by the National Institute of Child Health and Human Development to Leonard Abbeduto and by grant HD 03352 from the National Institute of Child Health and Human Development to the Waisman Center on Mental Retardation and Human Development.

PRODUCING AND UNDERSTANDING SPEECH ACTS

A speech act actually includes three different types of acts (Austin, 1962; Bach and Harnish, 1979; Levinson, 1983; Searle, 1969). Following Austin (1962), there is, first, the *locutionary act;* that is, the speaker makes reference to some person, place, or thing and predicates something of that referent. By uttering such a meaningful expression, a speaker intentionally performs a social function, or *illocutionary act.* In the right circumstances, for example, the utterance *I think it's a Mercedes* would be an act of assertion, the utterance *Move over* an act of requesting, and the utterance *I'll clean my room* an act of commitment. The distinction between the locutionary and illocutionary act is necessary because linguistic expressions can be used in different ways in different circumstances. For example, *That's mine* can be a request for the return of an object or merely a statement of fact. Finally, the utterance of a meaningful expression with a particular social function can have a variety of effects on the listener (e.g., the listener complies with a request, believes an assertion). The act of achieving such effects is typically referred to as the *perlocutionary act.* The distinction between illocutionary and perlocutionary acts is made because an illocutionary act may have different effects on different listeners or on the same listener at different times. *It's the best computer made* may be recognized as an assertion by two listeners, but only one may believe the assertion, for example. Nevertheless, the perlocutionary act is largely a by-product of the illocutionary act (Levinson, 1983), and so we have little to say about perlocutionary acts.

In the process of producing an utterance, language users are faced with a number of decisions about speech acts. A speaker must decide, first, which illocutionary act to perform at any given point in the interaction. This decision will be based, in part, on the speaker's interpersonal goals and motives. It also will be determined by the speaker's knowledge of the social acts that can be performed linguistically. In particular, speakers may find it difficult to code some interpersonal goals in linguistic utterances and so opt for nonverbal means for their expression. The specific illocutionary act that the speaker performs also will be influenced by his or her knowledge of the context. For example, a competent speaker probably would be more inclined to make a request of a co-worker than of a stern and aloof supervisor.

A speaker also must decide which locutionary act to use as the vehicle for the intended illocutionary act. This decision will be influenced by the speaker's knowledge of the illocutionary potential of the linguistic forms in his or her repertoire. For example, nondisabled adult speakers are aware that although forms such as *Can you close the window?* are questions literally, they can be used to request action (Abbeduto et al., 1989). Speakers who lack this knowledge will use these forms in a restricted manner. Which locutionary act a speaker uses for an illocutionary act also will be determined by his or her knowledge of the interpretive processes of listeners. For example, because a locutionary act often can be used to perform different illocutionary acts on different occasions, successful communication requires that a speaker use a linguistic form only if the current listener is likely to interpret it in the way intended.

Decisions about locutionary acts also will be affected by the degree to which the speaker is concerned with maintaining good social relations with the other participants. In particular, although an illocutionary act often can be conveyed by any of several different locutionary acts, not all of those locutionary acts may be socially acceptable. To request a signature, for example, a speaker could utter, among other things, *Sign this* or *Could I ask you to sign this?* The latter is a more indirect and thus polite way of making the request than is the former (Brown and Levinson, 1978). A competent speaker who is committed to maintaining good social relations, therefore, would most likely use the latter request form to obtain the desired signature.

The locutionary act that a competent speaker uses for an illocutionary act also will be determined by the context in which that act is to be embedded. For example, maintaining good social relations requires greater politeness in some contexts than in others. Thus, nondisabled adults are apt to use an extremely polite linguistic form (e.g., *May I please have another?*) when making a request of an angry listener, but a moderately polite form (e.g., *Can I have another?*) when the listener has a more positive affect. Moreover, there are contexts in which a speaker may not be concerned with maintaining good social relations with the listener. A speaker might have little interest in maintaining good relations with a listener, for instance, when requesting the return of a prized possession that was taken without permission.

Listeners too must make decisions about speech acts. In particular, for each utterance they hear, they must decide which illocutionary act the speaker intends to perform. Because many locutionary acts can be used to perform different illocutionary acts in different contexts, this decision typically cannot be based exclusively on what a speaker says. Instead, competent listeners also use the context of the speaker's utterance, and they do so in a manner that is consistent with the dictates of pragmatic rules (Bach and Harnish, 1979; Green, 1989; Levinson, 1983; Searle, 1975). Pragmatic rules are generalizations about how linguistic utterances relate to their contexts in the naturally occurring communicative exchanges of competent speakers. An example is the *answer obviousness* rule, which captures the generalization that competent speakers do not ask questions to which they already know the answers (Abbeduto et al., 1989; Clark, 1979). Competent listeners apparently assume that a speaker will adhere to this rule, and, consequently, they interpret a sentence such as *Could you roll this?* as a *yes-no* question only when the context suggests that the answer to the question posed is nonobvious to the speaker. Nondisabled adults, for example, are less likely to interpret *Could you roll this baseball?* as a *yes-no* question than they are *Could you roll this shoe box?* (Abbeduto et al., 1989). The difficulty of the action named in the latter sentence, as well as the difficulty of defining the criteria for successful performance of that action, makes the answer to the question posed nonobvious to the speaker.

In summary, the production and comprehension of speech acts are influenced by skills, knowledge, and concepts in a number of domains. Speech acts are linguistic events, and as such their production and comprehension depend on mastery of the linguistic system. Speech acts are also social acts, and consequently interpersonal goals and motives, knowledge about the minds of others, and other aspects of social cognition affect the production and comprehension of such acts in important ways. Cognitive abilities also play a role because such acts are intentional and thus require planning. Speech acts are not isolated events but instead are tied to the context of the speaker's utterance. Consideration of the context necessarily involves linguistic, cognitive, and social-cognitive skills and knowledge because the context includes the verbal and nonverbal behaviors of the participants, the nature of the interaction, the previous discourse, the knowledge and past experiences of the participants, and the physical setting of the talk (Bach & Harnish, 1979). Producing and understanding speech acts also requires recognition of the social uses of language, the dimensions of context relevant to particular speaking and listening decisions, the pragmatic constraints on those decisions, and other pragmatic knowledge. Thus, a speech act approach to speaking and listening is consistent with and has implications for process approaches to language performance and development, such as Child Talk. In both approaches, linguistic (i.e., syntactic, semantic, and phonological) knowledge is seen as being integrated into a larger system of knowledge about how to talk and listen in social interactions.

SPEECH ACT DEVELOPMENT

In this section we will describe some of the age-related changes that occur in the production and comprehension of illocutionary acts in typically developing children. We will also discuss studies involving persons with mental retardation, but this discussion is selective and is intended primarily to illuminate the connections between speech act development and acquisitions in language, cognition, social cognition, and pragmatic knowledge.

Producing Speech Acts

Types

Here we will consider the types of illocutionary acts that nondisabled children and individuals with mental retardation produce as they interact with other people. In studies addressing this issue, the usual approach has been to record the speech produced by a subject as he or she interacts with a parent, teacher, or one or more peers in a loosely structured setting such as free play. Each utterance is then classified as falling into one or more categories of illocutionary acts on the basis of the words spoken, the context (e.g., the participants' previous utterances), and the ways in which listeners react to the utterance (e.g., a *yes* response suggests that the prior utterance is an instance of the illocutionary act of questioning). These studies are motivated by the belief that an analysis of speech in terms of illocutionary acts will yield insights into the individual's conception of the social world and of the interactive goals that can be served by language (Dore, 1975). Consequently, Child Talk and other process models that see linguistic forms as being inextricably linked to the language user's interactive goals will need to consider such studies to identify the goals behind the talk of children at different ages.

Table 14–1 lists the illocutionary acts employed in three representative investigations involving nondisabled children. It is evident from the table that child language researchers have searched for somewhat different social acts in their young subjects' words. In part, this variability may be the result of differences in the ages of the children studied and the research questions of interest. We believe, however, that the variability is largely a reflection of the inherent difficulty of the task researchers have set for themselves—identifying the intentions behind the behaviors of individuals whose minds work in ways that we do not understand fully. Any set of illocutionary categories is simply a hypothesis about how children intend their words to be taken. We must be cautious in assuming that adult-generated categories such as "verbalizing nonexistence" or "tense markers" are psychologically real ones, that is, that they accurately describe the social acts intended by novice language users. Moreover, there are other, methodological problems that have plagued this endeavor (Chapman, 1981; Reeder, 1983; van Kleeck, Maxwell & Gunter, 1985).

Despite the obvious differences among the lists in Table 14–1, commonalities can be seen if we consider the types of illocutionary acts that have been used to describe the speech of nondisabled adult language users. Representative are the categories proposed by Searle (1976), who distinguishes between *assertives, directives, commissives, expressives,* and *declaratives.* Descriptions and examples of these categories are provided in Table 14–2. Assertives are utterances that function to express the speaker's belief in the truth of a proposition. In the case of directives, the

TABLE 14–1.
Examples of Categories of Illocutionary Acts Used by Child Language Researchers

Dore (1977)	Dale (1980)	van Kleeck et al. (1985)

Requests
  Solicit information, actions, or acknowledgment
Responses
  Directly complement preceding utterances
Description
  Represent observable or verifiable aspects of context
Statements
  Express analytic and institutional facts, beliefs, attitudes, emotions, reasons
Conversational devices
  Regulate contact and conversations
Performatives
  Accomplish acts by being said
	Naming
	  Descriptive labels for the environment
	Attributes
	  Labels for the environment that are perceivable attributes of objects
	Comments
	  Beyond immediate information to link with stored knowledge
	Tense markers
	  Comments on future or past actions
	Requests (present)
	  Requests for present objects, actions, or permission or approval
	Requests (absent)
	  Requests an absent object
	Request for information
	Verbalizing nonexistence
	  Expressing the absence or disappearance of an object
	Rejection
	Denial
	Affirmation
	Attention seeking
	Greeting
		Regulators (demand, suggest, request, invite)
		  Action
		  Object
		  Information
		  Acknowledgment
		  Clarification
		  Attention
		  Permission
		  Prohibit-reject-accept
		Comments
		  Label-name
		  Comment on situation
		  Specify
		  Affirm-negate
		  Personal report
		  Praise-criticize
		  Sound effects
		  Performed memorized language
		Other

TABLE 14–2.
Searle's Categories of Speech Acts*

Assertives	A speaker is committed in varying degrees to the truth of a proposition (e.g., *It's raining, I didn't do it.*)
Directives	A speaker tries to get the hearer to do something (e.g., *Move over, Clean your room.*)
Commissives	A speaker is committed in varying degrees to a certain course of action (e.g., *I will return, I promise to do my best.*)
Expressives	A speaker expresses an attitude about a state of affairs (e.g., *I'm sorry, Thanks for the gift.*)
Declaratives	A speaker alters the external status or condition of an object or situation solely by making the utterance (e.g., *You're fired, I baptize you.*)

*Adapted from Searle JR: *Lang Soc* 1976; 5:1–23.

speaker expresses a desire for the addressee to do something. Commissives function to commit the speaker to some future course of action. In an expressive, the speaker expresses his or her psychological state regarding a proposition. In a declarative, the speaker changes the world simply by uttering the linguistic expression. (Making a declaration requires that the speaker has the power to make such changes. For example, a boss can terminate an employee by saying *You're fired,* but an employee cannot end the boss's employment with those same words.)

The coding systems in Table 14–1, and all others of which we are aware, include categories that are instances of the major categories used to describe adult speech. For example, each of the subcategories of regulators of van Kleeck et al. (1985) falls into Searle's directive category and Dore's descriptions and statements categories are instances of assertives in the Searle scheme. The one exception is that most coding systems do not contain any category that would include only utterances that fit Searle's definition of commissives (Astington, 1988a, 1990).

Analyses of the speech of nondisabled children have provided examples of all of the major categories of illocutionary acts. For instance, 19 and 13 of Dale's (1980) 20 toddlers produced utterances in the naming (e.g., *bottle, ball*) and attribute (e.g., *blue*) categories, respectively. Both categories fall under Searle's heading of assertives. Dale also found that most of his subjects produced greetings (e.g., *night-night, bye-bye*) that would be classified as expressives by Searle, and better than half produced requests relating to the present (e.g., *want milk*), which are instances of Searle's directive category. Similar results have been obtained by Roth and Davidge (1985), who used Dale's coding system, and by Dore (1977). Dore (1977) also provides examples from preschoolers of utterances falling into the category of producing performatives, which is similar to Searle's category of declaratives. Although existing illocutionary coding systems are not informative about commissives, children as young as 5 years have little difficulty producing commissives when prompted to do so (Astington, 1988a, 1990).

These results suggest a basic similarity between nondisabled children and adults in their views of social interaction and of the social acts that can be performed linguistically. Young typically developing children, like adults, see social interaction as a forum for the expression of beliefs, desires, commitments, and feelings, and they see language as a vehicle for such expression. Thus, the categories of assertives, directives, commissives, expressives, and declaratives may reflect a mapping onto language of social-cognitive concepts that emerge early in development, probably during the prelinguistic period (Dore, 1975; Sugarman, 1984). Interestingly, adolescents and adults with moderate to borderline mental retardation, some of whom have lived for years in institutional settings, also produce numerous instances of these major categories of illocutionary acts (Abbeduto and Rosenberg, 1980; Owings and McManus, 1980; Owings et al., 1981; Zetlin and Sabsay, 1980). Such individuals have developed in environments that differ in many ways from those of nondisabled persons. That persons with and without mental retardation produce similar illocutionary acts in the face of such environmental differences suggests that the social-cognitive concepts underlying the major categories of illocutionary acts may reflect universal features of cognitive growth and of human social interaction.

Although all of the major categories of the adult system are used by young children, there are three important age-related changes in the production of illocutionary acts. First, the relative frequency with which these major categories are used changes with age (Dale, 1980; Halliday, 1975; Pellegrini, 1984; Roth and Davidge, 1985). These age-related variations in frequency of use may reflect differences in the communicative demands placed on children by their caregivers. Alternatively, these variations may reflect differences in the objects and events of interest to children. For example, preschoolers are especially interested in obtaining information (Piaget, 1929), whereas toddlers are probably more interested in obtaining objects (Shatz and O'Reilly, 1990). Whatever the interpretation, however, such findings reinforce Chapman et al.'s (see Chapter 1) claim that the frequency with which children produce particular types of utterances can be an important indicator of developmental progress.

Second, although the core concepts underlying the major categories of illocutionary acts may emerge early, the variety of expression within each category is narrower for the young child than for the mature language user. In particular, several investigators (Dale, 1980; Halliday, 1975; Roth and Davidge, 1985) have found that not all of the subcategories of the major illocutionary acts emerge simultaneously. Dale (1980), for example, found that utterances expressing nonexistence (e.g., *all gone*) appeared at a later age than did naming utterances despite the fact that both fall under the heading of assertives. Similarly, Astington (1988a, 1990) found that although 5- and 7-year-olds can be prompted to produce commissives such as *I will clean my room,* they seldom make explicit promises (e.g., *I promise I'll clean my room.*). Such developmental changes may reflect an increased knowledge of the linguistic means for coding particular subcategories of illocutionary acts or changes in the social-cognitive concepts that form the basis of those acts. Young schoolchildren may fail to make explicit promises, for example, because they are ignorant of the pragmatic function of the word *promise* or because they lack a detailed concept of social obligations and contracts.

The third age-related difference concerns children's very conception of a speech act. Nondisabled adults know that through the production of a locutionary act they perform an illocutionary act. They also know that they achieve an effect in their listener because he or she recognizes the intended illocutionary act. For example, nondisabled adult speakers know that *Could you move over?* expresses a desire for performance of the action named and that a listener who complies does so because, in part, he or she has recognized that desire. Young children may lack this sophisticated concept of the speech act. For instance, they may recognize that when they desire performance of an action, they can gain compliance by saying *Could you move over?,* but they may not understand how the listener knows to comply. That is, a speaker's words make clear how his or her mind works and listeners react accordingly. Children may know only that their words produce effects (Shatz and O'Reilly, 1990). In fact, Astington (1988b, 1988c) has provided evidence that nondisabled children's awareness of the processes by which speech acts are produced and understood continues to develop well into the school years.

The various age-related changes in nondisabled children's production of illocutionary acts that we have described may be caused, in part, by developments in social cognition, language, and cognition. In the domain of social cognition, advances in preschoolers' theory of the human mind may be necessary before they can understand the ways in which speech acts achieve effects (Shatz and O'Reilly, 1990). That language development plays a role is suggested by the finding that preschoolers with Down syndrome produce the same types of illocutionary acts and at precisely the same relative rates as do nondisabled children matched to them on measures of productive language level (Coggins et al., 1983; Owens and MacDonald, 1982). The role of cognitive development is demonstrated by the finding that the onset of intentional communication is related to sensorimotor advances (Sugarman, 1984). This relation is likely to continue during the early stages of language development (Roth and Davidge, 1985). Moreover, the Child Talk model leads to the prediction that young children's event representations should be a particularly important part of this relation, but this prediction has not been tested.

It is likely, however, that developments in the production of illocutionary acts are not simply a reflection of cognitive, social-cognitive, or linguistic developments. This is suggested by, for example, Dale's (1980) observation that the correlation between MLU and the number of illocutionary acts expressed by nondisabled 1- to 2-year-olds is quite low. Speakers also must possess pragmatic knowledge (e.g., about how language maps onto social-cognitive concepts), and the mechanisms by which this knowledge is acquired may not be the same as those responsible for linguistic, cognitive, and social-cognitive acquisitions. Later in the chapter we shall consider the implications of this observation for the Child Talk model.

Locutionary Acts and Contextual Influences

In this section, we will first consider the locutionary acts that nondisabled children and persons with mental retardation use for the performance of their illocutionary acts. We will then discuss contextual influences on the locutionary acts they use.

Most research on the locutionary acts used by nondisabled children for the expression of their illocutionary acts has focused on directives to act. This research has demonstrated that even 2-year-olds possess a large pool of potential directive forms. This pool includes the imperative (e.g., *Give me my toy.*), elliptical imperative (e.g., *Another toy.*) and various embedded imperatives (e.g., *Can you give me another toy?;* Ervin-Tripp and Gordon, 1986; Gordon and Ervin-Tripp, 1984; Newcombe and Zaslow, 1981). Preschoolers also occasionally soften their directives through the use of *please* (Bock and Hornsby, 1981; Read and Cherry, 1978). These findings suggest that preschoolers have learned that illocutionary acts map onto locutionary acts in a one-to-many fashion and that they know the illocutionary potential of many of the linguistic forms in their repertoires.

Nevertheless, there is a change with age in the directive forms used by typically developing children. For instance, permission requests (e.g., *Can I go outside?*), hints (e.g., *Are there any cookies left in the box?*), need and want statements (e.g., *I want more milk.*), and embedded imperatives increase in frequency over the preschool and early school years, whereas the use of imperatives declines (Ervin-Tripp and Gordon, 1986; Garvey, 1975; Gordon and Ervin-Tripp, 1984; Nippold et al., 1982). School-aged children also are more likely than preschoolers to include an explicit rationale for their directive (e.g., *Do you have a marker? Mine's broken.;* Gordon et al., 1980). The modal verbs included in embedded imperatives and permission requests also become more varied over the school years (Axia and Baroni, 1985; Nippold et al., 1982), and the frequency of *please* increases (Bock and Hornsby, 1981; Nippold et al., 1982).

These developmental changes reflect, in part, the increasing linguistic, social-cognitive, and cognitive sophistication of nondisabled children. For example, the auxiliary verb system of English, which is crucial to the production of a full range of embedded imperatives and permission directives, is not completely mastered until well into the school years (Coates, 1988). In the social-cognitive domain, improvements in perspective taking and increased knowledge of social roles are correlated with children's increasing use of *please* and various embedded imperatives (Bates and Silvern, 1977; Nippold et al., 1982). The role of cognitive development is demonstrated by the finding that the frequency with which polite directive forms are used is correlated with nonverbal mental age (Abbeduto, 1984; Bates and Silvern, 1977).

Two findings from research on persons with mental retardation, however, suggest that the linguistic, cognitive, and social-cognitive maturity of a speaker may not be the only determinants of the directive forms that he or she uses. The first is from a study by Abbeduto (1984), who used hypothetical situations to elicit directives to act from children with mild to borderline mental retardation and from nondisabled kindergarten children. Abbeduto (1984) found that many of the nondisabled children had a preferred linguistic form for their directives, that is, they used one form frequently and in a variety of situations. Few of the children with mental retardation had a preferred form. This difference between the groups emerged despite the fact that they were matched on nonverbal cognitive ability and productive language maturity. The second finding is from a study by Nuccio and Abbeduto (in press). These investigators found that 93% of the requests for toys made by nondisabled 5- to 10-year-olds were interrogative in form (e.g., *Can I have another puzzle?*), whereas the subjects with mental retardation frequently used impolite, noninterrogative, forms (e.g., *Another toy.*). These group differences were found despite the fact that the subjects with mental retardation were matched to the nondisabled children on mental age and were able to produce a variety of interrogative forms.

It is likely that differences between developing speakers in terms of the locutionary acts they use for their directives also are the result of differences in pragmatic knowledge. For example, nondisabled children's knowledge of the relative politeness of many directive forms (e.g., the permission directive) and various softeners (e.g., *please*) and intensifiers (e.g., *you have to*) continues to develop well into the school years (Becker, 1986; Nippold et al., 1982). Moreover, this pragmatic knowledge may be acquired, at least in part, through the efforts of parents who explicitly teach politeness (Becker, 1990; Gleason et al., 1984). Interestingly, explicit teaching by parents does not seem to play a major role in children's acquisition of the linguistic system. Thus, the process by which pragmatic knowledge is acquired may be different from the process involved in the acquisition of other types of language-relevant knowledge (e.g., syntactic knowledge). We will consider the implications of this observation for Child Talk and other process models of language development in a later section.

Nondisabled children not only have many directive forms available to them but also often use those forms in contextually appropriate ways. Preschoolers are more likely to be polite when the listener is more powerful, higher in status, or older than they are (Camras et al., 1985; Ervin-Tripp and Gordon, 1986; Gordon and Ervin-Tripp, 1984; James, 1978; Olson and Hildyard, 1981). Their familiarity with the listener also affects their politeness (Gordon and Ervin-Tripp, 1984). They also are more polite when seeking a favor than when attempting to end a violation of their rights (Gordon and Ervin-Tripp, 1984; James, 1978), and when "asking" than when "telling" (Bock and Hornsby, 1981). There also is evidence to suggest that preschoolers' affective states determine, in part, which forms they use for their directives. For example, preschoolers are more likely to use an imperative form for their directives when in the role of a story character who has an angry facial expression than when in the role of a character who has a neutral facial expression (Camras et al., 1985).

There is evidence from research on persons with mental retardation that a speaker's effectiveness in using contextually appropriate linguistic forms for illocutionary acts is influenced in important ways by his or her cognitive abilities. In particular, children and adolescents with mild to moderate mental retardation have been found to be as sensitive to various dimensions of the context as are nondisabled children matched to them on mental age. The dimensions of context studied have included the listener's age (Abbeduto, 1984), level of activity and affective state (Nuccio and Abbeduto, in press), the cause and goal of the request (Abbeduto, 1984), and the subject's familiarity with the listener (Bliss, 1985).

In closing, it is important to recognize that the fact that young nondisabled children use several polite forms and use them in contextually appropriate ways does not mean that they possess an adultlike concept of politeness or sophisticated rules for using linguistic politeness (Newcombe and Zaslow, 1981). Competent language users recognize that because a listener has his or her own goals and plans, (1) a directive imposes and (2) a listener's compliance cannot be assumed (Axia and Baroni, 1985; Gordon et al., 1980). This knowledge guides their politeness behavior. It leads them, for example, to use directives such as *Do you have a pencil?,* which acknowledge that compliance is not assumed by explicitly providing the listener an opportunity to deny that he or she has the ability to comply. It also leads competent language users to avoid directives such as *I need another,* which imply that the listener's knowledge of the speaker's desires is sufficient reason for the listener to comply. This knowledge also leads competent speakers to judge that any directive represents a greater imposition for a high-status listener than for a low-status listener (i.e., the former is under no obligation to do the speaker's bidding, whereas the latter may be). As a result, competent speakers use forms of differential politeness for listeners varying in status.

In fact, the results of three studies suggest that it is not until the age of 8 years or perhaps even later that nondisabled children understand the bases and rules of linguistic politeness. The first is that of Gordon et al. (1980), who found that when requesting an object from an adult, 5- to 7-year-olds' attempts at politeness were manifested in their use of politeness formulas, whereas older children used devices that explicitly dealt with the imposition created by their requests. For example, the former relied on *please* and *may I,* whereas the latter provided a rationale for imposing (e.g., *Can I have a pencil? Mine broke.*). The second study is that of Axia and Baroni (1985), who investigated the ways in which children dealt with an adult listener's noncompliance with their requests. These investigators found that 9-year-olds' rerequests were more polite when the listener provided a reason for not complying than when the listener simply was uncooperative. Presumably, a re-request poses a greater imposition in the former situation than in the latter. In contrast to the 9-year-olds, Axia and Baroni's 7-year-olds, who were quite polite, did not vary the politeness of their re-requests according to the nature of the listener's noncompliance. These results suggest that 9-year-olds recognize the link between linguistic politeness and issues involving listener imposition and compliance, whereas younger children recognize only that it is "good to be polite." The third study is that of Baroni and Axia (1989). They asked 7-year-olds first to decide whether directives of varying degrees of politeness were uttered by a speaker who was familiar with a listener or by a speaker who was unfamiliar with the listener and then to justify their decisions. In their justifications, the 7-year-olds focused on the formulaic devices contained in the directives (e.g., *please*) rather than on any rule about the link between politeness and familiarity.

If young nondisabled children do not understand the basis of linguistic politeness, how do we account for those instances in which they use linguistic politeness in contextually appropriate ways? How, for example, could preschoolers be more polite when making a request of an adult than when making a request of another child without an understanding of the rationale for such variations? One possibility is that such instances are simply a reflection of the memorization of conventions explicitly taught by adults (e.g., "be polite to grown-ups"). Another possibility is that these instances of contextually appropriate politeness result from the association of specific linguistic forms with specific events or contexts, as suggested by Chapman et al. (see Chapter 1). In either case, we believe that the rationale for linguistic politeness rules can be worked out only after further cognitive and social-cognitive advances have occurred.

Understanding Illocutionary Acts

Nondisabled children evidence a number of age-related changes in their comprehension of the illocutionary acts performed by others. These changes concern both their approach to the task of comprehension and the types of information they use. By and large, research in this area has focused on Searle's (1976) category of directives.

Nondisabled children seem initially to be more intent on responding to rather than interpreting utterances (Shatz and McCloskey, 1984). Between 1 and 2 years of age, they apparently search for cues that will tell them how to respond to an utterance. However, the responses triggered by such cues are derived from various—sometimes idiosyncratic—response strategies rather than from an understanding of what those cues indicate about the illocutionary act being performed. Thus, 1-year-olds focus on cues such as intonation and the presence of *wh-* words, with the result being that they respond differently to questions and nonquestions and to *wh-* and *yes-no* questions (Shatz and McCloskey, 1984). Their responses, however, are not consistently appropriate to either the locutionary or illocutionary act being performed (Shatz and McCloskey, 1984). Along with this response-based approach to language, 1-year-olds capitalize on only a limited number of the available cues, with their use of context apparently being limited to a relatively few frequently occurring, routinized cues (Shatz and McCloskey, 1984).

Between the ages of 2 and 2½ years, nondisabled children begin to respond differentially to a variety of *wh-* questions, and they show some progress in using context (Shatz and McCloskey, 1984). Nevertheless, they still appear to be guided largely by response strategies that are triggered by only a few features of the utterances they hear (Shatz and McCloskey, 1984). For example, children less than age 2½ years tend to respond to any adult utterance that mentions an action by performing that action (Shatz, 1978). In fact, Shatz (1978) has suggested that an important part of development in the third year of life and beyond is learning to recognize cues that indicate when to inhibit an action response.

By age 3 years, nondisabled children demonstrate an ability to interpret rather than simply respond to language. Now their goal often appears to be that of identifying the illocutionary act a speaker performs by talking (Reeder, 1980, 1990; Reeder et al., 1988; Reeder and Wakefield, 1987). A number of findings, however, suggest that the knowledge and skills underlying this new approach to comprehension are quite fragile in that even elementary school children sometimes can be induced to adopt strategies for responding to utterances that are based on a few salient linguistic or contextual cues rather than on the identification of the speaker's illocutionary act (Astington, 1988b; Elrod, 1983; Olson and Hildyard, 1981).

The range of contextual cues that nondisabled children appropriately use increases during the preschool years. By age 3 years, nondisabled children can use as context the speaker's previous utterances to them (Shatz, 1978) and the spatial arrangements of the participants and objects involved in the interaction (Reeder, 1980, 1990). By the age of 5 years, nondisabled children use their knowledge of objects and the actions they allow as context for deciding between a request for action and a request for information interpretation of sentences such as *Could you roll the shoe box?* (Abbeduto et al., 1988). Even young elementary school-aged children, however, do not always use the available context (Ackerman, 1978; Elrod, 1983), or they do so less effectively than do mature language users (Abbeduto et al., 1988). This suggests that these children have not learned the relevance of some types of contextual information or that they do not recognize all of the circumstances in which context is useful. Unfortunately, however, only a few contextual cues have been examined to date. As a result, we do not know if different types of contextual cues come to be used in a regular developmental sequence.

As nondisabled children's use of context improves over the preschool and early elementary school years, so does their ability to glean relevant information from a speaker's utterance and to coordinate the two types of cues. There is improvement, for example, in their recognition that negative directives (e.g., *Won't you color the circle blue?*) seek rather than prohibit the action named (Carrell, 1981; Eson and Shapiro, 1982; Leonard et al., 1978) and in their recognition of the illocutionary acts performed by hints such as *That candy looks great* (Carrell, 1981; Ervin-Tripp, 1977; Ervin-Tripp and Gordon, 1984; Ledbetter and Dent, 1988; Leonard et al., 1978). Moreover, preschool children sometimes have difficulty balancing utterance and contextual cues. In particular, when deciding on a speaker's illocutionary act, 3-year-olds sometimes ignore the speaker's words and rely exclusively on the context, whereas 4-year-olds sometimes attend only to the speaker's words and ignore relevant contextual information (Reeder, 1990; Reeder et al., 1988; Reeder and Wakefield, 1987).

There is evidence that cognitive skills are an important determinant of success in the area of illocutionary act comprehension. In particular, despite their relative skill in this area (Abbeduto and Rosenberg, 1980; Bedrosian and Prutting, 1978; Paul and Cohen, 1985; Zetlin and Sabsay, 1980), persons with mental retardation typically evidence below age-level comprehension of illocutionary acts (Abbeduto et al., 1988; Leifer and Lewis, 1984). Moreover, their ability to use their knowledge about objects and the actions they allow as context for comprehension increases reliably with increased nonverbal cognitive maturity (Abbeduto et al., 1988). Such findings raise the possibility that age-related changes in nondisabled children's illocutionary act comprehension, especially changes in their use of context, also are the result of cognitive advances.

Changes in linguistic ability also appear to be involved in the development of illocutionary act comprehension. There is correlational evidence, for example, that advances in nondisabled children's metalinguistic awareness (i.e., ability to reflect on and evaluate linguistic expressions) prompts the shift seen in the preschool years from an overreliance on context to a more balanced consideration of a speaker's utterance and its context (Reeder, 1990; Reeder et al., 1988). In addition, Ledbetter and Dent (1988) found that performance on a test of syntactic comprehension was related to the rate at which 4-year-olds appropriately responded to various direct and indirect directives.

Nevertheless, evidence from studies on mental retardation suggests that not all linguistic impairments will have an impact on a listener's ability to understand illocutionary acts. In particular, Abbeduto et al. (1988) found that school-aged children and adolescents with mental retardation used contextual and utterance cues to a speaker's illocutionary intent as effectively as did their nondisabled mental age matches despite the fact that the former evidenced a 1-year lag in their receptive language development compared with the latter. Similarly, Leifer and Lewis (1984) found that children with Down syndrome produced responses appropriate to the illocutionary intent of maternal directives at a higher rate than did nondisabled 18- to 23-month-olds matched to them on productive language level. These results suggest that developments in illocutionary act comprehension in nondisabled children, as well as in persons with mental retardation, are more than simply a reflection of growth in the linguistic system.

It is likely that some of the developmental changes in illocutionary act comprehension also are the result of acquiring new pragmatic knowledge. For example, nondisabled children begin to interpret a speaker's utterances in accordance with the maxim of relevance during the early school years (Ackerman, 1981; Conti and Camras, 1984). This maxim captures the generalization that speakers produce utterances relevant to the topic at hand (Grice, 1975). School-aged children assume that a speaker has adhered to this maxim and interpret his or her utterances accordingly. The lack of correlation between linguistic functioning and the comprehension of illocutionary acts for persons with mental retardation (Abbeduto et al., 1988; Leifer and Lewis, 1984) suggests that the processes by which such pragmatic knowledge is acquired are not identical to those underlying the acquisition of linguistic knowledge. What this observation means for Child Talk and other process models of language learning will be considered later in the chapter.

Summary

The research reviewed suggests that developmental changes in speech act performance are caused in part by acquisitions in language, cognition, and social cognition. Individuals with mental retardation, who exhibit linguistic, cognitive, and social-cognitive impairments (Brooks et al., 1984), evidence below age-level speech act performance. At the same time, many aspects of the speech act performance of individuals with mental retardation are commensurate with their levels of functioning in other domains. For example, they produce the same categories of illocutionary acts and at the same relative rates as do nondisabled children matched to them on measures of productive language. Similarly, children and adolescents with mental retardation show the same level of sensitivity to context in their production and comprehension of illocutionary acts as do nondisabled children matched to them on nonverbal cognitive ability. The role of social-cognitive functioning is supported by, for example, research on nondisabled children's use of polite forms when issuing directives.

Cognitive development appears to place particularly strong constraints on speech act performance. This is suggested by studies that have found that increases in mental age are associated with improvements in speech act performance within the population of persons with mental retardation. More important, however, is the fact that in no study did the speech act performance of persons with mental retardation, as a group, exceed that of nondisabled children matched to them on measures of cognitive functioning. This contrasts with comparisons involving language-matched groups with and without mental retardation. Interestingly, research on the performance of persons with mental retardation in other areas of linguistic communication (e.g., producing referentially informative messages, requesting clarification of problematic messages) also fails to uncover a single instance in which individuals with mental retardation, as a group, performed at a level above that expected on the basis of their mental ages (Abbeduto, 1991; Abbeduto and Rosenberg, 1992). Such results suggest that there are probably important cognitive prerequisites for many of the developments that occur in children's speech act performance.

Mastery of the linguistic system, in contrast, is not as strongly related to facility in speech act production and comprehension as has been supposed by many investigators in child language (Bates and MacWhinney, 1982) and speech and language disorders (Johnston, 1988). In particular, children and adolescents with mental retardation have been shown on occasion to perform better at speech act tasks than would be expected, given their levels of linguistic functioning. Even in studies of development in nondisabled children, the relation between language level and speech act performance has been found to be surprisingly weak at times (Dale, 1980). Such findings are not limited to a single period of development or to one performance mode. Moreover, similar findings characterize other aspects of communication in persons with mental retardation (Abbeduto, 1991; Abbeduto and Rosenberg, 1992) and persons with other developmental disabilities, including those with specific language impairment (Abbeduto and Nuccio, 1989). This is not to say that language impairments will have no impact on the development of communication. Producing and understanding speech acts logically require some facility with the linguistic system (Leonard and Fey, 1991). Our claim is, instead, that even persons with especially severe language impairments may have linguistic skills that are sufficient for the performance of many everyday speech act tasks.

The comprehension and production of speech acts also are influenced by pragmatic knowledge, and the mechanisms responsible for the acquisition of such knowledge appear to differ somewhat from those underlying the development of language, cognition, and social cognition. This is suggested by the finding that persons with mental retardation often evidence speech act performance that differs from that of nondisabled children matched to them on one or more measures of functioning in these other domains. Thus, there may be unique aspects of speech act development—aspects not explained in terms of the products or processes of development in cognition, social cognition, or even language (i.e., syntax, semantics, phonology). An important task for future research is to identify the experiences and learning strategies that are specific to the acquisition of pragmatic knowledge. Work on parental behavior (Becker, 1990; Bellinger, 1979) appears particularly promising in this regard.

Research involving persons with mental retardation also suggests that it is possible to find asynchronies across different aspects of speech act performance. In the task of illocutionary act comprehension, for example, children and adolescents with mental retardation are influenced by at least some types of contextual information in a manner commensurate with their levels of cognitive functioning. At the same time, they are less likely to use polite linguistic forms for their illocutionary acts than are their nondisabled mental age matches. Thus, developmental asynchrony between comprehension and production is possible. Asynchronies within either comprehension or production also are possible. In speech act production, for instance, individuals with mental retardation are below mental age in terms of the forms that they use for their illocutionary acts, but they are mental age appropriate in terms of their sensitivity to context.

In concluding this section, we must acknowledge several limitations of the research reviewed. First, the tasks used to assess speech act performance, especially for older children, often bear little resemblance to the daily interactions in which the children participate. Studies of contextual influences on directive production, for example, typically solicit such utterances in response to hypothetical dilemmas. Issues of generalizability from contrived to naturalistic contexts are particularly important when one is studying speech act development because an essential part of such development is learning what to do in different contexts. This is an especially important limitation from the perspective of the Child Talk model, which is based on the assumption that linguistic knowledge is inextricably linked to representations of the contexts in which it is learned and used. Second, no single study of speech act performance has included measures of functioning in each of the domains of language, cognition, and social cognition. This makes it difficult to determine the relative contributions of skills and knowledge in these domains to specific aspects of speech act performance. Finally, speech act performance has been examined largely in relation to gross, composite measures of cognitive, linguistic, and social-cognitive functioning. As a result, we know little about the ways in which specific developments in speech act performance are related to specific advances within these other domains (Abbeduto, 1991; Abbeduto and Rosenberg, 1992). For example, although the research reviewed suggests that certain cognitive advances probably function as prerequisites for speech act development, that research does not identify the particular cognitive advances involved (Abbeduto, 1991; Abbeduto and Rosenberg, 1992). The search for more precise relationships between advances in speech act performance and advances in other domains of functioning can benefit from process models of language learning such as Child Talk. Chapman et al.'s (see Chapter 1) model, for instance, leads to the prediction that the cognitive prerequisites for speech act development should include advances in event representation.

IMPLICATIONS FOR PROCESS MODELS OF CHILDREN'S LANGUAGE

The basic assumption of the Child Talk model (Chapman et al., see Chapter 1) and of many other process-oriented models (Bresnan, 1982) is that linguistic (i.e., syntactic, semantic, phonological) knowledge is not acquired or represented independently of procedures for its use. In the Child Talk model, linguistic knowledge is thought to be part of a network of knowledge about how to plan and carry out particular classes of goal-directed actions (i.e., speaking and listening actions) in specific social situations. In Chapter 1, Chapman et al.'s claims appear to extend to both the acquisition and use of linguistic knowledge. In this section, we will examine five predictions of the Child Talk model in light of the research on speech act development we have considered.

One prediction of the Chapman et al. model is that children should not afford special status to linguistic information (compared with nonlinguistic information) in the decisions that they make about speech acts. This prediction derives from their claim that linguistic knowledge is acquired, represented, and accessed in the same manner as is any other type of knowledge that is involved in goal-directed action. In keeping with this prediction, the research we have reviewed suggests that typically developing listeners less than age 2 years use both linguistic information and nonlinguistic context as cues about how to respond to another's utterance. Moreover, there is no evidence to suggest that they prefer or place greater trust in one type of information over the other, at least for purposes of response selection. Later in development, however, there is evidence to suggest that nondisabled children do distinguish between linguistic and nonlinguistic sources of information, with many 3-year-olds placing greater reliance on the context and many 4-year-olds attending more to linguistic properties of the speaker's utterance. This raises the possibility that the knowledge involved in linguistic performance becomes increasingly differentiated with age. Thus, the Child Talk model may be a more apt description of the earlier stages of development than of the later stages.

A second prediction of the Child Talk model is that children's utterances may not be the result of rules but of connectionist systems built by experience. Although Chapman et al. (see Chapter 1) make this prediction in the context of a discussion of the status of syntactic rules, presumably it extends to pragmatic rules as well. In fact, support for this prediction is provided by the finding that young nondisabled children can adjust the politeness of their directives to fit the context despite having little knowledge of the rationale or abstract rules on which those adjustments are based. This suggests that it would be useful to extend connectionist models to the pragmatic realm to see if other aspects of speech act performance can be explained without reference to pragmatic rules.

The third prediction of the Child Talk model that we consider concerns the relation between the comprehension and production of speech acts. A distinction between linguistic competence and performance (at least as traditionally drawn) is not made in the Chapman et al. model. Instead, the representation of linguistic knowledge is tied intimately to the ways and situations in which it is used. Because speaking and listening are associated with different goals and task requirements (e.g., modality), the Child Talk model leads to the prediction that speaking and listening can develop differently and show different degrees of impairments. In support of this prediction, the research on the speech act performance of persons with mental retardation reviewed in this chapter has uncovered several instances of asynchronous development across speaking and listening tasks.

A fourth prediction of the Chapman et al. model concerns the occurrence of developmental delays in linguistic performance. In the Child Talk model, children's linguistic performances are thought to be influenced in important ways by their conceptual knowledge and information processing capabilities. This is evident, for example, in the claim that the lexicon is organized in terms of event representations and the claim that linguistic knowledge is "acquired like any other developing knowledge of how to plan and carry out goal-directed action" (see Chapter 1). We believe that such claims lead to the prediction that delays in speaking and listening should be tied closely to impairments in the cognitive domain.

In fact, the research on speech acts reviewed in this chapter provides support for this prediction. This support comes from the previously mentioned finding that persons with mental retardation, as a group, never outdistance their cognitively matched nondisabled peers on measures of skill in speech act comprehension or expression. Support also is provided by the finding that nonverbal mental age is correlated with advances in the use of context in illocutionary act comprehension (Abbeduto et al., 1988). Thus, as predicted by the Child Talk model, there are strong cognitive constraints on speech act development.

The final prediction of the Child Talk model that we will consider also concerns developmental delays. We believe that the model leads to the prediction that delays in linguistic (i.e., syntactic, semantic, phonological) knowledge should be closely related to delays in the social uses of language, such as those seen in the areas of speech act performance. This prediction is suggested by Chapman et al.'s claim that the linguistic knowledge involved in speaking cannot be characterized without reference to the speaker's interpersonal goals, interactional role, and the context of the talk. The prediction also is consistent with their claim that linguistic knowledge is "generalized as utterance frames—given experiences that are based on the individual's knowledge of functional, pragmatic, discourse, and semantic relations or conceptual categories" (see Chapter 1).

The research on speech acts that we have reviewed, however, is not consistent with this prediction. In particular, as indicated previously, persons with mental retardation, as a group, evidence superior performance in some areas of speech act expression and comprehension than they do in tasks designed to tap their mastery of syntax or other aspects of the linguistic system. In addition, Curtiss (1988) has provided examples of individuals with mental retardation who evidence syntactic skills that are appropriate for their chronological ages despite having significant delays in pragmatic (including speech act) performance. Even for typically developing children, correlations between measures of speech act proficiency and linguistic maturity are often low. We interpret such findings as evidence that contrary to the predictions of the Child Talk model, pragmatic skills and linguistic knowledge are not acquired through or represented by the same mechanisms. Thus, Chapman et al.'s claims about the relation between pragmatic and linguistic skills during development may need to be revised.

IMPLICATIONS FOR CLINICAL PRACTICE

From the very earliest stages of language development, children's utterances reflect more than linguistic achievements; they reflect social acts as well. Children learn more than how to combine linguistic elements; they learn what social ends can be achieved by doing so. This social motivation for language needs to be acknowledged when one is working with individuals who have speech and language difficulties. For example, attempts to teach linguistic forms in the absence of information about the illocutionary potential of the forms are certain to fail (Leonard and Fey, 1991).

The research we have reviewed demonstrates that the acquisition of speech act skills is dependent not only on language but also on skills and knowledge in cognition, social cognition, and pragmatics. Problems in the area of speech acts, therefore, may arise because of impairments in any or all of these domains. Moreover, children who evidence superficially similar problems in the production and comprehension of speech acts may do so for very different reasons. One may lack the requisite linguistic skills, and another the cognitive skills needed for success. Understanding the nature of speech act problems, therefore, will require assessments in all four domains of language, cognition, social cognition, and pragmatic knowledge (Abbeduto and Nuccio, 1989; Wollner, 1983). Intervention will need to target one or more of these domains as well.

Quite naturally, attempts at ameliorating the communication difficulties of children and adults have traditionally focused largely on the linguistic sources of such difficulties (Leonard and Fey, 1991). The research we have reviewed, however, suggests that the strongest constraints on speech act development may be cognitive in nature. Thus, the traditional view of intervention will need to be expanded to include a wider variety of cognitive skills than targeted previously. Unfortunately, this new approach to intervention must wait until researchers abandon summary measures such as mental age and begin to examine relations between specific cognitive skills and specific developments in speech act performance.

Given the essential role of context in the production and comprehension of speech acts, children's speech act performance should be assessed across multiple contextual properties (Abbeduto and Nuccio, 1989). Children become sensitive to a full range of contextual cues only gradually over development, and, therefore, at any point in time they may demonstrate good linguistic performance in one context but not in others. Intervention also will need to be conducted in multiple contexts (e.g., in different physical and social settings, with various conversational partners). The Child Talk model suggests that assessment and intervention contexts should be selected with reference to the events and situations in which children typically participate as they learn language.

Clinicians should be aware that asynchronies can characterize an individual's speech act performance. Discrepancies can exist between a child's ability to produce and comprehend speech acts. Demonstrated facility with one does not dictate competence in the other. Even within comprehension and production, a child may evidence strengths and weaknesses. Assessment and intervention should be designed to deal with such asynchronies.

Research on speech acts, then, has the potential to greatly alter clinical practice. Informed assessment and intervention in speech act production and comprehension, however, are limited necessarily by the quality and quantity of empirical investigations. Researchers (1) must begin to study speech act performance in naturalistic interactions; (2) must examine speech act performance in relation to several other domains of mental and behavioral functioning simultaneously; and (3) must provide data about the relations between specific developments in speech act performance and specific acquisitions in the domains of language, cognition, social cognition, and pragmatic knowledge. Until this is done, the potential contribution of research on speech acts to clinical practice will not be realized.

REFERENCES

Abbeduto L: Situational influences on mentally retarded and nonretarded children's production of directives. *Appl Psycholinguist* 1984; 5:147–166.

Abbeduto L: Development of verbal communication in persons with moderate to mild mental retardation, in Bray N (ed): *International Review of Research in Mental Retardation.* New York, Academic Press, 1991, vol 17, pp 91–115.

Abbeduto L, Davies B, Furman L: The development of speech act comprehension in mentally retarded individuals and nonretarded children. *Child Dev* 1988; 59:1460–1472.

Abbeduto L, Furman L, Davies B: Identifying speech acts from contextual and linguistic information. *Language and Speech* 1989; 32:189–203.

Abbeduto L, Nuccio J: Evaluating the pragmatic aspects of communication in school-age children and adolescents: Insights from research on atypical development. *Sch Psychol Rev* 1989; 18:502–512.

Abbeduto L, Rosenberg S: The communicative competence of mildly retarded adults. *Appl Psycholinguist* 1980; 1:405–426.

Abbeduto L, Rosenberg S: The development of linguistic communication in persons with mental retardation, in Warren S, Reichle J (eds): *Causes and Effects in Communication and Language Intervention.* Baltimore, Brookes, 1992.

Ackerman BP: Children's understanding of speech acts in unconventional directive frames. *Child Dev* 1978; 49:311–318.

Ackerman BP: When is a question not answered? The understanding of young children of utterances violating or conforming to the rules of conversational sequencing. *J Exp Child Psychol* 1981; 31:487–507.

Astington J: Children's production of commissive speech acts. *J Child Lang* 1988a; 15:411–423.

Astington J: Children's understanding of the speech act of promising. *J Child Lang* 1988b; 15:157–173.

Astington J: Promises: Words or deeds? *First Lang* 1988c; 3:259–270.

Astington J: Metapragmatics: Children's conception of promising, in Conti-Ramsden G, Snow C (eds): *Children's Language.* Hillsdale, NJ, Lawrence Erlbaum Associates, 1990.

Austin JL: *How to Do Things With Words.* Oxford, Oxford University Press, 1962.

Axia G, Baroni MR: Linguistic politeness at different age levels. *Child Dev* 1985; 56:918–927.

Bach K, Harnish RM: *Linguistic Communication and Speech Acts.* Cambridge, Mass, MIT Press, 1979.

Baroni MR, Axia G: Children's metapragmatic abilities and the identification of polite and impolite requests. *First Lang* 1989; 9:285–297.

Bates E, MacWhinney B: Functionalist approaches to grammar, in Wanner E, Gleitman LR (eds): *Language Acquisition: The State of the Art.* New York, Cambridge University Press, 1982, pp 173–218.

Bates E, Silvern L: Social adjustment and politeness in preschoolers. *J Commun* 1977; 27:104–111.

Becker J: Bossy and nice requests: Children's production and interpretation. *Merrill-Palmer Q* 1986; 32:393–413.

Becker JA: Processes in the acquisition of pragmatic competence, in Conti-Ramsden G, Snow C (eds): *Children's Language.* Hillsdale, NJ, Lawrence Erlbaum Associates, 1990, vol 7, pp 7–24.

Bedrosian JL, Prutting C: Communicative performance of mentally retarded adults in four conversational settings. *J Speech Hear Res* 1978; 21:79–95.

Bellinger D: Changes in the explicitness of mother's directives as children age. *J Child Lang* 1979; 6:443–458.

Bliss LS: The development of persuasive strategies by mentally retarded children. *Appl Res Ment Retard* 1985; 6:437–447.

Bock JK, Hornsby ME: The development of directives: How children ask and tell. *J Child Lang* 1981; 8:151–163.

Bresnan J (ed): *The Mental Representation of Grammatical Relations.* Cambridge, Mass, MIT Press, 1982.

Brooks P, Sperber R, McCauley C: *Learning and Cognition in the Mentally Retarded.* Hillsdale, NJ, Lawrence Erlbaum Associates, 1984.

Brown P, Levinson S: Universals in language usage: Politeness phenomena, in Goody E (ed): *Questions and Politeness.*

New York, Cambridge University Press, 1978, pp 356–389.

Camras LA, Pristo TM, Brown MJK: Directive choice by children and adults: Affect, situation, and linguistic politeness. *Merrill-Palmer Q* 1985; 31:19–31.

Carrell PL: Children's understanding of indirect requests: Comparing child and adult comprehension. *J Child Lang* 1981; 8:329–345.

Chapman R: Exploring children's communicative intents, in Miller J (ed): *Assessing Language Production in Children.* Baltimore, Md, University Park Press, 1981, pp 111–136.

Clark HH: Responding to indirect speech acts. *Cognit Psychol* 1979; 11:430–477.

Coates J: The acquisition of the meanings of modality in children aged eight and twelve. *J Child Lang* 1988; 15:425–434.

Coggins TE, Carpenter RL, Owings NO: Examining early intentional communication Down's syndrome and nonretarded children. *Br J Disord Commun* 1983; 18:99–107.

Curtiss S: Abnormal language acquisition and the modularity of language, in Newmeyer FE (ed): *Linguistics. The Cambridge Survey,* vol II: *Linguistic Theory: Extensions and Implications.* New York, Cambridge University Press, 1988.

Dale PS: Is early pragmatic development measurable? *J Child Lang* 1980; 7:1–12.

Dore J: Holophrases, speech acts, and language universals. *J Child Lang* 1975; 2:21–41.

Dore J: Children's illocutionary acts, in Freedle RO (ed): *Discourse Productions and Comprehension.* Hillsdale, NJ, Lawrence Erlbaum Associates, 1977.

Elrod MM: Young children's responses to direct and indirect directives. *J Genet Psychol* 1983; 143:217–227.

Ervin-Tripp S: "Wait for me, Rollerskate!," in Mitchell-Kernan C, Ervin-Tripp S (eds): *Child Discourse.* New York, Academic Press, 1977.

Ervin-Tripp S, Gordon D: The development of requests, in Schiefelbusch RL (ed): *Communicative Competence: Assessment and Intervention.* Baltimore, Md, University Park Press, 1986.

Eson ME, Shapiro AS: When "don't" means "do": Pragmatic and cognitive development in understanding an indirect imperative. *First Lang* 1982; 3:83–91.

Garvey C: Requests and responses in children's speech. *J Child Lang* 1975; 2:41–60.

Gleason JB, Perlmann RY, Greif EB: What's the magic word: Learning language through politeness routines. *Discourse Processes* 1984; 7:493–502.

Gordon DP, Budwig N, Strage A, et al: Children's requests to unfamiliar adults: form, social function, age variations. Paper presented at the Boston University Conference on Language Development, Boston, October 1980.

Gordon DP, Ervin-Tripp S: The structure of children's requests, in Schiefelbusch RL, Pickar AJ (eds): *The Acquisition of Communicative Competence.* Baltimore, Md, University Park Press, 1984.

Green GM: *Pragmatics and Natural Language Understanding.* Hillsdale, NJ, Lawrence Erlbaum Associates, 1989.

Grice HP: Logic and conversation. The William James Lectures at Harvard University, Lesson II, 1967, in Cole P, Morgan JL (eds): *Syntax and Semantics—Speech Acts.* New York, Academic Press, 1975, pp 41–58.

Halliday MAK: *Learning How to Mean—Explorations in the Development of Language.* London, Edward Arnold, 1975.

James S: The effect of listener age and situation on the politeness of children's directives. *J Psycholinguist Res* 1978; 7:307–317.

Johnson J: Specific language disorders in children, in Lass N, McReynolds L, Northern TG, et al (eds): *Handbook of Speech and Language Pathology and Audiology*. New York, BC Decker, 1988, pp 685–715.

Ledbetter PJ, Dent CH: Young children's sensitivity to direct and indirect request structure. *First Lang* 1988; 8:227–246.

Leifer JS, Lewis M: Acquisition of conversational response skills by young Down syndrome and nonretarded young children. *Am J Ment Defic* 1984; 88:610–618.

Leonard LB, Fey ME: Facilitating grammatical development: The contribution of pragmatics, in Gallagher T (ed): *Pragmatics of Language: Clinical Practice Issues*. San Diego, Calif, Singular, 1991, pp 333–355.

Leonard LB, Wilcox MJ, Fulmer KC, et al: An investigation of children's comprehension of pragmatic meanings. *J Speech Hear Res* 1978; 21:528–537.

Levinson SC: *Pragmatics*. New York, Cambridge University Press, 1983.

Newcombe N, Zaslow M: Do 2½ -year-olds hint? A study of directive forms in speech of 2½-year-old children to adults. *Discourse Processes* 1981; 4:239–252.

Nippold MA, Leonard LB, Anastopoulos A: Development in the use and understanding of polite forms in children. *J Speech Hear Res* 1982; 25:193–202.

Nuccio JB, Abbeduto L: Dynamic contextual variables and the Directives of persons with mental retardation. *Am J Ment Retard* (in press).

Olson D, Hildyard A: Assent and compliance in children's language, in Dickson WP (ed): *Children's Oral Communication Skills*. New York, Academic Press, 1981, pp 313–335.

Owens RE Jr, MacDonald JD: Communicative uses of the early speech of nondelayed and Down syndrome children. *Am J Ment Defic* 1982; 86:503–510.

Owings NO, McManus MD: An analysis of communication functions in the speech of a deinstitutionalized adult mentally retarded client. *Ment Retard* 1980; 18:309–314.

Owings NO, McManus MD, Scherer N: A deinstitutionalized retarded adult's use of communication functions in a natural setting. *Br J Disord Commun* 1981; 16:119–128.

Paul R, Cohen DJ: Comprehension of indirect requests in adults with autistic disorders and mental retardation. *J Speech Hearing Res* 1985; 28:475–479.

Pellegrini AD: A speech analysis of preschooler's dyadic interaction. *Commun Cognit* 1984; 17:425–436.

Piaget J: *The Child's Conception of the World*. New York, Harcourt & Brace, 1929.

Read B, Cherry LJ: Preschool children's production of directive forms. *Discourse Processes* 1978; 1:233–245.

Reeder K: The emergence of illocutionary skills. *J Child Lang* 1980; 7:13–28.

Reeder K: Classifications of children's speech acts: A consumer's guide. *J Pragmat* 1983; 7:679–694.

Reeder K, Wakefield J: The development of young children's speech act comprehension: How much language is necessary? *Appl Psycholinguist* 1987; 8:1–18.

Reeder K, Wakefield J, Shapiro J: Children's speech act comprehension strategies and early literacy experiences. *First Lang* 1988; 8:29–48.

Reeder K: Text or context: The influence of early literate experience upon preschool children's speech act comprehension, in Conti-Ramsden G, Snow C (eds): *Children's*

Language. Hillsdale, NJ, Lawrence Erlbaum Associates, 1990, vol 7.

Roth FP, Davidge NS: Are early verbal communicative intentions universal? A preliminary investigation. *J Psycholinguist Res* 1985; 14:351–363.

Searle JR: *Speech Acts*. New York, Cambridge University Press, 1969.

Searle JR: Indirect speech acts, in Cole P, Morgan JL (eds): *Syntax and Semantics*. New York, Academic Press, 1975, vol 3, pp 59–82.

Searle JR: A classification of illocutionary acts. *Lang Soc* 1976; 5:1–23.

Shatz M: On the development of communicative understandings: An early strategy for interpreting and responding to messages. *Cognit Psychol* 1978; 10:271–301.

Shatz M, McCloskey L: Answering appropriately: A developmental perspective on conversational knowledge, in Kuczaj S II (ed): *Discourse Development: Progress in Cognitive Development Research*. New York, Springer-Verlag New York, 1984.

Shatz M, O'Reilly AW: Conversational or communicative skill? A reassessment of two-year-olds' behaviour in miscommunication episodes. *J Child Lang* 1990; 17:131–146.

Sugarman S: The development of preverbal communication: Its contribution and limits in promoting the development of language, in Schiefelbusch RL, Pickar J (eds): *The Acquisition of Communicative Competence*. Baltimore, Md, University Park Press, 1984, pp 23–67.

van Kleeck A, Maxwell M, Gunter C: A methodological study of illocutionary coding in adult-child interaction. *J Pragmat* 1985; 9:659–681.

Wollner SG: Communicating intentions: How well do language-impaired children do? *Top Lang Disord* 1983; 4:1–14.

Zetlin AG, Sabsay S: Characteristics of verbal interaction among moderately retarded peers. Paper presented at the Gatlinburg Conference on Research in Mental Retardation, Gatlinburg, Tenn, March 1980.

15 Individuals With Autism: Language Acquisition With Restricted Social and Emotional Knowledge

Nanette A. Negri, Ph.D.

The nature of the association between the cognitive, communicative, and social impairments of individuals with autism has been and remains a subject of debate (Baron-Cohen, 1987; Hermelin, 1982; Shah and Wing, 1986). However, there is no disagreement that an impairment in language production is cardinal in individuals with autism and has been since the syndrome was first identified (Kanner, 1943). The specific features of this language impairment have been described in detail by many researchers (Baltaxe, 1977; Hurtig et al., 1982; Menyuk and Quill, 1985; Paul, 1987; Prizant, 1982; Ricks and Wing, 1975; Tager-Flusberg, 1981) and include mutism, echolalia, literalness, affirmation by repetition, pronominal reversals, and metaphoric language that is unique to the individual. In addition, many individuals with autism also appear to have an excellent rote memory, coupled with an inability to use language in any other than a rote fashion (Fay and Schuler, 1980). But is this language impairment primary, or should it more appropriately be considered a secondary symptom, resulting from the different way in which these individuals experience the world and learn?

The purpose of this chapter is to show how the Child Talk model can be applied to understanding the language produced by children with autism. The chapter will begin with a description of the characteristics typically associated with autism and a review of current conceptualization of the syndrome, followed by a discussion of the potential effects of a different knowledge network on the formulation and use of language by individuals with autism. The chapter will end with a discussion of possible considerations for interventions to support such individuals.

WHAT ARE THE BASIC CHARACTERISTICS AND CURRENT CONCEPTUALIZATIONS OF INDIVIDUALS WITH AUTISM?

Language

Since the syndrome of autism was first identified by Kanner (1943), there have been considerable discussion and controversy over the nature of the language and communication deficits experienced by the individuals and the role that those deficits play in the definition of the syndrome. Language impairments affecting comprehension and expression are characteristic of all individuals with autism (Tager-Flusberg, 1985). The language abilities of even more able individuals with autism often are considerably less than their nonverbal cognitive functioning skills. Their language is often characterized as concrete and pedantic and includes "curious misinterpretations of meaning" (Dewey and Everard, 1974). For example, one young man with autism, when asked to characterize how people in a test photograph might feel, touched the photograph and replied, "soft" (Caparulo, 1982).

Some researchers have suggested that the language of individuals with autism represents a different underlying semantic knowledge (Menyuk and Quill, 1985). Thus, the language is often not easily shared. This sharing difficulty is most clearly reflected in the extended use of echolalic and delayed echolalic speech, which is typical during language development of more verbal individuals with autism (Newson et al., 1982). Although this period of development is delayed compared with the norm (Fay and Schuler, 1980), "more able" children with autism do gradually come to use their speech skills in meaningful ways (Newson et al., 1982), though not without some difficulties (Ricks and Wing, 1975; Simmons and Baltaxe, 1975).

Communication

Although some individuals with autism develop and use speech in meaningful ways, abnormalities in communication still remain (Newson and Dawson, 1983; Wing, 1981). From the earliest stages, children with autism demonstrate serious difficulties in key aspects of intentional communication. These difficulties are particularly apparent when communication is exclusively social interactive, as in establishing joint attention, informing, and initiating (Wetherby, 1986). At least half of all individuals with autism fail to develop language at all (Paul, 1987) and develop very limited communication skills. When language does develop, problematic communication characteristics include a lack of flow and stiltedness. One young woman with autism reported that it is very difficult for her to "feel when it is okay to take my turn in a conversation, especially if there is more than one other person there" (Grandin, 1987b). Conversations tend to be of the question and answer type only (Hurtig et al., 1982), with topics often limited to obsessions of the individual or the individual's needs (Newson et al., 1982). These abnormalities indicate difficulties at the discourse level of communication, most specifically in smooth conversational turn taking, and can be noted primarily in one or all three ways: (1) the individual tends to "drop the ball" rather than return it (Donnellan and Kilman, 1986; Kilman and Negri-Shoultz, 1987); (2) if it is returned, the individual has difficulty staying on topic or providing the necessary transition information or contextual cues for the listener, a problem involving decentering (Inhelder and Piaget, 1969); and (3) the impact of the conversational exchange is such that there are atypically long delays between speaker's turns (Mirenda and Donnellan, 1986).

Impaired language and communication skills remain a cardinal feature of the syndrome of autism. Some researchers, however, view the communication and language problems as secondary rather than primary and explanatory of the other symptoms seen across individuals with autism. They view the cognitive profile as key and as clearly reflected in the pattern of language development described (Shah and Wing, 1986).

Cognition

A number of investigators currently view the cognitive challenges of autism as primary. The inability of children with autism to encode stimuli meaningfully has been identified as their basic cognitive defect (Hermelin and O'Connor, 1970). For these individuals there appears to be a primary difference in the manner of sorting and storing information that reflects a defect in the ability to process information by meaning and with imagination. The children tend to impose stimulus-independent, simple, rigid, and repetitive patterns on random, as well as on structured, meaningful input. They show few specific deficits in terms of spatial performance, perceptual organization, and attentional short-term memory skills (Rutter, 1983; Wing and Attwood, 1987). Typically, for persons experiencing autism, information appears to be processed more easily in terms of perceptual attributes than in terms of meaningful, functional attributes. For example, one young woman with autism, trying on a pair of shoes with her mother, was asked to "walk up the store" to see how the shoes fit. The young woman looked anxious. She stood, searching the store with her eyes, until she spotted a ladder, which, of course, she quickly "walked up."

Further, parents have noted that even as young children these individuals often had good rote memories but rarely engaged in imaginative play (Newson et al., 1982). There have also been many reports of such children who have easily learned numbers and letters and yet had great difficulty knowing what those numbers and letters meant or what to do with them.

The processing differences in persons with autism have been described in terms of Gestalt vs. analytic modes of cognitive processing (Prizant, 1982). A gestalt mode of cognitive processing is one in which the "wholes" of events or stimuli are retained with relatively little analysis of the pieces (Hubbell, 1981). This indicates that an event or stimuli only has the meaning that is attached to it in a specific context. Outside of that context, the event has little or no meaning, and information about it cannot be abstracted and used. In contrast, an analytic mode of cognitive processing involves analyzing and segmenting experiences or events into meaningful components based on prior experience. Evidence from work with individuals with autism suggests that they do not code functional information in a meaningful way and that they code perceptual information more efficiently (Everard, 1976; Kilman, 1981; Park, 1986). Problems arise even for the most able individual with autism at the level where concept formation depends on the ability to manipulate instead of just store symbols (Ricks and Wing, 1975). Thus, individuals with autism have been described as processing primarily in the gestalt mode (Prizant, 1982), experiencing difficulty with abstraction. In an effort to gain a better understanding of autism, researchers have attempted to specify more clearly the nature of the cognitive challenges experienced by individuals with autism. Baron-Cohen et al. (1985) propose that a specific cognitive deficit in the development of second-order mental representations is actually at the heart of the disorder. This specific area is often referred to as social cognition.

Social Cognition

Social competence involves communication: these are not separate; they are overlapping areas of development, both of which depend on cognition (Selman, 1975). This overlap is at least part of the reason that individuals with autism have social adjustment difficulties. They seem to have a general lack of social know-how (Everard, 1976) and clear deficits regarding knowledge of how people think and feel as opposed to what they look like and what they do (Baron-Cohen et al., 1985; 1986; Frith, 1989; Hobson, 1986a; 1986b; Negri-Shoultz, 1987; Ungerer, 1989).

One most obvious characteristic, the impairment of two-way social interaction (Wing, 1981), appears to arise from an inability to understand and use the rules governing social behavior and a specific dysfunction in conceiving of mental states (Baron-Cohen et al., 1985, 1986). Conceiving of mental states, that is, knowing what other people know, want, or believe, is critical to social relatedness. Premack and Woodruff (1978) have called this knowing a "theory of mind," and the work of Baron-Cohen et al. (1985, 1986) demonstrates how the absence of a theory of mind could lead to many of the aspects of social ineptness often seen in individuals with autism.

To test the hypothesis that children with autism lack certain social-cognition skills, or a theory of mind, Baron-Cohen et al. (1985) examined the ability of more able children with autism, children with Down syndrome, and nonhandicapped preschoolers to recognize that different people can have different beliefs about the same situation. The researchers employed a paradigm designed by Wimmer and Perner (1983) that used two doll protagonists, Sally and Anne. While with Anne, Sally puts a marble into her own basket. Then she leaves the scene, and Anne moves the marble, hiding it in her box. When Sally returns, the child is asked the critical belief question, "Where will Sally look for her marble?" If the child points to Sally's basket, he or she passes, appreciating the doll's now false belief. If he or she points to Anne's box, the child fails, because the child had not taken into account the doll's belief. The children with Down syndrome and the nonhandicapped preschoolers were successful at this task; 16 of the 20 children with autism were not.

Skeptics asserted that perhaps the poor performance of the children with autism had more to do with their inability to engage in pretend play than in the specific absence of a theory of mind. The children were asked the same questions in different ways in some later experiments where real people took the part of Sally and Anne and where the marble was a coin, and the children performed exactly the same way as in the previous experiment (Leslie and Frith, 1990). As Frith (1989) points out, however, it is dangerous to rely on one paradigm when such striking group differences are found.

Thus, as a next step the same group of researchers developed another paradigm, this one using picture sequencing. The picture sequencing paradigm had been used by Bullock (1984) with very young children to study the understanding of causal relations. These studies gave a further line of evidence regarding the perspective taking and allowed the researchers to check for interpretation by the children. The researchers assessed the child's ability to sequence a series of pictures. This ability was taken to indicate the child's understanding of the story depicted in the sequence. Then understanding was checked in an analysis of narrations based on the sequences. Five conditions were used:

1. Mechanical 1: Objects interacting causally on each other.
2. Mechanical 2: People and objects acting causally on each other.
3. Behavioral 1: A single person acting in everyday routines not requiring attribution of mental states.
4. Behavioral 2: People acting in social routines, involving more

that one person, but not requiring attribution of mental states.

5. Intentional: People acting in everyday activities requiring attribution of mental states.

The three main conditions were compared, first for sequencing. On the mechanical condition the children with autism did significantly better than the other two groups. Baron-Cohen et al. (1986) assumed this reflected the higher mental age of the children with autism. On the behavioral condition, the children with autism and the nonhandicapped groups performed identically, whereas the children with Down syndrome did significantly worse. The children with autism did significantly worse than the nonhandicapped children or the children with Down syndrome on the intentional condition.

The three main conditions were then compared for narration, with narration being scored as causal, mental state, or descriptive. In the behavioral condition, all children used more descriptive utterances than any other kind. In the intentional condition, a significant difference was obtained between the children with autism and the rest. They used mental state expression much more rarely than either of the other two groups.

According to Baron-Cohen et al. (1986), these results suggest that the critical feature of social impairment in autism may not be "a general turning away from the realm of interpersonal interaction" but may possibly involve a specific dysfunction in conceiving of mental states. The disturbances manifest in children with autism, then, are very likely a function of their understanding of the world. Their lack of a theory of mind and a more gestalt mode of cognitive processing would make understanding discourse and other social interaction rules very difficult. Appreciation of the social context requires a knowledge of even more subtle and complex cues than is required for appreciation of discourse rules. Then, employing rules in social contexts (which by their very nature are everchanging) and recognizing the mental states of others are clearly a primary challenge for individuals with autism. Although there appears to be some improvement of social skills with age (Mesibov, 1984), even more able individuals with autism continue to have difficulty extracting meaning from social contexts whether the information is verbal or nonverbal. Many are aware of their difficulties. One very socially aware young man with autism noted, "People send each other messages with their eyes, and I don't understand those messages" (Newson, 1980, p. 7). For some, this awareness leads to depression (Park, 1986).

Affect

We have seen that messages are not always understood by individuals with autism. In addition, many times the messages are not sent by these individuals in a way that others can easily understand, or "read," them. As early as 1979, Ricks examined the vocal expressiveness of nonverbal 3- to 5-year-old children with autism, nonverbal children with mental retardation, and typically developing 8-month-olds and demonstrated this difference in affective expression. In his study, the children were presented with stimuli designed to elicit four affective states: surprise, pleasure, frustration, and need or request. In each situation the children's vocalizations were recorded, then parents were asked to match the vocalizations of each of the groups of children to the stimulus situation. All of the parents could reliably match the vocalizations of the 8-month-olds and the children with retardation to the correct affective state. The parents of the typically developing children and the children with retardation were not, however, able to identify the vocalizations of their own children. Thus, even though the vocalization of these two groups of children was clearly specific to the eliciting situation, it was also very similar across children. Parents of children with autism, however, were able to match the vocalizations of their own children with affective states but were unable to match the vocalizations of other children with autism. This indicated to Ricks (1979) that the vocalizations of children with autism were, in fact, expressive but idiosyncratic, holding meaning only for their parents, not other adults.

More recently Kasari et al. (1986; cited in Mundy and Sigman, 1989) demonstrated a similar phenomenon. In their study the facial expressions of eight children with autism were recorded during social interactions with an experimenter, and facial expression data on mental age– and chronological age–matched children with retardation and mental age–matched typically developing children were collected. Using a facial affect rating system, they found that children with autism displayed significantly more blends of facial expression than the other children. What is important to note is that the blends they displayed often included very different affects (e.g., anger and enjoyment), making their affective state in the situation difficult to read.

Another striking affective characteristic of autism, even in more able individuals, is a lack of social empathy. The delay in the development and conventional expression of social empathy and the continuation of egocentrism is well recognized as a major impediment to the development of appropriate social behavior (Piaget, 1932; Newson et al., 1982; Selman, 1975) and the ability to make friends (Park, 1986). Social empathy involves using appropriate discourse skills in a socially acceptable way within the proper social context. Social empathy involves the ability to decenter (Inhelder and Piaget, 1969) or to see things from another's point of view. Individuals with autism form social relationships, but they rarely form the kind of emotional relationships that result in being well tuned to the thoughts and feelings of others (Bemporad, 1979; DesLauriers, 1978; Dewey and Everard, 1974; Kanner et al., 1972, Negri-Shoultz, 1987; Volkmar and Cohen, 1985). Not only do these individuals have difficulty reading the emotions of others (Dewey & Everard, 1974), but they also often lack the ability to use body language, facial gestures, or paralinguistics (voice tone, word inflection, etc.) (Hermelin, 1982) to enhance the expression of their own emotions (Attwood, 1984). This is exacerbated by their tendency to take little notice of the emotional responses of others (Negri-Shoultz, 1987; Newson, 1980). The picture that emerges is one of a person who consistently misinterprets what is said, responds with little emotion, takes little note and expresses even less understanding of the feelings of others, and talks more "at you than to you" (Newson, 1980, p. 20). Such affective challenges and differences may in part be caused by a lack of information about emotions in the knowledge network of individuals with autism.

This lack of information about emotions has been demonstrated in a series of studies by Hobson (1986a; 1986b). Hobson examined the ability of children with autism to identify various components of emotional expression. In his first experiment, subjects were asked to match drawn or photographed faces to videotapes of a particular emotional expression. The children with autism were significantly impaired compared with matched children with retardation (no autism). In his second experiment, the tasks were designed to test whether children with autism were able to recognize which gestures are associated with particular facial and vocal expressions of emotion. Again, the children with autism were significantly impaired compared with matched children with retardation (no autism).

This difficulty was recently further demonstrated in a study designed to examine the abilities of more able individuals with autism (individuals having autism and not retardation) to identify and respond to the basic emotional states of others (Negri-Shoultz, 1987). The study developed an affective perspective-taking task and semistructured, open-ended interviews to be conducted with more able individuals with autism and a control group. The study was designed to ask the following questions:

1. How well do more able individuals with autism identify, describe, and respond to the emotional states of others in an affective perspective-taking task compared with their nonhandicapped peers?
2. How do more able individuals with autism report being able to identify and respond to the emotional expressions of others?
3. How do friends and family members report that the individual with autism identifies and responds to the emotional expressions of others?
4. Does information gathered from each source corroborate information from each other source?

The results from each component of this study indicated that the knowledge network of individuals with autism is restricted in terms of emotional and social information. Results from examining the first variable of interest, the correct identification of emotional states, are congruent with Hobson's (1986a, 1986b) findings. In the studies by Hobson and in my more recent study, few of the subjects with autism responded randomly but not always correctly, indicating restricted knowledge of emotions. In the study I conducted, subjects were asked to view a series of short videotaped sequences of an interacting dyad in which one member expressed one of the basic emotional states, happy, sad, or angry. They were then asked to describe what they had just seen. Accuracy of identification of emotional state expressed was one of the measured variables. Table 15–1 presents the percentages of correctly identified emotional states for individual subjects. The mean percentage correct for the experimental subjects (individuals with autism) was 67.6% compared with 94.8% for the control subjects (individuals not labeled or identified as having a disability). The standard deviation for the experimental subjects was 18.6 compared with 10.2 for the control subjects. The range for the experimental subjects was 33% to 100%; the range for the control subjects was 66% to 100%. As predicted, the control subjects performed significantly better than did the experimental subjects and with less variability.

Other variables examined in this study were the percentages of unprompted and prompted internal emo-

TABLE 15–1.
Percentage of Correctly Identified Emotional States

Experimental Subjects (n = 13)	% Correct	Control Subjects (n = 13)	% Correct
S01	50	C01	83
S02	66	C02	100
S03	83	C03	100
S04	50	C04	100
S05	100	C05	100
S06	66	C06	100
S07	83	C07	100
S08	33	C08	100
S09	83	C09	100
S10	66	C10	100
S11	50	C11	66
S12	83	C12	100
S13	66	C13	83
Mean % correct	67.6		94.8

tional state descriptors used in the subject's response. This portion of the study examined the subjects' ability to produce an internal emotional state descriptor. To do so, the subjects were required to do more than describe the behavior of the woman or man in the tape (she's crying, he's huffing and puffing, she's looking down); they were required to interpret the behavior of the person and ascribe to it an emotional state (she's happy, he's sad, she's very angry). Such a task requires the most basic level of affective perspective taking (Hoffman, 1975), that is, to infer an internal emotional state from another's external behavior, saying, in effect, he or she is behaving in X manner; thus, he or she must be feeling X. As in the experiments of Baron-Cohen et al. (1985; 1986), this portion of the task required being able to identify the internal feeling state of another. Experimental subjects in this study produced fewer unprompted and prompted internal emotional state propositions than did the control subjects. These results are congruent with those of Baron-Cohen et al. (1986) in their work with story constructions, indicating again that knowledge regarding the feeling states of others, a critical and necessary component for successful social interaction, is not as available to individuals with autism.

It appears, then, that emotional information is not as salient or as meaningful to individuals with autism. Interview and anecdotal information gathered in the course of this study supports this hypothesis as well. Several experimental subjects commented on the difficulty they had in identifying what the person in the tape was feeling. One man stated, "This is particularly hard for me because I have to look at their face, and you see, I don't get much information from faces." When he was asked how the task might have been made easier for him, he responded, "Well, captions of what emotion was being presented would have helped." One of the young women indicated she was surprised that the logic she had learned in honors English was not helping her much in the task, and she had thought it would. These can be contrasted to the comments made by several of the control subjects who felt what they were being asked to describe was quite "obvious" and that often there was really "only one thing you can say."

Another portion of the study examined subjects' abilities to identify the appropriate response to one of the given emotional states and to develop a hypothesis regarding the source of the expressed emotional state. This is a more socially related aspect of affective perspective taking. The experimental subjects were less able than their peers to identify correctly a conventional response to the presented emotion and produced significantly fewer hypotheses across the six scenes than did the control group. One possible explanation for this result has to do with the difficulty individuals with autism have with emotional tuning (Kilman, 1987).

Emotional tuning develops out of the infant's ability to engage in attunement with his or her caregiver and requires amodal perception and processing (Stern, 1985). Several researchers have demonstrated that individuals with autism have difficulty integrating and transferring information from various sources (Lovaas et al., 1971; Schwartz, 1981). Stern (1985) discusses the ability to integrate information across various modalities (amodaly) as that which allows nonhandicapped infants to respond to and benefit from the affective attunement of their caregivers. He believes that such attunement is necessary for affective development and the development of the self. The ability to transfer information form one modality to another allows the infant to experience a world of perceptual unity. If, as Frith and Baron-Cohen (1987) assert, the child with autism processes information specific to the modality of input, such perceptual unity is not likely to exist for him, and affective development is likely to be impaired. With a knowledge network developing in such a way, the world may seem a very disordered place, and behavior others perceive as unconventional may, in fact, be reasonable reactions carrying communicative message value of confusion, fear, or frustration (Donnellan et al., 1984). An affective impairment resulting from an inability to benefit from attunement with one's caregiver could make understanding and producing conventional emotional responses, language, and social interaction difficult.

Sensory Processing

The world is further confused for many individuals with autism because of their overresponsiveness to some stimuli and undersensitivity to others (Ayers, 1979; Ornitz, 1974; Ritvo, 1976). One more able woman with autism who can recall and report childhood memories has stated, "As a young child I was very sensitive to sudden loud noises, but I was able to tune out continuous noises" (Grandin, 1984). Specific and observable deviant responses to raw sensory stimuli occur in most children with autism when they are observed before age 6 years (Ornitz et al., 1977, 1978). Ornitz (1974, 1989) has proposed a neurophysiological model of autism that stresses disturbances such as those experienced by Grandin (1987) and observed in these children. His model stresses disturbances in sensory modulation and motility. The disturbances of sensory modulation involve all sensory modalities and are manifested as both underactivity and overreactivity to sensory stimuli and as self-stimulation (e.g., watching spinning objects). Some of the motility disturbances, such as hand flapping, may provide the individual with input through the proprioceptive and kinesthetic channels and thus provide necessary stabilization or stimulation for them.

Ornitz (1989) claims that autism is clearly more than a language-processing disorder or the result of even a specific cognitive defect. His position is that such views do not account for the complex symptoms associated with autism and asserts further that the failure of even more able individuals with autism to respond to social cues and nuances suggests some subtle cognitive dysfunction that can be considered in the context of information processing. He proposes that the behavior of individuals with autism can be understood as a disorder of directed attention and conceptualizes it as occurring at the interface between sensory processing and information processing (Ornitz, 1989).

Distortions of sensory input during sensory processing can compromise the conversion of sensation into information. Thus, when individuals with autism experience undersensitivity or oversensitivity to stimuli, there follows a distortion of information processing. Ornitz (1989) suggests that the disturbances of language and cognition suggest cortical dysfunction, and the disturbances of sensory modulation and motility suggest subcortical dysfunction. Distortions of sensory input and a disorder of directed attention would clearly impact the construction of the child's knowledge network.

Other researchers concur that current data implicate both subcortical and cortical dysfunction (Dawson and Lewy, 1989). They cite abnormalities in vestibular responses and autonomic abnormalities, including elevated heart rate, increased peripheral blood flow, increased heart rate variability, and a failure to exhibit normal orienting responses by individuals with autism as indicative of subcortical dysfunction. Cortical dysfunction is suggested by studies of event-related potentials in persons with autism, in which a reduced P3 wave has been found (Courchesne et al., 1984, 1985), and by studies of functional brain lateralization, in which an increased incidence of reversed or absent lateralization has been reported (Dawson and Lewy, 1989).

Dawson and Lewy (1989) propose that autism involves dysfunction of the cortical-limbic-reticular system, which is the basis for attention to novelty. They suggest overactivation of the right hemisphere, which, in theory, may lead to increased sensitivity to novelty and arousal; this would account for the child with autism's tendency to respond to novel stimuli of normal intensity with aversive reactions. As they point out, this would selectively impair processing of social (including linguistic) information compared with visual-spatial information, because such information is, by nature, novel and unpredictable. In their recent review of research in this area, Dawson and Lewy (1989) indicate that the research strongly supports involvement of all levels of brain processing and that even subtle changes in the degree of novelty and predictability may have significant consequences for information processing and, thus, the development of world knowledge for individuals with autism.

IMPLICATIONS FOR PROCESS MODELS OF CHILDREN'S LANGUAGE

In developing Child Talk, we have come to believe that knowledge of how to talk is (1) process based (understanding or production); (2) embedded in world knowledge; (3) multiply entered in memory, including the context of understanding or production; (4) automatized by use; (5) generalized as lexical scripts; and (6) generalized as utterance frames, given experiences that are based on the individual's knowledge of functional, pragmatic, discourse, and semantic relations or conceptual categories. A consequence of the Child Talk assumptions about language production is the prediction for early development that delays or deviancy in cognitive and social development and limitations of linguistic, cognitive, and social experience will be associated with later language delay. Autism is one such case in point.

It does appear that because of any variety of etiologies, individuals with autism come into the world with an innate inability to enter into emotional contact with other people (Baron-Cohen, 1989), as was originally proposed by Kanner (1943) when he described these children as having "disturbances of affective contact." Since Kanner's original description, researchers have identified the various characteristics outlined in the earlier part of this chapter and conceptualized autism in a number of ways. Given what we now know about the cognitive style of processing most often used by individuals with autism, given what we know about their lack of a theory of mind, given what we know about their severe affective impairment, and given what we know about how such individuals respond to and use sensory input, it is easier to understand that these individuals very likely do construct a knowledge network that is very different from many of the rest of us. Duchan's (1984) work on sense making supports this hypothesis, suggesting that persons with autism frequently have a different sense about activities than do the persons with whom they are interacting. With such a different understanding of the world, of activities, of scripts, and of language, the development of language and communication systems that lack appreciation for the perspective of others, that are devoid of certain types of expressions, and that do not always appear conventional is, as the Child Talk model asserts, predictable. Without the same sense of an event, the fluency and clarity of an interaction will be affected. For example, the statement, "He might have a fever," being repeated when an individual is in pain or is upset, may have little apparent relation to the situational context in which it is being repeated.

Pragmatic deviance is one of the most striking features of language in autism. This is even more striking when contrasted to the pragmatic competence of very young children, children with language delays, children with Down syndrome, and adolescents and adults with mental handicaps (Baron-Cohen, 1989). The pragmatic deficits in autism can be predicted given the restricted emotional and social knowledge of these individuals, as the kind of social understanding that appears to be missing for these individuals are important precursors for language development and use (Mundy and Sigman, 1989).

Child Talk assumes that early language learning is a part of learning about the social and physical world. The kinds of cognitive, social, affective, and sensory processing challenges of autism can be clearly associated with the later language delays and deviances noted throughout the literature and by the families and professionals involved in supporting such individuals.

IMPLICATIONS FOR CLINICAL PRACTICE

Whether a cognitive, social, affective, or sensory processing perspective is most valid for defining the primary deficits in autism is, at least to me, not clear. Perhaps, as is suggested by Tager-Flusberg (1989), future progress in delineating the core deficit in autism will come from understanding more about the interrelationships among the different components of functioning than from scrutinizing each. Although attempts are being made toward that delineation, individuals with autism continue to require facilitation and support in the development of skills that will allow them to fit more smoothly into a world that is clearly confusing and difficult for them to understand. What we do know about their experience of the world can provide us with some direction in providing more effective and meaningful support to them.

Supportive Mentor

It seems clear that individuals experiencing the problems associated with autism, even if they do not also have retardation, would benefit from a supportive mentor as originally proposed by Bemporad (1979), regardless of the service system or systems with which they are associated. This supportive mentor would need an in-depth understanding of the syndrome and, with that, would facilitate and support the individual with autism as he or she attempts to make sense of the world. He or she would help the individual more fully develop his or her knowledge network. A supportive mentor who understands the specific nature of this social impairment could help such individuals interpret their experiences in a world that is likely very confusing and unpredictable.

Visual Cueing

We know that visual-spatial and rote memory skills are strengths for individuals with autism (Bemporad, 1979; Grandin, 1986; Newson et al., 1982; Rutter, 1983). Thus, techniques that include some visualization and visual imagery work (Groden & Cautela, 1984) might be considered to support the individual's difficulties in interpersonal relationships. In a report of her own experiences as an individual with autism, Grandin (1984) discusses the use of visualizing relationships with people as being similar to walking through sliding glass doors; both are fragile and must be approached slowly and not with force. This visualization helped her think about how to approach people and enter into interactions with them. Similar visualization strategies have been employed by Kilman (1987). In an attempt to help a young man learn to relax in situations that made him nervous, she had him visualize butter and ice melting. Any time a visualization or visual aid can be used, the individual with autism is more likely to be able to grasp the concept.

This extends beyond the development of social skills. Tasks of any kind should most often be laid out in such a way that there is a very clear beginning and a very clear endpoint, making predictability about it easier. The use of concrete visual cues will almost always facilitate performance, particularly when an individual is attempting to learn a new and novel task.

Friends and family members of individuals with autism have reported that the individual's ability to recognize and respond to the emotional states of others seemed to increase with the saliency of the emotions expressed (Negri-Shoultz, 1987). Thus, dramatic modeling and dramatic role playing may also facilitate development of social interactive skills and responsiveness for the person with autism.

Ecological Manipulations

Behavior occurs within a context and often is a function of that person's physical, interpersonal, and programmatic environment. Ecological manipulations that might be considered to support individuals with autism and to facilitate management of their behavior could include at least the following: changing the setting (perhaps there are too many or too few students in a class for him or her), changing the number and quality of the interactions (perhaps he or she is being asked too many questions or not being given enough processing time), changing the instructional methods (perhaps he or she needs more concrete cues), changing the instructional goals (perhaps through a parallel or adapted curriculum), and removing or controlling environmental pollutants (perhaps some environments are too noisy or not stimulating enough for him or her). These kinds of manipulations are an attempt to "smooth the fit" for the individual with autism at school, at work, or at home.

Positive Programming

Because of the difficulties they have in experiencing and interacting with their world, all individuals with autism require the base of a solid positive educational or training program before we can begin to help them manage any of their challenging or nonconventional behavior. A positive program is referred to as a longitudinal instructional program designed to facilitate and teach greater skills and competencies that will contribute to the social integration of the individual. This will include at least academic skills training, social skills training, adaptive skills training, communication skills training, relaxation skills training, and vocational skills training.

Relaxation Training

If one is to help individuals with autism cope with their autism and with a confusing and unpredictable world, relaxation training is critical. Such training could be done at home, at school, or at work. Strategies for conducting such training are outlined by Cautela and Groden (1978).

Social Skills Training

The difficulties experienced by most individuals with autism in the acquisition of social skills were reviewed earlier. Clearly they have a need for training in this area. Such training can occur both individually or in small groups. There are a number of approaches to social skills training, many of which are appropriate (Donnellan and Kilman, 1986; Odom & McConnell, 1985; Odom and Strain, 1984a, 1984b). Whatever approach is chosen, special consideration must be given to the communication and learning style of the individual with autism and adaptations created, if necessary.

Facilitated Communication

In the previous discussion, what we know about the experience of individuals with autism has suggested ways of providing more effective and meaningful support to them. Recently a new approach for supporting and communicating with individuals with autism has surfaced, and the results of this new approach, facilitated communication, have brought into question much of what we thought we understood about autism. Now there may be a way to support them that is allowing us to learn more about them.

Facilitated communication is a method of providing physical support under the forearm or at the hand to aid a person in isolating an index finger for pointing to make choices (about objects, pictures, words, or letters, etc.) (Biklen, 1990; Crossley, 1990). The method was originated by Rosemary Crossley, an Australian educator, while she was involved in supporting individuals with cerebral palsy during the 1970s. According to Crossley (1988), facilitated communication differs from other hands-on training methods such as graduated guidance and coactive movement in which the movements are performed by both student and teacher together and it does not matter if the teacher's movement is stronger than that of the student (at least not at the start of training). With the method she developed, it is vital that the choices made be those of the aid user. The aid user's movements should be stronger than those of their facilitator, who gives the minimum assistance required.

Physical assistance is not a new approach in helping individuals with autism perform. What has been different with facilitated communication is the kind of physical assistance being provided and the results of this assistance. When given this kind of assistance on letter boards or other kinds of communication devices, individuals with autism who have been nonverbal (and often considered to have retardation as well) have been able to spell out original sentences, statements, and requests by pointing to appropriate letter selections (Biklen, 1990; Crossley, 1988, 1990). Perhaps even more interesting is that often the statements made by many of these individuals include considerable social and emotional content, sometimes even reflecting a clear ability to take the perspective of another individual. Not surprisingly, the reports of such outcomes and the experiences of facilitators in the field are being responded to with interest, hope, confusion, and sometimes skepticism. There is even some documented evidence against the validity of facilitation (Cummins and Prior, 1991). In a study of a limited number of facilitated communicators, Cummins and Prior (1991) demonstrated that in some cases it was the facilitator who was answering and not the aid user. This has caused some to question the entire approach.

However, families and practitioners in the field continue to experience what they believe is unquestionable success as they document over and over that with facilitation many individuals with autism seem to be able to communicate complex, novel, and emotion-laden communications via the written word (Donnellan et al., in press). In a more complete review of the topic than can be covered here, Donnellan et al. (in press) discuss the complexities facing researchers in this area. They suggest that much of the confusion surrounding this approach results from merging facilitation (touch or physical assistance), communication, and the written word. In their review they establish links between previous research data and good practice that may help us to better understand how each of these components operates in facilitated communication.

They begin by examining the component of facilitation, or touch. As they point out, the use of physical touch, usually through prompts, has long been established as a technique of choice for teaching a wide variety of tasks to children with autism (Donnellan-Walsh et al., 1976; Koegel and Rincover, 1977; Woods, 1987). Both Crossley (1990) and Biklen (1990) describe how this physical touch and support may help overcome the problems students with autism experience with motor expressive behavior. Facilitation and prompting are not the same, but together they add weight to the notion that touch may be a critical sense modality for individuals with autism (Ayers, 1979; Donnellan et al., in press).

In observing and directly facilitating communication, one can see that there is something more than just physical assistance contributing to the success of the individuals with autism. In fact, there have been many cases in which different facilitators, using what appears to be the same kind and level of physical assistance, are not able to successfully facilitate the same individual. An important but conceptually difficult variable in the process appears to be the influence of the communication partnership between the user and the facilitator (Donnellan et al., in press). The critical nature of this relationship to successful communication has been addressed by both Crossley (1988) and Biklen (1990). They stress how important the facilitator's attitudes and belief in the communicator's competence are. Perhaps because of the difficulties that individuals with autism experience in developing relationships, little attention has heretofore been given to the kinds of relationships that are most supportive for them. Work in the area of facilitated communication has provided us the opportunity to look at that variable in a way we never have before, because it seems clear that the relationship factor, although difficult to define, is a critical one. Interestingly, Donnellan et al. (in press) have suggested examining the touch and relationship issue as one when considered as "attunement" (Stern, 1984).

Stern (1984) discusses three general features of a behavior that can be matched: (1) intensity, (2) timing, and (3) shape. He then further divides the three dimensions into six more specific types of matches: (1) absolute intensity, (2) intensity contour, (3) temporal beat, (4) rhythm, (5) duration, and (6) shape. This matching forms the basis of an attunement, and, as previously mentioned, it is attunement that is important in developing normal social interaction in infants (Stern, 1984). Is a trusting and positive relationship necessary for attunement to occur? Is attunement necessary for more connected communication and interaction? Donnellan et al. (in press) have posed additional provocative questions regarding attunement, autism, and facilitated communication: Does touch provide a compensatory tuning during facilitation? Does facilitation provide a sense of timing or rhythm from the facilitator to the communicator, producing a communication dance that makes it easier for the communicator to perform? These and many more questions remain.

Perhaps easier to sort out is the influence of the written word in this whole process. For years reports on autism referred to surprising reading abilities of individuals with autism (Goodwin and Goodwin, 1969; Kanner, 1943). Because of its visual and static nature, the written word has often served as a very useful prompt or adaptation for individuals with autism. The current experience with facilitated communication suggests that the written word is an additional augmentative communication option for a wider range of individuals with autism than previously considered possible, and although the quality of the communication produced does go well beyond what one might have expected from the literature (Cummins and Prior, 1991), the fact that individuals with autism demonstrate unusual or unpredictable facility is not unprecedented (Donnellan et al., in press). Again, Donnellan et al. (in press) pose some provocative questions: Will the facilitated communication of the written word enhance the learning of spoken language? Might it inhibit such learning? How does the written word fit in with other communication the individual already uses? Can the written word systems be made more efficient? Clearly there are many more questions to be answered about facilitated communication.

CONCLUSION

Interestingly, the experience of facilitated communication raises questions about the very nature of the syndrome of autism. We may now have an opportunity rarely available to us before—an opportunity to ask individuals directly about their experiences of autism. Will their responses prove our hypotheses accurate? What more can they tell us about their knowledge network and how it develops? Has our support to them been useful? What else do they need and want from us? In learning more about them, what more will we be able to learn about ourselves? Future research holds many of these answers, and, no doubt, many more questions.

REFERENCES

Attwood A: The gestures of autistic children. Doctoral dissertation, London, University of London, 1984.

Ayers AJ: *Sensory Integration and the Child.* Los Angeles, Western Psychological Services, 1979.

Baltaxe CAM: Pragmatic deficits in the language of adolescent autistics. *J Pediatr Psychol* 1977; 2:176–180.

Baron-Cohen S: Autism and symbolic play. *Br J Dev Psychol* 1987; 5:139–148.

Baron-Cohen S: The autistic child's theory of mind: A case of specific developmental delay. *J Child Psychol Psychiatry* 1989; 30:285–297.

Baron-Cohen S, Leslie AM, Firth U: Does the autistic child have a "theory of mind"? *Cognition* 1985; 21:37–46.

Baron-Cohen S, Leslie AM, Firth U: Mechanical, behavioural and intentional understanding of picture stories in autistic children. *Br J Dev Psychol* 1986; 4:113–125.

Bemporad JR: Adult recollections of a formerly autistic child. *J Autism Dev Disord* 1979; 9:179–197.

Biklen D: Communication unbound: Autism and praxis. *Harvard Educ Rev* 1990; 60:291–314.

Bullock M: Preschool children's understanding of causal connections. *Br J Dev Psychol* 1984; 2:139–148.

Caparulo B: Address to the Annual Conference of the National Society for Autistic Children. Boston, 1982.

Cautela JR, Groden J: *Relaxation: A Comprehensive Manual for Adults, Children, and Children With Special Needs*. Champaign, Ill, Research Press, 1978.

Courchesne E, Kilman BA, Galambos R, et al: Autism: Processing of novel auditory information assessed by event-related brain potentials. *Electroencephalogr Clin Neurophysiol* 1984; 59:239–248.

Courchesne E, Lincoln AJ, Kilman BA, et al: Event-related brain potential correlates of the processing of novel visual and auditory information in autism. *J Autism Dev Disord* 1985; 15:55–75.

Crossley R: Unexpected communication attainments by persons diagnosed as autistic and mentally impaired. Paper delivered at the Biennial ISSAC Conference, Anaheim, Calif, 1988.

Crossley R: Communication training involving facilitated communication. Paper presented at the Annual Conference of the Australian Association of Special Education, Canberra, Australia, 1990.

Cummins R, Prior M: Autism and assisted communication: A reply to Biklen. *Harvard Educ Res* (in press).

Dawson G, Lewy A: Reciprocal subcortical-cortical influences, in Dawson G (ed): *Autism, Nature, Diagnosis, and Treatment.* New York, Guilford Press, 1989, pp 144–173.

DesLauriers AM: The cognitive-affective dilemma in early infantile autism: The case of Clarence. *J Autism Child Schizophr* 1978; 8:219–228.

Dewey M, Everard P: The near-normal autistic adolescent. *J Autism Child Schizophr* 1974; 4:348–355.

Donnellan AM, Kilman BA: Behavioral approaches to social skill development in autism, in Schopler E, Mesibov G (eds): *Social Behavior in Autism*. New York, Plenum Press, 1986, pp 213–235.

Donnellan AM, Mirenda P, Mesaros R, et al: Analyzing the communicative functions of aberrant behavior. *J Assoc Persons Severe Handicaps* 1984; 9:201–212.

Donnellan AM, Sabin LA, Majure LA: Facilitated communication: Beyond the quandary to the questions. *Topics Lang Disord* (in press.)

Donnellan-Walsh A, Gossage LD, LaVigna GW, et al: *Teaching Makes a Difference.* Sacramento, Calif, California State Department of Education, 1976.

Duchan J: Clinical interactions with autistic children: The role of theory. *Top Lang Disord* 1984; 4:62–71.

Duchan J: Autistic behavior: Deviant or different. *Aust J Hum Commun Disord* 1985; 13:3–8.

Everard MP: Mildly autistic young people and their problems. Paper presented at the International Symposium on Autism, St Gallens, Switzerland, 1976.

Fay W, Schuler A: *Emerging Language in Autistic Children.* Baltimore, Md, University Park Press, 1980.

Frith U: Autism and "theory of mind," in Gillberg C (ed): *Diagnosis and Treatment of Autism.* New York, Plenum Press, 1989, pp 33–52.

Frith U, Baron-Cohen R: Perception in autistic children, in Cohen D, Donnellan AM (eds): *Handbook of Autism and Pervasive Developmental Disorders.* New York, John Wiley & Sons, 1987, pp 85–102.

Goodwin M, Goodwin T: In a dark mirror. *Ment Hyg* 1969; 53:550–563.

Grandin T: My experiences as an autistic child and review of selected literature. *J Orthomolec Psychiatry* 1984; 3:144–174.

Grandin T: *Emergence: Labeled Autistic.* Novato, Calif, Arena Press, 1987a.

Grandin T: Personal communication, 1987b.

Groden J, Cautela JR: Use of imagery procedures with students labeled "trainable retarded." *Psychol Rep* 1984; 54:595–605.

Hermelin B: Thoughts and feelings. *Aust Autism Rev* 1982; 1:10–19.

Hermelin B, O'Connor N: *Psychological Experiments With Autistic Children.* New York, Pergamon Press, 1970.

Hobson RP: The autistic child's appraisal of expressions of emotion. *J Child Psychol Psychiatry* 1986a; 27:321–342.

Hobson RP: The autistic child's appraisal of expressions of emotion: A further study. *J Child Psychol Psychiatry* 1986b; 27:671–680.

Hoffman ML: Developmental synthesis of affect and cognition and its implications for altruistic motivation. *Dev Psychol* 1975; 11:607–622.

Hubbell R: *Children's Language Disorder—an Integrated Approach.* Englewood Cliffs, NJ, Prentice-Hall, 1981.

Hurtig R, Ensrud S, Tomblin J: The communicative function of question production in autistic children. *J Autism Dev Disord* 1982; 12:57–69.

Inhelder B, Piaget J: *Early Growth of Logic in the Child.* New York, Norton, 1969.

Kanner L: Autistic disturbances of affective contact. *Nerv Child* 1943; 2:217–250.

Kanner L, Rodriguez A, Ashenden B: How far can autistic children go in matters of social adaptation? *J Autism Child Schizophr* 1972; 2:9–33.

Kilman B: Developing social skills for children and adolescents with autism, in Park D (eds): *The Proceedings of the 1981 International Conference on Autism.* Washington, DC, National Society for Children and Adults With Autism, 1981, pp 318–327.

Kilman BA: The development of social interaction in children and adolescents with autism. 1987 (unpublished).

Kilman B, Negri-Shoultz N: Characteristics of near-normal persons with autism, in Cohen DJ, Donnellan AM (eds): *Handbook of Autism and Pervasive Developmental Disorders.* New York, John Wiley & Sons, 1987, pp 440–451.

Koegel RL, Rincover A: Research on the difference between generalization and maintenance in extra-therapy responding. *J Appl Behav Anal* 1977; 10:1–16.

Leslie AM, Frith U: Prospects for a neuropsychology of autism: Hobson's choice. *Psychol Rev* 1989; 97:122–131.

Lovaas OI, Schriebman L, Koegel R, et al: Selective responding by autistic children to multiple sensory input. *J Abnorm Psychol* 1971; 77:211–222.

Menyuk P, Quill K: Semantic problems in autistic children, in Schopler E, Mesibov G (eds): *Communication Problems in Autism.* New York, Plenum Press, 1985, pp 127–145.

Mesibov GB: Current perspectives and issues in autism and adolescence, in Schopler E, Mesibov G (eds): *Autism in Adolescents and Adults.* New York, Plenum Press, 1984, pp 337–353.

Mirenda PL, Donnellan AM: Effects of adult interaction style on conversational behavior in students with severe communication problems. *Lang Speech Hear Services Sch* 1986; 17:126–141.

Mundy P, Sigman M: Specifying the nature of the social impairment in autism, in Dawson G (ed): *Autism, Nature, Diagnosis, and Treatment.* New York, Guilford Press, 1989, pp 3–21.

Negri-Shoultz NA: Affective perspective-taking skills in more able individuals with autism. Doctoral dissertation, Madison, University of Wisconsin, 1987.

Newson E: The socially aware autistic child and adult. Paper presented at the International Conference of the National Society for Autistic Children, Coventry, England, Warwick University, 1980.

Newson E, Dawson M: Autism and intelligence: A study of barriers. Paper presented at the Autism Europe, Paris Conference, Paris, 1983.

Newson E, Dawson M, Everard P: The natural history of able autistic people: Their management and functioning in social context. University Park, Nottingham, England, University of Nottingham, Child Development Research Unit, 1982 (unpublished).

Odom SL, McConnell SR: A performance-based conceptualization of social competence of handicapped preschool children: Implication for assessment. *Top Early Child Spec Educ* 1985; 4:1–19.

Odom SL, Strain PS: Classroom-based social skills instruction for severely handicapped preschool children. *Top Early Child Spec Educ* 1984a; 4:97–116.

Odom SL, Strain PS: Peer-mediated approaches to promoting children's social interaction: A review. *Am J Orthopsychiatry* 1984b; 54:544–577.

Ornitz EM: The modulation of sensory input and motor output in autistic children. *J Autism Child Schizophr* 1974; 4:197–215.

Ornitz EM: Autism at the interface between sensory and information processing, in Dawson G (ed): *Autism, Nature, Diagnosis, and Treatment.* New York, Guilford Press, 1989, pp 174–207.

Ornitz EM, Guthrie D, Farley AJ: The early development of autistic children. *J Autism Child Schizophr* 1977; 7:207–229.

Ornitz EM, Guthrie D, Farley AJ: The early symptoms of childhood autism, in Serban G (ed): *Cognitive Defects in the Development of Mental Illness.* New York, Brunner/Mazel, 1978, pp 24–42.

Park CC: Social growth in autism: A parent's perspective, in Schopler E, Mesibov G (eds): *Social Behavior in Autism.* New York, Plenum Press, 1986, pp 81–99.

Paul R: Communication in autism, in Cohen DJ, Donnellan AM (eds): *Handbook of Autism and Pervasive Developmental Disorders.* New York, John Wiley & Sons, 1987, pp 61–84.

Piaget J: *The Moral Judgement of the Child.* New York, Harcourt Press, 1932.

Premack D, Woodruff G: Does the chimpanzee have a theory of mind? *Behav Brain Sci* 1978; 4:515–526.

Prizant B: Gestalt language and gestalt processing in autism. *Top Lang Disord* 1982; 3:16–23.

Ricks D: Making sense of experience to make sensible sounds, in Bullowa M (ed): *Before Speech: The Beginning of Interpersonal Communication.* New York, Cambridge University Press, 1979, pp 245–268.

Ricks D, Wing L: Language, communication and the use of symbols in normal and autistic children. *J Autism Child Schizophr* 1975; 5:191–221.

Ritvo ER (ed): *Autism: Diagnosis, Current Research, and Management.* New York, Spectrum, 1976.

Rutter M: Cognitive deficits in the pathogenesis of autism. *J Child Psychol Psychiatry* 1983; 24:513–531.

Schwartz S: Language disabilities in infantile autism: A brief review and comment. *Appl Psycholinguist* 1981; 22:25–31.

Selman RL: Taking another's perspective: Role-taking development in early childhood. *Child Dev* 1975; 42:1721–1734.

Shah A, Wing L: Cognitive impairments affecting social behavior in autism, in Schopler E, Mesibov GB (eds): *Social Behavior and Autism.* New York, Plenum Press, 1986, pp 153–169.

Simmons JQ, Baltaxe C: Language patterns of adolescent autistics. *J Autism Child Schizophr* 1975; 5:333–351.

Stern DN: Affective attunement, in Call J, Galenson E, Tyson R (eds): *Frontiers of Infant Psychiatry*. New York, Basic Books, 1984, pp 3–14.

Stern DN: *The Interpersonal World of the Infant: A View From Psychoanalysis and Developmental Psychology*. New York, Basic Books, 1985.

Tager-Flusberg H: On the nature of linguistic functioning in early infantile autism. *J Autism Dev Disord* 1981; 11:45–56.

Tager-Flusberg H: Psycholinguistic approaches to language and communication in autism, in Schopler E, Mesibov G (eds): *Communication Problems in Autism*. New York, Plenum Press, 1985, pp 69–87.

Tager-Flusberg H: A psycholinguistic perspective on language development in the autistic child, in Dawson G (ed): *Autism, Nature, Diagnosis, and Treatment*. New York, Guilford Press, 1989, pp 92–120.

Ungerer JA: The early development of autistic children: Implications for defining primary deficits, in Dawson G (ed): *Autism, Nature, Diagnosis, and Treatment*. New York, Guilford Press, 1989, pp 75–91.

Volkmar FR, Cohen DJ: The experience of infantile autism: A first-person account by Tony W. *J Autism Dev Disord* 1985; 15:47–54.

Wetherby AM: Ontogeny of communication functions in autism. *J Autism Dev Disord* 1986; 16:295–316.

Wimmer H, Perner J: Beliefs about beliefs: Representation and constraining function of wrong beliefs in young children's understanding of deception. *Cognition* 1983; 13:103–128.

Wing L: Asperger's syndrome: A clinical account. *Psychol Med* 1981; 11:115–129.

Wing L, Attwood A: Syndromes of autism and atypical development, in Cohen DJ, Donnellan AM (eds): *Handbook of Autism and Pervasive Developmental Disorders*. New York, John Wiley & Sons, 1987, pp 3–19.

Woods T: The technology of instruction: A behavior analytic approach, in Cohen D, Donnellan AM (eds): *Handbook of Autism and Pervasive Developmental Disorders*. New York, John Wiley & Sons, 1987, pp 251–272.

INDEX

L

M